THE
TWELVE RELIGIONS
OF THE
BIBLE

W9-DCN-372

ROLLAND WOLFE

**Studies in the Bible
and Early Christianity
Volume 2**

**The Edwin Mellen Press
New York and Toronto**

Library of Congress Cataloging in Publication Data

Wolfe, Rolland E., (Rolland Emerson), 1902–
    The Twelve religions of the Bible.

    (Studies in the Bible and early Christianity ; v. 2)
    Includes bibliographical references.
    1. Bible--Criticism, interpretations, etc.
2. Near East--Religion. I. Title. II. Title: 12
religions of the Bible. III. Series.
BS511.2.W64 1982   220.6   82-20401
ISBN 0-88946-600-9

Portfolio of paintings by Diane Krueger

Studies in the Bible and Early Christianity
ISBN 0-88946-913-X

        The Edwin Mellen Press
        P.O. Box 450
        Lewiston, New York   14092

Printed in the United States of America

CONTENTS

Illustrations of Biblical Themes
    by Diane Krueger

(following page 248)

FOREWORD

In spite of all the sermons preached, the classes taught, and the myriads of books that have been written, the Bible remains a relatively unknown literature. Most people quote from it selectively, gleaning from it what they like and rather unconsciously discarding the rest. Few people go far toward comprehending the great sweep of historical and religious development in the Scriptures.

Usually the Bible has been assumed to have a monolithic structure, giving essentially the same message from beginning to end. Rather grudgingly, it is recognized that there are two religions in the Bible, Judaism and Christianity. Even so, most writers on the Bible insist that the two Testaments are basically a unit production, narrating a single story of redemption. Pursuant to this view, the Old Testament often is spoken of as the New Testament "prefigured," and the New, as the the Old "revealed."

That a measure of unity prevails throughout the Scriptures is true, but it is only half of the story. That there is considerable diversity is true also. No longer can it be assumed that the Bible is a smoothly flowing river of spiritual discovery, relatively indistinguishable in its various parts, coursing its way uninterrupted from Genesis to Revelation. Discerning study shows it to be more like a kaleidoscopic succession of spiritual dramas, each with acts and scenes that reveal its own distinctive message.

Since a number of these successive stages in mankind's upward spiritual progress are covered by the Bible, the time has come to look on these in a new way. This writer believes the differences between the various parts of the Scriptures are so pronounced that they portray a series of twelve relatively distinct religions. Transition from one to another usually has been precipitated by some national or theological crisis.

These variations follow a fundamental law of cultural development, that each age has its own distinctive problems and produces its own government, its own social institutions, and its own perspectives. In the same manner, each age tends to have its own religion, with the innovative variables often more important than the presumed ongoing constants. This is how it has happened that the three thousand years covered by biblical history have displayed a panorama of religions.

In contrast with most other publications, which stress the unity of the Bible, the present book is devoted to observing the special features of its distinctive parts. As such, this study attempts to portray the successive stages in the rise and development of the Judaeo-Christian tradition during the course of biblical history. Stops will be made at the various way-stations in the course of retracing the long, and sometimes tortuous, pathway of religious searching which mankind has traveled.

The Bible is the only book from antiquity that most people ever encounter. Readers tend not to realize that there is a science of interpreting ancient documents. For instance, early biblical writers often misconstrued strangers as gods, God, or angels walking the earth. Regarding such mistaken identity, I John 4:12 states that "No man has seen God at any time." Also, biblical people had no concept of a brain that is able to create ideas. It accordingly was self-evident to those writers that every new thought was a message from some god. Therefore they could say "Thus saith the Lord."

In the light of such considerations it is evident
that translating the Bible from Hebrew, Aramaic, and
Greek into English is only the first step in mediating
the Scriptures to the present age. One must go on to
the more difficult task of translating the primitive
thought modes which prevailed in antiquity into the
thought modes of the present day. The following pages
have been written with this imperative in mind, thus
making the Bible more meaningful.

Another aid to interpretation lies in comprehending
that the canonizers' dividing the first part of the
Bible into seventeen historical books means little. It
is fundamental to realize that those writings were produced largely by three editors in extensive strands that
originally were not divided into books.

(1)   A valuable sequence of well-written material
gives a masterful world history from creation to the
time of King Solomon around 925 B.C. That strand extends
through Genesis, Exodus, Numbers, Joshua, Judges, Samuel
and I Kings. As one of the world's first real historians,
that author had reverence for facts and portrayed history truthfully. In scholarly writings he and his work
are designated as the Jehovistic editor and the J strand.
In the following pages he is referred to simply as the
early editor, and his work as the early historical writing or the early source.

(2)   What is commonly called P in scholarly publications is a rewriting at approximately 440 B.C. of
the early valid JE history in a parallel strand which
extends through Genesis, Exodus, Leviticus, Numbers,
and Joshua. That extensive revision will be referred
to in coming pages simply as the late priestly strand
or late strand, and its author as the late editor,
priestly editor, or postexilic editor. This strand tends
to miraclize historical events, retroject postexilic

institutions and ideas into the early history, monotheise all the early writings, distort events, and is
a travesty on truthful portrayal. Although this supposed
history is far more extensive and spectacular, it is
misleading and regrettable.

(3) The Deuteronomic editor or school, whose work
usually is referred to in the books as D, produced
Deuteronomy, conserved valuable sources from the judges
and monarchy periods, and wove those documents into the
Judges-Samuel-Kings valuable history. A true historian,
this editor pieced his sources together without altering
them, revealing his own ideas only in the editorial
transitions between primary documents.

From these three paragraphs it is evident that the
early part of the Bible is not a simple writing but very
complex. In the following pages it is attempted to make
this historical maze as simple as possible. Only by
reckoning fully with this documentary arrangement of
the early biblical books can one approach toward full
appreciation of those early Scriptures.

In citing biblical episodes, and where conclusions
may be questioned, references are given within the text
for the convenience of readers in checking the scriptural sources. Where the numberings of Hebrew and English
verses differ, the Hebrew is given in brackets. Where
evidence is overwhelming and generally recognized, references are not cited. All quotations from the Bible
are in the author's own translation.

Proper rendition of divine names is extremely important. An annoying factor is that the plural *elohim*
(gods) continued to be used after the Hebrews became
monotheists. The context therefore is the determining
factor in each instance as to whether *elohim* should be
translated gods or God. In the following translations
"god" indicates polytheistic reference while "God" is

reserved for the one God of the universe. The divine
name with consonants *yhwh* -- god of the Midianites,
Israel, and Palestine -- is rendered according to its
original pronunciation as "Yahweh," in contrast with
the improperly transliterated "Jehovah" in some versions.

The demands of space have made it impossible to
list the various views of scholars at most places. This
book is essentially an attempt to see what the Bible
has to say about itself. Nevertheless, this author is
deeply grateful to the body of biblical scholarship
which has made such a study possible. Greatest indebtedness is to the vast amount of archaeological contributions upon which the following pages rely heavily for
illuminating the biblical records. The archaeologically
corrected chronology used throughout is that devised
by William F. Albright.

There may be a bit of magic in the number twelve:
the twelve sons of Ishmael, the twelve tribes of Israel,
the twelve minor prophets, the twelve disciples, and
now, perchance, the twelve religions of the Bible. It
has been an exciting search to bring this new dimension
in biblical study into reality and it is hoped greater
spiritual infilling may result from this treatment of
the Bible in more meaningful ways.

These explorations into the Bible's twelve religions are dedicated to all who would learn more about
the origins of our faith, with the long upward trail,
and sometimes downward, that has brought us where we
are. This quest may also be an adventure in ecumenicity
since more than three fourths of the Bible records the
"common Scriptures" shared by Jews and Christians.

CHAPTER 1

THE SUMERO-AKKADIAN RELIGION OF GENESIS 1-11

As might have been expected, the Bible's earliest religion is found in its opening book, Genesis, which means origins or beginnings and whose first Hebrew word is translated "In the beginning." Someone had the courage to set down in writing some prevailing ancient beliefs concerning origins of the universe and everything in it.

That notable treatise on beginnings is confined to the first eleven chapters of the Bible, which ought to be set aside as a separate book. The source materials in those chapters were derived from early authors who lived in the Tigris and Euphrates valleys and inscribed their researches on clay tablets with cuneiform wedge-shaped writing.

The initial concern of those authors was with what they comprehended of the universe, which they called "the heavens and earth." Even in those days, some five thousand years ago, there were differing views of how the world and its celestial environs were created. Two of those variant stories found their way even into the Bible. One author was content to hypothesize creation of only a primeval garden of the gods, the Garden of Eden, brought into being by a creator god in one day (Gen. 2:4-24). The other was sufficiently daring as to account for creation of the celestial universe, the world, and all natural phenomena within it in the course of seven days (1:1-2:3).

Both accounts give theories regarding how mankind came to be created. The Garden account assumes that humanity began with a single pair, Adam and Eve, created respectively out of a lump of clay and an extracted rib. The other version has no room for primeval pairs of animals or people but assumes that all sentient life was created in mass, including mankind.

Genesis 1-11 also gives a list of firsts: the first man, the first woman, the first child, the first farmer, the first herdsman, the first murderer, the first city builder, the first polygamist, the first nomad, the first musician, the first smith, the first vineyardman, the first drunkard, and the first line of settlers along the upper Euphrates River (Gen. 2; 4; 9:20-27; 11:10-32). Passages deal also with the origin of sin, origin of religion, origin of the rainbow, and origin of languages (3; 4:26; 9:12-17; 11:1-9). There is also the story of a disastrous flood that swept the Tigris-Euphrates valleys and how one family escaped by building an ark (chs. 6-9).

In antiquity that land of Mesopotamia ("between the two rivers") was occupied in succession by two great nations. Earliest were the Sumerians who are thought to have been driven from their original homeland in southern Asia. As a refugee people, they settled along the Tigris and Euphrates Rivers in the relatively uninhabited swampy areas of what is now southern Iraq. Although handicapped by having no stone, metals, or substantial wood, and menaced by malaria and tropical diseases, these persevering Sumerians developed the world's first great civilization during the fourth and third millenniums B.C.

About 2400 B.C. the Akkadians of central Mesopotamia conquered the Sumerians. As frequently in such situations, the victors adopted as their own the superior culture and literature of the vanquished. With certain

Akkadian elements added, the resultant blending eventuated in the Sumero-Akkadian achievement in literature,
arts, crafts, government, and religion.

The editor of Genesis paid tribute to that pioneering Sumero-Akkadian civilization by allotting to it the
place of honor as the beginning of the Bible. Accordingly, most of Genesis 1-11 consists of digests and fragments borrowed by the Hebrews from the mythological and
historical writings of those forebears who were in their
prime during the two millennia before Abraham, the first
Israelite, appeared on the scene of history. Although
revised considerably by the biblical editor, those
eleven chapters of myths and legends concerning creation, flood, and social origins reflect the religious
beliefs held by the early dwellers of Mesopotamia who
developed mankind's first advanced faith.

THE HEAVENLY PANTHEON AND EARTH DEITIES

Sumero-Akkadian religion is focused on an extensive
pantheon of diverse deities. The Genesis editor went
far toward making the writings adopted from that primeval faith compatible with Hebrew religion by eliminating
the more glaring polytheisms and by placing monotheistic
coloring over others to obscure them. However, by looking beneath that monotheistic coloring, and observing
those places where the more vague polytheisms slipped
through uncensored, one finds in those eleven chapters
indications of the many gods worshiped by the ancient
Mesopotamians.

Reference to multiple deities of a heavenly court
are visible at several places. In Genesis 1:26 the Hebrew editor apparently tired for a moment in his monotheistic emending of the document he was following. He
accordingly let slip through his censoring touch a quo-

tation from the chief of the pantheon, speaking to the
company of gods concerning his plan to create mankind:
"Let us make man in our image, after our likeness." Attempts to rationalize away the "us" and "our" as plurals
of majesty, the blessed trinity, or the editorial "we"
are probably not valid alternatives to the native polytheism which survives in that verse.

Certain more subdued references to multiple deities
are found within this supposedly monotheistic first
chapter of Genesis. In 1:16-18 the biblical editor slipped into repeating a pair of old polytheistic phrases
as he told how the "two great lights" were set "in the
firmament of Heaven . . . to rule over the day and over
the night," with "the greater light to rule the day and
the lesser light to rule the night." This expresses the
ancient belief that the sun and moon were considered
gods. Since "the stars also" was a phrase attached to
the ruling statement, this reflects how they were also
regarded in antiquity as personal deities, guarding individuals on earth.

An elusive clause in Genesis 1:2 reflects a variant
view of creation, that the earth originated from a cosmic egg. After making her floating nest on the surface
of the primeval water, the female bird deity laid one
egg on it. Upon incubation, this hatched out to become
the earth. Unable to get away completely from this
imagery, the biblical editor sublimated it into "and
the spirit of God was brooding upon the face of the
waters."

There were gods of chaos as well as deities of
order. The classic Akkadian Enuma Elish epic of creation
asserts that everything began with two primeval whale-
like female and male godmonsters of chaos, Tiamat and
Behemoth. They swam around in the abyss and ruled the

primeval waters. In course of time the phrase "Tiamat
and Behemoth" became abstracted in Hebrew into *tohu* and
bohu meaning "waste and void." When it is said in Genesis 1:2, "And the earth was waste (*tohu*) and void
(*bohu*)," the editor was inadvertently, but nevertheless
revealingly, commending to all readers the early
Akkadian belief that what is now the earth was originally only a watery abyss, with the two deities of chaos,
Tiamat and Behemoth, swimming about therein.

A reflection of the heavenly pantheon is seen in
Genesis 3:22 as the creator of Adam and Eve reported
failure with the primeval pair to his heavenly superiors: "Behold, the man has become as one of us to know
good and evil. And now, lest he put forth his hand and
take also from the tree of life, and eat, and live forever. . .?" Apparently the end of this question was censored out, as well as the reply of the heavenly respondent. Verse 23 indicates this garden deity was advised
to drive his man and woman from that place of delight
so they no longer would have access to the second tree.

The Cain and Abel story in Genesis 4 is an adaptation into the Adamic family-context of the Sumerian
classic concerning two brothers, Emesh and Enten. Emesh
was god of herds while Enten was god of fields and farmers. Both were anxious to win the special favor of their
father, the air-god Enlil. After each presented his plea
before their father-god in Nippur, Enlil chose to bestow
his special favor upon the farmer-god Enten. This resulted in enmity between the two brothers. In the course
of transcribing that ancient story into the Bible, the
Genesis editor demythologized Emesh and Enten from gods
into human beings, and renamed them Cain and Abel.[1]

Genesis 6:1-4 tells of mass apostasy from the heavenly assembly of deities when "the sons of god saw that

the daughters of men were beautiful, and they took wives for themselves of all whom they chose, and . . . the sons of god had sex relations with the daughters of men and they bare children to them." "Sons of god" was an idiomatic name for "gods," as "sons of Israel" was idiom for Israelites; "sons of the prophets," for prophets; "sons of men," for human beings, etc.

It is not clear whether this passage means to say that a portion of the gods abdicated the heavenly abode to live permanently on earth and enjoy human sexuality, or if this luxury was achieved only by frequent forays from Heaven to earth. To eliminate the resultant hybrid progeny, part god and part human, was the prime biblical reason for bringing a flood on the earth.

The Tower of Babel episode also alludes to the heavenly council of gods, when people in the land of Shinar were in the process of building a tower to Heaven. Frightened by this prospect of having the celestial domain invaded and colonized by earth people, a heavenly alarmist addressed the company of gods, saying, "Come, let us go down, and there confuse their language so they cannot understand each other's speech" (Gen. 11:7).

YAHWEH-GOD IN THE GARDEN OF EDEN

The graphic version of origins in 2:4-3:24 is the only place in Genesis 1-11 where a Sumerian-based account has been taken into the Bible without significant revision. Whatever the explanation for this abstinence, that narrative is left to portray its diversity of earth gods, with no attempt at monotheising.

Chief in Eden was the anthropomorphic (manlike) being called Yahweh-god. Operating without any clear design, he blundered along in an improvident hand-to-mouth manner. This deity had to work hard, moulding his man by hand in the clay pit. Having no place to put Adam in that dry desert, Yahweh-god was driven to the thought of making an oasis. It soon dawned on him that a garden paradise would need shade, so trees were supplied. Then water for the trees became a necessity, hence the river.

Eventually Yahweh-god came to see that, if there was to be an ongoing human race, Adam would need a mate. So this god plunged again into the clay pit for an ordeal of prolonged and unfruitful labor in so far as his immediate design was concerned. According to Genesis 2:18-20, every species of animal he formed was an abortive attempt to secure a desirable partner for Adam. In desperation this trial-and-error god resorted to physical surgery, removing one of Adam's ribs in an attempt to make a satisfactory mate out of it.

This was a god who had other serious disabilities. He failed in providing a reliable guardian for the tree of knowledge. As soon as Eve was made, she disobeyed him and upset the whole plan for the future of his creation. Whether for pleasure or to keep in trim, he was accustomed to "walking in the Garden in the cool of the day." He had no better vision than humans, since he could not find Adam and Eve when they hid themselves "among the trees of the Garden" (Gen. 3:1-9).

Yahweh-god was unpardonably rash in passing sentences upon the Eden offenders (Gen. 3:14-19), and was unable to think of an expedient by which he might extricate himself from the predicament into which he had been placed by the disobedient pair. When in desperation he sought counsel as to a way out, he was a completely frustrated deity (3:22). Although Yahweh-god had considerable creative power, this was outweighed by his multiple inadequacies.

That deity's domain was very small, confined to the desert oasis he had created. His jurisdiction extended only as high as the treetops and only a short distance outside the garden wall (Gen. 4:14-16). Beyond that were the territories presided over by other comparable area gods.

KITCHEN STAFF AND SERPENT GUARDIAN

In addition to Yahweh-god, there were also other gods in Eden. Most elusive of these were the deities that were thought to reside within the two special trees. Such belief is made more plausible as one observes supposedly god-inhabited trees in isolated regions of the Near East today.

The two tree deities in that Garden constituted the kitchen staff of the gods. One produced the magic fruit that gave divine knowledge (wisdom) to all who ate its fruit. The other bestowed life (immortality) upon all who partook of it. Assuming gods were gods because of what they ate, the Eden formula was: fruit from the tree of knowledge plus fruit from the tree of life equals deity.

Since the two special trees in that garden of the gods produced food of the gods, mortals normally were to be denied access to them. The pantheon of deities thereby tried to insure against encroachments into their numbers by humans. None other than Yahweh-god himself committed the first act of insubordination in Eden by leaving the tree of life unguarded. In this he ostensibly was disobeying his superior heavenly deities by tacitly inviting Eve and Adam to eat the fruit from the tree of life, thereby achieve the immortality of the gods, and to that extent become demigods.

Most spectacular in that garden of the gods was the serpent, one of the esteemed earth-deities. Serpents

were venerated throughout the ancient world as guardians
of whatever was treasured. In bas-reliefs at doors and
along the tops of retaining walls, serpent-gods were
believed to prevent anyone from entering temples with
ill intent. Carved or painted on the outside and often
inside tombs and sarcophagi, these deities were supposed
to protect bodies of the departed from tomb robbers.
During high royal periods in Egypt, one or more serpents
were worn on a Pharoah's crown as the ultimate in
security. In Eden the serpent's role was to guard the
tree of knowledge and prevent Adam and Eve from eating
its forbidden fruit.

In polytheistic mythologies it was not uncommon
for subordinate deities to disobey a superior, when the
lesser god's wisdom regarded that type of procedure desirable. This was the situation in Eden when Yahweh-
god's orders were disregarded by the serpent who proved
himself an unfaithful guardian of the tree whose sanctity was entrusted to him.

More benevolent to Eve and Adam than Yahweh-god,
the serpent deity urged this original pair to eat also
from the tree of knowledge and attain full deity. He
pointed out to Eve that Yahweh-god had lied in saying
"in the day that you eat thereof you shall surely die"
(Gen. 2:17). Then that snake stated the truth of matters, telling how Yahweh-god "knows that in the day you
eat thereof, then your eyes shall be opened, and you
shall be as gods, knowing good and evil" (3:5).

The great mistake of that primeval pair, after having eaten the fruit of knowledge, lay in not rushing
over quickly to the tree of life and eating of its
fruit. Then, according to Sumerian belief, nothing in
Heaven or on earth could have taken from them the everlasting full deity which thereby would have been achieved. According to this story, subsequent millennia

of mankind therefore have had to be content with possessing the wisdom of the gods, but not their immortality.

HEAVENLY CONSULTANTS AND CHERUB GUARDIANS

A pantheon of gods is reflected in Genesis 3:22
as Yahweh-god supposedly went to his heavenly superiors,
reported his failures with the primeval pair, and sought
advice from the council of gods: "Behold, the man has
become as one of us to know good and evil. And now, lest
he put forth his hand and take also from the tree of
life, and eat, and live forever . . . ?" The end of this
question and the reply of the heavenly respondent apparently were censored out by the Genesis editor. Verse
23 indicates this seeking god was advised to drive his
man and woman from that place of delight so they no
longer would have access to the second tree.

To prevent Adam and Eve from re-entering, Yahweh-
god "placed at the east of the Garden of Eden the cherubim, with flickering flaming swords, to guard the way
to the tree of life" (Gen. 3:24). Such cherubim (Hebrew
plural) usually appeared as here in pairs, one cherub
on each side of precious objects, doorways, or gates.

By contrast with the representations in late
medieval and modern art, archaeological recoveries show
that cherubs of the ancient Near East were composite
deities with the body of a lion or bull, the wings of
a bird, and the head of a man. They were gigantesque
creatures, usually of stone and weighing as much as fifty or more tons. European museums have a number of them,
especially the British and Berlin Museums and the Lou-
vre. Two magnificent specimens from Khorsabad can be
seen in the Semitic Museum of Harvard University and
the Oriental Institute at the University of Chicago.
Two giant ones remain in position, guarding entrance

to the northwest gate of Nineveh. The best *in situ* demonstration is at Calah, in northern Iraq, where three
pair, in almost perfect preservation, continue guarding
approaches to ancient palaces.

In Hittite lands one finds many stela and statues
of the storm god Adad holding a flickering shaft of
lightning that looks like a flaming sword. Each cherub
in Genesis 3:24 is pictured as having one of these
menacing weapons in hand. With such giant deities flanking Eden's gate, armed with their flickering lightning
shafts to be used in striking intruders, Adam and Eve
never tried to re-enter this garden of the gods.

These pages have shown what a surprising number
of deities wholly or partially escaped the monotheising
process in the Bible's earliest chapters. This imposing
total offers a glimpse into the many types of gods worshiped by the people of Sumer and Akkad in antiquity.

THE SUMERIAN CLASSICS ON BROTHERHOOD

Although adherents of so-called monotheistic religions usually assume that ancient polytheistic faiths
had little or no value, this is not true. Instead of
rating religions according to the number of their deities, a better test lies in the comparative moral discernment attributed to the gods or God worshiped in
each. According to this more valid test, ancient Sumero-
Akkadian religion appears to have been well developed.

The already-cited narrative underlying the Cain
and Abel account shows the importance placed on harmonious relationships in Sumerian society. In that Emesh
and Enten myth these two brother gods settled their an-
tagonisms peacefully.[2] Concern for brotherhood is observed also in three similar stories. In the one called
Cattle and Grain, Lahar, the cattle-god, and his sister
Ashnan, the grain-goddess, quarreled on the farms and

in the fields. However, they eventually overcame their differences, as brothers and sisters should, with that narrative ending in restoration of friendship.[3] The Dumuzi and Enkidmu Myth records that the shepherd-god and the farmer-god got into conflict. This dispute between brother deities also was settled peacefully.[4] The same theme of antagonism and eventual reconciliation is developed in the Enmerkar and Ensukushsiranna poem.[5] These four compositions show how highly brotherhood was treasured in ancient Sumerian life.

One might have expected that the editor who incorporated the theme underlying these four classics of brotherhood into the Bible at approximately 440 B.C. would have accented further the ethical elements in these foreign sources. To one's amazement, the opposite has taken place as four derogatory changes were made in the story.

In all four of these Sumerian narratives, featuring the conflict between siblings, the difficulties were settled peacefully, ending with restoration of friendship between them. This accentuation of the positive contrasts with the biblical version where the story is made to end in the negativism of murder. Would it not have been in the range of a higher morality to have been taught how brothers and sisters can surmount their difficulties, than to have the anger go unchecked as in the lowered biblical version where rage triumphs in brother killing brother?

A further perverting of the Sumerian story concerned the validity of sacrifices. Cain represented the advanced Sumerian agricultural view that if sacrifices were offered to a deity, they should consist of grain or vegetables to be acceptable, and not burned but simply "presented." Animal sacrifices were looked upon as inhuman, cruel, and revolting. Enlightened Sumerians regarded it as absurd that any god should forgive the sins of a worshiper in consequence of his slashing an animal's throat and offering up the flesh on an altar as odoriferous food for deity.

Since most early Hebrews were herdsmen rather than farmers, the object of divine approval was reversed, with Abel, the herdsman, in favor, and Cain, the farmer, disgraced. The biblical editor thereby condemned agricultural sacrifices as unacceptable to the Hebrew Yahweh in Genesis 4. For not having offered a blood sacrifice, that editor stigmatized Cain as a villain. This amounted to placing at the Bible's beginning an eternal command that only animal sacrifice is acceptable to God. From that re-editing the Bible was to become saturated with the dictum that "without the shedding of blood there can be no remission."

Strange as it might seem, it was to take the biblical deity several more millennia before he would attain the stage of advancement already achieved in this regard at the Bible's beginning by Cain. In the Hebrew tradition this was a hard-fought battle, with the abolition of animal sacrifice not finally achieved until destruction of the Jerusalem temple at A.D. 70.

The most unpardonable element in this series of biblical revisions lay in giving an ethnic twist to the story through the renamings, making Abel represent the divinely favored Hebrews and Cain, the despised Canaanites whose territory Israel wanted. The precedent of driving Cain "out from the presence of Yahweh" to become "a fugitive and a wanderer . . . in the earth" (Gen. 4:12-16) gave Israel the right to drive out the Canaanites and take over their territory. How tragic that a quartet of brotherhood stories could have been so perverted into a vehicle of hatred!

Where would a child be best off -- studying the negativisms of murder, ritualism, ethnicism, and hate in Sabbath schools and Christian Sunday schools, or learning the fine art of brotherhood in an ancient Sumerian religious class?

DEITY DISSENT OVER THE FLOOD

Early Mesopotamian accounts, from which the biblical version has been taken, show high moral sensitivity when they state that other deities protested against the supreme god Enlil's brutality in causing the flood. A six-column Sumerian fragment excavated at Nippur records that when news of the plan was divulged, the sorrowing of the "mourning goddess" was notable as she burst into tears over the impending fate of earth's inhabitants.

Then did Nintu weep like a . . . ,
The pure Inanna set up a lament for its people.[6]

In the Akkadian Gilgamesh Epic the protest of other deities was even more pronounced. The goddess Ishtar was so depressed over the barbarity of the flood that she said she never could be happy again. This she expressed by saying that whenever she would look at the prized stone in her necklace henceforth, she would be able to think only of that terrible decimation.

Ye gods here, as surely as this lapis
Upon my neck I shall not forget, I shall be
Mindful of these days, forgetting (them) never.[7]

When the Akkadian hero of the ark presented his offerings in thankfulness that the flood had ended, Ishtar appealed to all other members of the divine pantheon that, because of his cruelty, Enlil, who brought the flood, should not be allowed to come and partake with them of the sacrifice.

> Let the gods come to the offering;
>
> (But) let not Enlil come to the offering,
>
> For he, unreasoning, brought on the deluge
>
> And my people consigned to destruction.[8]

Enlil was enraged because advance information about the coming flood had leaked to the other gods and goddesses and they had provided for the one man and his family to be saved.

> As soon as Enlil arrived,
>
> And saw the ship, Enlil was wroth,
>
> He was filled with wrath against the Igigi gods:
>
> "Has some living soul escaped?
>
> No man was to survive the destruction!"[9]

The god Ea closed the protest by accusing Enlil of never having thought through the consequences of the flood.

> How couldst thou, unreasoning, bring on the deluge?[10]

Ea further reminded Enlil that any one of four alternate lesser punishments would have been more appropriate than flood for the sins of mankind.[11]

This chorus of protests on the part of subordinate more ethically discerning deities, against the cruelty of their father-god in his heartless drowning of earth's population, was denied admittance into the Bible. In his monotheistic revising, the Genesis editor retained only the merciless villain of the gods. Changing Enlil's name to Yahweh, this inconsiderate deity became the unchallenged brutal hero in the biblical version of the flood.

The high level of Mesopotamian religion is observed also in the flood story's ending where the Sumerian originals conclude in a grand climax. For having built and manned the ark, thereby saving the human race and every species of animal, Ziusudra, the Sumerian Noah, was highly rewarded by the minority deities. This consisted in being given "life like a god," "breath eternal like a god," and in being taken to reside thereafter in Dilmun, abode of the gods.[12]

By contrast, the editor of Genesis gave an amazing downward twist to the flood story by making it conclude in a drunken debauch, with Noah exposing his nakedness (Gen. 9:20-27). This indicates poor judgment on the part of the biblical deity in having chosen Noah as the seed of a new humanity.

Here too, in the flood story and its sequel, a child in an ancient Sumerian religious school was taught a more moral story than is true in the modification now found in our Bibles.

THE HIGH POSITION OF WOMEN

Equality of women with men was another achievement that was basic in documents underlying the Genesis 1-11 re-editings. This was in harmony with so-called primitive religions in general, where there were goddesses as well as gods, priestesses as well as priests. In Akkadian-based Genesis 1:27 men and women appeared in equality as mankind was created "male and female." In the Sumerian original garden account a male ate the forbidden fruit, and no woman was involved.[13] As already seen, in one Sumerian prototype of the Cain and Abel story, the sister was the heroine and goddesses led the protest against the barbarity of the male-contrived flood.[14] The Indo-European Sumerians granted women a high place in society and allowed them to hold property the same as men.

The Genesis re-editings changed all this as that high view of women was replaced by the Semitic low

opinion of them. In the Eden version, Eve was the after-
thought and insignificant tail end of creation. In contrast with the Sumerian garden account, in which a male
was the culprit, the Genesis editor substituted Eve as
the individual who yielded to temptation, disobeyed
Yahweh-god by eating from the forbidden tree, and induc-
ed her husband Adam to do likewise. She at once disrupt-
ed Yahweh-god's plan and became the cause of all mankind's basic troubles, from that day to the end of time.

The spectacularness of the Genesis 2-3 presentation
has been considerably responsible for making this disparaging appraisal of women normative in Jewish, Christian, and Muslim circles, consigning them generally to
menial tasks and positions. Only in this twentieth century are we in process of liberating ourselves from that
perversion. With regard to the franchise, New Zealand
was the first nation to give women the right to vote
(1893) and the United States was sixteenth (1920). At
the moment of this writing, efforts are somewhat stalled
over granting women equal rights and ordination.

It should be humiliating to realize that after five
millennia our religions have not caught up with the
ancient Sumerian precedents in regard to the position
of women.

THE PROBLEM OF INDIVIDUAL RESPONSIBILITY

When there was an infraction of propriety in Sumerian
society, appropriate penalty was administered, and only
the culprit was punished. As those early epics became
revised by the editor of Genesis 1-11, an amazing reversal took place. Very strangely, the biblical versions
have the respective punishments heaped largely or wholly
on the innocent rather than the guilty.

In contrast with the one fruit eaten in Genesis,
eight forbidden plants were partaken of by Enki in the

Sumerian story. However, for these eight transgressions no one but Enki was punished, and he, only slightly.

Thereupon Ninhursag cursed the name of Enki:
"Until he is dead I shall not look upon him with the eye of life."[15]

By contrast with this moderate reproof, when revising this story the editor of Genesis made his Yahweh-god to over-react in 3:14-19 by striking vengefully with his punishments in all directions at once, with little thought of propriety. Upon the serpent he inflicted penalties of being the most cursed of all animals, having the legs removed, going on the belly, striking at people's heels, hated by women, victim of eternal antagonism, and to be destroyed by all people. Eve was victimized into excessive sexual desire, constant childbearing, pain in childbirth, and being ruled over by man. Adam was consigned to labor, sweat, and slaving in producing enough food to remain alive. Upon both human offenders was imposed the doom of death. All this for their disobedience in eating fruit from the tree of knowledge!

But far more! Every serpent, every woman, and every man, who would inhabit this planet to the end of time, were consigned to suffer the same punishment as the three Eden principals. In addition, all the soil on this earth was cursed by being made to grow weeds uch as "thorns and thistles," and withhold its fertility as a further plague upon mankind. In total, all but an infinitesimal per cent of the punishment was heaped upon the innocent. This is an astounding example of punishing them for sins of the guilty, something not found in the original Mesopotamian account.

If that offense was as heinous as Yahweh-god thought, it seems he should have killed Adam and Eve

on the spot, and created a new pair so the world population could have been restarted in proper manner. In that
way the punishment would have fallen exclusively on the
guilty, and the innocent throughout the ages would not
have been made to bear the almost total brunt of it.

Appropriate punishment in the Tower of Babel story
would have been for Yahweh to have gone down, demolish
the tower, and punish the builders, as in early Mesopotamian archaeological representations. Instead, the Genesis editor had his biblical Yahweh inflict the curses
of divisiveness and diversity of languages on the entire
human race, intending to make it impossible for people
after Babel to co-operate on any project. Again, except
for the extremely small per cent upon the culprits, most
of the punishment is heaped on the successive generations of their innocent descendants throughout all history.

The most notable example of misdirected punishment
is in the story of Noah's becoming intoxicated and displaying his nakedness in Genesis 9:20-27. Instead of
punishing Noah for his drunkenness and pornographic exposure, or Ham for looking upon his father's nudity,
the Genesis editor has made the punishment to be inflicted wholly upon Ham's son, who was not even present
when the episode occurred. Not only was the innocent
Canaan punished but every one of his descendants was
made "a servant of servants," thereby dooming them to
be a slave population to Israel in perpetuity. The biblical writer even confused his family derivations, for
the Canaanites were Semites, descendants of Shem, rather
than Hamites, descendants of Ham. By this revision the
Genesis editor made the flood story to end in punishment,
all heaped on an innocent person and his innocent posterity to the end of time.

The Sumerian and Akkadian originals have such misdirected punishment at only one place, when the flood
was carried out by Enlil, head of the pantheon. The lesser deities were outraged over his indiscriminate drowning of the innocent animal world and the innocent segment of humanity with the guilty. Their protest was expressed best in the words of the god Ea when reproving
Enlil for his inconsiderateness.

On the sinner impose his sin,

On the transgressor impose his transgression![16]

This statement marks one of the highest moral at-
tainments in Mesopotamian religion. It shows that those
ancients in their "Epic of Gilgamesh" already had arrived at the belief in individual responsibility.

Punishing the innocent for sins of the guilty was
routine not only in the Hebrew rewritings of the Mesopotamian mythological epics. An appendix to Moses' Decalogue pictures Yahweh punishing children for sins of
their parents to the third and fourth generations
(Exod. 20:5). Deuteronomy, written at approximately
620 B.C., asserts that Yahweh was accustomed to punish
children to the tenth generation for their parentage
(Deut. 23:2-3 [3-4 in Hebrew]). Punishing an innocent
animal victim, instead of the guilty worshiper, was the
basis of the biblical sacrificial system. It survives
in the orthodox Christian belief that God could not forgive the inherited sins of the post-Eden human race and
grant salvation to mankind until he had the satisfaction
of seeing his own innocent son's blood shed on the cross.

It is ironic that it should ever have been thought,
as in the Genesis 1-11 re-editings and their sequels,
that God punishes the innocent for sins of the wicked.
This is in sharp contrast with the sense of justice and
ethical discernment that already had been attained in
Mesopotamian religion at the dawn of recorded history.

ECHOES FROM EDEN, BABYLON, AND UR

In spite of the percentage loss in ethical perspective due to the re-editings in Genesis 1-11, numerous elements of Sumero-Akkadian religion reflected in those chapters have radiated from them to become permeated in both the Jewish and Christian traditions.

The assumption that gods are gods because of what they eat has survived to the present with the revised meaning that worshipers become religious by what they eat. Although the sacramental elements have changed, partaking of two select foods became adopted into the Hebrew faith as bread and wine on the table of showbread were offered by priests to worshipers in the temple. This passed over into Christianity as the eucharist, in which communicants achieve the ultimate in religion and assurance of immortality by eating a bite of bread and drinking a swallow of wine. Every time Christians partake of communion in the two elements they stand indebted to its ultimate Sumero-Akkadian origin with the two foods of the gods in Eden's garden.

The snake deity of Genesis 3 also has survived in subsequent religion. One Hebrew word for serpent is *saraph* or seraph, with the plural seraphim. Isaiah 6 portrays a fleet of six-winged seraphs flying over the head of the Lord, protecting him from harm. This imagery has been taken also into the Christian tradition. However, since the Italian masters, who established the norms of modern art, did not know these were serpentine deities, they were reimaged as long-winged human-sized beings. As such, artists ever since have pictured "seraphim" hovering protectively over the heads of Christ or God. Since the stinging bite of snakes led to their being thought of as fiery creatures, this has persisted in usually coloring seraphim red.

It is much the same with the guardians of Eden's east gate as cherubim also became an element in subsequent biblical religions. This is attested by the eighty-eight times the names cherub or cherubim occur in post-Eden Scripture. Thousands of them appeared at three focal points: in the furnishings provided for Moses' tent of meeting, Solomon's temple, and the second temple. Cherubim served as divine guardians of those sacred structures, and especially of Yahweh himself. In Ezekiel 1 they became alive and continued so thereafter. Ignorant also as to what they were, the Italian painters portrayed cherubim as chubby cupids with tiny wings and dimpled cheeks. In this modified form, the masters saturated Christian art, especially in the baroque age, in picturing "cherubim" accompanying the divine presence.

Both orders survive within Christian hymnody in such lines as "O higher than the cherubim, more glorious than the seraphim" and "Cherubim and seraphim falling down before thee."

In intertestament literature the Garden of Eden itself was thought to have been elevated into regions supernal, occupying the second of the three-Heaven structure, or third of the seven Heavens, when so conceived.

Two essentials of Eden are mentioned in Revelation as present in the Christian Heaven. One is the river watering the Garden. "And he showed me a river of life, bright as crystal, proceeding out of the throne of God" (Rev. 22:1). This is the heavenly river referred to in Christian poetry and hymnody as "Crossing the Bar" and "Shall We gather at the River?"

Although both Eden magical trees were transported with the Garden to Heaven, the prohibited one became transformed into a second tree of life. "And on this side of the river and on that was a tree of life,bearing twelve crops of fruit, producing its fruit every month, and the trees' leaves were for the healing of the nations" (Rev. 22:2).

The Fourth Gospel and Revelation give a variant -- a countryman's idea of Heaven as a walled fortress,within which is a cubical high-rise apartment building, approximately fifteen hundred miles square and fifteen hundred miles high, with an infinite number of rooms (Rev. 21:10-21; John 14:2). However, the increasingly urbanized world of today prefers to think of Heaven as portrayed in that portion of Revelation which preserves the Eden touch. The Qur'an and Muslim tradition also have visualized the next life occurring in that garden paradise of delights.

The Tower of Babel has become perpetuated in Christianity and multiplied into the many spires of cathedrals and churches as they suggest that worshipers look to Heaven. To most congregations a place of gathering would not be a church unless it has a spire, be it ever so small in these penurious days. By inspiring such pointings to Heaven, the people of ancient Babylon have immortalized themselves all over the world as perhaps the inhabitants of no other city on earth.

THE SUMERO-AKKADIAN RELIGIOUS HERITAGE

Although not reflected in Genesis 1-11, a basic element in Sumero-Akkadian religion deserves mention here. Centuries before Moses issued his ten commandments, ancient Mesopotamian legal documents served as charts to personal morality and ethical conduct.Earliest were the three Sumerian codes formulated in succession by Ur-Nammu, Bilalama, and Lipit-Ishtar.[17] The later Code of Hammurabi built heavily on the three earlier ones. These four have served as the foundation of the legal and ethical structuring of the nearer Orient and Western world.

Even the earliest of these was amazingly advanced, as witnessed by Ur-Nammu's assertion that in his administration "the orphan did not fall a prey to the wealthy," "the widow did not fall a prey to the powerful," and "the man of one shekel did not fall a prey to the man of one mina (sixty shekels)."[18]From Ur-Nammu, and through these later codes, this concern for the oppressed -- orphan, widow and poor -- permeated the whole biblical tradition and remains one of the brightest stars in the galaxy of Judaeo-Christian faith.

Among its other contributions, Sumerian religion gave to our world its first great literary breakthrough, the art of writing. This was developed by temple priests at Uruk in what is now southern Iraq between the years 3400 and 3100 B.C. From there this literary innovation quickly spread, through adopting or by inspiring indigenous parallel developments, to all the world.

The same diffusion occurred with the cosmologies originated by the Sumerians and further developed by the Akkadians and Assyrians. These concepts of beginings also moved out toward all points of the compass, establishing the patterns of metaphysical thinking for the subsequent religions and philosophies of most peoples on our planet.

The Sumero-Akkadian heritage that radiated through Genesis 1-11 became the foundation of the Judaeo-Christian-Islamic achievement. The canonizers added 908 more chapters to make the complete Hebrew Scriptures, Christians appended the New Testament, and Muslims produced the Qur'an. Nevertheless, for all three of these faiths the basically Sumero-Akkadian graphic stories of Genesis 1-11 remain the best-remembered portion of their sacred literatures -- creation according to Sumero-Akkadian concepts, the primeval garden, conflict between Cain and Abel, a great flood that covered the earth, the ark by which one man saved seed of all life for a new beginning, and the Tower of Babel.

The observations in this chapter cause one to marvel before the high levels of life achieved by those early Mesopotamians who developed exalted ethical perspectives some thirteen centuries before Abraham, the first Hebrew, appeared on the world scene. Since so many of those contributions have spread throughout the Bible, and have become part of the three related communions that regard it as their holy book, this is a great tribute to the world's first advanced religion, the Sumero-Akkadian faith.

NOTES TO CHAPTER 1

1.   Samuel N. Kramer, *Sumerian Mythology*, Philadelphia, American Philosophical Society, Memoirs, Vol. XXI, 1944, pp. 43, 49-51.

2.   See Note 1 above.

3.   Kramer, *From the Tablets of Sumer* , Indian Hills, Falcon's Wing Press, 1956, pp. 144-146.

4.   James Pritchard, *Ancient Near Eastern Texts* , Princeton, Princeton University Press, 1st. ed., 1950, pp. 41-42.

5.   *Ibid.*, p. 41, Note 1.

6.   Kramer, *Tablets of Sumer*, p. 179.

7.   Pritchard, *Op. cit.*, p. 95.

8.   See Note 7 above.

9.   See Note 7 above.

10.   See Note 7 above.

11.   See Note 7 above.

12.   Kramer, *Tablets of Sumer*, pp. 180-181.

13.   *Ibid.*, p. 174.

14.   See Notes 6 and 7.

15.   See Note 13.

16.   Pritchard, *Op. cit.*, p. 95.

17.   Kramer, *Tablets of Sumer*, pp. 47-48.

18.   *Ibid.*, pp. 49-50.

CHAPTER 2

ARAMAEAN RELIGION OF THE PATRIARCHAL NOMADS

The Bible's second religion is portrayed in Genesis 12-50 which contains the first truly historical writing in the Scriptures. In somewhat legendized form those thirty-nine chapters present certain outstanding events in the lives of the four generations of prominent individuals who in that day were called patriarchs.

Greatest of those patriarchs was Abraham, the first important historical character in the Bible. He was the person from whose initial influence virtually everything in its sixty-six books was ultimately derived. He might be called the father of religions. Through his son Isaac he became the progenitor of the Hebrew people and, as such, the father of Judaism. Through his son Ishmael Abraham became the revered ancestor of all Arab peoples, and thereby the father of the Islamic faith. Through his grandson Esau -- with alternative name Edom -- Abraham became the father of the once-important Edomite religion. Since Christianity is the offshoot of Judaism, Abraham also is reckoned as the ultimate father of Christianity.

Abraham's tomb at Hebron in southern Palestine has been regarded as a sacred shrine by all these religions. The Bible says he, Sarah, and Jacob were buried there (Gen. 23:19-20; 25:9; 50:13). Isaac, Rebekah, Leah, and Joseph may have been interred there also (50:25). Over that cave of the patriarchs Muslims have constructed the Mosque of Hebron, their fourth most sacred shrine as a tribute to their spiritual father.

THE CHANGE OF STAGE SETTING WITHIN GENESIS

In moving from   Genesis 1-11 to 12-50 practically everything changes. First, there is a different geographical setting. The events described in Genesis   1-11 have their locale in Lower Mesopotamia but the occurrences described in Genesis 12-50 took place in northern Syria, Palestine, and Egypt.

The golden age of Mesopotamian religion spanned the years 3200 to 1800 B.C. but the patriarchal age was later, approximately 1750 to 1550 B.C.

Even though these patriarchal Aramaeans lived later, they followed more primitive types of religion than the   earlier   Mesopotamians.   The   Aramaean   religion   of Genesis 12-50 therefore was quite different from the Mesopotamian faith underlying Genesis 1-11.

The documents underlying Genesis 1-11 appeared in the cuneiform wedge-shaped scripts of the Sumerians, Akkadians, and Assyrians, but there is a complete linguistic change in moving to Genesis 12-50 where the basic language is Aramaean. Since Aram was the ancient name for both Damascus and the nation of which it was the capital, the language used in that country was fittingly called Aramaean. Numerous traces of that original form of Aramaic are found among the Hebrew versions of those Aramaean stories as transcribed in Genesis 12-50.

While Genesis 1-11 dealt   with the peoples and cities of antiquity, Genesis 12-50 is concerned with only one family. Although other personages are inevitably interlocked with it, those thirty-nine chapters present basically the history of four tribal leaders: Abraham, Isaac, Jacob, and Joseph.

In contrast with the first eleven chapters, where people lived sedentary lives, the latter thirty-nine portray a nomadic existence. That saga of migration

began in Syria as Abraham left the ancestral home
(Gen. 12:1-5). It was revisted by his servant in seeking
a wife for Isaac in chapter 24 and by Jacob in his
flight and accumulation of two wives in chapters 29 - 31.
Journey's end eventually led for the grand finale to
Egypt for most events in the closing chapters 39-50.
The heart of the action, during intervening portions,
was occupied with wanderings in the lands of Canaan and
Gerar.

The ancestral home was at Haran in Aram-naharaim,
"Aram of the two rivers" (Gen. 24:10). Most translations
render that location rather misleadingly as "Mesopotamia." Aram-naharaim was the portion of northern Aram
between the Tigris and Euphrates Rivers. The particular
section from which Abraham came was called Paddan-aram,
the Plain of Aram, as referred to in Genesis 25:20; 28:2,
5, 6, 7; 31:18; 35:9, 26; 46:15; and 48:7 (only Paddan).
That "Plain of Aram" is called Al-Jeziret today, located
some hundred and fifteen miles northeast of Aleppo in
north Syria.

Genesis 12-50 speaks freely of the patriarchal relationship as Aramaean. Isaac's wife is referred to as
"Rebekah, the daughter of Bethuel, the Aramaean of
Paddan-aram, the sister of Laban, the Aramaean" (25:20).
Jacob's father-in-law is spoken of as "Laban, son of
Bethuel, the Aramaean" (28:5). Deuteronomy prescribes
that, when first fruits are presented at the altar, the
offerer "shall answer and say before Yahweh, your god,
'My father was an Aramaean, about to perish, when he
went down into Egypt and sojourned there, few in numbers, but he became there a great, mighty, and populous
nation'" (Deut. 26:5).

Inasmuch as Abraham and his descendants were Aramaeans, and spoke the Aramaean language, it is fitting
to describe their spiritual outreach as Aramaean

religion. Since in the course of centuries the old name
Aram became replaced by the equivalent Syria it can be
said that Abraham, Isaac, Jacob, and Joseph were Syrians, that they spoke the Syrian language, and that they
were adherents of Syrian religion. For this reason, some
translations use the later terms Syria and Syrian rather
than the Aram and Aramaean of the Hebrew text.

Because ancient religions are most distinct from
each other with respect to their concepts of deity, the
Aramaean type may best be approached from that angle.
Although a monotheistic revision of these patriarchal
tales was attempted by the editor or editors of Genesis,
this was carried through even less successfully than
in Genesis 1-11. From the unrevised portions, comprising
most of the thirty-nine chapters, it is possible to see
what the religion of Abraham, Isaac, and Jacob was like.
It is found that they worshiped various categories of
deities.

NATURE DEITIES IN WOOD, STONE, AND WATER

The most elementary   Aramaean practice consisted
in continuing primitive stone-age worship of nature deities. This was based on the belief that certain trees,
stones, and bodies of water had gods or numina within
them. If a person had a special religious experience
at one of these, usually in a dream, it indicated a deity resided in the tree, rock, or body of water and had
brought that theophany upon the individual.

That the patriarchs considered tree-gods an essential part of their worship is indicated by the important
place supposedly sacred trees played in their wanderings. Presumably that he might dwell under the shadow
of deity, Abraham pitched his tent under the "oak of
Moreh" at Shechem. Shortly thereafter he "moved his tent
and came and dwelt by the oaks of Mamre which are in

Hebron, and there he built an altar" (Gen. 12:6; 13:18).
In Beer-sheba he planted a tamarisk that eventually became such a cult tree (21:33).

When returning from his servitude to Laban, Jacob
feared his Aramaean religious treasures and his wife's
Aramaean jewelry might be stolen in that Canaanite land.
He therefore deposited a pot containing both under the
sacred oak at Shechem (Gen. 35:4). In this he was following the accepted custom of those times, depositing
coins and precious objects for safe-keeping in the care
of some tree-god. According to the sanctions in those
days, no person would have dared dig up and steal a
cache of entrusted valuables, because of the calamity
the god in care would heap on any such thief.

When Rebekah's nurse died, "she was buried below
Beth-el under the oak, and the name of it was called
Allon-bacuth" (the oak of weeping). This god was thought
to specialize in watching over the dead who were buried
around that tree (Gen. 35:8).

That the patriarchs worshiped tree gods is made
more plausible by observing such continuing practices
as they survive today at out-of-the-way places in the
Near East. One of the best examples is seen at Aqra,
in northern Iraq on the Iranian border. Worshipers deck
the branches of that tree with ribbons of all colors,
each tied there to remind that deity of a petitioner's
request. Upon being granted, a suppliant removes the
ribbon he or she had placed there, so as not to bother
further the god in question. At the base of that tree
is a low oval altar on which worshipers leave flowers,
money, choice objects, or other sacrificial gifts. A
vast cemetery surrounds the tree, as these people are
intent on laying their dead in the protective care of
deity.

Some two miles northwest of Hebron the oaks of
Mamre, under which Abraham pitched his tent, remain as
a shrine today. An iron fence to protect the clump surrounds it. Attention concentrates on the giant trunk
of the partially fallen tree. Since the Palestinian oak
is extremely slow in growth, and this trunk is two feet
in diameter, this may be the surviving portion from one
of the actual trees under which Abraham worshiped, or
a sprout thereof.

The patriarchs also worshiped gods believed to reside in certain stones, usually referred to as pillars,
masseboth, or monoliths. Genesis 28 shows how one such
rock came to be regarded as god-inhabited. While fleeing
from his enraged brother, Jacob spent one night on a
hill thirteen miles north of Jerusalem, using a stone
for a pillow. In his dream he saw a ladder reaching to
Heaven, with angels "ascending and descending on it."
Suddenly, a god stood beside Jacob and spoke, giving
him all that land, promising progeny "as the dust of
the earth," and assuring him safety in his journey and
return.

As Jacob awakened he said, "'Surely a god is in
this place, and I knew it not.' And he was afraid, and
he said: 'How awful is this place! This is none other
than a dwelling place of gods, and this is a gate to
the heavens.'" The editor evidently replaced the original "a god" with "Yahweh."

Genesis 28:16-19 tells how Jacob "took the stone
he had put under his head and set it up for a pillar,
and poured oil upon the top of it, and he called the
name of that place Beth-el" (dwelling place of a god.)
Anointing the stone was a symbolic recognition of the
deity within it. Setting it up as a pillar marked either
the beginning of the Beth-el shrine or addition of

another god. Genesis 35:7 indicates that, in course of
time, the deity inhabiting that sacred stone came to
be called El Beth-el (god of Beth-el).Next to Jerusalem,
that shrine became the leading place of worship in Palestine.

It also is related how the holy place at Mizpah
was established. "And Jacob took a stone and set it up
for a pillar" (Gen. 31:45), thereby constituting it as
the habitat of a god delegated to enforce the covenant
made there between Jacob and Laban. "Then they took
stones and made a heap" which, in their Aramaean language was called Jegar-sahadutha (the heap of witness).
Every person present placed a stone at the foot of the
pillar as his or her witness to the covenant made between the two principals. Then a sacrifice was offered
before the pillar (vss. 46-47, 54).

The guardian deity, who by their prayers and rituals supposedly took residence in that Mizpah (watch
tower), was then implored, in the words of Laban, to
"watch between me and you, while we are absent, one from
the other, . . . That I will not pass beyond this heap
to you, and that you will not pass beyond this heap and
this pillar to me, for harm" (vss. 49, 52).

Genesis 33:20 states that at Shechem Jacob "erected
an altar and called it El-elohe-Israel." Because of the
similarly sounding consonants in *mzbh* (altar) and *mtsbh*
(pillar), a mistake likely has been made here in transcribing the Hebrew text. In contrast with "built," the
usual word for making an altar, the verb used here is
the one customarily employed in "erecting" a pillar,
i.e., setting it on end. Another reason favoring this
restoration is the fact that altars elsewhere are never
called gods. Of stone structures, only "pillars" carried
such designations. In light of these reasons, this text
should be corrected to read that Jacob "erected a pillar

and called it El-elohe-Israel" (god of the gods of
Israel). The name of this monolith indicates the patriarchs worshiped many gods in a polytheistic complex.
It also shows that Jacob regarded this god at Shechem
as the most important of all those deities. When Shechem
was excavated, a standing pillar, and bases which originally held other pillars, were found at that central
shrine in Palestine.

The patriarchs undoubtedly also worshiped gods who
were supposed to reside in many other sacred pillars.
The significance of Genesis' special attention to Beth-
el, Mizpah, and Shechem lies in describing the origin
of these three leading shrines where deities residing
in their respective pillars henceforth were worshiped
by multitudes of Israelites.

Since such stone monoliths are not subject, as
trees, to death and decay, this phase of patriarchal
worship remains evident in the hundreds of such supposedly god-inhabited pillars that survive today
throughout the biblical world. They occur in greatest
profusion in Trans-Jordan, such as Ader (one standing
and two fallen) and nearby Lejjun (twelve still standing
and eleven fallen).

In addition to venerating deities in trees and
stone pillars, the patriarchs also worshiped gods in
bodies of water. While fleeing from her mistress Sarah,
Hagar had a theophonic experience "by a fountain of water in the wilderness, by the fountain on the way to
Shur" (Gen. 16:7). She concluded that the deity who resided in that spring, and "who spoke to her," was a god
who sees." Henceforth (vss. 13-14), that fountain was
called Beer-lahai-roi (well of the living one who sees
me). After the death of Abraham, Isaac pitched his tent
and dwelt by that sacred well (25:11).

Beer-sheba (well of seven), the leading place of worship in southernmost Palestine, was thought to be the home of another water deity. Abraham built an altar there, ostensibly to worship the god in that fountain. He called that particular deity "the everlasting god," in the sense his supply of water was never-failing (Gen. 21:33). Verses 14-19 indicate Hagar had a previous theophonic experience there.

Every well and fountain was a source of blessing in a land where water supplies were not plentiful, but the fountains at Beer-lahai-roi and Beer-sheba were special wells in which deities were supposed to reside.

This is the basis of water baptism, washed free of one's sins by the enfolding deified waters through immersion. Survival of water-god worship is most evident in India where even today every river is believed to have its indwelling god and the Ganges offers the most dramatic mass purification rites in its cleansing waters of deity.

That belief in deities with these three types of embodiments continues in remote areas of the Near East, southern Asia, and Africa does not mean that Aramaean religion survives today. Rather, it indicates some contemporary hang-over of stone-age nature religion which worshiped gods in trees, stones, and water -- a primitive world religion in which the patriarchs participated.

EL ELYON AND THE GOD WHO PROVIDES

It appears that on occasion Abraham worshiped El Elyon (god most high), chief deity in the north Semitic pantheon. This god was worshiped by Phoenicians, Syrians, Canaanites, and especially Priest-King Melchizedek in his city of Salem (peace), the ancient name for Amorite

Jerusalem. The four citations in the five verses of Genesis 14:18-22 indicate the pre-eminent place occupied by El Elyon worship in that key city.

Genesis 14 describes the return of Abraham and his soldiers after having rescued the people of Sodom who had been captured and carried as far as Damascus. When the triumphal procession was passing Jerusalem, Priest-King Melchizedek went out to meet these heroes and staged a victory mass for Abraham by administering the Amoritic sacrament of bread and wine in the name of El Elyon. On that occasion it appears that Abraham joined in worshiping El Elyon (god most high) as he said, "I have lifted up my hand unto . . . El Elyon, maker of Heaven and earth" (Gen. 14:18-22).

The Genesis editor apparently was shocked by having the great patriarch worship an Amoritic Canaanite god and therefore inserted a "Yahweh" in verse 22 to make Abraham worship Yahweh on that occasion. However, the other three unredacted references to El Elyon indicate Yahweh was not in the original picture.

This eucharistic ritual climaxed in Melchizedek's pronouncing the blessing of his god El Elyon on Abraham:

> And he blessed him, and said, "Blessed be Abram
> of El Elyon, maker of Heaven and earth, and
> blessed by El Elyon who has delivered your
> enemies into your hand."

In reciprocation, that patriarch gave to Melchizedek as an offering a tenth of the loot, since tithing was a requirement in the Amoritic form of Canaanite religion that prevailed in Jerusalem (Gen. 14:19-20). Communion of the bread and wine, and giving the tenth, thereby moved from Canaanite religion into the Judaeo-Christian faith.

One must not be disturbed by the ascription "possessor of Heaven and earth" or "maker of Heaven and

earth" in Genesis 14:19 and 22. Such statements are typical of the effusive claims made by many an ancient
idolator for his or her particular god.

Later on, presumably at Melchizedek's command,
Abraham proceeded to offer his son Isaac as a human sacrifice to this same El Elyon at his altar on Mount
Moriah (Gen. 22:2). This episode, combined with Abraham's participation in worship of El Elyon in Genesis
14, shows Abraham sufficiently ecumenical to accept the
blessings of the north-Semitic deity, El Elyon, and go
considerable distance in being obedient to that god's
demands, as enunciated by the Amorite Canaanite Priest-
King Melchizedek.

However, when Abraham came to the summit of Mount
Moriah he decided to make his own altar and offer Isaac
on it. Because of finding the substitute lamb, Abraham
called the deity of that newly-made shrine "the god who
provides" (Gen. 22:9-14).

In this way a new Aramaean deity, "the god who provides," came to assume joint jurisdiction with the
Canaanite "god most high" (El Elyon) over Jerusalem's
seven hills. As the editor of Genesis was unable to tolerate such polytheism, he rewrote Genesis 22 making
Yahweh "the god who provides."

It is significant that this hilltop place of worship, shared henceforth by the pair of Canaanite (El
Elyon, god most high) and Aramaean (the god who provides) deities, became the most holy spot in Palestine,
the location to be chosen later as the site for Solomon's temple.

TERAPHIM OR HOUSEHOLD DEITIES

Another type of deity in Aramaean religion consisted of the teraphim or household gods. Each of these had
his or her own distinctive vocation, such as bestowing

tribal wealth, health of persons, conception of wives and handmaids, male fertility, health of flocks, protection from thieves, success in warfare, etc. Since they were the functional gods worshiped daily, the welfare and prosperity of the tribe was thought to depend primarily on their bounties. Since they were passed on as part of the tribal inheritance, the patriarch who possessed these gods held title to all tribal wealth.

It therefore was a daring theft when "Rachel stole the teraphim that were her father's" as she and Jacob left her home by stealth (Gen. 31:19). When Laban overtook Jacob and his company, the father-in-law's question was (vs. 30), "Why have you stolen my gods?" The seriousness of this offense was indicated by the response of Jacob, who did not know Rachel had taken them: "with whomsoever you find your gods, he shall not live" (vs. 32).

The size of teraphim is indicated by the fact Rachel was able to conceal them in the saddlebag on which she sat (Gen. 31:34-35). These household gods usually were small figurines, from four to six inches tall, and have been dug up by the hundreds of thousands in excavations.

As migrating tribes traveled from country to country, they had to leave behind the nature and area deities who could not move their places of residence. Nomads therefore had to adopt new nature and area deities when coming into a different community. By contrast, since they were mobile, the teraphim brought an element of continuity into the religious needs of wandering peoples. This made the household gods highly revered in Aramaean religion.

With regard to those teraphim that Rachel stole from her father and took along to Palestine, upon nearing Beth-el

> Jacob said to his household, and to all who
> were with him: "Put away the foreign gods that
> are among you, . . . and let us arise and go
> up to Beth-el," . . . And they gave to Jacob
> all the foreign gods that were in their posses-
> sion, . . . and Jacob hid them under the oak
> which was by Shechem (Gen. 35:2-4).

There is no evidence they ever were removed from that
place of deposit to be worshiped again.

This suggests that Abraham was a religious pioneer
with respect to worshiping images, as there is no record
that he, Isaac, or Jacob (except while journeying from
the Aramaean heartland to Shechem) had teraphim in their
possession. It appears that Abraham transcended normative Aramaean religion by abandoning worship of household gods. For this reason Jacob feared to bring into
Canaan the teraphim Rachel stole from her father.Against
the background of universally worshiping household gods
in that age, Abraham's banishing them from the Israelite
form of Aramaean religion was one of the contributions
made by him, as he established an imageless worship in
Israel.

INDIVIDUAL PERSONAL DEITIES OF THE PATRIARCHS

The Aramaeans also had more nebulous gods, not associated with material objects or locations. Strange
as it may appear to us, each patriarch seems to have
had his own personal deity.

Abraham's individual god is represented as having
addressed Isaac, "I am the god of Abraham, your father"
(Gen. 26:24). This personal deity of Abraham was implored four times, by the servant seeking a wife for Isaac,
as the "god of my master Abraham" (24:12, 27, 42, 48).
When speaking to Jacob, Laban once felt the need of

imploring the grandfather's deity, "the god of Abraham"
(Gen. 31:53).

Isaac's personal deity was called by Jacob "the
god of my father" and was spoken of by Laban to Jacob
as "the god of your father" (Gen. 31:5, 29). Addressing
Jacob directly, Isaac's deity was quoted as having said,
"I am the god, the god of your father" (46:3). On that
occasion Jacob "offered sacrifices to the god of his
father Isaac" (46:1). This special god of Isaac seems
to have had a definite name, for it is said that "Jacob
swore by the Fear of his father Isaac" (31:53). That
deity is mentioned once as simply "The Fear of Isaac"
(31:42).

Jacob's specific god was mentioned when the brothers begged Joseph to "forgive the transgression of the
servants of the god of your father" (Gen. 50:17) and
when Jacob blessed the brothers (49:25).

Occasionally the gods of two successive generations
were cited. Jacob told how "the god of Abraham and the
Fear of Isaac had been with me" (Gen. 31:42). Joseph's
steward spoke to the brothers in terms of "your god and
the god of your father" (43:23).

If the whole tribal complex had worshiped the same
deity, such special dialings of an individual patriarch's god would not have been necessary. That the original phrases such as god of Abraham, god of Isaac, Fear
of Isaac, and god of Jacob have survived the editor's
monotheising effort, and that they appear so frequently
and at times in multiples, would seen adequate indication of separate deities.

It appears that a patriarch's personal god had power over the son as long as the father was alive. The
personal deity of a younger desginate took over full
jurisdiction in family and tribal circles only after
the father patriarch had died. Since Abraham and Isaac

were long-lived, for most of their years Isaac and Jacob
had to deal with "the gods of their fathers," as it was
phrased. Their own deities therefore did not come into
full powers until comparatively late in the lives of
these two patriarchs.

Existence of such personal gods was essentially
the same as with the persisting belief in guardian
angels today. This type of supernatural being supposedly
is assigned to an infant at birth and watches over the
entrusted person as guardian, by day and night, throughout that mortal's lifetime. At the death of this individual, that particular angel is transferred to watch over
another human in process of being born.

From the contexts it would appear that these personal gods of the respective patriarchs were regarded
as more important than any of the three kinds of
Aramaean deities previously considered.

EL SHADDAI, HIGHEST IN THE PANTHEON

In their profusion of concepts regarding existence
of supernatural beings, the patriarchs believed in a
still higher deity called El Shaddai. By contrast with
the individual lifetime-bound personal deities of the various patriarchs, El Shaddai was god of the whole ongoing
Israelite tribal family. Although translators have almost universally rendered the name "God Almighty," this
is questionable. The root idea is to "deal violently"
or "to devastate." Since the specific meaning is uncertain, it is perhaps best to leave it untranslated.

El Shaddai was represented as having proclaimed his
covenant with the Israelite people initially to Abraham,
the first Israelite. It contained ultragenerous promises
of numberless progeny, inheriting the land of Canaan,
political achievement, and endless prosperity as a
"multitude of nations" (Gen. 17:1-8).

When fleeing from home because of his brother's wrath, Jacob had this god's blessing bestowed upon him by his father Isaac.

And El Shaddai bless you, and make you fruitful, and multiply you, that you may become
a company of peoples, and give you the blessing of Abraham, to you, and to your descendants
with you, that you may inherit the land of
your sojournings which he (the orgiainal reading via Gen.17:1-8) gave to Abraham (Gen.28:3-4).

As Jacob returned to Palestine from his twenty years with Laban, El Shaddai again renewed the covenant by saying,

I am El Shaddai. Be fruitful and multiply.
A nation and a company of nations shall emerge
from you, and kings shall come out of your
loins, and the land which I gave to Abraham
and to Isaac, to you I will give it, and to
your descendants after you I will give the
land (Gen. 35:11-12).

Jacob's blessing the sons of Joseph in Genesis 48, to renew the covenant and include them in it, was again done in the name of El Shaddai (vs. 3). The blessing bestowed by Jacob upon all his sons in Genesis 49:25 also was made in the name of El Shaddai, as attested by three Hebrew manuscripts, the Samaritan codex, Greek Septuagint, and Syriac:

From the god of your father who shall help you ;
and by El Shaddai, who shall bless you.

From these observations it appears El Shaddai was believed to renew his covenant with Israel in every gen-eration by commissioning each new patriarchal leader.

However, this deity had a major disability. Since it was believed El Shaddai could love and bless only

one patriarchal aspirant in each generation, all other
sons of an incumbent had to be banished from the tribe.
With Abraham this meant recognizing Isaac as the patriarchal heir, but driving into eastern deserts Ishmael
and the six sons of Abraham's second wife Keturah
(Gen. 16:11-12; 25:1-6).

The edict at Ishmael's banishment was, "And he shall
be a wild ass among men -- his hand against every man,
and every man's hand against him, and he shall dwell
to the east of all his brothers" (Gen. 16:12). Of Abraham's other offspring it is said, "And while he yet
lived he sent them away from Isaac, his son, into the
east country" (25:5-6). The enmities engendered by those
expulsions from fertile Palestine into the inhospitable
and unwanted desert areas of Arabia were to prove incal-
culable.

These exilings of unchosen sons led to a radical
disproportion between discarded sons of Abraham, whose
descendants became the Arabs, and the chosen son of
Abraham, whose descendants became the Jews. At the end
of that first generation the score of sons was 7 for
the Arabs and 1 for Israel.

By the end of the second generation the disparity
had become catastrophic. On the Arab side now were to
be numbered the twelve sons of Ishmael, the two sons
of Jockshan, and the five sons of Midian (Gen. 25:3-4,
12-16). Since the number of progeny begotten by the other four sons of Keturah is not listed, one can only
guess at their number. Inasmuch as Jockshan and Midian
had seven between them, it would seem a safe minimal
number to suggest that the other four sons had a total
of fourteen offspring. The discarded Esau also was driv-
en into the Arab camp. This made the score at the end
of the second Abrahamic generation 34 men (plus the un-
named concubines' sons and their sons in 25:6) for the

Arabs to 1 for Israel. In such a short time, the disproportion between the two groups had become frightening.

Jacob perceived that if El Shaddai continued to
choose only one son in each generation, while consigning
the others to a desert existence, his branch of the
Abrahamic family would be destined to meet a quick and
doomful end by reason of emerging enmities and comparative numbers. Jacob therefore blessed all twelve of his
sons, plus the sons of Joseph, even though they had an
Egyptian mother (Gen. 48-49).

However, the harm already had been done. Even
though El Shaddai, the highest deity of the patriarchal
age, was revered for only a relatively short period of
approximately two hundred years, that worship inflicted
upon Israel an irreparable damage which was destined
to plague her for all time to come. The resultant antipathy between Arabs and the Israeli people remains una-
bated today as the perennial conflict of the ages continues within the family of Abraham between the dis-
inherited Arabs and the Jews, upon whom El Shaddai
chose to shower all his bounties.

MONOTHEISING THE PATRIARCHAL NARRATIVES

From these pages it has become apparent that the
Abrahamic family and progeny, for the four generations
recorded in the patriarchal stories, worshiped a conglomerate of five different types of deities. Imploring
those many gods, with proper devotion, constituted the
heart, and almost the whole, of the Aramaean religion.

The Hebrew editor (or editors) of Genesis 12-50
must have been shocked by this polytheistic amalgam that
appeared in those histories of Israel's forebears. Consequently, an attempt was made at remedying the situation by proceeding to monotheise the patriarchal accounts, with the intent of making them acceptable for

inclusion in the Bible. This was done by inserting the
later names Yahweh or God (*elohim*) throughout the narratives. This remade the patriarchs and their people
into worshipers of the supreme and only God, or the
Yahweh approximation thereto.

The designated trees, stones, fountains and geographical areas then became not residences of primitive
deities but special places where Yahweh or God appeared
to the patriarchs. The more ethereal deities (god of
Abraham, god of Isaac, god of Jacob, and El Shaddai)
were similarly reinterpreted as only varying references
to Yahweh or God.

Although such a monotheistic revision of these
patriarchal narratives in chapters 12-50 was attempted
by the Genesis editor, this was carried through even
less successfully than in Genesis 1-11. The vast amount
of unmodified materials in the final thirty-nine chapters has made it possible to reconstruct the real theological orientation of the patriarchal period.Its deity-
centered faith has been seen as a complex of polytheisms, with even the highest god, El Shaddai, far from
the monotheistic level.

SIGNIFICANT ABSENCES IN ARAMAEAN RELIGION

Most of the components, rather generally considered
essential to religion, were missing in this Aramaean
worship. There was no professional religious class or
even semblance of any priesthood. The father of the family was the leader in all religious acts. There were
no designated or regular holy days, no mass religious
gatherings, no cult assembly buildings, no formal rituals, no stated feasts, and no fasts. People worshiped
in a spontaneous manner at home or at holy places, whenever and wherever they felt the urge to do so.

The only cult paraphernalia mentioned were altars, but we are not told how they were built or how worship was conducted at those structures. In nine cases it is stated only that Abraham (Gen. 12:7, 8; 13:4, 18; 26:25) and Jacob (33:20; 35:1, 3, 7) "built" altars and there "called on the name of" some deity. It is recorded that Jacob presented sacrifices on two occasions, but in neither instance is there any statement as to what is meant by "sacrifices," and if altars were involved (Gen. 31:54; 46:1). It is clear that the "seven ewe lambs" which figured in naming Beer-sheba (well of seven) were not sacrificed on that altar by Abraham. After giving them as a present to Abimelech, Abraham then worshiped (21:27-32).

Since no animals are mentioned as having been burnt up to deity in any of these twelve instances, it appears the patriarchal people already had risen above the crude belief that the gods lived on the smell of animals presented as burnt sacrifices. Near the end of this chapter attention will be given to the strategic event which brought about that remarkable abstention.

If not for presenting burnt offerings, what then was the purpose of Abraham and Jacob in constructing altars? In light of the love for divine fragrance in the ancient Near East, some probably were altars of incense. Others may have been simply small heaped-up mounds of earth that served as fire altars, with the ascending flames and smoke carrying the patriarchal prayers and petitions to their respective deities. The only certainty is that these modest structures were places of worship.

When all the abstentions are taken into consideration, it becomes apparent that this Aramaean religion of the patriarchs was a matter of outreach toward deity

in religious experience that avoided the usual ritualistic formalities of religion.

PASSIONATE LONGING FOR CHILDREN

Passionate longing for children amounted to an essential element in Aramaean religion, for survival
through their progeny was the only form of immortality
the patriarchs envisioned. They strove especially for
numbers since children served to develop a work force
and to make the tribe's future militarily strong by
ability to conquer potential enemies: "And your offspring shall possess the gate of his enemies" (Gen. 22:17).

In this megalomania, the patriarchs are represented
visualizing descendants so numerous "as the stars of
the heavens and as the sand which is upon the seashore"
(Gen. 22:17 cf. 15:5; 26:4; 32:12). With such daring
hopes, it was anticipated that Israel would become not
only one great people but a whole complex of nations:

> but your name shall be Abraham, for I have ap-
> pointed you the father of a multitude of na-
> tions (Gen. 17:5 cf. 17:4, 6, 16; 48:19).

Although these exotic promises are in the wording of
the Genesis editor, they express the patriarchs' great
concern for descendants.

This was true even more of the wives who, in their
mania for children, developed a psychopathic fear of
barrenness. To bypass this, the Aramaeans had developed
their system of handmaidenship. As implied in Genesis,
and clearly stated in the Nuzi documents, it was customary for the father to give the bride, as her wedding
gift, a handmaiden who would serve as child insurance.
This standby was the bride's proxy whom she would give
to her husband in case of barrenness, that thereby the
wife might obtain children for herself.

The best picture of how the handmaiden system operated is observed in Gen. 29:31-30:24, with Jacob's two
wives and the two handmaidens. Since unloved Leah got
started in childbearing first, the score at the end of
the first inning was Leah 4 and Rachel 0. Frightened
at this trend, Rachel gave Jacob her handmaid Bilhah
who gave birth to two children, thereby changing the
count to Leah 4 and (by proxy) Rachel 2. Thwarted by
her own seemingly emerging barrenness, and the possibility of Rachel's catching up, Leah gave her handmaid Zil-
pah to Jacob and obtained two proxy sons in that way,
with the resultant number, Leah 6 and Rachel 2. By eating aphrodisiac mandrakes, Leah resumed conception and
gave birth to two more sons and a daughter, Dinah, with
a semifinal number of sons, Leah 8 and Rachel 2. Belatedly, Rachel became pregnant (30:24; 35:16-18) and had
Joseph and Benjamin. With the game over, the final score
of sons was Leah 8 and Rachel 4.

Undoubtedly girl babies also were born to these
four mothers, but are not mentioned because female
children were considered relatively worthless. The only
reason for listing Dinah was that she became the object
of a first-rate intertribal scandal and conflict (Gen.
34:1-31).

The agonizing cry of Rachel to her husband, "Give
me children or else I die," and the scramble of both
wives for the aphrodisiac mandrakes and sex relations
was pathetic (Gen. 30:1, 14-24). The psychological back-
firing of this mania for children appears to have been
severe in producing either childlessness or limited conception. Jacob's four partners had only three and a
quarter known children per mother, Isaac's wife Rebekah
had only a single conception (twin sons), while Sarah
and Hagar had but one child each.

Abraham's loyalty to Sarah's handmaid deserves special commendation. After protesting against his wife's jealousy, callousness, and illegality in banishing Hagar from the homestead, he showed his loyalty to this handmaiden by sending supplies of food and water with her (Gen. 21:11, 14).

The Aramaean system of handmaidenship was not thought in any way immoral but a proper marital procedure. However, it had its undertow of debits. The jealousies between wife and handmaid are observable between Sarah and Hagar. Especially when compounded with polygamy, as in Jacob's case, this custom resulted in domestic disharmony, with a complex of rivalries between the two wives, wives and handmaids, the two handmaids, and between the respective children of these four.

All this contributed toward making Genesis 12-50 a drama of conflicting favoritisms. Although well-meaning, the practice of handmaidenship must be viewed as a debit in the Aramaean religious system.

LIES, AND RUMORS OF LIES

The lowest point in the patriarchal stories consisted in the lying that was tolerated. The biblical text states that Abraham twice denied Sarah was his wife by declaring to both Pharaoh and Abimelech she was his sister. The same deception is recorded as having been perpetrated by Isaac against Abimelech. In each instance the motive for such deception was personal safety and possibly desire of wealth by way of blackmail (Gen. 12:10-20; 20:1-18; 26:1-11). Since these accounts probably represent three versions of a single event, with varying identification of persons and places, the debit is reduced by two-thirds.

One saga of prevarication was inexcusably satanic. This occurred in connection with the Aramaean custom of a patriarch's giving his ancestral blessing when death was approaching. That was all-important, since it involved bestowing the entire tribal wealth and prestige upon a successor. This occurred when Rebekah and son Jacob took advantage of the senility and blindness of a husband and father, supposedly facing death, by executing a succession of brazen lies (Gen. 27:5-45).

When Isaac asked, "Who are you, my son?" Jacob replied, "I am Esau, your first-born" (vss. 18-19). Isaac requested that Esau go to the hunting ranges and "hunt venison" and prepare "tasty food." Even though Jacob had not been out of the tent area, he shamelessly said, "I have done according as you requested me" (vss. 3-4, 19). Although presenting only the lying food of goat's meat, this deceiver said to his father, "sit up and eat of my venison, that your soul may bless me" (vss. 9-14, 19). When Isaac questioned how this could have been done so soon, Jacob not only perjured himself but also brought Isaac's god into the lying by saying, "Because the lord your god brought me success" (vs. 20). Although eliciting the immortal response, "The voice is Jacob's voice, but the hands are the hands of Esau," the lying wrists and neck, covered with sparse-haired goat skins, were in a measure convincing (vss. 11-13, 16, 21-23). Still doubting somewhat, Isaac said, "Are you really my son Esau?" to which Jacob brazenly replied "I am" (vs. 24). By resorting to the lying kiss, a virtual sacramental seal of certification that the one inviting the blessing was Esau, Jacob was committing also a religious outrage (vs. 27). The clincher proved to be the lying clothing, since Rebekah had placed Esau's "best garments," on her pet son. When Isaac "smelled the smell" of Esau's clothes, this was taken as the decisive indication the candidate for blessing before him was Esau (vss. 15, 27). Ultimately convinced by this

shamelessly executed amalgam of eight lies that his misgivings had been but the groundless misjudgments of
old age, with failing powers and blindness Isaac finally
bestowed the patriarchal blessing and tribal inheritance
upon Jacob.

If a moral story is one in which wickedness is punished and righteousness is rewarded, that anecdote appears immoral. This is shown in the deceiver's receiving
all the blessings while curses were heaped upon the hon-
est son who was consigned to perpetual servitude and
driven "away from the fatness of the earth" into the
arid regions which came to be called Edom (Gen. 27:39-
41). Rebekah had no moral scruples, and Jacob's hesitancy was only because of fear he might be caught in this
deceptive scheme and be punished (vss. 11-13). It is
amazing that the editor of Genesis should have included
in the Bible an account so unfavorable to his people.

The last Genesis generation was plagued by another
tragedy of deceptions. This was initiated by the lying
of the brothers to their father when they brought
Joseph's blood-stained coat and said (Gen. 37:32), "We
have found this. Do you know whether it is your son's
coat or not?" They had not "found" the coat, they pre-
tended they were not certain it was their brother's garment, and their father was made to believe his beloved
son had been killed. These three lies were compounded
tenfold by reason of the ten brothers' complicity in
them. Until his thirtieth year (41:46) Joseph was forced
to live under the torment initiated by that triad of
falsehoods. During all that time Jacob's life was tortured with the thought of having lost his beloved son.
This dishonesty must have troubled even the ten brothers
every day of those deceptive years.

Since the Aramaean religion of the patriarchs was
marred by its overshadowing falsehoods, the Genesis

narratives can have value at these points only in impressing the need for truthfulness in daily living.

AT PEACE WITH NEIGHBORING PEOPLES

A laudable element in the lives of the patriarchs
consisted in their peaceful relations with non-
Israelite peoples. Abraham set the example by his resolve to be a good neighbor and a blessing to all with
whom he came into contact, so "all the families of the
land" (the preferred translation) would be blessed by
his presence among them (Gen. 12:2-3). This is shown
especially in his generous dealings with the Hittites,
in purchasing a burial site for Sarah (23:7-20). Those
attitudes carried over to Isaac who also strove to be
at peace with other tribes. He even left his developed
territory to the Gerarites rather than fight to retain
it (26:17-22).

Jacob also was scrupulous about having good relations with other ethnic groups. He was outraged when
his sons Simeon and Levi massacred all males in Shechem,
and plundered that city. In exasperation he cried out,
"You have troubled me, to make me odious before the inhabitants of the land." However, as with his hesitancy
in pursuing the stolen blessing, expediency rather than
principle seemed to be Jacob's chief motivation: "Since
I am few in numbers, they will gather themselves together against me and attack me, and I shall be destroyed;
I and my household" (Gen. 34:30). In spite of this lowered motive with Jacob, by contrast with Abraham and
Isaac, passion for being in harmony with all peoples
was one of the high points in the Aramaean religion of
the patriarchs.

One of the jewels in this crown of friendship was
the method of settling disputes. When in conflict, patriarchs settled disagreements peaceably by making a

covenant with the actual or potential opponent. In Abraham's covenant with Abimelech it was promised that

> you will not deal falsely with me, nor with my
> offspring, nor with my posterity; but according to the kindness that I have done to you,
> you shall do to me and to the land wherein you
> have sojourned . . . and the two of them made
> a covenant (Gen. 21:23, 27).

This carried even an ecological touch, for it terminated in the promise that no harm would be done "to the land."

Notable also were the ensuing covenant meals by which such agreements were sealed. When Laban and Jacob parted, vowing there would be no further enmities between them, that promise was consummated by such a sacred feast: "and they ate there by the heap . . . And they ate bread, and tarried all night in the mountain" (Gen. 31:46, 54). This early sacrament of friendship was to develop into the original Passover custom of spending the whole night at the festal table (Deut. 16:7).

These holy covenant meals, in which deity supposedly participated, were prototypes also of the Christian Lord's Supper and the anticipated heavenly banquet. The belief that Abraham and his god were bound together in covenant, renewed with Isaac and Jacob, found overtones even in the scriptural designations Old Covenant (Old Testament) and New Covenant (New Testament), and in some Christian groups calling themselves "covenanters."

ABRAHAM'S COMPASSION FOR THE SODOMITES

Abraham's superb qualities were revealed at their highest in his relationships with Lot. The uncle was generous in giving to that nephew the choice of territory, and in accepting the less-desirable land for himself (Gen. 13:5-12). Selecting the fertile Jordan valley was understandable, but Abraham was jolted when Lot made his home in Sodom, the most immoral city in Palestine. Even so, Abraham remained loyal to his rather inconsiderate nephew. When Lot and the people of Sodom were captured by enemy armies, Abraham went to the rescue. Using his own three hundred and eighteen tribal warriors, and with help from the confederated tribes of Aner, Eshcol, and Mamre, Abraham pursued as far as Damascus. There he recovered the captured goods and all the people, including Lot and his family (14:11-24).

The next event in which these three chieftains participated is recorded in Genesis 18-19. They are called "men" in the unrevised portions of that story (Gen.18:2, 16, 22; 19:5, 8, 10, 12, and 16). However, the editor of Genesis mythologized these two chapters to the extent of making the leader into "Yahweh" at fourteen places and into "the Lord" in four verses. The two lesser members of the trio were transformed into "angels" in 19:1 and 15. By demythologizing the chapters at these points, the account of destroying the wicked cities of Sodom and Gomorrah can be reduced again to good history.

When those three confederates of Abraham (Gen. 14:13, 24; 18:2) plotted to annihilate the twin cities of corruption, Abraham insisted that the people of Sodom not be destroyed. He was at his best when pleading before Aner, who remained behind to enlist the help of Abraham and his three hundred and eighteen trained warriors, even though the other two chieftains already were on the way to join their armies and destroy those cities.

Unable to conceive of anyone so brutal as to incinerate innocent people with the wicked, Abraham issued a dual challenge to Aner: "Will you consume the righteous with the wicked?" and "Shall not the judge of all the land do right?" Abraham begged that Sodom be saved

if fifty righteous people could be found in it, then
forty-five, forty, thirty, twenty, and finally ten, to
all of which Aner agreed (Gen. 18:23-32).

There was no doubt in Abraham's mind but that ten
righteous people could be found in Sodom. He had faith
in man, which is the essence of democracy and almost
as important as faith in deity. When he left the meeting
that day he went home in glee, feeling confident he
had saved the city. On the other hand, Aner was equally
certain ten righteous people were not to be found in
Sodom, and therefore the way was clear for the federated
armies to embark on their genocidal plan to destroy that
"gay" city of homosexuals.

This was done the following morning when Sodom and
Gomorrah were taken by surprise before daybreak and put
to the torch while the inhabitants were still asleep.
The Genesis editor mythologized this attack by making
the fire descend from Heaven, as the author of Revelation was to do later in describing Nero's supposed burning of Rome (Rev. 13:13).

Abraham's heart sank when he awoke in the morning
and

> looked toward Sodom and Gomorrah, and toward
> all the land of the Plain, and beheld, and lo,
> the smoke of the land went up as the smoke of
> a furnace (Gen. 19:28).

If it were necessary to worship one of these two
leaders, and they were Abraham and God, as exegetes commonly assume, one would have had to choose Abraham,
since that patriarch was superior in possessing those
qualities of morality, discernment, and mercy we associate with deity. His pleading that even wicked cities
should not be ruthlessly destroyed, but should be given
opportunity to repent, was a diamond moment in Abraham's
life and religion.

ELIMINATION OF HUMAN AND ANIMAL SACRIFICE

Another place Abraham appears at his best was with respect to sacrificing his son Isaac in Genesis 22.Among some neighboring peoples it was customary to sacrifice the first-born son on the eighth day (Exod. 22:29-30). It was believed deity demanded the first-born male of both flocks and humans as a burnt sacrifice, otherwise the god in question would grant no more progeny. The fact that Abraham and Sarah did not comply with this theological imperative, and were granted no more children by their god, supposedly proved the rule.

Suffering under the stigma of being irreligious, these parents endured increasing ostracism at the hands of their neighbors for something like ten to thirteen years. Abraham finally capitulated to community pressure, slipped Isaac secretly out of the tent early one morning, unknown to Sarah, and departed for the place of sacrifice. While climbing Mount Moriah the father's heart must have sank as the innocent lad, carrying the load of wood (key to his age) that soon was to burn him alive, said, "Behold the fire and the wood, but where is the lamb for a burnt offering?" (Gen. 22:7).

At the top, this patriarch weakened in his intended compliance with Melchizedek's presumed demand that Isaac be sacrificed on the altar of the Amorite deity, "god most high." Instead, Abraham hastily built an Aramaean altar nearby, the only recorded place in the patriarchal narratives that an altar was built to present a burnt sacrifice.

After having arranged the wood on the altar, he quickly tied up Isaac and placed him thereon. Raising his knife, this fond father was at the point of slashing his beloved son to death. At that moment Abraham was overcome by the impending gruesomeness of the deed he was about to perform. He could not go through with it.

Several pointed questions may have overpowered him. How could any deity be so sadistic as to take delight at seeing an innocent child suffer by being stabbed to death and incinerated as a burnt sacrifice? By what strain of the imagination could such an abhorrent act bring well-being and forgiveness of sins to the burning child's parents? Could any god be so dull of perception, unable to tell whether Abraham was righteous without putting an innocent lad through such a traumatic experience that would torment his dreams for life?

Abraham dropped the knife, untied his terrified son, and proceeded to sacrifice instead "a ram caught in the thicket by his horns" (Gen. 22:13). Apparently this patriarch reacted with almost equal decisiveness at seeing that innocent animal suffer in a human's place, ostensibly to placate an offended god, and vowed never to do such a deed again.

In abandoning religious practices so generally observed throughout antiquity, Abraham set a daring precedent. His turning against human sacrifice, and resolving never ceremonially to slit another animal's throat, apparently resulted in eliminating both human and animal sacrifice from the subsequent two centuries of patriarchal religion. An even more amazing result was that his Amorite neighbors came to have such respect for his action that they also seem to have abandoned the practice of child sacrifice.

In harmony with the Near Eastern practice of often changing a man's name upon attaining an especially significant achievement, in succession two later designations were applied to Abraham. At Isaac's birth his father's original name Heber, from which comes Heberites or Hebrews, was changed to Abram (exalted father). After refusal to sacrifice this son, the name was altered further from Abram (exalted father) to Abraham (compassionate father).

The Genesis editor has each of these changes take place too early. Losing the first name, the second (Abram) has been moved back to this patriarch's birth. As to the final name Abraham, the editor mistook one consonant within it, ascribed the change to the god El Shaddai, retrojected it to the time Isaac's birth was annunciated, and its philology was misconstrued as "father of a multitude" rather than "compassionate father" (Gen. 17:1-5).

This terminal renaming probably was made by surrounding peoples in recognition of that patriarch's love and compassion for his son Isaac. To honor Abraham further, the name of the village near his home was changed (Gen. 23:2) from Kiriath-arba (delightful city) to Hebron (Heber's city), the designation it has borne from that day to the present.

These name changes indicate the high regard accorded Abraham by his own and other tribes, perhaps largely because of his eliminating both human and animal sacrifices from the religion of his day.

THE FLOWERING OF ARAMAEAN RELIGION

At the close of Genesis, Joseph provided a blessed benediction to Aramaean religion. His highest merit consisted in abiding by his principles, whatever the cost. This was observed at its best in refusal to betray the trust Potiphar had placed in him (Gen. 39). Joseph's dependability in whatever he did, and vision of a famineless nation, caused this son of a patriarchal nomad to be exalted into a position of high power in the land of Egypt (ch. 41).

After meeting and needling his brothers sufficiently to make them remorseful for their deed, his forgiveness and bestowing bounty on them was a magnificent example of returning good for evil (chs. 42-45). It is a delight to have the Book of Genesis end in moral triumph with this keen and upright young man for whom one can have only praise.

However, as the people in Genesis 12-50 recede into the distant past, the spotlight of attention remains focused on the first in that succession. Although basic religion of the patriarchs was Aramaean, Abraham became a religious pioneer who elevated the Palestinian segment of that faith to much higher spiritual levels. This towering individual became progenitor of the remarkable family that was to become Israel. As the source from which all three have come, Abraham laid the initial foundations upon which Judaism, Christianity and Islam have been built. Consequently, all adherents of these three faiths look back to him as their spiritual father.

He left to posterity a free worship, unencumbered by ritualistic appurtenances that usually crystallize about cult practices. Abraham's religion was one of faith in all people, passion for peace with all humanity, and concern for even the least. Rising above both human and animal sacrifice, that religion consisted basically in outreach and upreach toward deity.

The sunset of patriarchal religion left a delightful afterglow. Although these four men and their people were still enmeshed in a rabble of deities, and never achieved a concept of God, in other respects they had discovered many of the fundamentals in religion. In spite of the failings connected with that age, the worthy qualities of their heightened Aramaean religion provide a floodlight of spirituality that illumines the entire Bible.

CHAPTER 3

THE EGYPTO-MIDIANITE RELIGION OF MOSES

The Bible's third religion was produced by Moses who was to accomplish the herculean task of liberating his Israelites from their bondage in Egypt. Without armies, and only faith in divine help, he outwitted the Egyptian hosts. Millennia of children have been thrilled over his dramatic escape by parting the supposed Red Sea waters and crossing on dry land. Generations of the faithful have treasured the picture of the great lawgiver conversing with God face to face and coming down from the holy mountain with those tablets of the immortal ten commandments.

Moses finally succeeded in bringing those reluctant refugees to the edge of that anticipated land of promise. Then he died, after only seeing from the top of Mount Nebo that land believed to be "flowing with milk and honey."

Moses is recorded to have staged the greatest miracles over nature in the Bible. However, miracle is but the glamor and tinsel with which heroes of the dim past are often adorned by their devoted followers. The task today is to demythologize the glamorized Moses into the real but far more modest historical character. Even on that level of truth one discovers a great national and religious hero.

The first item to remember about the Bible's third religion is how far it was removed in point of time from the Aramaean religion of the patriarchs. Exodus 12:40 reckons the lapse of time from the close of Genesis to the beginning of Exodus as four hundred and thirty years. Apparently the late priestly editor made Abraham

predict that interval as four hundred years (Gen.15:13).
According to present archaeologically based dating, the
time from Joseph's death about 1550 B.C. to Moses' liberation of the Israelites around 1223 B.C. was approximately three hundred and twenty-seven years. Even that
was a very long period.

By the time the curtain rose to terminate that interval of silence, the Israelites had degenerated into
but an inert mass of dispirited slaves. Ground into cultural death by their masters, these descendants of Jacob
did not have sufficient vitality to preserve any record
of their life while in Egypt. Consequently, not one word
has survived in the Bible concerning what transpired
during that third of a millennium.

It is also necessary to realize that by no means
all of Jacob's descendants were left in Egypt at the
time of Moses. In chapter 5 it will be shown that only
Judah and Levi remained there. Consequently, only those
two straggling tribes were in need of liberation.

In the course of those disintegrative centuries,
the patriarchal way of life and the Aramaean religion
associated with it had become abandoned as these Israelites capitulated to their environment. By the beginning
of Exodus they had adopted what was essentially a brand
of Egyptian theology. This was the foundation religion
which initiated the Mosaic age.

Although the late priestly editor had done some
elaborating and changing in the Genesis narratives,
he splurged when it came to revising the Mosaic accounts.
This is true to such an extent that the authentic materials are almost completely overshadowed by the approximately ninety per cent of Exodus, Leviticus and Numbers
that consists of spurious materials added by this editor,
or the late priestly school of which he was a member.

With so little of the authentic portions remaining, and since Moses' religion was so largely a gradual build-up from episode to episode, it is important to point out at each stage the essential facts as recorded in the few surviving genuine Mosaic fragments. As most people's supposed knowledge of this great liberator, law-giver, and national leader is based on the false statements in the editorial elaborations, it is enlightening to see what the editor has done to the authentic nucleus of truth at strategic places. The pressing task is to liberate the real Moses, and his modest religion, from the editor's spectacular fabrications.

This third religion of the Bible is essentially that of one person, Moses, whose spiritual perspectives evolved gradually through some forty years of bitter trial.

RELIGION WITH A PASSION FOR JUSTICE

Moses' new faith for a new age found its first expression in three significant episodes. The first occurred when this youth went to observe the public works and saw an Egyptian taskmaster lashing an Israelite slave. Outraged, Moses proceeded to stop this brutality, first by words and then by action. Whatever the details of the tussel that followed, it ended as the taskmaster lay dead and Moses buried him in the sand (Exod.2:11-12).

Continuing his observations the following day, Moses saw one Israelite beating another. This youth's sense of justice again asserted itself as he asked the offender what justification he had for doing such an act. The villain insolently replied, "Are you intending to kill me as you killed the Egyptian?" Realizing that news of his deed the previous day had spread, and upon hearing that the government was taking steps to apprehend and kill him, Moses fled from Egypt across the marshes to the land of Midian (Exod. 2:13-15).

In that arid territory this refugee came to a well where shepherdesses had drawn water for their flocks,but were being driven away by shepherds bringing their sheep to the troughs the girls had filled. Observing this, Moses must have said to himself, "This isn't right." Thereupon he drove the shepherds away, allowing the shepherdesses to water their flocks in peace (Exod. 2:15- 17).

Those three episodes reveal a young man with one dominant concern, a passion for justice. This was the foundation upon which Moses' religion was to rest. There was nothing theological about it, with no mention of any deity. It was an existential involvement in response to situations of exploitation and cruelty. Throughout the exodus and wilderness periods, this strong passion for justice became intensified as a basic component of Mosaic religion.

DISCOVERING THE MIDIANITE RELIGION OF YAHWISM

When the girls returned so soon and told of the "Egyptian" who had befriended them, their father had them return to the well and bring Moses to the tent.This Midianite patriarch, listed as Reuel in Exodus 2:18 but Jethro elsewhere, admired this guest and gave him the oldest daughter Zipporah for a wife (Exod.2:19-22).

Those were momentous days, since Moses found himself encountering a wholly new religion. As Jethro was a priest in that faith, the time spent in his tent placed Moses at the center of Midianite religion. During evenings spent around the campfire, one can imagine the aging priest indoctrinating his young son-in-law in the essentials of that belief. Central in all this was

Moses' discovery of a new and worthy deity, Yahweh, god
of the Midianite people.

The most determining event in Moses' life was his
encounter with Yahweh while watching Jethro's flocks at
"the back of the wilderness" near "the mountain of god"
(Exod. 3:1). Since the continuing dialogue in verses 4
and 7 was between Yahweh and Moses, it is evident that
verse 2 originally read:

And Yahweh appeared to him in a flame of fire
from the midst of a bush. And he looked, and
behold, the bush burned with fire,but the bush
was not consumed.

Those who have been near a tree when being struck
by lightning can appreciate the aptness of Moses' description. One minute it is all aflame with fire, but the
next, it appears not to have been burned in the least.
However, with the passing of hours it is a different
story, as the scorched leaves soon wilt, and by the following day become brown.

In the theology of that time, every shaft of lightning was an arrow shot by a god at some individual for
a particular purpose. In harmony with Oriental custom,
this shepherd's first impulse was to remove the shoes
from his feet because this theophonic manifestation indicated he was standing on "holy ground" (Exod. 3:5).

After the first shock, Moses tried to determine why
this experience had come to him. He had felt conscience-
stricken often during those days in Midian for having
deserted the Israelite slaves in Egypt and having fled
for his own personal safety, but he always had dismissed
the thought. Now it seized him with force. Could Yahweh
be taking him to task for his cowardice? Although trying
to reason this conclusion out of his mind, Moses could
hear only the repeated divine summons that he must go

back and liberate those oppressed people from their
curse of bondage (Exod. 3:6-10).

If he should attempt this task, where would he take
those suffering slaves? In almost an instant there
flashed before this young shepherd what he construed as
Yahweh's plan to lead them into the land of Canaan
(Exod. 3:8b).

Through this spectacular encounter, Moses came to
see that the compassion of Midianite Yahweh was extending beyond tribal bounds to the Israelite slaves in
Egypt. Ensuing reliance on that god was to become a
religion of liberation for Israel and, by implication,
for all oppressed peoples.

FROM DISTRACTING DOUBTS TO INVINCIBLE FAITH

Great as that religious experience was at the burning bush, a series of doubts immediately engulfed Moses.
He feared he could not perform such a herculean under-
taking. However, on further thought he came to the conclusion that, with Yahweh's help, he would be able to
carry out this difficult assignment. Moses would bring
the redeemed slaves to this mountain so they could stand
on that holy spot where he had his epochal experience
before the once-burning bush. There, they too could become acquainted intimately with this new god
(Exod. 3:11-12).

The quandary then arose over how to convince these
skeptical refugees of this new god's reality and that
he had spoken at the burning bush. Moses thought to
solve this dilemma by relaying to Israel the divine words
"I am Yahweh" and informing them that "Yahweh has sent
me to you" (Exod. 3:13-14).

Because that occasion, when the name of this new
god Yahweh was revealed directly to Israel, became construed by later generations as the most sacred moment

in Israel's history, the advent of this divine name in Exodus 3:14 came to be regarded as too sacred to pronounce in synagogue reading. To avoid this, it has been twice surrogated in the Hebrew text of that verse into the meaningless substitute "I am" instead of "Yahweh." Since these are similar in Hebrew, the substituted term avoids the supersacred word but still suggests it. This is how the enigmatical "I am who is I am" and "I am has sent me to you" have come to replace the original "I am Yahweh" and "Yahweh has sent me to you." Since the surrogation was not carried beyond that strategic verse, the original "Yahweh" has been left remaining in the Hebrew throughout the balance of this narrative: Exod. 3:15, 16, 18; 4:1, 2, 4, 5, 6, etc.

The amount of mileage gotten out of that simple surrogate "I am" in Exodus 3:14 is seen in the profusion of theological treatises and sermons derived therefrom. This is regarded as the chief biblical proof for the eternal existence of God. All this theology is extracted from what was but a device to avoid pronouncing, in synagogue reading, the name of the Midianite regional god Yahweh when introduced to Israel at Mount Sinai.

Hundreds of such surrogates remain in daily speech today for words of reverence or abomination: my land for my Lord, gosh for God, je crouts for Jesus Christ, goodness knows for God knows, heck for Hell, darn for dam, the deuce for the devil, etc. The surrogate usually has enough similarity that thoughtful people can discern the obscured words.

Moses' third doubt concerned how he could convince the Israelite slaves that this deity would help them. He became reassured at this point as he resolved to tell how Yahweh had appeared before him, asking that he relay to them the urgent message:

I indeed have given attention to you and what
is being done to you in Egypt,and I have said,
I will bring you up out of the affliction in
Egypt.

This god of Mount Sinai and surrounding areas had been
observing the oppression of the Israelites, presumably
sanctioned by the Egyptian deities, and had resolved to
slip across the border and rescue that slave people.
Moses felt assured by Yahweh that they would respond
(Exod. 3:15-18).

Doubting that the people would believe him, Moses
triumphed over this by his most fragile and unworthy re-
assurance, that he would resort to magic to convince opponents (Exod. 4:1-9).

Moses' project collapsed once more as he thought of
how he had done no public speaking, and was not eloquent.
This doubt was surmounted as he envisioned Yahweh saying
to him, "I shall be with your mouth, and I will teach
you what you shall speak" (Exod. 4:10-12).

Nevertheless, that same doubt resurged itself even
more strongly as Moses begged Yahweh to have someone
else do the speaking. At this point the text says, "And
the anger of Yahweh was kindled against Moses." He finally decided to rely on his brother Aaron for doing the
speaking (Exod.4:13-16). Even though having bypassed reliance on Yahweh to the extent of using Aaron as a crutch,
Moses finally felt confident for his task.

How could such a record of inner experience have
survived? On many an evening during the wilderness wanderings the Israelite refugees may have said to Moses,
"Tell us again about your experience at the burning bush
and Yahweh's calling you to this service." At each invitation one can imagine Moses repeating that enchanting
story to his interested listeners. Enough of them remembered it with a fair degree of accuracy that, when

Israel's early traditions came to be written down some three centuries later, this record found its rightful place near the head of the Mosaic corpus. This ranks among the most remarkable records of inner religious experience for all time.

Even though adulterated somewhat by this series of alternations between doubt and faith, the power of divine compulsion experienced by this young man at that burning bush was sufficient to make him the liberator of his people. It kept him pursuing his ultimate goal through all the discouragements that were to come during the ensuing forty years of wilderness wanderings at the head of an obtuse people. This shows what power for a whole lifetime can be generated in a few moments by a single, but meaningful, experience of worship.

THE IMPERATIVE OF CIRCUMCISION

No sooner had Moses begun the return trip to Egypt, with Zipporah and a young son, than adversity struck. Record of that episode has survived in a puzzling account (Exod. 4:24-26).

> And it came to pass on the way, at the lodgingplace, that Yahweh met him and tried to kill him. Then Zipporah took a flint and cut off the foreskin of her son, and cast it at his feet. And she said, "You surely are to me a bloody bridegroom." So he let him alone. Then she said, "A bloody bridegroom because of the circumcision!"

This is one of those cases where the writing is telegraphically brief. Translating such an account from Hebrew into English is only a portion of the task. The other part is to fill out the thought by clarifying the concentrated wording. When so treated, this seemingly

insignificant fragment becomes a classic in portraying
the thought modes of that time.

The key to interpretation lies in the observation
that this episode occurred at a "lodging-place." The
best guess is that Moses ate contaminated food there and
became deathly sick with ptomaine poisoning. The sudden
stroke of this acute illness prompted a succession of
reasonings.

First came the diagnosis, that Yahweh was attempting to kill Moses. This was a strange conclusion, since
this god supposedly had ordered Moses' return to Egypt
and now was trying to kill him for complying.

The question regarding particulars now emerged,
"Why was Yahweh trying to kill Moses?" This led to
secondary diagnosis and review of possible causes. After
examining all options, it was concluded Yahweh had proceeded to kill Moses because of taking an uncircumcised
son into Egypt.

Conflict between Midianite and Egyptian cultures
was the basic factor in this situation. From time immemorial Egyptians had practiced circumcision of male
children. The Mosaic family was facing potential scandal
if they were to take an uncircumcised son into Egypt.

Since Moses had been disabled, Zipporah took matters in hand and circumcised the offending son. As
Midianite life was neolithic, not yet having advanced
to the stage of adopting metal tools, a sharp flint
stone was used to perform this operation. She then cast
the severed foreskin at Moses' feet as evidence to Yahweh that the omission had been taken care of. Moses recovered, which indicated to all concerned that both the
primary and secondary diagnoses had been correct.

The generalization from this sequence was that
Israel's god demands circumcision of all males. By Abraham's and now Moses' capitulation to Egyptian influence,

the rite of circumcision became an integral element in subsequent Israelite religious practice. This episode shows how an essentially casual event can initiate a religious ritual and taboo that is assumed henceforth to have eternal validity and importance.

RELIGION OF SOCIAL ACTION

In today's parlance, Moses was a labor agitator or organizer. He asked for no increased pay or improved working conditions but only a single fringe benefit (Exod. 5:1-2). It was phrased in the words:

Thus says Yahweh, the god of Israel, "Let my people go, that they may celebrate a feast unto me in the desert."

This demand was met with a flat rejection as Pharaoh said:

Who is Yahweh, that I should listen to his request to let Israel go?

Repeating the demand, the amount of time off was made specific as three days for this worship. In response, Pharaoh gave an even more decisive reply:

Wherefore do you, Moses and Aaron, release the people from their works? Get to your burdens (Exod. 5:3-4).

Later that same day Pharaoh issued a retaliatory decree requiring these slaves to gather their straw in addition and still produce the same quota of bricks per day. When the Israelite workmen protested against the impossibility of meeting the new requirements, the complainants were beaten and Pharaoh re-enunciated his demands with increased severity (Exod. 5:5-18).

By restricting privileges of the workmen, Pharaoh hoped they would drive out this union organizer. This method worked well for Pharaoh, as the "officers of the Israelites" met with Moses and requested that he desist from further agitation. They said,

> You have caused our reputations to be abominat-
> ed in the eyes of Pharaoh, and in the eyes of
> his servants, to put a sword in their hand to
> slay us (Exod. 5:19-21).

At that moment Moses' cause was lost, for not only
the Egyptians but also his own Israelite people had
turned against him. Faced with that situation, one would
have expected Moses to have been crushed. However, he
was not the type of person to accept defeat. He still
had his faith in Yahweh to inspire him and keep him
working. Resorting to prayer, he sought further support
and guidance from this Midianite deity (Exod. 5:22-6:1).

THE GOD WHO ACTS THROUGH HISTORY

A series of plagues saved the day for Moses (Exod.
7:20-12:30). By looking carefully at the few surviving
remnants of the old historical strand, it is possible
to determine the identity of each adversity. These are
the types of maladies which have afflicted Egypt from
time immemorial. Although introduction of flood, pest,
and disease controls have reduced the severity of all
except the first, seventh, and ninth plagues, residents
in Egypt continue to be inflicted with most of them in
one area or another, at least mildly, in any twelve-
month period.

The first two plagues concerned the Nile. (1) Water
turned to blood and killed all fish. This was *gymnodium
breve*, a dinoflagellite type of algae which is normally
present in warm waters to the extent of one thousand to
the quart. When population explosions occur, as many as
sixty million are found per quart, with the water becoming red, syrupy, and poisonous, killing all marine life.
This occurs rather regularly in tropical waters around
the world. This is how the Red Sea got its name. On the

gulf coast of Florida this "red tide" becomes disastrous every two or three years. (2) When the rising waters of the Nile took place while frogs were at the river for their annual breeding season, they were swept on by the flooding waters, resulting in frogs, live and dead, in houses, wells, and everywhere.

Four plagues consisted of endemic diseases. (3) First among those visitations was the deadly plague of typhus, which is transmitted from person to person by body lice. (4) When the plague of flies gets bad in Egypt today, those who would avoid them must wave a fly-chaser from daylight to sunset to keep them out of their eyes. This was the blinding eye disease of trachoma, which the flies spread from eye to eye. (5) The cattle disease was probably anthrax, which still sweeps along river valleys in Africa and the Near East, killing live-stock. (6) The plague of boils, affecting humans, likely was impetigo with its watery pustules on the skin, a disease that remained in America as late as the early twentieth century.

Three plagues were disturbances in nature. (7) Hail speaks for itself. Although uncommon in Egypt, when it does occur, it strikes with vengeance. (8) Before the advent of modern insecticide controls, locusts were the most dreaded plagues in that part of the world as these insects left devastation in their path. (9) The three-day darkness was caused by sandclouds blown over Egypt from the three thousand miles of Sahara, shutting out light of the sun for the duration.

(10) Although unnoticed by most readers, a clue to the final plague is found in Exodus 11:7.

But a dog shall not point his tongue toward
any of the Israelite people, toward either man
or beast.

Since there were no controls over rabies in those days,

when mad dogs began biting other dogs, other animals,
and people, the ensuing epidemic of rabies could be
disastrous.

What caused this series of plagues? In the context
of those days it was assumed each one had a theological
causation. Displeased with the conduct of an individual
or group, some god had inflicted each plague as appropriate punishment. The problem was to determine the offender and the offense in each instance.

In the mind of Moses there was no question at this
point. With the advent of each visitation he went to
Pharaoh, telling him it had been sent by Yahweh because
of the oppression inflicted on Israel. Although each
confrontation ended with the appeal, "Let my people go,"
this request invariably met with ridicule and refusal.
At the ninth palace-call Pharaoh was so exasperated that
he told Moses he would kill him if he should appear
there again (Exod. 10:28).

Nevertheless, it may be guessed Pharaoh had been
weakening somewhat during the seventh, eighth, and ninth
plagues, with a slight feeling that Moses was right.
When the tenth arrived and Pharaoh's eldest son, who
would have succeeded to the throne, lay dead of the
rabies, this monarch was brought low. Not wishing to
take further chances, Pharaoh

> called for Moses and Aaron at night and said,
> "Get up, get you forth from among my people,
> both you and the Israelites, and go, serve
> Yahweh, as you have requested" (Exod. 12:31).

This permission evidently came when the women had
prepared their dough for baking the following day, but
had not yet leavened it. Fearing Pharaoh might change
his mind, after the initial grief over loss of his son
wore off, Moses was not taking any chances. Requesting
the people to take their dough unleavened as it was, he

ordered them to be on their journey at once. With only what personal belongings they could carry, by night the hosts of Israel began their march toward freedom (Exod. 12:34, 39).

Those ten plagues had turned hopeless defeat into triumphant victory. Through them the Israelites came to look on Yahweh as the benevolent and powerful savior of their people. This was the deity who acted through history.

LATER THEOLOGIZED VERSION OF THE PLAGUES

This story of the plagues, and their eventual accomplishment, was not sufficiently dramatic for the late priestly editor who could not find God in history but only in the supernatural. The editor therefore added elaborate supplements which transformed those occurrences into a series of spectacular miracles.

(1) Never having lived in Egypt, that editor revised those ten visitations, from more or less common types which have always plagued that country, into unique disasters which never have occurred in Egypt before or since. (2) From time immemorial to the present, most Egyptian plagues have extended over only some restricted portion of the nation. By contrast, the late priestly editor portrayed every one of the ten as spread over the entire land of Egypt.

(3) By reason of their manner of life and residing in the relatively isolated steppe region of Goshen, the Israelites were exempt from at least four of the plagues. These consisted of the bloody waters and frogs because they did not live along the Nile; anthrax, since they did not keep cattle; and the tenth plague of rabies by reason of having no dogs. Not decisive enough for the late editor, he made the Israelites exempt from all ten plagues. (4) Instead of taking place sporadically over

a year or more, the editor made them occur quickly, in timed succession. (5) Rather than being occasioned by maladjustments in nature and stopped when that imbalance was corrected, the late editor had them caused and ended by Moses, often raising his magic rod.

(6) What was done to the tenth and final plague makes an especially interesting study. Even though many people and animals had died from that plague of rabies, the spotlight of national attention focused on the palace where Pharaoh's son lay dead (Exod. 11:5; 12:29). The loss of that first-born son caught the late editor's attention and from it he carelessly generalized this from the plague of rabies into the plague of killing the first-born male in every home throughout Egypt, including the first-born of all animals. He had this done in one night of terror as the angel of death at midnight visited every home in Egypt that did not have the Israelite sign of blood smeared on doorposts and lintels (11:4-6; 12:7, 22-30). In these transformations of the final plague, the late editor pictured his sadistic deity wreaking ghastly terror over the whole land.

One of the greatest differences between the editor and his sources (7) consisted in the reason for Pharaoh's actions by asserting that Yahweh "hardened" that monarch's heart (Exod. 4:21; 7:3; 8:19; 9:12; 10:1, 20, 27; 11:10) so he was powerless to let Israel go until all ten plagues had run their respective courses.

This delay was so that exhibitionist deity, hitherto unknown to both Egyptians and Israelites, could prate his powers in showoff manner before both groups to exalt his prestige. Since Pharaoh was but the innocent tool of Yahweh's will, there was no thought here of that deity's punishing Pharaoh. Instead, the millions of Egyptian citizens were made the innocent victims of the ten plagues by being subjected to untold sufferings and

even death in those visitations by this megalomanic deity. In this way the worthy god of Moses was degraded by
postexilic   re-editing   into   an   irresponsible   self-
glorifying brute.

Most readers of the Bible never discover the real
god of Moses as portrayed in the primary documents. They
see only the more spectacular perverted deity of the
late exilic editor. Only as this cruel, gruesome, and
repulsively exhibitionist god is put aside does one find
in the more modest portions of the plague account the
worthy and attractive god of that great religious
leader.

RELIGION OF LIBERATION FOR THE OPPRESSED

Moses' second seemingly final defeat was suffered
at the first full-night encampment on the journey. His
worst fears, of Pharaoh's changing his mind, came to be
realized as that monarch sent a portion of his army to
pursue the Israelites and bring them back. Arriving in
the evening, these Egyptian hosts pinned the escapees
against that swampy barrier known as the Sea of Reeds.
With Pharaoh's objective as good as accomplished, the
armies rested for the night. In the morning they would
capture the entrapped slaves and return them to new
bondage (Exod. 14:5-6, 9-10).

That was a night of terror for the Israelites, and
especially for Moses. They reproached him for having
done such a foolhardy act as to take them from their
comfortable homes and deliver them to this impending
death (Exod. 14:11-12).

The following morning Moses' faith was vindicated
as another dramatic escape took place. During the night
a strong wind from the northeast had blown the shallow
waters out of the *yam suph* , Sea of Reeds if translated
correctly in Exodus 15:22, and into the Gulf of Suez.

Realizing the water level had lowered to the point they could wade across those marshlands, the fleeing Israelites lost no time in doing so.

Belatedly, the Egyptians pursued. However, when they struck those swamplands their chariots and horses became mired and wheels came off. Suddenly the wind changed, the waters came back with a rush, and many Egyptians were drowned. The early account of that brilliant escape is as follows.

> And Yahweh caused the sea to go back by a strong east wind all the night, and made the sea dry land. And the people of Israel went on the dry ground. And the Egyptians pursued, and he bound their chariot wheels and made them to drive heavily, so that the Egyptians said, "Let us flee from the presence of Israel, for Yahweh is fighting for them." And when the morning dawned, the sea returned to its normal level, and the Egyptians fled before it, but the waters returned and covered the chariots and the horsemen. Thus Yahweh saved Israel that day out of the hand of the Egyptians, and Israel saw the Egyptians dead upon the seashore. And Israel saw the great work which Yahweh did upon the Egyptians, and the people feared Yahweh, and they believed in Yahweh, and in his servant Moses (Exod. 14:21-31).

Like the plagues, that strong east wind also was not unique but occurs today, two or three times a year. Before it was excavated to present depth, those winds blew even the waters of the Suez Canal into the Gulf of Suez, often making the canal inoperative two or three days at a time.

It never will be possible to determine whether that intense wind came on that particular night by coincidence or whether it was a miraculous occurrence. However, there is no doubt but that Moses credited Yahweh with having brought those winds to save Israel from being captured and returned to more bitter slavery in Egypt.

This second saving of Israel through a normalcy of nature, although unusual, as with the historical plagues again was not sufficient miracle for the late priestly editor. He had Moses deliberately entrap the Israelites twice so Yahweh's exhibitionist triumph over the pursuing hosts could be more spectacular.

As the first of his contrived escapes the late editor had these refugees "turn back" and tantalizingly encamp in a hopeless situation between the desert and the sea, within sight of the approaching Egyptians (Exod. 14:1-4). In that precarious situation he had Israel saved by "the angel of God" who placed a cloud between the two groups so the attackers could not see their supposed victims (14:19-20).

Not satisfied with the Israelites taking advantage of receding waters by hobbling across the swampy Sea of Reeds, this editor had the Israelites make the second unbelievable move of journeying south along the western (Egyptian) shore of the Gulf of Suez. There they are represented as having become hopelessly entrapped against the Red Sea, with those vast waters barring the way to Sinai. This formed the setting for his superspectacular saving of Israel.

At that critical emergency those Red Sea waters suddenly were made to part, with the refugees marching triumphantly to freedom through the narrow corridor, and Pharoah's hosts in hot pursuit. The ultimate occurred when the two walls of water came together, drowning Pharoah's army in those Red Sea waters. By the late editor's additions, omitted from the translation of Exodus 14:21-31 as given in the sixth previous paragraph,

he reminds readers nine times that this great escape did
not take place at the Sea of Reeds but rather on the
gulf floor "in the midst" of the Red Sea, and that "the
waters were a wall unto them on their right hand and
on their left."

The late editor again misrepresented Moses as finding divine working only in events that were spectacular and contrary to nature. This editor should have been
reminded that truth is a more secure foundation for religion than false reconstruction of history, punctuated
with miracle.

A RELIGION OF SCIENCE FOR TIMES OF CRISIS

Partly to avoid military interception, Moses felt
compelled to take his people to Canaan through back-
paths, by the holy mountain of Sinai. This involved
leading them through the forbidding Deserts of Shur and
Sin.

Three days in Shur found the Israelites famishing
with thirst. Eventually they came to an oasis with some
springs but the water was undrinkable because of being
alkaline, or "bitter" as the refugees said. Here one
discovers further emergence in the Bible of religion for
an age of science. From his years with Jethro's flocks
Moses had learned how to make such brackish waters
palatable by producing a simple chemical reaction. The
Bible says he took "a tree," "cast it into the waters,
and the waters were made sweet" (Exod. 15:22-25). Resorting to this procedure, hallowed through centuries
or even millennia of use by the residents of that oasis,
Moses felt this was the method deity had provided man
for making bitter waters sweet.

As in Moses' day, the same fountain pool with its
clear alkaline water can be seen today at that oasis of
Marah en route to Sinai. The Bedouin inhabitants of that

area continue to use the method employed by Moses. There
is enough acidity in the camel bush, which they gather
and put in the water, to dealkalize an appropriate
quantity and make it drinkable.

The problem of food became acute as these refugees
journeyed through the Desert of Sin (the moon god), pronounced "seen". They were in such distress that they
     murmered against Moses and Aaron saying, "Would
     that we had died by the hand of Yahweh in the
     land of Egypt, when we reclined by the flesh-
     pots, when we ate bread to the full -- but you
     have led us out into this desert, to kill this
     whole company with hunger" (Exod. 16:2-3).

This time manna saved the day. Researches conducted
by the author in the Sinaitic area have led to the conclusion that the usual explanation of manna, as sap ex-
uded from the tamarisk tree, is baseless. The key to
proper interpretation survives in the old-source nota-
tions that both occurrences of manna were associated
with moisture (Exod. 16:13-14; Num. 11:9). Evidently the
famished refugees were saved by the spring rains which
caused edible fungi to spring up from the desert sands.
These growths appear virtually by scientific formula:
heat plus moisture plus spores equals fungi. On occasional rainy springs, the Bedouin in those parts continue to live on those potato-like fungus growths today,
often for weeks at a time. Not having encountered such
food in Egypt, and not knowing any name for it, the Israelites called it *manna* , translated "What is it?" or
simply "What's it?"

The early authentic account of the first occurrence
is found in Exodus 16:13b-17, 19-21. The late editor's
radically revised version in verses 16:4-13a, 18, 22-36
shows seven contrasts. Three of these concern differences in origin, identity, and taste. (1) In the original

account the manna sprang out of the ground, but the late editor said it came down from the sky. (2) Although in reality only a species of fungi, he assumed it to have been the bread of Heaven. In Egypt today mushrooms continue popularly to be regarded as divine and magic food sent from Heaven. (3) Even though the historical narrative says the taste was "like fresh oil" and unappetizing (Num 11:6-9), this did not deter the editor from ascribing to it an exquisite taste, like "honey wafers" (Exod. 16:31).

As this postexilic editor assumed the Sabbath already was in existence at Mosaic times, he departed further from truth by making the manna's coming observe postexilic Sabbath laws in two respects. (4) Since work, such as gathering manna, was prohibited on the Sabbath, the editor assumed that double rations of two omers per person were provided on Friday morning, and none fell on the Saturday Sabbath (Exod. 16:25-30). (5) In the historical account spoilage occurred quickly, so that in twenty-four hours the manna was wormy and stank (16:19-21). By contrast, while in the miraclized version the spoilage period remained twenty-four hours on the first five days of the week, it was doubled to forty-eight over Friday and the Sabbath (16:24).

The editor also made two notable changes with regard to the amounts of manna received. (6) In the original, Moses pled with the people to gather no more than an omer per person -- what they could eat. However, many picked more, with the result that the surplus spoiled while the unlucky obtained little or no manna (Exod. 16:16-17). By contrast, the editor assumed there was a miraculous rationing system by which those who gathered much had only an omer upon arrival in camp, while those who got little or nothing found their container to have a full omer of manna in it upon their

return (16:18). (7) The most radical of all changes concerned the total number of days on which manna was
found. The authentic account tells of finding this food
only on two occasions, one before Sinai and the other
after (Exod. 16 and Num. 11:6-9). Quite differently,
the late priestly editor asserts that God provided the
Israelites with manna every day for the forty years of
wilderness wandering (Exod. 16:35).

With his scientific interest, Moses found divine
working again in the phenomena of nature. In moments of
desperation, he implemented his prayers for help by taking the utmost advantage of natural occurrences as they
came to the rescue of his people. The nighttime wind at
the Sea of Reeds, the plagues, the bitter waters, and
the manna form a notable quartet in which Moses used
science as the handmaiden of religion.

THE TEN COMMANDMENTS, THEISM BUT NOT MONOTHEISM

Battling the terrors of famishing and starvation
through the Deserts of Shur and Sin left little time or
energy for high thought. Final arrival at the oasis of
Sinai offered temporary security, sufficient for some
stocktaking on Moses' part. By then it had become evident that the washed-out type of Egyptian religion this
unwieldy host had brought with them, would not be adequate for the demanding future that lay ahead.

If this refugee group was to avoid disintegration,
these people would need some basic principles of law and
order to govern them. Toward this end Moses took the opportunity for an undisturbed retreat to the top of Mount
Sinai. Away from the cares of the world, he felt a special closeness to Yahweh during his meditations in that
unbroken silence. From the inspiration of those moments
there emerged the ten commandments, which this lawgiver

inscribed on two stone slabs that spelled out the specifics of the Israelites' commitment to Yahweh and to
each other.

The first tablet makes explicit the Midianite components in the Sinaitic covenant.Lingering popular misunderstandings make imperative a careful look at those
initial five laws.

Although the first commandment is commonly understood as stating there is only one God in existence,that
law makes no such assertion. It says, "You shall have
no other gods before me," i.e., before my face
(Exod. 20:3). This means what it says. That "other gods"
are recognized is implied. This first commandment allowed the Israelites to worship as many lesser gods as they
might wish, provided they kept worship of their savior-
god Yahweh pre-eminent over other deities.

This interpretation is supported by the fact that
the desert deity Azazel (strong god) was worshiped during the wilderness wanderings and was given a place almost equal to Yahweh in the Day of Atonement ritual of
the two goats, "one lot for Yahweh and the other lot for
Azazel" (Lev. 16:8). While the one goat was sacrificed
to Yahweh at camp as a sin-offering, after being loaded
with the sins of Israel the other was driven into the
desert to the abode of Azazel. As this scapegoat was presented to him, that desert deity was thought annually
to complete the remission of Israel's sins (vss. 7-10).
This recognition of Azazel as god was done at the supposed instigation of Yahweh (16:1).

When snakebites were a menace to the wanderers,
Yahweh is recorded as having ordered Moses to make a
brass serpent god. Yahweh promised that whenever anyone
was bitten, if that person looked to this serpent deity
and worshiped it the snakebite would not be fatal
(Num. 21:6-9).

Exodus 25:18-22; 37:7-9 and Numbers 7:89 represent Yahweh as having ordered Moses to make two golden cherub gods and place them facing each other on the ark of the covenant's lid, ostensibly to guard Yahweh's presence when giving his messages from the mercy seat between them. It is said that Yahweh ordered Moses to have cherub gods embroidered all over its curtains (Exod. 26:1, 31; 36:8, 35), presumably to keep unworthy people from entering that tent of meeting.

Seeing that Moses made the brass serpent god for worship in the wilderness, why did he react so violently against Aaron's making the golden calf in Exodus 32? The answer lies not in his opposing divine images as such but in what that particular one signified. It was an Egyptian god which was to lead the Israelites back to bondage in that country. This particular deity of retreat and new slavery was not to be tolerated because it would have undermined everything for which Yahweh had stood, and for which Moses was giving his life and effort. Therefore he demolished this treasonous god at once.

These observations show that Moses was not the founder of monotheism. To assert that he was, continues as a major falsity in both Jewish and Christian dominant theologies. True historical perspective indicates that monotheism was not to develop in Israel until almost seven centuries after Moses' time.

HONOR AND TRUTHFULNESS TO GOD AND PARENTS

The second command also has generally been misunderstood. Since the third century A.D., Orthodox Judaism has interpreted that law as banning all pictorial representation. Muslims have agreed, but have concluded that geometric art is permissible. Protestants have thought this commandment prohibits all idols and religious images.

Moses again said exactly what he meant: "You shall not make for yourselves a graven image," i.e., an engraved or tooled image for worship (Exod. 20:4). This prohibition leaves permissible images made by pouring molten metal into a mould formed in the sand. Such molten images had been the traditional type of deities worshiped by the Israelites.

Moses' purpose in enunciating this law was to keep a margin of difference between Israelite worship and that of the Canaanites into whose land he was leading these people, where elaborate tooled and engraved images were common. By this law he was trying to insure that his Egypto-Midianite Yahwism would not be swallowed up by Canaanite religion.

The third commandment presents another misunderstood prescription. Most people take this law as prohibiting profanity, not realizing that profanity is a modern development, unknown in the ancient world. When Moses said, "You shall not take the name of Yahweh, your god, in vain," he was referring to taking oath or swearing in the sense it is used in courts, congressional investigations, taking the oath of office, etc. (Exod. 20:7).

Moses could vaguely foresee what has become a travesty -- people taking oath (often on the Bible) that they "will tell the truth, the whole truth, and nothing but the truth" and then proceed "under oath" to outlie the opposition. When giving this law he was virtually saying, "Speak the truth, especially when you invoke the name of your deity as attestation to a statement." He realized that a worthy court system, as well as a stable social and economic structure, can be built only on the solid foundation of truth.

The fourth commandment has been inadequately rendered in all English Bibles. In the authentic original law, as confined to Exodus 20:8, the key word should not be transliterated. If fully translated, this commandment should read: "Remember the day of the cessation, to keep it holy." In his supplement to this law (Exod. 20:9-11), the postexilic editor misinterpreted Moses' commandment as applying to the seventh-day Sabbath, which was not to develop for almost six centuries after the great law-giver's date.

In Moses' time, when regular holy days had not yet come into observance, he was referring to people's taking time off for the purpose of going on pilgrimage to some shrine where a day or more would be spent in festivities. Moses was concerned over the shallowness and often irreverence on such occasions. Drunken carousing and sacred prostitution were the two major evils rather commonly associated with the often hilarious rites at such supposed holy places. He accordingly insisted that all worship be a meaningful and holy experience. Because "the day of the cessation" is a cumbersome expression, it seems best to translate the command freely: "Remember the holy day to keep it sacred." Considering the age in which Moses lived, this was an important forward step in religion.

Moses gave as his fifth command, "Honor your father and your mother that your days may be long in the land" (Exod. 20:12). He realized that mutual respect of age for youth and youth for age is a necessary rock foundation without which no enduring civilization can be built. He was concerned about getting his people established properly in the land to which he was taking them.

THE QUINQUELOGUE FROM EGYPTIAN SCRIPTURES
Although having gained inspiration for his first five laws from the Midianite religious heritage, the thought of issuing a second tablet regarding personal

conduct came to Moses from his Egyptian religious background. May this difference in origins be the reason he
placed his laws on two stone slabs instead of one?

The latter five commandments were taken from the
125th chapter of the Egyptian collected pyramid and mor-
tuary texts called the Book of the Dead. Moses' attention centered on the so-called "negative confession"
which describes the weighing of the soul by the gods as
it seeks to enter the next life. In that most important
chapter, religion is reduced to abstention from forty-
two basic evils of daily conduct. Presupposing those
questions which the court of the gods puts to each
aspiring soul, it gives the responses required of all
who would seek everlasting bliss. Moses further reduced
these forty-two concerns to the five ultimates in religious conduct (Exod. 20:13-17).

Turning the negatives into positives, these last
five of Moses' laws were taken over virtually intact
from that Book of the Dead (James B. Pritchard, Ancient
Near Eastern Texts, Princeton University Press, 1950,
1st. ed., pp.34-35). Using Pritchard's numbering, item
B 5 in the Book of the Dead, "I have not killed men,"
became law 6 in Moses' Decalogue, "You shall not kill."
B 19, "I have not committed adultery," became law 7,
"You shall not commit adultery." B 2,"I have not stol-
en," became law 8, "You shall not steal." B 9, "I have
not told lies," became law 9, "You shall not bear false
witness." B 3, "I have not been covetous," became law
10, "You shall not covet." These five are the basic laws
of life, the fundamentals of ethical conduct in society.
As the Egyptians had discovered before him, you cannot
have a tolerable social structure if you have murder,
stealing, adultery, lying, and coveting.

With their original Aramaean tongue long since forgotten, and not yet having made contact with the

language that would be called Hebrew, Moses and his Israelite hosts evidently spoke Egyptian at the Exodus and
during their forty years of wandering between Sinai and
Canaan. By the same token, it is fairly certain that the
ten commandments were written in the Egyptian language.

This Decalogue is especially notable as the shortest promulgation of laws ever offered to mankind. The
original portion of each, as arranged in the Masoretic
Bible text (Exod. 20:1-17), consists of only 5, 2, 5,
4, 3, 2, 2, 2, 3, and 2 Hebrew words respectively, making a total of only thirty. Slightly hyperbolizing their
brevity, the Decalogue is often referred to as "the ten
words."

Four of these laws remain in their original brief
unredacted form -- the first, sixth, seventh, and
eighth. The other six have been elaborated by later writers rather tragically, usually blunting the point of
the laws, weakening rather than strengthening them, and
obscuring their terseness.

Moses may have chosen the number ten to make it a
uniquely memorable code. With one for each finger and
thumb, all Israelites carried these ten laws with them
at all times, day and night, wherever they went. The ten
digits accordingly became constant reminders of the corresponding ten laws.

This code is immortal also in its comprehensiveness, including within itself the essentials of religious and moral duty.

FROM SIMPLE RELIGION TO THE ULTIMATE IN RITUALISM

By force of circumstance, Moses' religion was almost completely devoid of material accompaniments. Leaving in the panic of an instant order, most of those
fleeing refugees brought along only what they could carry. If any wagons were taken, they were lost in crossing

the Sea of Reeds. If any livestock had been along, and succeeded in getting through the marshlands, they were eaten by these starving people or soon perished in the deserts. Because of difficulty in lugging them along, most of what few possessions had been taken on that arduous trip were soon dropped along the way.

The only cult object of that age seems to have been the crude box Moses made at Mount Sinai. In that container the two decalogue tablets were transported as Israel moved from place to place. At each stop Moses may have removed the stone slabs and stood them up beside the ark at the central point of encampment so all who walked by would be reminded of those ten socio-religious imperatives. Referred to as the "ark of the covenant," this treasure chest soon became revered as the dwelling place of Yahweh, whom these refugees thought they were carrying with them to Palestine (Num. 10:35-36). That simple box was destined to become the nucleus of the whole later Israelite ritualistic complex.

In the early historical strand there is no mention of Moses ever having made an altar, or having worshiped at one by presenting incense or burnt offerings. Since there were no altars, there accordingly were no priests in the Mosaic period. There is no mention of worship at local shrines along the way. Inasmuch as these were wandering people much of the time, there were no religious structures. Mosaic religion came about as near as possible to having no material accompaniments.

Strange as it may seem, this simple nonritualistic religion of Moses, as observed in the early strand, was changed into the opposite by postexilic editors in their interpolated materials. In these supplements, the highly developed ritualistic paraphernalia of 700-400 B.C. were retrojected back by five to eight centuries to Moses' time at 1225-1185 B.C. That lawgiver thereby was made to initiate and sanctify the elaborate cult practices of late pre-exilic and early postexilic religion by hallowing them with Sinaitic origin.

The amount of these untrue reassignments that were retrojected back to Moses by late editors is amazing. They constitute all the material in chapters 24-31 and 33-40 of Exodus, all 27 chapters of Leviticus, and chapters 1-9, 15, 17-19, and 28-30 of Numbers. These fifty-nine chapers of cult prescriptions, the combined equivalent in size of two average biblical books, has come to be called the Priestly Code.

This elaborate codification includes authorizations of the seventh-day Sabbath, Passover, all other feasts, and how each was to be observed. In addition, there is the vast compendium of meticulous instructions telling how the various types of sacrifices were to be presented, how the priests were to dress, and how they were to conduct themselves in the priestly office.

One of this editor's greatest fictions consisted in making Aaron and his sons the very active priests of that era. Most of the 285 verses that mention Aaron in Exodus, Leviticus, and Numbers feature him as founder of the Israelite priesthood. This role is rather inconceivable for an Aaron who built the golden calf and in the early historical strand opposed Moses for most of the forty years.

In addition to the fifty-nine chapters of cult prescriptions, it has been observed that this late editor also freely revised the intervening chapters which record historical happenings during the wilderness wanderings. He also appended his profuse untruthful supplements. In all these ways the late priestly editor committed the unpardonable sin of misrepresenting Moses' life at almost every stage. This falsifying of the

Mosaic period is the greatest travesty on truth in the
Bible.

THE FICTIONAL TENT OF MEETING

The late editor achieved his extravaganza when
creating his fictional tabernacle or "tent of meeting"
and its fictional furnishings. Deuteronomy (chapter 12,
especially) at 620 B.C. contained the edict that worship
could be conducted only at Solomon's temple. This law
seemed to rule out all worship in the Mosaic age. Since
it was considered inconceivable that Moses and his people would not have been able to worship during those
forty years of wandering, the late editor resorted to
the supposition that Moses must have constructed at
Sinai a portable prototype of the Jerusalem temple which
his people could carry with them and set up wherever
they went (Exod. 35-40).

According to that editor's fanciful reconstruction,
Moses would have needed a group of factories at Sinai
to have manufactured that supposed tent and all its ac-
coutrements: 10 sections of embroidered tentcloth for
the tabernacle, each 42 x 6 feet; 11 sections 45 x 6
feet for the tent over the tabernacle, with ram's skins
and sealskins for the roof; 450 feet of this material
to curtain from view the outer court; 56 or 58 boards,
at least 40 of which were 15 feet long and 2 1/4 feet
wide; and 70 long tentpole pillars, filletted with silver, their capitals overlaid with silver, and set in
brass sockets (Exod. 36:8-34; 38:9-20).

There were also the elaborate furnishings: the ark
overlaid with gold, gold mercy seat, and two golden
cherubs; table of showbread and its staves, all overlaid
with gold, with its spoons, bowls, and flagons, all
of pure gold; the six-branched golden candlestick and
its vessels; the altar of incense, overlaid with gold;

and the altar of burnt-offering, with its pots, shovels, basins, flesh-hooks, firepans, laver, and gratings, all made of brass (Exod. 37:1-38:8).

In addition, a multitude of smaller articles were listed as associated with the setup or worship in this gigantic tent: tremendous supplies of rope, silver hooks and fillets, four brass pillars, brass pins, brass clasps, bars, screens, hangings, mirrors, staves, ephod inner-priestly garments, outer vestments, censors, and horns (Exod. 36:14-40:38).

The editor seems never to have thought of the scores of tons that such a massive tent, its furnishings, and cult objects would have weighed. Although this tent of meeting was supposed to have been transported from place to place on six covered wagons drawn by twelve oxen, it is stated that the furnishings were carried on the shoulders of priestly subordinates (Num. 7:3-9). The difficulties involved in setting up such a complicated tent structure and taking it down day by day never seem to have occurred to this unrealistic editor.

Also, how could all that gold, silver, copper, brass, wool, cloth, oil, incense, hides, and spices have been secured in a relatively uninhabited area where none of these materials would have been available? Nor did the editor realize that Mount Sinai has such scant water supply that a multitude could have remained there only a very limited time at most.

A persistent question in the editor's mind was, how did Moses know where to transport the tent of meeting and its worshipers? Assuming that God gave visible guidance, the conclusion reached was that a pillar of cloud must have led the way by day and a pillar of fire by night. This editor's ultranaivete is seen in having

the Israelites follow their traveling tent by both day
and night, twenty-four hours a day.

   This editor's extreme warping and fictionizing of
Moses' religion, climaxing in the tent of meeting, is
one of the most amazing phenomena in the Bible.

A RELIGION OF NONVIOLENCE

   It might have been assumed that slaying the
Egyptian taskmaster would have set the pattern for a
life of violence (Exod. 2:11-12). However, the reactions
to that event appear to have had the opposite effect,
convincing Moses that this was not the way to achieve
desired ends. Accordingly, his religion after that event
seems to have been one of nonviolence.

   The campaign to liberate his people from slavery
in Egypt was conducted throughout by peaceful negotia-
tions with the authorities. Moses never organized any
semblance of even a passive resistance movement among
the Israelite slaves. He went to Pharaoh repeatedly,
requesting that he allow the Israelites to go on a vaca-
tion for the purpose of sacrificing to their god Yahweh
(Exod. 5:1-3; 7:2, 10, 15-16; 8:1, 25-30; 9:1, 13;
10:1-3). It already has been observed that in the early
source Moses had nothing to do with the plagues, or the
backwash that drowned the Egyptians, except that he used
those events for his ends. Only the late editor, in his
miraclizing, made Moses by his raised rod cause those
terrors of destruction and death. Probably never has
a great liberation been attained with such complete nonviolence.

   The real Moses is seen in his reaction to the
golden-calf episode. He was so outraged by that action
that he "cast the tables (of the law) out of his hands
and broke them" (Exod. 32:19). He burned the calf, reduced the ashes to powder, put it in their water, and

as a token of chastisement made the offenders drink it
(vs. 20). That was as far as he went in bringing punishment. After reminding the guilty that they had "sinned
a great sin," he went up the mountain to "make atonement" for them (32:30). Here one observes the non-violent
religion of Moses, with its ready forgiveness.

The late editor could not bear to leave, as the
final word regarding the golden-calf episode, a response
that must have seemed so spineless. Therefore he placed
on Moses' lips a ruthless order: "Put you, every man,
his sword upon his thigh, and go back and forth throughout the camp from gate to gate, and let every man slay
his brother, and every man his companion, and every man
his neighbor" (Exod. 32:27). It is stated that the
priestly Levi tribe, idol of the late editor, responded
by killing three thousand Israelites (vs. 28). This
editor thoughtlessly assumed that every man possessed
a sword, when there probably was not even one in the
entire encampment. By such appendages within the priestly strand, Moses has been changed at strategic places
from the meek man of peace into a cruel and vengeful
person, as barbaric as the sadistic god the late editor
worshiped.

In harmony with his nonviolent religion, Moses resolved that entrance of his people into the land of
Canaan was not to be through forcible invasion. However,
when Israel was poised on the southern edge, men of the
militaristic faction were determined to fight their way
in by using gorilla tactics. Moses pled with them to
stop their plans, stating that this military approach
was against Yahweh's will. Even though he would not allow these aggressive ones to take the ark of the covenant into battle, this militant group persisted. The result was a bitter defeat at Hormah (Num. 14:40-45).

By thus alerting the Canaanites to an apparent
invasion, this violent element had spoiled Moses' plan
of having his Israelites make a peaceful movement into
the land of Canaan from the south. To avoid further conflict, he withdrew his people to the oasis of Kadesh.
This tragic alienation of the Canaanites caused Israel
irreparable damage by losing the next forty years in
a stalemated existence, south of the border.

Finally giving up the idea of a penetration from
that direction, Moses moved his people toward the east
to enter Canaan through Trans-Jordan. The shortest way
of accomplishing this was to follow the southeast shore
of the Dead Sea, skirting the land of Edom. He sent mes-
sengers to that king, reminding him of Israel's hardships and requesting the privilege of passing through
his country in transit. Moses promised that his people
would take no food from the Edomite fields or vineyards
and would drink none of the precious water from their
wells, but would go through on a nonstop basis. Although
greatly disappointed at the adamant king's refusal, that
settled the matter for Moses who neither argued nor
thought of fighting his way through (Num. 20:14-22).

To avoid conflict with the Edomites, and other settled peoples along the way, Moses led his refugees south
to the Gulf of Aqaba and around the Mount Seir range.
Upon moving northward he bypassed most of Trans-Jordan
by detouring along the edge of the Arabian Desert, hoping to enter Canaan peaceably from the east. This shows
him so devoted to the priciple of nonviolence that he
was willing to undergo the hardships of some two hundred
added miles of arduous travel through semi-desert regions in order to keep peace with dwellers along the
way.

During a lifetime under circumstances when the
temptation to take the path of violence was extremely

inviting, it is a credit to the poise of Moses that he stuck throughout those forty years to the nonviolence principle in his religion. In spite of the late editor's reversing the picture by remaking him into a ruthless punisher who trusted in military might, the true picture of Moses as a man devoted to achieving his ends through peaceful means hovers as a benediction over the Israelite people. They can justly be proud to have had as their liberator one who achieved such remarkable results without violence.

MOSES, THE LONG-SUFFERING

The supreme tragedy of Moses' life was that, during those years of leadership, he usually was unappreciated and had little support from his people. Only fear of the greater slavery that would have been inflicted upon them prevented the Israelites from repudiating his leadership and returning to the flesh-pots of Egypt (Exod. 16:3; Num. 11:4-5).

Even before arriving at Sinai Moses prayed in desperation to Yahweh, saying, "What shall I do to this people? They are almost ready to stone me" (Exod.17:4). While he was on the mountain his brother Aaron organized a revolt that was intended to lead these escaped ones back to Egypt (32:1-4).

In journeying from Mount Sinai to Canaan, these refugees found themselves in the deserts or semideserts of Paran, Negeb, and the Arabian fringe. The result was forty agonizing years of thirst, hunger, and laments over the lot Moses had inflicted upon his people. A chorus of complaints against him was the daily undertone of those years, at times subdued but often with extreme loudness. The biblical account states fifteen times how these wanderers murmured against him

(Exod. 15:24; 16:2, 7, 8, 9, 12; 17:3; Num. 11:1-10; 14:2, 27, 29, 36; 16:11, 41; 17:5).

Periodically, this opposition erupted into major rebellions against Moses' leadership. When he married the black Cushite woman, both his brother Aaron and sister Miriam joined in protest and tried to take over leadership in this first example of race prejudice in the Bible (Num. 12:1-15). On another occasion the people said "one to another, 'Let us appoint a captain and let us return to Egypt'" (Exod. 14:4). Subsequently Korah, with two hundred and fifty of Israel's prominent men, tried to depose both Moses and Aaron and take over (16:1-3). Even at the oasis of Kadesh there was a widespread rebellion against Moses (20:2-4).

Although he had deep love for these ungrateful people and endured so much for their welfare and future, those wilderness wanderers regarded Moses as the person who had gotten them into all kinds of trouble. Disgusted with him, most of the people he had led to Canaan probably welcomed his death. Because of these attitudes, very little of his exalted religion rubbed off on those unresponsive masses. In so far as most Israelites were concerned, the Egypto-Midianite religion of Moses died with him and was soon forgotten.

REQUIEM AND BENEDICTION

In spite of all this opposition, and the tragic turn of events following his death, Moses' influence lived on. In time the more thoughtful people came to appreciate the service he had rendered. However, this recognition came only gradually. Although his work was done in the years 1225-1185 B.C., his worth was largely unappreciated for the following three centuries. Fortunately, enough individuals remembered parts of the dramatic story concerning his liberating the Israelites from slavery and bringing them to a land of promise that the fairly complete story was passed on orally from generation to generation.

Moses received his first major recognition when the account of his life and work was incorporated into Israel's first history, produced around 900 B.C. During exilic and postexilic time, when the need for new liberations became imperative, he was to be magnified into the greatest individual in the Hebrew biblical tradition. This consisted in coming to be revered as the liberator of his people and the spiritual father of his country.

Although he wrote only the "ten words" of the Decalogue, or possibly nothing more than the ten numerals suggesting them, Moses became credited in time with being a great author. The first five books of the Bible in particular were attributed to him. Although called the Pentateuch or Torah, they commonly have been referred to as "the five books of Moses." He also came to be thought of as the inspirer of the whole corpus of Hebrew sacred Scripture.

Looking back through the smogs of later fictionizings, three monumental achievements appear to have immortalized Moses' work. When facing the many situations that appeared hopeless, during the forty years of leading his people from Egypt to Canaan, Moses' invincible faith refused to capitulate before the succession of seemingly inevitable defeats. As a result, his life was a saga of turning supposed failures into brilliant triumphs. This "perseverance of the saints" was one of the prime characteristics of his religion, which flowered forth especially in times of adversity when those about him had succumbed to despair.

Moses' two greatest religious triumphs took place at Mount Sinai. One of these, his major theological innovation, consisted in formally introducing these fleeing refugees to the Midianite deity Yahweh. Moses virtually married the Israelite people to Yahweh in a national wedding ceremony at the foot of that sacred mountain. This tribal and area Midianite deity thereby became chief god of the Israelite people. Moses expanded this religion of Yahwism to include treasured and intangible qualities of the spirit such as passion for justice, freedom for all peoples, social action, divine providence, invincible faith in deity, nonviolence, and longsuffering forbearance, with upreach to deity and prayer as the mainspring of worship. As transformed by him, that higher Yahwism was to become the focus of Israelite religion for the ensuing six or seven centuries.

The greatest religious monument to Moses is the ten commandments. He is to be credited with having devised in that Decalogue the most immortal code of laws this world has ever known -- immortal in their brevity, comprehensiveness, and memorableness. These commandments have served as the rock foundation upon which rests the religious and moral structure of the Near East and Western world. They are the most prized common jewel of Judaism, Christianity, and Islam. They are a light to the world, summoning all mankind to higher ways.

Numbers 12:3 records a worthy tribute to this great leader: "Now the man Moses was very meek, above all the men who were upon the face of the earth." A fitting benediction to his life and work is found in eulogy epitaph among the closing words of the Torah (Deut.34:5-12):

> So Moses, the servant of Yahweh, died there
> in the land of Moab, . . . And the people of
> Israel wept for Moses in the plains of Moab
> thirty days: . . . And there has not risen

since in Israel a prophet like unto Moses,whom
Yahweh knew face to face.

CHAPTER 4

JOSHUA'S RELIGION OF GENOCIDE

After the mountain peaks of Sinai and Nebo, it is a great comedown to descend into the forbidding and dark canyons of Joshua. This is indeed a matter of passing into "the valley of the shadow of death."

There are two notable Joshuas in the Bible, this one and the New Testament Joshua who appears in the Greek language as Jesus. So one can speak of Jesus as the Joshua of the New Testament or Joshua as the Jesus of the Old. But there the analogy ends, for the respective parents had no power to determine the extent to which each offspring would live up to the name's meaning of "He saves" or simply "Savior."

Joshua has been glamorized with parting Jordan's waters and tumbling the walls of Jericho in response to the weird strains and vibrations of the rams' horns. Then he burned that great metropolis and every person in it, saving only the harlot Rahab and her relatives. In the case of Joshua more demythologizing needs to be done, not at so many places but more radical at the points of special need.

This is the chapter that never should have been written, but it has had to be written. Israel never should have been plagued by the religion of Joshua, but it unfortunately came into existence, found itself recorded on the pages of the Bible, and therefore cannot be ignored even though it chronicles one of the most deplorable chapters in political and religious history.

That "each action produces an equal and opposite reaction" often is as true in human affairs as in physics. An excellent example of this is observed as

the religion of Joshua suddenly reversed about everything in the religion of Moses. The multitude of wanderers being led to their hoped-for new national homeland
was the same in each instance. This new turn in Israelite destiny was due to a radical change in leadership
when Moses, the peaceful person, came to be replaced
by a man of war.

This sharp break with the past became evident at
once as Moses' ten commandments, and most of the associated spiritual heritage, became discarded in the zeal
for conquest. Except for the god Yahweh -- although
tragically misconstrued -- and the ark of the covenant,
all vestiges of Mosaic religion were soon lost. The Book
of Joshua therefore marks the advent of another almost
wholly new religion. As the Egypto-Midianite religion
of the Exodus was the achievement of one towering individual, Moses, the succeeding religion of genocide
was that of one man, Joshua.

JOSHUA, ISRAEL'S PROBLEM CHILD

To understand how this fourth religion of the Bible
could develop, examination must be given to the bio-
graphical information about Joshua in the wilderness
records. From the earliest days of the Exodus he had
been Israel's problem child. This young man of great
ability and charisma had come to be looked upon as the
natural leader of the youth coalition.

When the desert-famished wanderers descended upon
the little oasis of Rephidim, the Israelites found themselves in conflict with its Amalekite residents. In the
ensuing scramble for the limited supplies of food and
water, Joshua's incipient militaristic spirit flared
forth. "And Joshua laid low Amalek and his people with
the edge of the sword" (Exod. 17:13). Although the late
priestly editor ascribed this genocidal determination

to "blot out completely the remembrance of Amalek from under Heaven" to Yahweh and Moses (vs. 14), its cruelty and injustice to the unsuspecting people who lived in that oasis seems to bear Joshua's trademark.

From that episode Moses could envision troubles ahead. Possibly to preserve rapport with the younger generation, he took Joshua along when going for rest and meditation to the top of Mount Sinai (Exod. 24:13; 32:17). Or was it to prevent this ambitious youth from organizing an opposition movement while Moses sought spiritual guidance on the mountaintop? Probably as an aid toward preserving a measure of unity among those unruly refugees he chose to make this highly talented youth his personal attendant (Exod. 24:13; 33:11; Num. 11:28; Josh. 1:1).

Fear of what a serious generation gap could do to his liberation movement would seem to have been in the mind of that lawgiver as he formed his fifth commandment (Exod. 20:12). Perhaps the purpose in prescribing honor to father and mother was to bridge the generation gap between his own peaceful intents, supported by many adult followers, and the restiveness of the youthful militants under Joshua's inspiration.

A revealing episode occurred when Moses was about to reach his destination and desired to enter Palestine from the south. He sent ahead a group of twelve advance men to see what Canaan and its people were like and presumably to find a location where the Israelites could settle and make their home peacefully in that land of promise. Under Joshua's influence, these explorers could think only in terms of militaristic conquest. Upon return, ten of these twelve spies reported that the Canaanites could not be conquered by this unarmed refugee group of such small comparative stature and numbers.

Joshua and Caleb dissented from the majority verdict and insisted upon assault at once. Believing Israel
would be able to conquer the Canaanites, this pair organized the aggressive ones into a force for immediate
attack. Joshua was intent on annihilating the Palestine
residents as he shouted, "They are bread for us." That
was his way of saying, "We will devour them" (Num. 13:1-
14:9). Armed only with the confidence Yahweh would give
them victory, this invading band was decisively defeated
(14:40-45).

When approaching the land of promise from the east
some years later, Moses was in failing health and feared
death at any time. Under the circumstances he yielded
to popular pressure by commissioning Joshua (Num. 27:15-
23). Handing the reins of leadership to Joshua was probably the greatest mistake Moses ever made.

In true ecumenical spirit the friendly Midianites
invited Moses' newcomers to a religious festival. People
of the conservative faction were outraged that so many
Israelites attended. Although the late editor has the
directive given by Yahweh and delivered through Moses,
probably it was Joshua, leader of the militaristic faction, who issued the order: "Vex the Midianites and
smite them, for they vex you with their wiles, wherewith
they have beguiled you" (Num. 25:17-18).

Since Joshua was the military leader throughout
those wilderness years, it may be assumed that he led
the attack against the Midianites. His newly formed army
descended with ferocity upon those unsuspecting people
by proceeding to annihilate them as the Israelite hosts
"slew every male. . . And they burnt with fire all their
cities, in the places where they dwelt, and all their
encampments. And they took all the spoil, and all the
prey, both of man and of beast" (Num. 31:7-11). Verse
40 states that 16,000 Midianites were slain, of whom

thirty-two were sacrificed as a burnt offering to Yahweh.

This brutal annihilation was carried out, even though the Midianites had given Israel their god Yahweh, even though the main constituent of Moses' faith comprised the fundamentals of Midianite religion as learned from his father-in-law Jethro, priest of Midian, and even though the Midianite prophet Balaam had protected Israel by his blessings on the way toward Palestine (Num.22-24).

Joshua's wrath proceeded with even greater venom against all Israelites who attended that service, formulating a supposed divine edict that all offending Israelites and their sympathizers be killed. "Take all the chiefs of the people and hang them up unto Yahweh before the sun, that the fierce anger of Yahweh may turn away from Israel . . . Slay you, every one, his people who have joined themselves to Baal-peor." Apparently not regarding all this slaughter as sufficient reproof of ecumenism, it is recorded that Yahweh himself got into the act by sending a plague which killed 24,000 additional Israelites (Num. 25:1-5,9). The ultimate indignity lay in the biblical editor's assigning the order for this Joshuan hate and bloodshed to Moses and God. This ruthless massacre was a foretaste of the new Joshua and events to come.

HIGH WORTHINESS OF CANAANITE CIVILIZATION

Through the centuries there has been a general misunderstanding of the Canaanites, whom Joshua's people were about to face upon approaching their destination. This has resulted from following the late priestly editor's prejudiced opinion of them. According to him, the Canaanites were a primitive and depraved people, with a religion that was an abomination in the sight of God. This view was built into a theology which gave Israel

divine right and authority to annihilate the Canaanites
and destroy everything pertaining to them.

The truth of matters is almost the reverse, for
at that moment the residents of Canaan were highly civilized. Canaanites and Phoenicians were essentially the
same people. Canaanites often were called South Phoenicians, and Phoenicians, North Canaanites. In addition
to seamanship and other contributions, these twin peoples gave to the world one of the greatest literary
breakthroughs of all time -- invention of the alphabet.
That literary device has been borrowed and adopted, in
slightly varying forms, as the basis of all written
languages in the Western world. Use of the alphabet has
been one of the major causes for the pre-eminence of
the Occident and nearer Orient, through the centuries,
over the Far East where civilizations have clung tena-
ciously to more primitive sign languages, with their
myriads of characters.

The Canaanites had achieved a world of peace, to
the point they had little in the way of armaments at
Joshua's time. Although continuing to live in ancient
walled cities, these people had forgotten how to make
war. Their heritage of world peace is illustrated by
four lines from "The Poems about Baal and Anath"
(Pritchard, James, Ancient Near Eastern Texts, Princeton,
1950, p. 136).

Take war (away) from the earth,
        Banish (all) strife from the soil;
Pour peace into earth's very bowels,
        Much amity into earth's bosom.

The Canaanites were highly cultured and had a
worthy religion. Through the centuries people have shuddered when the name Baal, chief god of the Canaanites,
is mentioned. Most readers of the Bible do not realize
that Canaanite *baal* means Lord, as Hebrew *adonai* means

Lord. The abominations commonly ascribed to Baal worship were mostly those of the Transjordanian Ammonites. Cannaanite culture focused on Jericho, often rated as the world's oldest city. It is important to get this revised picture of a misunderstood and biblically maligned people.

The conquest of Canaan must be looked upon as an assault by uncultured invaders, maddened by forty years of desert wanderings, upon a highly civilized people who could not conceive of unprovoked conquest, and who had no war facilities since they felt certain they were living in a world of peace. This is how it was possible for Joshua to annihilate them and their cities, one by one, as sitting ducks in his path. Before such brutal conquerors, the peace-minded Canaanites seemed powerless to resist.

THE RUTHLESS CONQUEST OF CANAAN

It apparently never entered the mind of Joshua that he might have entered Canaan peacefully. This is indicated by the fact he had no communication with Canaanite authorities. His only negotiation was through spies with Rahab, the harlot of Jericho, probably using her family as a fifth column to let the invaders enter that city (Josh. 2).

Facing Jericho, Joshua had a vision of "the prince of Yahweh's host" with "his sword drawn in his hand," intimating that Yahweh's heavenly armies would aid in conquering the city (Josh. 5:13-15). Thereupon Joshua planned a seven-day war of nerves. Headed by Yahweh, carried in his ark of the covenant, the invading hosts marched around Jericho in silence, and then retreated to camp. This was done each day for six days. To climax this psychological warfare, that procession marched around the city seven times on the seventh day. At

conclusion of the final circuit the rams' horns were
blown, the invaders all shouted, "and the wall fell down
flat" (6:1-20).

Unfortunately, the early truthful account of this
conquest is almost completely missing from the biblical
record. Joshua 6:1-20 gives the late editor's highly
spectacularized version of the attack. If the walls of
Jericho had "fallen down flat" literally, the inhabitants would not have been trapped in the city but could
have escaped for their lives in every direction. Excavation of Jericho shows the surviving wall portions still
standing rather than "fallen down flat" as the late editor asserted.

One may guess the assault occurred at night as Rahab and her family opened the gate to the invaders at
the signaled time. With all inhabitants trapped inside
the walls, Joshua and his people proceeded to kill every
person in the city except Rahab and her relatives. It
is one of the most ghastly stories in the Bible, as witnessed by the following shred of the otherwise-lost early historical account:

> the people went up into the city, every man
> straight before him, and they took the city.
> And they completely destroyed everything that
> was in the city, women as well as men, young as
> well as old, and ox, and sheep, and ass with
> the edge of the sword.

Then

> they burnt the city with fire, and everything
> that was in it (Josh. 6:20-21, 24).

Archaeological excavation witnesses to the incineration of this metropolis on that occasion.

Joshua next took Ai by ambush, "and they smote them
so that they let none of them remain or escape"
(Josh. 8:22). Thereupon he met the defenders of the five

Amorite cities and conquered them, as "Joshua and the
people of Israel made an end of slaying them with a very
great slaughter, till they were annihilated" (10:20).
In turn he swept through the great highland cities,
destroying each in succession. This campaign left in
its wake seven maledictions of terror (10:28-39).

1. MAKKEDAH: (vs. 28). "He completely destroyed them,
   all the people who were in it -- he left none remaining."

2. LIBNAH: (vs. 30). "He destroyed it with the edge of
   the sword, even all the people who were in it -- he
   left none remaining therein."

3. LACHISH: (vs. 32). "He destroyed it with the edge
   of the sword, even all the people who were in it."

4. GEZER: (vs.33). "And Joshua destroyed him and his
   people until he had left him none remaining."

5. EGLON: (vs. 35). "And he desroyed it with the edge
   of the sword, even all the people who were in it,
   he completely destroyed that day."

6. HEBRON: (vs. 37). "They took it and destroyed it
   with the edge of the sword, . . . even all the people who were in it, he left none remaining
   . . . but he completely destroyed it, even all the
   people who were in it."

7. DEBIR: (vs. 39). "He completely destroyed all the
   people who were in it -- he left none remaining."

As the late editor looked back on Joshua's genocidal campaign, of wiping the Canaanite people out of
existence, he summed it up in the Bible's most terrible
words. Although meant as a triple benediction, it is
in reality a triple malediction upon Joshua's work, telling how his scourge of annihilation spread as a deadly
plague over southern Palestine (Josh. 10:40; 11:11, 14).

> He left none remaining, and he completely de-
> stroyed everything that breathed, as Yahweh,
> the god of Israel, had commanded . . . .And they
> smote all the people who were therein with the
> edge of the sword, completely destroying them
> -- there was nothing left that breathed. . . .
> But every person they smote with the edge of
> the sword until they had destroyed them, nei-
> ther did they leave anything that breathed.

Annihilation was the lot also for Israelites who
disobeyed Joshua's dictatorial decrees or in any way
impeded his endeavors. He commanded that all such individuals be put to death. Evidently delivered in the
first person, his order was,

> Whoever he be that . . . shall not obey my
> words in all that I command him, he shall be
> put to death (Josh. 1:18).

The Achan account indicates that slaying such offenders often was dramatized by gruesome public execu-
tions. Even though the invading Israelites had been commanded by Joshua not to do any personal looting, the
riches of Jericho proved too much temptation for Achan.
He took

> a valuable Babylonish garment, and two hundred
> shekels of silver, and a wedge of gold

and hid them in his tent (Josh. 7:10-21).

When Joshua found out about this, he commanded
all Israel to assemble at Achan's tent.

> And Joshua, and all Israel with him,took Achan
> the son of Zerah, and the silver, and the gar-
> ment, and the wedge of gold, and his sons, and
> his daughters, and his oxen, and his asses,and
> his sheep, and his tent, and everything that
> he had, and they brought them up into the Val-
> ley of Achor . . . And all Israel stoned him

with stones, and they   burned them with fire,
and stoned them with stones   (Josh. 7:22-26).

Stoning to death and incinerating the innocent
sons, the innocent daughters, the innocent livestock,
and all Achan's material possessions shows how venemous
Joshua could be toward even his own people when they
disobeyed the slightest of his commands.

ECHOES AND RE-ECHOINGS OF JOSHUA'S RELIGION

One of the greatest misfortunes in Israelite history was the failing health of Moses and his death on
Mount Nebo before reaching the land of promise. If
physical strength had allowed him to lead his people
into Canaan, he likely would not have entered that country unless he could have done so without conflict. In
that event, the subsequent history of Israel and her
attitudes toward other peoples might have been different, with much of the antiforeignism avoided.

Joshua virtually reduced all religion to only one
oft-repeated word which reverberated through the days
of his leadership. That magic word was "kill." He heard
Yahweh telling him to kill every person of every nation
that lay in the way of Israel's expansion, from the
Mediterranean Sea to the Euphrates River (Josh. 1:4).
Such a religion of genocide, with its ostensible divinely ordered annihilation of whole peoples, is a frightful
thing to have in any supposedly holy book.

Insofar as worthy religion is concerned, the Joshua
period was almost wholly negative. He imposed on the
future of his people only religious perversions, three
in number.

Moses' yearning to take his people to a "land of
promise" (i.e., a promising land), where he might find
a peaceable home and economic opportunity for his wanderers, was laudable. However, Joshua turned that into

the doctrine of "the Promised Land." This included the
territories of all countries from the Mediterranean Sea
to the Euphrates River. All these lands were supposedly
wrested by Yahweh from their rightful owners and given
to Israel for all time to come.

Laudable also was the concept of Israel as "the
choosing people," who chose at Sinai to give their future allegiance to Yahweh by covenant. This was degraded
by Joshua into the doctrine of "The Chosen People,"
based on the assertion that Israelites are better than
other people and are the only ones in this world for
whom God really cares. This laid the way for arrogance
on the part of those who were to regard themselves objects of divine preference.

The Israelite invaders were charged with having
erred tragically by not obliterating all non-Israelite
peoples from the land of Canaan and contiguous territories (Num 33:50-56; Josh. 23:12-13). Popularization
of this view by the late editor led to the postexilic
belief that all subsequent serious maladies of Israel
during the biblical period were caused basically by
Joshua and his successors not carrying the genocide program far enough.

At approximately 440 B.C. the late priestly editor
revised the tenth-century B.C. Jehovistic valid historical records of Israel's past, supplementing them into
a six-volume history of Israel from creation to the end
of Joshua's life. This master production is known as
the Hexateuch. When its first five divisions came to
be regarded as sacred Scripture, at approximately 400
B.C., the Book of Joshua was cut off and not included.
This left only five books as the Bible of that day, called variously the Torah, Law, Five Books of Moses, or
Pentateuch.

Did those canonizers have discernment sufficient to realize that such a sadistic writing as the Book of Joshua should not be included in any "holy book"? By contrast, those who formulated the second collection of Hebrew Scripture, at approximately 200 B.C., showed a lapse in judgment by including the Book of Joshua in that canon of "The Prophets."

Joshua's religion of genocide, however reprehensible, did not die with him. Although the book that bears his name is the lowest point in the Hebrew Scriptures, the echoes reverberating from that writing have endured through the centuries and continue to exert an influence even in this supposedly modern world.

The greatest devotee of Joshua's genocide religion has emerged during the twentieth century in none other than the person of Adolph Hitler. He read his Bible carefully, found Joshua's religion of genocide the most worthy part of the Scriptures, and resolved to implement it. While in that book the Israelites set out to destroy all other peoples and make a Gentile-free biblical world, Hitler proceeded to reverse the process. He resolved to destroy all Jews and make a Jew-free world. By the time that movement collapsed he already had incinerated some six million Jews in the gas furnaces of the concentration camps, probably the greatest demonstration of genocide in human history.

Even toward the end of the twentieth century, the possibility of further genocides remained on the horizon. In December 1948 the International Convention on the Prevention and Punishment of the Crime of Genocide was adopted unanimously by the United Nations General Assembly. At the time of this writing almost a hundred nations have ratified this international agreement which makes it a crime to attempt the destruction of national,

ethnic, racial, or religious groups, but the United
States has not signed.

CHAPTER 5

CANAANITE-HEBREW RELIGION OF THE JUDGES AND KINGS

Five entire books are devoted to the Bible's fifth religion: Judges, I & II Samuel, and I & II Kings. Those writings cover more than eight centuries of biblical history, from approximately 1400 to 586 B.C. During those centuries most of the Israelite religious institutions came into existence.

That period began with a loose federation of brother tribes, each ruled by a judge: Deborah, Gideon, Jephthah, Samson, and Samuel being the most notable. The judgship developed into a theocratic monarchy which endured from 1020 to 922 B.C. That century, under Kings Saul, David and Solomon, marked the highest period of political achievement in Israel's history. This governmental triumph was marred in 922 B.C. by division into rival monarchies, the Southern and Northern Kingdoms of two and ten tribes respectively.

During the time of the early judges four constituent faiths became merged to form this fifth Old Testament religion.

(1) The basic initial ingredient consisted of what natively prevailed in the land of Palestine, the religion of the Canaanites.

(2) This was joined by the second major stream, the Aramaean religion of the Israelite tribes that settled early in the land of Canaan: Simeon, Benjamin, Dan, Ephraim, Manasseh, Issachar, Zebulon, Naphtali, and Asher, located in this order from south to north. Shortly after the death of Joseph, around 1550 B.C., those nine left Egypt and settled in Canaan between the

Mediterranean Sea and the Jordan River. Contrary to the
late exilic editor who asserted that all twelve tribes
left Egypt with Moses at approximaely 1225 B.C., two
types of indicators show a much earlier exodus for the
nine tribes. (a) There is the archaeological evidence
in the clay-tablet Tel el-Amarna letters, correspondence
of east-Mediterranean native princes and governors with
Pharaohs Amenhotep III and Akhenaten (1413-1362 B.C.).
These letters virtually state that the Habiru (maraud-
ers), presumably the encroaching Israelite tribes in
this context, were already in their positions by 1400
B.C. (b) This conclusion fits information in the Book
of Judges which records historic episodes and crises
of those nine tribes from well before 1400 B.C. and onward, as demonstrated by the recorded lengths of judge-
ships and number of years between them.

It is therefore evident that these nine northern
tribes were consolidating their settlement in Palestine
during the three centuries before Moses led the last
two remaining tribes out of Egypt. Since those nine
tribes left the land of the Pharaohs before becoming
Egyptianized, their religious development assumed the
form of a gradual transition from the ancestral patriarchal Aramaean religion of Genesis 12-50 to adopting
largely the religion of Canaan.

(3) Another instreaming occurred, perhaps around
1250 B.C., when the two tribes of Gad and Reuben, with
their Egyptian religion, left that country and proceeded
to the Trans-Jordan area. There they ruthlessly annihilated the Amorites and Bashanites, and settled in their
territories. The record of that campaign in Numbers
21:10-35 (clearly a foreign intrusion into the Mosaic
sequence) and Deuteronomy 2-3 evidently has been wrongly
attributed to Moses. These two tribes became loosely
affiliated with the previous nine to form the eleven

northern tribes of Israel. The Books of Judges and I Samuel record episodes in the political and religious development of those eleven tribes from the time they arrived in Canaan until the death of King Saul at 1000 B.C.

(4) The final stream that flowed into this Israelite coalition in Canaan consisted of the Judah and Levi tribes. They came belatedly with their Egypto-Midianite religion, introducing the component of Yahwism into that complex amalgam. These newcomers entered south Canaan at approximately 1183 B.C., wedging their way west of the Jordan River between the territories occupied by Simeon and Benjamin. Only the late editor portrays Joshua's program of genocide as having extended over all Palestine (Josh. 11; 24). The early historical parts of that book in chapters 1-10 indicate his slaughter was confined largely to the Jericho-Ai-Gibeah axis and southward.

Although able to subdue the Canaanites militarily, the Israelites in the northern tribes capitulated culturally and religiously to the extent of adopting and adapting many religious practices from their more highly civilized subjects. As observed in the Book of Judges, this assimilation had gone on for more than three centuries in the north before Joshua led the two straggling tribes into South Canaan. Since the northerners were unaffected by the carnage Joshua perpetrated in the south, most of the Canaanites in the territories controlled by the northern tribes became incorporated into those Israelite communities. By 950 B.C., in King Solomon's reign, those two peoples had become almost completely merged. From that point onward, the three religions brought in by the Israelites (Aramaean, Egyptian, and Midianite) found themselves rather completely blended with the native Canaanite worship into what may be called the Canaanite-Hebrew faith.

When the three groups of tribes entered Canaan between 1550 and 1183 B.C. they spoke Aramaean, Egyptian, or both. However, it was inevitable that these Israelites should adopt the more advanced alphabetical Phoenician-Canaanite language. Except for Aramaic portions in Ezra and Daniel, the entire Old Testament was to be written in that adopted language. Renamed Hebrew by the new possessors, this has continued as the sacred language of Judaism.

WORSHIP AT THE HIGH PLACES

Normative Canaanite worship during the judges and monarchy periods was carried on at local shrines, usually situated on hills or mountaintops. Therefore they were called "high places." The numerous references in pre-exilic literature indicate there were great numbers of such shrines in Palestine and that Israelite as well as Canaanite worshipers patronized them.

I Kings 3:2 states that worship at the high places was the accepted rule among Israelite people until Solomon's temple was dedicated in 950 B.C. as "the people sacrificed only in the high places, because no house had been built for the name of Yahweh until those days." It is recorded that Solomon himself "sacrificed and burnt incense at the high places" and constructed new ones for his foreign wives (I Kings 3:3; 11:1-8). Even after the temple was built, Solomon's son, Rehoboam, inaugurated an extensive program of constructing new high places over all Judah: "For they also built themselves high places . . . on every high hill and under every green tree" (I Kings 14:23).

King Jeroboam, Rehoboam's counterpart in the north, also carried on a campaign of establishing new high places through his realm. At Beth-el, Jeroboam himself offered sacrifices, burned incense, and instituted new national religious festivals (I Kings 12:28-33; Amos 7:13). The importance of such high places is suggested by the fact that Beth-el is mentioned more often in the Bible than any other location except Jerusalem. There also were other classic pilgrimage sites such as Beer-sheba, Gibeon, Gilgal, Mizpah, and Shechem. Undoubtedly numbers of less important high places, whose names have not survived, were patronized by local worshipers.

That rites observed on the high places enjoyed orthodox religious sanction, as well as state approval, is indicated by the important governmental decisions and celebrations which occurred there. Samuel dined Saul with considerable drama at the high place in the land of Zuph and upon parting anointed him as Israel's first king (I Sam. 9:5-10:1). King David customarily worshiped at a high place on the Mount of Olives (II Sam.15:30-32). King Solomon made his coronation sacrifice at "the great high place " in Gibeon where the altar was large enough for him to present "a thousand burnt-offerings" (I Kings 3:3-4). It is recorded that Ahaz of Judah, one of the better kings, "sacrificed and burnt incense in the high places, and on the hills, and under every green tree" (II Kings 16:4).

Widespread support is indicated by the fact that religious "reformers," before the 621 B.C. advent of Deuteronomy, never thought of abolishing the popularly patronized high places. After stating that the reforming King Asa did not remove them, the Deuteronomic editor said of him "nevertheless, the heart of Asa was perfect with Yahweh all his days" (I Kings 15:14). Even though the same editor noted that five subsequent reformers did not remove the high places, each is credited with having been "right in the eyes of Yahweh" (I Kings 22:43; II Kings 12:2-3 (3-4 in Hebrew); 14:3-4; 15:3-4, 34-35). The religious history of the northern Israelite tribes was summarized in the words,

> they built for themselves high places in all
> their cities, . . . upon every high hill, and
> under every green tree, and there they burnt
> incense in all the high places (II Kings 17:9-
> 11).

The tirades against the high places by the Deuteronomic editor of Judges-Kings must be discounted as the
adverse judgments of a later age which insisted that
Jerusalem was the only legitimate place of worship. By
contrast, the sources he was revising and supplementing
show that worship at the outlying shrines was acceptable
throughout the judges and monarchical period until
the advent of Deuteronomy in 621 B.C.

The main patrons of the high places were the common people who prized the simple worship at local
shrines. Most of these high places were modest unpretentious worship locations beneath the inspiring open sky
and before sacred trees or stones. With Israel these
"groves were God's first temples."

FROM SIMPLE SHRINE TO LUXURIOUS TEMPLE

Since the patriarchs and Moses spent most of their
lives moving from place to place, they had no opportunity to construct buildings devoted to worship. Not until
in this fifth religion of the Old Testament did their
descendants begin erecting such structures. This innovation was made possible when the Israelites became settled in fixed territories and may have been inspired
by the Canaanite Baal temples as well as the structures
in neighboring Philistine and Syrian religions
(Judg. 9:4, 27, 46; I Sam. 5:2-5; I Kings 16:32; II
Kings 5:18; 10:21-27; 11:18).

The earliest biblical record of a building erected
by an Israelite for purposes of worship is found in

Judges 17:5. This verse tells of an Ephraimite by the name of Micah who constructed near his home a "house of gods" as a private family shrine.

The first major temple in Israelite history was located at Shiloh. It apparently had been constructed by the Canaanites and later was captured or simply taken over by the Hebrews. Called "the House of Yahweh" (I Sam. 1:7), it served initially as the place of worship for the tribe of Ephraim (1:1-3) and, eventually, for all Israel (I Sam. 2:14, 22, 28-29; 3:11; 4:1).

As soon as Samuel was weaned, Hannah brought this first-born son to Shiloh and left him there to be reared as a temple servant (I Sam. 1-3). Although an important place of worship while it lasted, the Shiloh temple suddenly vanished from history. It probably was destroyed by the Philistines during the military debacle described in I Samuel 4 when "the glory departed from Israel."

King Solomon had an edifice complex. This led him to construct on Mount Moriah in Jerusalem the most magnificent place of worship in Israel's history. It seemingly was designed on the theory that the more luxurious the structure, the grander the religion. Solomon's glamorous temple replaced the tent shrine (II Sam. 6:17) pitched shortly after 1000 B.C. by King David. That site had been made doubly sacred by Milchizedek's establishing there his altar to "god most high" (Gen. 14:18-22) and by Abraham's token offering of his son Isaac as a burnt sacrifice (Gen. 22).

Three structures at the approach to Solomon's temple commanded attention. Most imposing was the high altar with its column of smoke ascending to Heaven from the flaming sacrificial offerings. The artistically designed molten sea was located between altar and temple. Its mammoth brass bowl was fifty feet in circumference, rested on twelve brass oxen, and contained twenty

thousand gallons of water for the temple supply (I Kings
7:23-26). Flanking the temple entrance on the porch
stood two highly ornamented brass columns, each eighteen
feet in circumference and twenty-seven feet high. These
may have been used to burn incense from their bowled
tops on state occasions (7:15-22).

The Holy Place, or assembly hall, was sixty feet
long, thirty feet wide, and forty-five feet high (I Kings
6:2, 17). Its cedar walls were ornamented with "carved
figures of cherubim and palm trees and open flowers,
within and without."

And the whole house he overlaid with gold,
. . . He even overlaid the floor of the house
with gold, within and without (I Kings 6:22-30).

The Holy of Holies (thirty feet in length, width,
and height) was entered from the Holy Place by a door,
with a golden chain across it. The walls, floor, and
ceiling of this oracle were covered with gold (I Kings
6:20-21). Since that dark Holy of Holies was thought to
be the earthly dwelling place of Yahweh, his assumed
presence there made Jerusalem to be regarded as the Holy
City.

As if religion could be measured by the amount of
gold in evidence, most funishings in the temple were
of solid gold. These included the altar of incense, the
table of showbread, ten candelabra, flowers, lamps, door
hinges, and all utensils used in the services such as
tongs, snuffers, cups, basins, spoons, and firepans
(I Kings 7:48-50). In light of the profuse use of that
precious metal, this remarkable architectural creation
came to be called "the temple of gold" (7:50).

Upon division of the united monarchy, King Jeroboam
feared for the continuing separateness of his ten tribes
if any substantial number of his people were to continue
worshiping in the south at Jerusalem. To discourage this

practice he erected houses for worship at many high places in his realm (I Kings 12:31; 13:32). At the southern
and northern gateways to his country he expanded the
ancient holy places of Beth-el and Dan to become
national shrines. State celebrations were held at those
royal sanctuaries and it was intended that the special
worship of all northerners would be carried on at those
two designated places (I Kings 12:26-33).

After only thirty-three years of untarnished mag-
nificence (950-917 B.C.), the glory of Solomon's temple
began to fade as "Shishak, King of Egypt, came up a-
gainst Jerusalem and took away the treasures of the
house of Yahweh" (I Kings 14:25-26). During the following two and a half centuries the floors, walls, and
ceilings were progressively stripped of their gold to
pay war indemnity or tribute. The solid gold vessels,
furnishings, and their silver replacements met the same
fate (I Kinqs 15:18; II Kings 12:18-19; 14:14; 16:8-9;
18:16). Even so, Solomon's temple remained an imposing
structure that was the place of elite worship for four
centuries. However, it never won the support of the common people and the poor. They reacted against its opu-
lence and were unable to afford the copious sacrifices
that were required. Therefore the majority of citizens
continued to worship at the high places.

Certain psalms, which can be recognized as pre-
exilic by their use of the term Yahweh for deity, express the joy experienced by those who came to worship
in the sacred precincts of Solomon's temple. Most notable is Psalm 84 whose author expressed his longing to
return for another worship experience in the immortal
words,

> How lovely are your tabernacles, O Yahweh of
> hosts. My soul longs, yes, even faints, for
> Yahweh's courts.

Then he went on to tell how he envied the sparrows and swallows that nested there, the priests and altar attendants who lived there, and even the most menial janitor. That psalmist concluded that one day of worship in the temple was worth more than a thousand spent elsewhere since, by contrast, all other places were but "tents of wickedness."

THE ARK OF THE COVENANT

The central object upon which Israelite worship focused in the Canaanite-Hebrew period was the treasure chest made by Moses to carry the two slabs of decalogue. It was carried by the Judah and Levi tribes through the wilderness for forty years and across the Jordan River. For a century thereafter it dropped out of sight but turned up eventually at Beth-el (Judg. 20:26-28).

The ark's next home was in the temple at Shiloh. I Samuel 3:3-15 relates that Yahweh called four times from the ark and then gave a message to the boy Samuel. Giving such an oracle was in harmony with belief since the wilderness wanderings that Yahweh resided in the ark of the covenant, from which he delivered directions and predictions.

Since the Israelites regarded Yahweh as the ultimate in militancy and therefore the most valuable asset in war, he was carried in the ark at the head of their armies when they attacked. Psalm 24:7-10 (an early psalm appended to the postexilic Psalm 24:1-6) describes the return of Yahweh Militant at night after a victory. The bearers called for the city gates, presumably of Shiloh, to be opened so Yahweh in the ark might be returned to his temple.

I Samuel 4-5 tells of a later occasion when the ark was taken from the Shiloh temple to lead an attack against the Philistines. This time the endeavor was not successful, as the ark was captured and in Philistine possession a considerable length of time. Suspecting that Yahweh was

causing the bubonic plague which the ark and its bearers
spread from city to city, the Philistines eventually sent
it home to Israel on a cart drawn by two cows (I Sam. 6:1-12).

Exultation over having Yahweh and his ark returned
soon changed to grief as the plague broke out among the
residents of Beth-shemesh who received this sacred box.
Fearing Yahweh had caused the outbreak, they requested
the people of nearby Kiriath-jearim to come and get the
ark. A delegation from that town brought this Mosaic
trophy and placed it in the house of Abinadab where it
remained twenty years and produced no more plague
(I Sam. 6:13-7:2). King Saul is said to have taken it
into battle once and it brought victory (14:18). Since
the epidemic at Beth-shemesh was regarded as Yahweh's
punishment upon the people of that city for having looked
inside, thereafter the ark was considered unopenable.

One of David's first resolves on becoming king was
to bring this ark of the covenant into his new capital
at Jerusalem. On the way lightning struck the ark, stun-
ning the oxen and killing Uzzah who touched it as he
fell. Not wishing to encounter Yahweh's ostensible anger further, David had the ark placed in the home of a
Philistine named Obed-edom (II Sam. 6:1-11). Because
it popularly was assumed that Uzzah had been killed because of having touched that sacred object, the ark
henceforth was regarded as untouchable except by the
carrying staves.

Since the household of Obed-edom prospered while
the ark was there, David decided he would make another
attempt to bring it into his capital city. With great
ceremony this precious box was successfully transported
to Jerusalem and was placed in a tent on the top of
Mount Moriah (II Sam. 6:12 - 7:2). When Solomon built
his temple this ark was moved into the Holy of Holies

(I Kings 8:1-21). In that gold-enshrined darkness it remained unseeable by nonpriestly eyes except on rare occasions. This was the ultimate home of the ark of the covenant, with whose sacredness no other religious object in Palestine could compare.

An important accompaniment of the holy ark was the sanctuary light which likely was in the Shiloh temple when taken over from the Canaanites. It may have been suspended from the ceiling above or in front of the ark. Each morning it had to be refilled and relit since its font did not contain enough oil to burn all night (I Sam. 3:3). In Solomon's temple this sanctuary light was placed over the entrance to the Holy of Holies.

This ever-burning light survives to the present before torah shrines in Jewish synagogues and temples, before the mihrab in Islamic mosques, and over altars as well as before icons or images of saints in Eastern Orthodox and Roman Catholic churches. It is significant that this Canaanite vigil of the eternal light has immortalized itself through all these centuries in Judaism, Islam, and the liturgical segments of Christianity.

EMERGENCE OF A PROFESSIONAL PRIESTHOOD

According to previous chapters, the early authentic records indicate no semblance of religious professionals in the Bible's first four religions. However, development of a priesthood was inevitable in Israel's fifth religion since holy places and the holy ark came to play such important roles. The fact that the Canaanites had their priests to Baal (II Kings 10:19; 11:18) may have influenced the Hebrews into developing corresponding priests to Yahweh.

On festal occasions self-appointed local individuals likely served as priests at the less important Canaanite-Hebrew high places. Micah, the Ephraimite, made the innovation of appointing one of his sons to perform the rituals at his shrine (Judg. 17:1-6). Following suit, Abinadab "consecrated Eleazar, his son, to keep the ark of Yahweh" while it was in his home (I Sam. 7:1). In the Northern Kingdom, during the monarchy, officiants were assigned to the high places by kings as a matter of political patronage (I Kings 12:31-32; 13:2, 33; II Kings 23:8-20; Amos 7:10). However, none of these sporadic starts developed into any continuous priestly line.

Jonathan, grandson of Moses, was the first priestly professional in the Bible. While "looking for a position" he was employed by Micah to serve his gods as a levitical priest. When members of the Danite tribe came by that "house of gods" while migrating to the extreme north of Palestine, they heard Jonathan officiating and either enticed him to go with them or kidnaped him. In this way Jonathan and his offspring became a line of priests serving the tribe of Dan (Judg. 17-18).

The Bible offers no information concerning the origins of Eli who came on the scene half a century later. He may have been a son of Jonathan. If so, Eli would have been a great-grandson of Moses. Whatever his origins, Eli appeared at the Shiloh temple as priest to the tribe of Ephraim, with his two sons whom he also had consecrated (I Sam. 1:3; 2:12-22). Since he sat on a dais by the temple door, counseling and judging apparently were among his chief functions. When he and those sons met death in consequence of a military defeat at the hands of the Philistines, that priestly line seemingly came to an inglorious end (4:11-18).

However, long after the Shiloh temple had been destroyed by the Philistines, Ahijah, great-grandson of Eli, was found officiating "under the pomegranate tree in Migron" (I Sam. 14:2-36). Another great-grandson

(14:3 cf. 22:20), Ahimelech, had become head of a group of eighty-six priests located at a sanctuary in Nob, the north suburb of Jerusalem. King Saul slew eighty-five of those priests for having befriended David, and destroyed that "city of the priests." Only one escaped alive, a youth by the name of Abiathar. He became priest to David and his refugee group (I Sam. 21-22). This great-great-grandson of Eli served as David's priest during that king's forty-year reign.

Because of having supported Adonijah's claim to the throne, Abiathar was defrocked by King Solomon and was exiled from the capital city (I Kings 1:5-10; 2:26 - 27). In Anathoth, several miles northeast of Jerusalem, Abiathar and his progeny in time became a village of priests, although without portfolio. Because of popular reverence for David, many people sought out Abiathar and his successors for priestly services as they became somewhat of a rival to the Jerusalem priesthood.

During David's kingship when the priestly duties had become too heavy for Abiathar, his uncle Zadok, great-grandson of Eli was brought as priest into the royal cabinet to assist (II Sam. 8:17). When King Solomon deposed Abiathar, Zadok became chief priest and founder of the whole subsequent line of temple offici-ants. In the centuries after 961 B.C. these Zadokites became a powerful professional class.

The initial priestly duties consisted in caring for the ark of the covenant, transporting it during pre-Solomonic days from place to place, and performing pro-per rituals before it.

Priests also functioned at holy meals. As shown in I Samuel 1-2, the presumed earliest "sacrifice" in this period was not done by burning up an animal to Yah-weh upon an altar. Rather, it consisted in boiling the cut-up animal in a caldron at the holy place. When well

boiled, a priest jabbed in with a large three-pronged
fork and drew out all it could hold as their portion.
Then those making the offering partook of the remainder.

In the course of time worship became increasingly a
daytime affair -- more frequent and formalized into
stated priestly rituals. Burning incense on the small
altar set aside for that purpose was the simplest and
most frequent duty. For affluent worshipers the priests
sacrificed goats, sheep, or cattle on the high altar.
When presenting peace offerings only part of the meat was
burned, or blood was merely sprinkled on the altar
(II Kings 16:13). Priests also served worshipers who
brought the more aesthetic nonblood grain, meal, or
drink offerings. Vows, such as the complicated Nazarite
vow of abstaining from wine, liquor, unclean food, and
cutting the hair, also were heard and administered by
the priests (Num. 6:13-21; Judg. 13:4-7, 14; 16:17).

Along both sides of Solomon's temple there were
three floors of rooms for priests. In addition to ritualistic duties, these religious professionals were responsible for maintaining the temple in good condition
and for initiating and overseeing all repairs (II Kings
12:9-16; 22:3-10). Priests received and disbursed all
temple funds gained from sacrificial fees, from the offering chest at the temple door, and from all other
gratuities paid by worshipers. II Kings 11 indicates
even changing the temple military guard was done under
priestly supervision.

Priests also played important governmental roles
and were political functionaries in ways not specifical-
ly recorded. Such is indicated by the fact that King
David had two priests in his cabinet of seven
(II Sam. 20:23-26) and Solomon had three in his cabinet
of eleven (I Kings 4:1-6). As observed at the accessions
of Saul, Solomon, and Joash, priests played a key role

in designating who should accede to the throne when a
king died. Usually, a priest anointed the incoming
monarch with oil as the consecrating rite of coronation.
A major priestly duty was to counsel kings, especially
in regard to foreign affairs and military proposals.

Priests wore the linen ephod, the original vestment
(vest) from which subsequent Judaeo-Christian vestments
have come. The ephod had a pocket in which were kept the
sacred stones or primitive dice called Urim (Num.27:21;
I Sam. 28:6). When suppliants wished to know what Yahweh
wanted done in a particular situation or desired advance
knowledge concerning future events and their outcome,
these predictive objects were thrown to the ground or
floor where the manner of falling was believed to give
the requested divine information. Usually they were cast
before the ark, i.e., before Yahweh. However, no matter
where he was, if the priest had on his ephod it was assumed he could determine Yahweh's will by "casting the
lot," as the process was idiomatically called.

The ritualized sacrament of communion, an adoption
from Canaanite religion, appeared during King Saul's
reign. The ever-present holy bread on the altar was
first observed in the sanctuary at Nob and later on the
table of showbread in Solomon's temple. An important
part of priestly functioning consisted in administering
to all worshipers who sought that token of spiritual
infilling, the holy bread that was infused with the
divine spirit (I Sam. 21:3-6; I Kings 7:48).

Two practices that survive in Roman Catholicism
today already were present in this Canaanite-Hebrew
religion. (1) Communion to the worshipers seems to have
been only in the "one kind" of bread, with the wine reserved for the priests. (2) This showbread or presence
bread always had to be on the altar. The only exception
to this in Roman Catholicism is that the "host"

(eucharistic bread) is removed from the altar each year from Good Friday afternoon until Easter morning.

The foregoing observations show that the priests gradually carved out for themselves an important place in Israelite life as they performed the rituals connected with presenting all types of offerings, conveyed to Yahweh worshipers' thanks for past favors, presented suppliants' special requests, sought for the perplexed that divine information which it was believed deity alone could supply, and on behalf of the distressed implored Yahweh for present or future help. Through the opportunities for pompous priestly functioning in Solomon's temple, this fifth Old Testament religion became gradually changed from one without religious professionals, in the days of the judges, to an elaborate priestly religion with its temple cult.

THE COVENANT OF HUMAN SACRIFICE

By a coalition of circumstances Samuel supplied a new law code for a new era in Israel's life. That innovation resulted from widespread clamor for the establishment of a monarchy because people feared Samuel's renegade sons would be judges over the nation after his death. Faced with that pressure, he strove to resist the oppostion and retain his position by modifying his rule into a constitutional judgeship. He accordingly gathered into the form of a new law code the principles by which he guaranteed thereafter to judge the people, and "wrote it in a book which he placed before Yahweh," i.e., before the ark of the covenant (I Sam. 10:25).

Since this made Samuel Israel's second lawgiver, the canonizers placed his code in Exodus 20:23-23:33, immediately following the ten "words" of Israel's first great lawgiver. If law codes were to be judged by size,

Samuel's would be much superior, approximately twenty times larger than Moses' unredacted short Decalogue as he delivered it.

Exodus 22:29-30 contains the most astonishing law in this new code. "You shall give to me the first-born of your sons. You shall do likewise with your oxen and with your sheep. Seven days it shall be with its mother; on the eighth day you shall give it to me." Most surprising is this demand that first-born males of humans had to be offered up in the same way the first-born of animals were sacrificed. Although Abraham's refusal to sacrifice his son Isaac should have ended human sacrifice in Israel for all time, here it turned up again, prescribed by law in Samuel's Code of the Covenant.

The most dramatic human sacrifice took place in a national military emergency and may have been strategic in fastening that practice upon the judges period. Realizing that his darling daughter likely would be first to meet him when he would return home from battle, Jephthah euphemistically vowed to sacrifice her if Yahweh would give him victory over the Ammonites,

> Then the spirit of Yahweh came upon Jephthah
> . . . . And Jephthah made a vow to Yahweh,
> and said, "If you will indeed deliver the peo-
> ple of Ammon into my hand, then it shall be,
> that whatsoever comes out from the doors of my
> house to meet me, when I return in peace from
> the people of Ammon, it shall be Yahweh's and
> I will offer it up for a burnt offering"
> (Judg. 11:29-31).

Since it is recorded that this god granted his judge victory over those enemies, Jephthah fulfilled his vow by presenting this beloved and only child as a burnt offering to Yahweh.

Strange as it may seem to us, everyone concerned was happy over that human sacrifice. Yahweh was thought happy because of having such a delightful burnt sacrifice offered to him. Jephthah was happy because Yahweh, by reason of this promised sacrifice, had given victory to his judge. All Israel was happy because this sacrifice had freed their country from foreign domination. Even Jephthah's daughter was happy at the thought of having been, through her promised sacrifice, the savior of her nation in the hour of trial.

The only regret was that she would be dying a virgin, childless, and therefore bereft of any immortality. For that reason Jephthah gave her permission to go with her girlfriends on a retreat into the mountains "to bewail her virginity." This was not to bewail the fact that she was about to be burned alive on an altar. The subsequent four-day annual feast "to celebrate the daughter of Jephthah" must have impressed that whole generation with the belief that Yahweh was delighted with human sacrifice and that all godly people might well follow Jephthah's example (Judg. 11:34-40).

As the builder who took the contract to reconstruct the walls of Jericho, Hiel "laid its foundations with the loss of his first-born, Abiram, and hung its gates with the loss of his youngest son, Segub" (I Kings 16:34). That one son met death when the contract was begun and the other, when it was completed suggests two more examples of human sacrifice rather than death from natural causes. Evidently in those days a contractor required an adequate supply of sons to sacrifice as building insurance that the structures he erected would not fall down. As with Jephthah's daughter, this indicates human sacrifice was not confined to presenting first-born sons.

From there on human sacrifice gradually acceler-
ated, with development of a standard euphemism to foil
objectors' outrage over such events. In a grave military
situation King Ahaz of Judah "made his son to pass
through the fire" (II Kings 16:3). King Manasseh also
"made his son to pass through the fire" (21:6).
II Kings 17:17 tells how this rite of human sacrifice
was commonly practiced by the people of Israel who
"caused their sons and their daughters to pass through
the fire." It may be assumed that Samuel's law demanding
human sacrifice was obeyed far more than the largely
expurgated records of Israelite practice would lead one
to believe.

The underlying theology was that Yahweh demands
the best in sacrifice: the best of one's animals, grains,
fruits, etc. Since the ultimate best was found in the
family's choicest possession, their children, it was
thought these were demanded as the most efficacious presentation. Sacrifice of the first-born of animals and
mankind was based on the further assumption that unless
Yahweh was made pleased by receiving in advance his
share of the whole birth succession he would not grant
the female animal or human mother more offspring.

Sacrifice of children on the eighth day has survived in sublimated forms to the present. Within Judaism
the token sacrifice of the male via circumcision takes
place on the eighth day. The overtone of human sacrifice
is seen also in Orthodoxy's redemption of the first-born
son by payment of a price. The liturgical segments of
Christianity pay silent memory to human sacrifice on
the eighth day by baptizing infants on the eighth day
and by frequently designating the first-born son for
religious orders.

WORSHIP OF CANAANITE-HEBREW AND NEIGHBORING GODS

Samuel's Code of the Covenant has valuable information also concerning the gods worshiped during this period. Most revealing is the prescription for making an
Israelite a permanent slave. Samuel allowed his people
to enslave a fellow Hebrew for a maximum of six years
but in the seventh such a slave was to be freed. In
Exodus 21:2-6 this new lawgiver dealt with the case
of a slave who had been given a slave wife by his master
and the couple had slave children. This man liked his
master, did not want to sever his family relationships
by leaving, and therefore chose to forfeit the freedom
option by requesting that he be made a slave for life.
Samuel ordered that in such a situation

his master shall bring him to the gods, and
shall bring him to the door, or to the doorpost,and his master shall bore through his ear
with an awl, and he shall serve him for ever.

This indicates that the normative Hebrew home at
Samuel's time had household gods on the god-shelf beside
the entrance door. By placing the slave's ear against
the door or doorpost for this tattooing ceremony, the
gods on that god-shelf would be witnesses. Thereby these
deities were made the enforcement officers so that if
he ever should disavow his slavery they would punish
him.

The household gods and god-shelf survive today in
sublimated form in Orthodox Judaism where the mezuzah
is attached to the doorpost. This is a capsule a few
inches long into which have been inserted several key
pasages of Scripture. Every Jew who places a mezuzah
at a door is unknowingly paying tribute to the day when
his people had their household gods on the god-shelf
by the door to protect the house against anyone's entering it with evil design. Echoes of such household gods

survive also in some Christian countries, notably Italy, where the shelf remains by the front door but with the images on it construed as saints.

Another law in Samuel's Code of the Covenant tells how gods might not be made. Moses commanded in the Decalogue, "You shall not make for yourself a graven image" (Exod. 20:4). That this law was being disregarded among the late judges is indicated by Judges 17:3-4 which tells of newly made graven and molten images. It appears that Samuel had given up trying to stop his people from making graven images and now was content to prohibit making deities of silver and gold, as was increasingly common in Canaanite usage.

> You shall not make with me gods of silver or gods of gold -- you shall not make for yourselves (Exod. 20:23).

This interpretation is made more plausible by observing Samuel's companion law concerning altar construction. The traditional Israelite altar, and still the most desirable according to Samuel, was but an improvised scooped-up pile of earth. By contrast, the Canaanites built high altars of hewn stones, with steps to the top. Since the Israelites were beginning to follow suit, Samuel felt forced to allow stone altars, provided they were made of unhewn field stones and not high with steps (Exod. 20:24-26).

Even though Samuel felt forced to make such compromises, these laws concerning images of precious metals and altar construction show that he was determined to restrain his people into keeping a margin of difference between Canaanite and Hebrew religious practice.

At one point Samuel reacted with greater severity than any one before him. "He who sacrifices to any god, except to Yahweh only, shall be utterly destroyed"

(Exod. 22:20). How could the death penalty for worshiping other gods be prescribed here when household deities
were sactioned a chapter earlier in Exodus 21:2-6? The
objection in 22:20 apparently was not with worshiping
other gods as such but with the treason involved in patronizing national deities of enemy peoples. That this
law by Samuel fell largely on deaf ears is indicated
by the maze of references to Israelites venerating the
gods of their neighbors.

Throughout the judges period Canaanite worship had
occasionally replaced Yahweh religion. As the first recorded act of Deborah's judgeship "new gods were chosen"
(Judg. 5:8). Gideon's first move also was to change gods
and after his death the situation was reversed
(6:25-32; 8:33). Following Jair's judgeship a similar
interchange took place (10:6-16).

Judges 3:7 indicates that the Israelites were
strongly attracted to the chief Canaanite god Baal
(Lord). Gideon's family patronized the local Baal altar
and this judge's acquired name was Jerub-baal, "Let Baal
Contend" (Judg.6:25-32; 8:27-29). The first religious
structure of this period was a Baal temple (9:4). King
Saul, Israel's first monarch, named one of his sons Ish-
baal, "Man of Baal." Jonathan, David's most intimate
friend, had a son named Merib-baal, "Baal is my Advocate" (I Chron. 8:34; 9:40). Such names in high places
reveal the important role Baal worship occupied among
the judges and members of Israel's first royal family.

Embarrassed over this situation, the Deuteronomic
editor of Samuel and Kings always surrogated the baal
component in the names of Saul's and Jonathan's sons
into "shame." By this change Ish-baal (Man of Baal) was
turned into Ish-bosheth (Man of Shame) in II Samuel 2:8-
15; 3:7-15; and 4:5-12. In the same way Merib-baal (Baal
is my Advocate), with some further alteration of conson-

ants, was degraded into Mephi-bosheth (Shame is my Advocate) in II Samuel 4:4; 9:6-13; 16:1-4; 19:24-30; and
21:7-8).

With King Ahab and Queen Jezebel of Israel, and
their daughter Queen Athaliah of Judah, Baalism for a
time became even the state religion in each kingdom (I
Kings 16:31-33; 18:1-40; II Kings 11:1-16). Some sixteen
references indicate Baal's consort, the Canaanite mother goddess Astarte (Esther), was widely worshiped. Gods
of the Transjordanian nations also received considerable
veneration. Because of these incursions into Israel
there was a chorus of polemic against Molech and Milcom
of Ammon as well as Chemosh of Moab (I Kings 11:5-7,
33; II Kings 23:10-13).

The popular high places were devoted principally
to local deities. Usually these gods were thought to
be found in sacred trees, such as "the oak that was in
Ophrah," "the oak of the pillar that was in Shechem,"
"the oak of Meonenim," "the oak of Tabor," the pomegranate tree which is in Migron," etc. Such deified trees,
or remnants thereof, are rendered in translations usually as asherah, oak, terebinth, grove, or their respective
plurals. Gods were thought to reside also in holy
stones, set upright and called "pillars" (Judg. 6:11-
30; 9:6, 37; I Sam. 10:3; 14:2; I Kings 14:15, 23;
15:13; 16:33; II Kings 13:6; 17:10). This religion at
the high places, throughout the judges-kings period,
was for the most part a surviving stone-age worship of
nature gods.

This roll-call of marginal deities in the Old Testament's fifth religion shows that the Israelites in that
period worshiped primitive nature gods in trees, stones,
and water, household deities that were kept on god-
shelves by the door, gods of neighboring nations, and
especially Canaanite Baal and his wife Astarte.

Worshiping such a diversity of deities during the
Judges, Samuel, and Kings period indicates there was little if any thought that such pluralism was prohibited,
either by Moses' first commandment or by Samuel's Code
of the Covenant.

DEITIES AUTHORIZED FOR TEMPLE WORSHIP

Even Solomon's temple was not theistically monolithic since its worship clustered around a trinity
of gods. With their imposing bull bodies, bird wings,
and human heads, a pair of cherubim dominated the Holy
of Holies as master deities. They were made of olive
wood overlaid with gold in harmony with the golden ceiling, golden walls, and golden floor. Approximately fifteen feet tall, each had an outstretched wingspread of
fifteen feet, with combined wingspread reaching from
wall to wall. This pair of gigantesque associate deities
stood guard over the ark of the covenant, the assumed
earthly dwelling place of Yahweh who was protected by
their overshadowing wings (I Kings 6:23-28; 8:6-7;
II Kings 19:15).

Thousands more of these divine creatures were carved on the walls of both the Holy of Holies and the Holy
Place, on the temple doors, and on the furnishings. By
this multitude of guardian cherub deities, the temple
and all its parts were provided the supposed maximum
security of supernatural protection to keep all unworthy
persons from entering and degrading its rituals (I Kings
6:29-35; 7:29, 36).

As suggested by archaeological recoveries of Near
Eastern temple and palace architecture, the two lions
that formed the sides of Solomon's throne probably also
were protective cherub deities. The same was likely true
of the twelve "lions" at ends of the six steps approaching that throne. The "golden calves" stationed at the

two borders of Jeroboam's kingdom in Dan and Beth-el also may have been cherub gods guarding those main entrances to the nation (I Kings 10:19-20; 12:28-29).

There also was the bronze serpent deity Moses made to be worshiped by victims of snake bites during the wilderness wanderings (Num. 21:6-9). That image was worshiped by Israelites during succeeding centuries as a seraphic (from Hebrew *saraph*, serpent) deity. When Solomon's temple was built, this brass serpent was mounted over the door to the Holy of Holies as one of the Hebrew people's most treasured gods. According to Isaiah 6:2 it played an important part when that prophet had his prophetic call during a coronation service in the temple. On that occasion the fleecy curls of smoke rising from the altar of incense seemed to cut that image into sections. In his mystic mood the dreamy Isaiah accordingly visualized this *saraph* (snake) as a group of six-winged serpents (seraphim) flying about over the prospective king's head while waiting for his crown. II Kings 18:4 notes that "unto those days the people of Israel burnt incense to it, and it was called Nehushtan," *nahash* being another name for snake.

Although accompanied by these subsidiaries, Yahweh was the chief deity upon whom all Israelite religion eventually focused. Transported to the land of Canaan in the ark of the covenant, he soon came to be thought of as the god of Israel and the god of Palestine. The reforming judges were considered appointed and empowered by Yahweh. Since the ensuing monarchy was construed as a theocracy under Yahweh's guidance and inspiration, the king was revered as "Yahweh's anointed." These rulers were judged religiously by the degree to which each fostered devotion to Yahweh and the Yahwistic program for the nation. Even though many other gods were part of the picture along the way, Yahweh was to triumph over them all. That was the greatest achievement of this fifth Old Testament religion.

HOLY AND FESTAL DAYS

When the priestly editor's retrojection of late institutions back into Israel's early history is discounted, it becomes evident there was no weekly Sabbath in any of the Old Testament's previous four religions, or even in this fifth.

The first move in the direction of a regular day for worship is observed in the time of Samuel, at approximately 1080 B.C., as shown in I Samuel 1:3-23; 2:12-20. Elkanah and his wives arrived at the Shiloh temple in the afternoon with a three-year-old bullock, a bushel of flour, and a skin of wine. While the men dressed the bullock, cut it up, and placed the pieces in a caldron to boil, the women baked cakes. With all in readiness by late evening, the worshipers gathered about and partook of those delicacies during a night of feasting. In the morning, after performing benedictive rituals, the family returned home, joyful over having fulfilled their religious duties for another year. I Samuel 20:5-29 identifies this as the new-moon festival.

Several deductions can be drawn from these passages. From the point of view of the individual family it was an annual religious reunion, on the particular new moon each relationship had chosen for its celebration. However, at the Shiloh temple, and other major places of worship, it was a monthly observance since one or more families were present each month.

With its greater illumination for nighttime, the more spectacular full moon eventually asserted its claims also. The observance at that time of the month was called sabbath, from *shabbatu* , the Akkadian word

for full moon. When prophets or historical writers spoke
of "new moon and sabbath" they were referring to these
two lunar festivals per month (Amos 8:5; Hosea 2:11).
Psalm 81:3 (4 in Hebrew) reflects this period when it
says: "Blow the trumpet at the new moon, at the full
moon, on our feast day." In II Kings 4:23 surprise is
expressed that any one should have wished to visit a
holy place except on new moon or sabbath. By the time
of Amos 8:5, at approximately 750 B.C., business activity and work were supposed to cease as those days became
devoted to religious ceremonials. This was the ultimate
development with regard to regular worship in the Old
Testament's fifth religion -- two holy days, on the
first and fifteenth of each month, dedicated to worshiping the moon deity.

In addition, three major annual festivals, commonly
called "the set feasts," were prescribed by Samuel in
his Code of the Covenant (Exod. 23:14-17). These agricultural celebrations likely had been taken over from
the Canaanites. (1) The spring sheepshearing festival
of one week duration was reinterpreted as the Feast of
Unleavened Bread. The seven days devoted to eating unleavened bread were to remind all Israelites of their
liberation from the house of bondage in Egypt. (2) The
Feast of Harvest celebrated the beginning of grain reap-
ing. Since this took place seven weeks after the spring
festival it was renamed the Feast of Weeks. (3) A third
observance, the Feast of Ingathering, took place in aut-
umn when the grapes ripened. Entire families went into
the vineyards to live in improvised shelters as a week
was spent gathering the year's crop of grapes. In time,
this outdoor fall jubilation assumed the name Feast
of Succoth, i.e., the Feast of Booths.

The command in Amos 4:4 to "bring . . . your tithes
every three days" did not mean every third day, but on

the three great festal occasions. On those most important religious celebrations of each year King Solomon
asserted his royal prerogative as the ultimate priest
by offering the temple sacrifices himself (I Kings 9:25).
That trio of basically agricultural sacred holidays
overshadowed the new moons and sabbaths and served to
make Judaism a religion of feast days. Those three religious festivals were to be transformed into the Christian Easter, Pentecost, and Harvest Festival or Thanksgiving.

It has been seen how the Israelites adopted the
Canaanites' language (renaming it Hebrew) and much of
their religion. The cycle of Canaanite-Hebrew holy observances found their completion as the new-moon and
full-moon festivals of worshiping the lunar deity became
supplemented by the three annual agricultural Baal festivals. The main Hebrew additions consisted in an emerging priesthood, worship at Solomon's temple, and ever-
mounting devotion to Yahweh. This conglomerate became
the Bible's fifth religion, the Canaanite-Hebrew faith.

SPIRITUAL ACHIEVEMENTS BY SAMUEL AND DAVID

Samuel left a memorable utterance as he said to
King Saul, "To obey is better than sacrifice, and to
hearken, than the fat of rams" (I Sam. 15:22). In that
tense moment Samuel became vaguely aware of a higher
dimension in religion.

If one can judge a faith by the people it produces,
David was the showpiece of this fifth religion. During
shepherd days he perfected his poise and marksmanship
to the point of being able to face calmly bears, lions,
and eventually Goliath (I Sam. 17:34-51). While shep-
herding his flock David became skilled at playing the
lyre. As a pioneer in music therapy, when summoned to
court this lad brought King Saul out of his demented

moods (II Sam. 16:23). This young musician became the chief exponent of Hebrew psalmody and was called "the sweet psalmist of Israel" (II Sam. 23:1).

Unable to tolerate this youth's popularity throughout the realm, King Saul tried repeatedly to have him killed. This was done by attempting to spear David while playing the harp on three occasions, by giving him a succession of dangerous military assignments in which he supposedly would be killed, by repeatedly trying to have him arrested and brought so Saul could kill him, and by sending full armies into the field four times to capture and kill this elusive youth. These add up to seventeen times King Saul tried to kill David, many having been multiple attempts. David's returning good for evil on all such occasions was his greatest ethical achievement (I Sam. 18:10-26:25).

Most revealing are the two episodes when David risked his life by passing the guards and standing beside the sleeping king at night. Both times this refugee had opportunities to kill this person who had been unspeakably murderous toward him on so many occasions. However, David only cut off a snip of Saul's garment the first night and carried off his flask and spear on the second. When the king was awake the following morning and at safe distance, in each instance David held up these trophies of good will, showing how he had those two opportunities to kill King Saul, but did not take them (I Sam. 24, 26).

Since David regarded the enthroned one as the Lord's anointed, the royal person was to be respected as sacred. When an Amalekite asserted he had killed Saul, David had that claimant executed at once for having slain "Yahweh's anointed" (II Sam. 1:14-15). When two opportunists decapitated a king of the northern tribes and brought his head to David, he immediately had them

put to death and hung by the pool in Hebron as an object
lesson to all who would do violence to the person of
any ruler, even undesirable ones (II Sam. 4:12).

These examples of respect for public officials made
such an indelible impression upon succeeding ages that
the Southern Kingdom of Judah continued almost half a
millennium, from 1000 B.C. to the Babylonian exile in
586 B.C., without an assassination of any validly a-
nointed ruling king. This contrasted with the Northern
Kingdom, where the Davidic tradition was absent, which
met its ruin by slipping into the caldron of assassination and counterassassination. To the citizens of every
age and nation there comes from David the call to have
respect for the office and person of government officials, even when disagreeing with their policies.

His lament over the death of Saul and Jonathan in
II Samuel 1:19-27 shows that David was able to appreciate opponents' accomplishments as he freely called them
to public attention. This magnificent example should
be a challenge to every political aspirant and voter
to recognize the good contributions of opposition par-
ties and their leaders.

One of the most notable friendships of all time developed between David and Jonathan. Chief credit goes
to this first-born son who was destined to follow King
Saul on the throne of Israel. This royal son was objective enough to realize that David would make a better
king. Jonathan also was a big enough person to yield
his right of succession to this friend whom he so admired. Because

Jonathan loved him as his own soul. . . . Jonathan stripped himself of the robe that was upon him, and gave it to David (I Sam. 18:1-4).
Such unselfishness and magnanimity are seldom found in
human annals.

Although David had faults, with women especially and in raising his children, his virtues so outweighed those failings that he was popularly regarded as the man after his god's own heart.

KING SOLOMON, IN ALL HIS GLORY

Solomon brought the Israelite people to their highest point of national achievement during pre-exilic days. He built his palace, the luxurious temple, and six store cities for famine protection and national defense (I Kings 6-7; 9:15-22). As an industrial magnate he exported copper from the mines and refineries he developed, and imported gold. To carry on this trade he constructed a fleet of merchant ships that plied the Red Sea and the Indian Ocean (9:26-28; 10:11-12, 22). He was Israel's first scholar, author, and educator -- introducing the arts, crafts, and sciences of horticulture, botany, zoology, ornithology, entomology, ichthyology, metallurgy, proverbialism, psalmody, and theology (4:29-34).

The Old Testament's best example of an individual with both piety and good judgment is observed when "Yahweh appeared to Solomon in a dream by night" at Gibeon. His humility upon taking office, and dependence upon divine aid in carrying out his governmental role, are illustrated by the words of his inaugural prayer.

"I am but a little child. I do not know how to go out or come in. . . . Therefore, give your servant an understanding mind to govern your people, that I may discern between good and evil." . . . And the petition was pleasing in the eyes of the Lord, that Solomon had made this request. And god said to him, "Because you have made this request, and have not requested long life for yourself, neither have

requested riches for yourself, nor have requested the life of your enemies, . . . lo, I
have given you a wise and an understanding
mind; . . . And I also have given you that
which you have not requested, both riches and
honor, . . . And . . . I will lengthen your
days." . . . And god gave Solomon exceeding
much wisdom and understanding, and largeness
of heart even as the sand that is on the seashore (I Kings 3:5-15; 4:29).

Although the Deuteronomic editor criticized Solomon
harshly for worshiping other gods, therein lay one of
that king's major contributions to the development of
religion. In his ecumenicity Solomon constructed, on
the Mount of Olives, shrines where the leading types
of foreign worships could be carried on by diplomats
assigned to his court and by his foreign wives (I Kings
3:3; 11:1-8). Even though Solomon often joined ecumeni-
cally in their rites on the special feast days of those
faiths, such occasional expressions of interreligious
friendship did not diminish his total commitment to Yahweh and the religion of Israel. In all this, Solomon
was the pioneering voice of religious liberty in the
Bible, believing each person should have the right to
worship according to the dictates of his or her own
conscience. Although we take this principle for granted
today, for Solomon's time it was an innovative and revolutionary religious precedent.

Solomon struck the ultimate in ecumenism as he constructed his temple with a world outreach. He built it

that all the peoples of the earth may know your
name, . . . that all the peoples of the earth
may know that Yahweh, he is god (I Kings 8:43,
60).

The spirit and intent of Solomon in building his temple, as expressed best in Micah 4:1-2, may serve as the benediction to this fifth religion of the Old Testament, the Canaanite-Hebrew faith.

The mountain of Yahweh's house shall be established at the head of the mountains, and it shall be exalted above the hills, and peoples shall flow unto it. And many nations shall go and say, "Come, and let us go up to the mountain of Yahweh, even to the house of the god of Jacob; and he will teach us of his ways, and we will walk in his paths, for out of Zion shall go forth the law, and the word of Yahweh from Jerusalem."

CHAPTER 6

THE REVOLUTIONARY RELIGION OF ISRAEL'S PROPHETS

In history the milestones of progress are set by pioneers who envision something better and set out with vigor to attain it. This was characteristic of the Bible's sixth religion, developed by a few hardy souls who forged ahead remarkably into things religious. To retrace the mature achievements contributed by those geniuses is to embark on an odyssey of spiritual discovery.

Although there were several pioneering individuals, what is called the great prophetic succession began under Canaanite-Hebrew religion with Amos at approximately 750 B.C. and continued in Judaism which began at 722 B.C. The succession ended with the writing of Jonah at 300-250 B.C.

These prophets commonly have been classified as three major (Isaiah, Jeremiah, and Ezekiel) and twelve minor (Hosea, Joel, Amos, Obadiah, Jonah, Micah, Nahum, Habakkuk, Zephaniah, Haggai, Zechariah, and Malachi). That rating is very artificial, based not on the comparative quality of their work but only on how many pages of each prophet's writings or speeches have survived in the Bible.

The prophetic movement was a succession of enervated individuals, each of whom caught a transcendent spiritual gleam from his predecessor and passed the message on, usually amplified and readapted to the unique problems of a succeeding age. This chain of talented and devoted individuals developed a superior religion that was at home in the rarified heights by contrast with the mediocre popular types that flourished below. Nevertheless, the prophets exerted a transforming influence that

always was pulling the accepted religions of the day
up to higher dimensions of faith.

By reason of their vision, the biblical prophets
were lone voices of the future, with few friends. In
many instances it was one man against the whole nation
of Israel. These individuals challenged a fundamental
assumption of democracy, that the majority is always
right and that "the voice of the people is the voice
of God."

Because the prophets heralded a new future, they
faced two opposing segments of society. As in every
age, a substantial portion of those to whom these spiritual pioneers spoke revered the past and longed to return there. Another large per cent worshiped the status
quo and were pained by any one who wanted to transform
or replace it.

In face of this combined devotion to past and present, these few high-powered prophetic voices "crying
in the wilderness" were commonly regarded by the mass
of society as unpardonable meddlers and disturbers of
the peace, iconoclasts set on destroying both civilization and religion. With some prophets, opposition went
to the point of being executed by the reactionary and
complacent power structure -- Amos after only two or
three months of work, Isaiah sawed in two, Zephaniah
after having delivered a single address, Uriah slain
by King Jehoiakim, and Zechariah stoned to death before
the altar.

CONTINUING MISUNDERSTANDINGS OF THE PROPHETS

Appreciation of the prophets today is smogged over
by popular misunderstandings of them. Usually these individuals are pictured as tottery old men with bald
heads, often leaning on a cane, and with one foot in
the grave. The truth is the exact opposite. These were

young people in the full flush of idealism. Although
Isaiah and Jeremiah managed to continue prophetic activity for approximately forty and forty-three years respectively, they began as youths. These young people
in Israel formed perhaps the greatest religious youth
movement of all time.

A second major misunderstanding consists in regarding the prophets as predictors of a long-range future,
hundreds and thousands of years beyond their age, or
even to the end of time. Careful study shows that this
assumption also is untrue. Those prophets were basically
forthtellers, not *foretellers*. Predictions requiring
more than ten or twenty years for fulfillment usually
were inserted into the prophetic documents by the pre-
sumptuous eschatologists of later generations.

The common Christian belief that the primary role
of these prophets was to predict the coming of Jesus
is proved by the best research to be a third prevalent
misconception. Most "Messianic" expectations were inserted into the pre-exilic writings after the exile when
Palestine had lost her king, for which Messiah (the a-
nointed) was the underground name. These passages anticipated a day when political independence would be restored and a righteous king again would sit on the
throne of Israel. In their bondage and persecution these
Messianists envisioned the coming king as virtually
divine and well-nigh perfect. They anticipated the joy
when he would be born and the righteous acts he would
perform. Although Jesus was a man of peace and righteousness, he did not fulfill the Messianic expectations
of being a king sitting on a throne, setting up a government, and defending it with an army.

If not old men, predictors of long-range future,
or foretellers of Jesus, who then were these religious
leaders? Israel's prophets were the superb preachers

and teachers of those centuries. They were the liberals of the Old Testament period, working to liberate the people of their day from all that cramped or destroyed. These inspired young men were existentialists who dealt with contemporary problems in a grappling manner. The Hebrew word *nabi* (prophet) comes from the root meaning "to foam at the mouth." These young men were wrought up over the corruption of their times and spoke out a-gainst it with such vigor that they foamed at the mouth. They were the activists and reformers who had visions of a transformed humanity and gave their lives to bring it about. The prophets lived ahead of their times, al-ways discovering higher concepts of deity and working for the better world they believed humanity was created to enjoy.

The importance of Israel's prophets was recognized by the canonizers who devoted approximately one third of the Old Testament to the addreses, writings, and bio-graphical items about those young religious leaders whose souls were on fire with the divine spirit. This body of literature comprises information about activi-ties of the prophets as found in the Books of Judges, Samuel, and Kings; the reform Book of Deuteronomy which put prophetic principles into law; and the fifteen books in what is called the prophetic canon.

FORERUNNERS OF THE NEW PROPHECY

Three individuals heralded the advent of prophetic activity as each attained for a moment the high voltage which was characteristic of that impending movement. The first of these pioneering pre-prophets was Nathan. He was chosen for a cabinet position as David establish-ed the monarchy, following the precedents set by neigh-boring nations such as Phoenicia and Egypt in having court prophets. Nathan's duties were to serve as royal chaplain, to advise the king on things spiritual, and to inform him concerning the divine will on issue after issue.

A good illustration of how Nathan performed his prophetic task occurred when David lusted after his neighbor's wife, Bathsheba, and caused her to conceive a child while her husband was at the front fighting the king's battles (II Sam. 11). When David learned of the conception he granted her husband a furlough so people would think he was the coming child's father. Since Uriah already had heard rumors of what had been going on, he went to the palace gate instead of returning to his wife. Even though the king sent royal foods to the house, urged this furloughed soldier to return home, and plied him with wine, Uriah refused to leave the palace gate. In that way he publicly dramatized King David's adultery.

Since this attempted coverup backfired, David returned Uriah to the front. The king added insult to injury by having this soldier carry and deliver to the commanding officer a sealed royal note ordering that the bearer be placed in the front line where he would surely be killed. When the welcomed death was reported to King David, feigning innocence he nonchalantly remarked that in war "the sword devours one as another." When Bathsheba's days of pretentious mourning were over, the king took her to himself and she became his wife.

Shortly thereafter the prophet Nathan came to the palace, ostensibly to report a terrible deed. He told of a city in which lived two men, one rich and the other poor. Instead of taking a lamb from his own "exceedingly many flocks and herds," the rich man stole the lamb from that poor man who had only one, killed it, roasted it, and served it to his guests.

King David was outraged at hearing about such actions and at once pronounced judgment: "The man who has done this is worthy to die." Then, pointing to the king, the prophet said "You are the man" (II Sam. 12:1-7). Nathan was notably successful in this first glimmer of the prophetic movement's sunrise. David repented and thereafter was a changed man.

Elijah was the second notable pre-prophet to emerge. When Queen Jezebel of Israel wanted Naboth's vineyard for an herb garden, he would not sell because it was his beloved ancestral estate. During a banquet arranged supposedly to honor him, this queen had two slanderers announce that Naboth "had cursed god and the king." Without further evidence, she had him taken out and stoned to death.

The next morning, when her husband went to take possession of the vineyard, Elijah was there awaiting the king. Upon seeing the prophet Ahab said, "Have you found me, O my enemy?" Elijah replied with thundering vehemence:

> I have found you, because you have sold your-
> self to do that which is evil in the sight
> of Yahweh. Behold, I will bring catastrophe
> upon you, and will completely sweep you away,
> . . . for the provocation with which you have
> provoked me to anger and have made Israel to
> sin.

In response to this devastating judgment even such a hardened king as Ahab

> rent his clothes, and put sackcloth upon his
> body, and fasted, and slept in sackcloth, and
> went about humbly (I Kings 21:19-27).

Third in this notable trio was Micaiah, the son of Imlah. I Kings 22 describes an occasion when King Ahab of Israel was trying to get Jehoshaphat, King of

Judah, to join in war against Syria. The reluctant Jehoshaphat wanted divine authorization for the war and
promise of victory before joining his forces. To render
such a verdict King Ahab brought four hundred of his
court prophets into the open square before the palace
and put the issue to them, "Shall I go to battle against
Ramoth-gilead, or shall I refrain?" The four hundred
responded by staging a bull dance before the two kings.
They held real or imaginary horns at their heads, in
simulation of goring the enemy to death, and said in
unison, "Go up, for the Lord will deliver it into the
hand of the king."

Jehoshaphat was suspicious of this verdict and
asked,

> Is there not here some other prophet of Yahweh
> that we may inquire of him?

King Ahab replied,

> There is one other man by whom we may inquire
> of Yahweh, Micaiah, the son of Imlah, but I
> hate him, for he does not prophesy good con-
> cerning me, but evil.

Jehoshaphat urged that Micaiah be consulted and he was
summoned by the reluctant king.

Under directive from Ahab the messenger who brought
Micaiah advised him to give the same verdict as the four
hundred prophets. When presented with the problem publicly before the kings, prophets, and hosts, Micaiah
obeyed and gave the same answer, but in mimicry. King
Ahab reproved Micaiah for this mockery and cautioned
him to tell the truth. In response, this lone prophet
said, "I saw all Israel scattered upon the mountains,
as sheep that have no shepherd." This was Micaiah's way
of predicting that Israel would be defeated and Ahab
would be killed in any such attack. Then, in theologized

language, Micaiah proceeded to call the four hundred prophets a bunch of liars.

King Ahab at once ordered Micaiah imprisoned, to be fed only on "bread of affliction and with water of affliction" until the army should return victorious. In the ensuing battle King Ahab met his death. Micaiah never was heard of again, which may indicate that he perished in prison or was blamed for the defeat and executed.

Nathan, Elijah, and Micaiah were hearing a higher voice than was true of the hundreds of majority prophets who had sold out to the establishment echoing whatever kings desired and clothing those royal wishes with the halo of divine sanctity. These three true servants of Yahweh were not afraid to stand up and be counted as they denounced royal misconduct. Nathan and Elijah were successful, for in each instance the king repented of his misdeed and bowed in contrition. These men lit three candles in the darkness, foregleams of the prophetic illumination which was to follow.

AMOS, THE SHEPHERD LAD FROM TEKOA

The full-scale prophetic movement was initiated by Amos, a shepherd youth from the semi-desert area of Tekoa, between Bethlehem and the Dead Sea. He had spent much time thinking about reports concerning immorality and corruption in the cities of Judah and Israel. When a lion pounced on a sheep in his flock and he was able to recover only two leg bones and part of an ear, Amos took this as an indication Yahweh was about to wreak similar destruction upon the sinful nation. That episode inspired this young man to become a prophet and warn Israel of impending doom (Amos 3:8, 12; 7:14-15).

Amos resolved to begin at Samaria, capital of the North, where corruption was reputed to be at its worst.

He appears to have arrived when a political celebration
was about to begin. This young man took that opportunity
to deliver his message, mounted the speaker's platform,
and spoke. In succession he pronounced judgment on
Syria, Ammon, and Moab -- three traditional enemies that
had been thorns in the side of Israel through the centuries (Amos 1:3-5, 13-15; 2:1-3). The applause may have
been so tumultuous that he had to quiet it with raised
hand, for he had a few more words to speak.

In that final stanza Amos denounced Israel for exploiting the righteous, victimizing the needy, tramp-
ling on the poor, denying court access to the lower
classes, practicing sacred prostitution at holy places,
and turning religious feasts into drunken carousals.
While the other nations were to be chastised for one
sin in which each had unpardonably overstepped the
bounds of propriety, Israel was to be punished for "all"
of her many iniquities. Because she had enjoyed greater
opportunities for good, her punishment would be corres-
pondingly more severe (Amos 2:6-8; 3:1-2). By contrast
with the applause that undoubtedly greeted previous
stanzas, the silence following this one must have been
ominous.

Amos was a master psychologist who played on the
international hatreds of his listeners as a musician
plays an instrument. After having put his audience completely off guard, he suddenly had thrust in his decisive blow. By having used this strategy of surprise, Amos
had made that first address in Israel most memorable.

This prophet even intruded himself at the palace
when the queen was having a reception for the elite
wives of that realm. As he looked at such overweight
women they reminded him of the fat cattle he once had
observed on the slopes of Bashan. He therefore addressed
those luxury-sated society belles as "cows of Bashan,"

accusing them of "oppressing the poor," "crushing the
needy," and making the nation so morally rotten it was
about to collapse. Amos ended by showing what the fall
of Israel would mean to these ladies of the realm as
they would be raped to death by invading soldiers. With
deadly seriousness he portrayed the catastrophe their
demands for indulgence inevitably would bring upon themselves (Amos 4:1-3).

This youth was astounded upon observing the shallowness of religious practices at the holy places of
Beth-el and Gilgal. People thought all they needed to
get their manifold sins removed was to burn up animals
as sacrifices. Then they could commit a new galaxy of
sins (Amos 4:4-5). The religious climax of this prophet
came when he represented Yahweh as saying,

> I hate, I despise your feasts, and I take no
> delight in your sanctimonious assemblies . . . .
> Take away from me the noise of your songs,
> even the melody of your harps I refuse to hear.
> But let justice pour forth as waters, and
> righteousness as an ever-flowing stream (Amos
> 5:21-24).

Amos was amazed at the perversion of justice he
observed in the courts. This was so glaring that he
spoke out in public session, denouncing judges

> who turn justice into bitterness, and cast
> down righteousness to the earth. . . . They
> hate him who reproves in the gate, and abhor
> those who witness truthfully . . . .You who
> harass the just, who take bribes, and who turn
> aside the needy in the gate   (Amos 5:7,10,12).

That prophet spoke also to merchants in the market
place, chiding them for selling shoddy products, charg-
ing exhorbitant prices, using scant measures, and giving
short weights. His greatest condemnation was against

exploiting commercially the poor and needy (Amos 8:4-7). This may have been the first time in history that the pulpit passed judgment on prevailing business practices.

What appears to have been Amos' final confrontation was with Amaziah, the high priest of Beth-el. This cleric tried to stop the prophet from speaking at that royal shrine, but he did not choose to remain silent. As these two determined individuals got into altercation, Amos likely was arrested, imprisoned, and soon executed (Amos 7:10-17). Such an early and tragic end to a great prophet's work is suggested by the fact that he never was heard of again.

This was a young man with only one idea -- righteousness -- but he did something about it. He began by changing the concept of Yahweh from a god of caprice, who blessed anyone who fed him sacrifices, to a god of righteousness and justice. Amos transformed religion by showing that it must include ethics and foster righteousness. He also applied these principles to daily life by originating the concept of a just society. He thereby became founder of the social gospel and all social action movements.

Although Amos' brilliant torch of the spirit had illuminated the Palestinian horizon for only two or three months, that light was passed on to other pioneering souls. As a result, this religious genius was followed by a succession of fifteen more prophets who echoed and amplified his message. Such was the amazing accomplishment of that Tekoan youth who never had attended a school, who could neither read nor write, but who became a literary and religious master of the spoken word.

HOSEA, THE FARMER WITH THE FAITHLESS WIFE

Amos' immediate successor was Hosea, a farmer in the Northern Kingdom. His call to prophetic service e-volved gradually as a series of overtones from his home-life.

This enterprising farmer thought he was marrying one of the most upright young women who could be found. Betrothal, wedding, and the days immediately thereafter were glorious. Little did Hosea suspect he had married "a woman of harlotry," i.e., a woman with the tendency toward harlotry (Hosea 1:2). His life was saddened as he found this to be true, especially when she left him for the company of other lovers.

In his sorrowings over this situation Hosea came to realize that Yahweh was in a similar predicament. That deity had married Israel in love, with the wedding taking place at Mount Sinai and the honeymoon alone with Israel in the wilderness years. However, upon arrival in Palestine the nation strayed from Yahweh and played the harlot with other gods.

What was Hosea to do in that situation, and what was Yahweh to do? This prophet could not help continuing to love Gomer in spite of her adulteries. One day he came to see that Yahweh must have been feeling similarly toward Israel. In that way the concept of love at the heart of deity came into existence. Even though Amos had brought about an epochal development in theology by conceiving of Yahweh no longer as a god of caprice but as a god of justice, this was still only the classic eye for eye and tooth for tooth. Hosea's discovery of love as the chief essence of deity was a further great forward step.

ISAIAH, THE ROYAL COURTIER OF JERUSALEM

By contrast with Amos and Hosea, who prophesied in northern Israel, Isaiah was the first great prophet in the Southern Kingdom. This scion of the royal aristocracy received his call through a mystical experience while attending the coronation of King Ahaz at 735 B.C. in the Jerusalem temple (Isaiah 6). Isaiah realized that the people of his nation were politically and religiously deaf, dumb, and blind. Nevertheless, feeling forced to accept the divine summons, he said, "Here am I, send me"(vss. 8-10). That one service generated enough power to launch Isaiah on his prophetic vocation and keep him at the task for some forty years in spite of encountering indifference and opposition.

Isaiah's first prophetic years were devoted to keeping his country from embarking on hazardous military ventures (Isa. 7:1-16). He could see that Judah would likely be ground to bits between the great powers if such an insignificant country should implicate itself in military alliances. For a time he was successful in getting his small nation to follow a course of honorable independence. He accomplished this goal by keeping Judah from joining the military alliance against Assyria. Defeat of that alliance was destined to bring an end to Syria in 732 B.C. and Israel in 722 B.C. This measure of success shows how a prophet could save a nation politically when his advice was followed.

However, Isaiah became increasingly doubtful that his nation was worth being saved. He portrayed Judah as the vineyard Yahweh had planted, with harvests of luscious fruit anticipated. Since delight was being turned to disappointment upon finding that the supposedly choice vineyard was producing only sour grapes, Isaiah feared Yahweh might be at the point of destroying such a worthless vineyard. The deity had expected justice and righteousness, but was finding only oppression and exploitation (Isa. 5:1-7).

For a season Isaiah turned his attention to social concerns. He stamped indelibly upon Israel's conscious-ness, for all time to come, regard for the underprivi-leged poor, orphans, and widows (Isa. 1:23; 10:2). This was the first prophet to point out the evils of land monopoly as greedy landlords were extending their hold-ings. The disaster in such seizures and foreclosings lay in pushing into cities the landless, who, once there, would likely find themselves degenerating into a slum existence. Isaiah pointed out that the inevitable result of such exploitation would be destruction of the nation from within (Isa. 5:8-9). By such demographic insights he became the prophet of the urban problem.

Isaiah also stressed the disintegrative effects of luxury and indulgence (Isa. 3:16-17, 24). The curse of alcoholism received attention, especially the innova-tion of producing and using distilled liquors. This pro-phet's classic introduction to that subject was

Woe to those who drink wine in excess,
and the men who excel at mixing distilled
liquor (Isa.5:11-12, 22).

Isaiah had seen even "priests and prophets reeling with distilled liquor." He could not forget having observed a drunken priest vomiting over the communion table of showbread while officiating (Isa. 28:7-8).

This prophet's later days were turned to more dis-tinctly religious matters. He was distressed about the reversed values in vogue among his people who were call-ing

evil good, and good evil, . . . putting darkness for light and light for darkness, . . .
bitter for sweet and sweet for bitter (Isa.5:20).

Isaiah believed that once-faithful Jerusalem had become a city of rebels, thieves, bribers, and exploiters -- as depraved as ancient Sodom and Gomorrah. He envisioned Yahweh as disgusted with the sacrifices presented by such people, abominating the incense rising from their altars, wearied by their solemn assemblies, hating the great annual religious festivals, shutting his ears from hearing their many prayers, and closing his eyes so he would not need to observe the ritualistic antics of the priests (Isa. 1:10-23).

The whole program of this prophet was summed up in the words:

> Wash yourselves, make yourselves clean, put away the evil of your doings from my eyes, cease to do evil, learn to do what is right, seek justice, relieve the oppressed, judge the fatherless, plead for the widow (Isa.1:16-17).

In 701 B.C. Assyria's great western campaign swept toward Palestine. Since Hezekiah ignored Isaiah's warnings against trying to stop the tidal wave of war by militaristic means, that king almost brought ruin to Judah. As all cities were annihilated except Jerusalem, which barely escaped, the prophet was grieved to see his beloved country "desolate" and its "cities burned with fire" (Isa. 1:7-9; II Kings 18:13-19:37).

Although Isaiah attempted to nurse this depressed people back to spiritual health, he found war-ravaged Judah a "sinful nation, a people weighted down with wrongdoing, offspring of evil-doers, children who behave corruptly" and who "have despised the Holy One of Israel." This prophet finally was forced to conclude that "The ox recognizes his owner, and the ass his master's crib; but Israel does not know, my people do not discern" (Isa. 1:3-4).

Isaiah's callous countrymen found themselves unable
to tolerate his calls for ethical conduct and righteousness any longer. His fate is recorded in the intertestament book called the Martyrdom of Isaiah. To avoid seeing him suffer, this prophet was placed inside a hollow
log which then was sawed in two. In this way the residents of Jerusalem silenced the prophetic voice which
had haunted them for four decades.

MICAH, THE ARTISAN OF MARESHAH

During Isaiah's later years of functioning among
royalty and the upper classes of Jerusalem, a younger
contemporary began spreading the prophetic spirit among
the laboring classes in outlying regions. Micah followed
in the footsteps of Elijah by going about naked except
for a loincloth. This lack of dress was to impress on
his people that they soon would be carried away as naked
captives if they were to persist in their destructive
ways. With such sensational appearance this prophet went
through the foothill region of southern Palestine warning each city and village of Assyria's impending approach (Mic. 1:1-16).

Micah was grieved at oppression of the masses for
selfish gain. He deplored how unscrupulous overlords
spent their nights devising schemes of exploitation and
their days executing the dastardly plots (Mic. 2:1-2).
He accused these upper classes of being bloody butchers,
skinning the masses alive and devouring them (3:2-3).
This prophet championed especially the rights of mothers
and orphans by insisting that the practice of ruthlessly
throwing them into the streets by foreclosures must
stop. He viewed such dehumanizing of women and children
as mortgaging the nation's future (2:9).

Micah was astounded at the way his calls to righteous conduct were being spurned. He placed chief blame

on the unprincipled priests and majority prophets who
were giving divine permission to the vile requests of
any petitioner who would bring money, gifts, and food
(Mic. 3:5-7). The ultimate was a drunken pretender who,
in return for the promise of another drink, told his
patrons what they wanted to hear. Even such an impostor
was being accepted as "the prophet of this people"
Mic. 2:11).

"With what shall I come before Yahweh, and bow my-
self before the high god?" was the fundamental question
asked by Micah. In answer, he proclaimed a deity displeased with "burnt offerings," "calves a year old,"
"thousands of rams," or even "ten thousands of rivers
of oil." Rising to his finest hour in 6:6-8, this prophet summed up all religious duty in the immortal statement,

> What does Yahweh require of you but to do
> justly, and to love kindness, and to walk hum-
> bly before your god?

These words served as a good summary to eighth-century
prophecy and are one of the Bible's notable statements
concerning the essence of religion.

JEREMIAH, TOWER OF SEVENTH-CENTURY PROPHECY

With respect to religious creativity, the eighth-
century prophetic achievement was one of the greatest
in the Bible. However, with the passing of that illustrious quartet of spiritual geniuses the golden period
of Israelite prophecy came to a sudden end. That religious pioneering was followed by eight decades of pagan
reaction. During those tragic years the streets of Jerusalem ran red with blood as the "sword devoured" prophets "like a destroying lion" (Jer. 2:30).

Jeremiah was the first individual to be successful
in confronting the apostasies of those destructive

years. Throughout boyhood he was inspired by the memories of Amos, Hosea, Isaiah, and Micah, whose voices continued echoing over the Judaean hills. This lad came
to feel that he had been set aside by divine commission,
even before birth, to take up the torch laid down by
the eighth-century prophets and illuminate his dark age
with the light of prophecy (Jer. 1:4-6).

This youth well realized that it would be an almost
impossible assignment. He would need to fight

> against the whole land, against the kings of
> Judah, against the princes thereof, against
> the priests thereof, and against the people
> of the land (Jer. 1:18).

Before he could "build and plant" a new age of
righteousness, he would need "to pluck up, and to break
down, and to destroy, and to overthrow" the pagan civilization that was in power. Even so, Jeremiah felt confident of eventual success as he heard Yahweh saying to
him:

> Do not say "I am a child," for you shall go
> on whatever assignment I send you, and you
> shall speak whatever I command you. Do not
> be afraid because of them, for I will be with
> you to deliver you (Jer. 1:7-10).

Jeremiah regarded the religious establishment as
the greatest impediment to progress. He was outraged
by the priests and hundreds of guild prophets with their
self-serving popularity-seeking religion. In sweeping
manner he said, "from the prophet even to the priest,
everyone deals falsely." He accused them of ignoring
corruption by "saying 'Peace, Peace,' when there is no
peace" (Jer. 6:13-14; 8:10-11). This statement means
that when those supposed religious leaders were confronted by evil, exploitation, or difficult problems,
they would virtually say, "Take it easy. Don't get all

wrought up. If you only keep quiet, things will adjust themselves." By contrast, Jeremiah desired action in undesirable situations, and quickly. By such insistence he became a rebuke to the peace-of-mind clerics in all generations.

Jeremiah was distressed by the popular toleration of religious exploitation. It seemed to him that people even loved to be victimized by their clergy.

> An appalling and outrageous thing has come
> to pass in the land. The prophets prophesy
> falsely and the priests bear rule with their
> support, and my people love to have it so
> (Jer. 5:30-31).

Jeremiah's indictment of the temple administration came to its climax in 7:11 when he called out, "Has this house, which is called by my name, become a den of robbers?"

The forces of reaction felt that this young man had gone too far. They joined against him with such antagonism that his life thereafter was a continuous battle. Even the home-town people of Anathoth plotted his death (Jer. 11:18-23). The impasse came when he preached one of his denunciatory sermons in the temple precincts. Pashur, the priest in charge of that supposed holy place, put Jeremiah in the stocks. The prophet was forced to languish in that torture all night while the misleaders of that city, and the misled, slept in peace (20:1-3).

Jeremiah regarded national and international affairs as a fundamental province of religion. He accordingly became self-appointed counselor to the last five kings of Judah, encouraging them when they made constructive choices and reproving those rulers when he felt they had gone wrong. His sharpest words were to King Jehoiakim.

Woe to him who builds his house by unrighteousness, and his chambers by injustice: . . .
your eyes and your heart are for nothing but
your covetousness, and for shedding innocent
blood, and for oppression, and for violence,
to do it (Jer. 22:13-19).

In spite of Jeremiah's vehement protests, the government persisted in following what he regarded as a
ruinous course that was threatening destruction to what
little remained of his nation. With Babylonia in control
of the international scene during Judah's final days,
Jeremiah advised tribute payment and peaceful submission
as the only way his country could survive. Since King
Zedekiah regarded this policy as treason, and concluded
that such a subversive person could not be left at
large, this prophet was subjected to a succession of
imprisonments.

Jeremiah was placed first in the palace prison
(Jer. 32:2; 33:1). Next, it was house arrest (36:5).
In a military interval he started for Anathoth to take
possession of a field he had bought. Jeremiah got no
farther than the city gate when he was intercepted, arrested, charged with attempted desertion to the enemy,
beaten, and placed in a dungeon (37:11-16). When brought
for consultation to the palace, Jeremiah begged not to
be placed again in that terrible pit. King Zedekiah was
touched by this plea and had the prophet returned to
the palace prison (37:17-21).

After the siege of Jerusalem began, Jeremiah called
through his jail window to all who went by, suggesting
that they should desert their unwise king and his impo-
tent armies and flee to the Babylonians. Four princes,
who regarded such supposed treason intolerable, appealed
to the king who gave them permission to do as they
pleased with Jeremiah. Thereupon they dropped him into

a deep cistern with mud in the bottom. Stuck in the mire, he suffered for days. An Ethiopian court servant finally took mercy on Jeremiah and obtained the king's permission to rescue the prophet. He was placed once more in the guard-house prison by the city gate. Jerusalem eventually fell, and Jeremiah's most dire predictions were realized (Jer. 38; II Kings 25).

Jeremiah must have been an invincible person to have continued prophetic work for forty-two or forty-three years against such determined opposition. He was like a "fortified city, and an iron pillar, and bronze walls," and his words were "like a hammer that breaks the rock in pieces" (Jer. 1:18; 23:29).A man of sorrows, he wished he could have cried his eyes out because of Judah's sins (8:18-9:1). When tempted to stop his seemingly thankless task, the "burning fire shut up in" his bones always kept Jeremiah going on (20:7-9).

Once, while silenced by house arrest, this prophet conceived the idea of extending his influence by putting into a book the prophecies he had delivered from the beginning. He hired a scribe and dictated them to him. Scribe Baruch took the completed work to the temple on a fast day and read it to the worshipers. Later, at the palace, it was heard by the princes. When the book was read to the king, he slashed it to pieces with his pen-knife and fed the manuscript to the flames in his brazier (Jer. 36:1-26).

Undaunted, the prophet bought a second scroll and dictated the manuscript again, enlarging it considerably (Jer. 36:27-32). This was the first time a prophet wrote down his utterances, even if by dictation. That document has been included in the Bible as the Book of Jeremiah.

It was tragic that those who were ruining what little remained of Judah continued in authority and were widely followed. By contrast, this man of vision,

perhaps the only one who could have saved his country
in its hour of crisis, was ignored, persecuted, and imprisoned. The net result was the destruction of Jerusalem and the exiling of her remaining residents to Babylon in 586 B.C.

SECOND ISAIAH, PROPHET IN EXILE

The individual who may have been the greatest of
the prophets wrote at least Isaiah 35 and 40-55. For
want of a better name, this anonymous person usually
is called Second Isaiah or Deutero-Isaiah. He produced
his work in Babylon, during the exile, at approximately
540 B.C. That was no time for blaming or chiding, since
the nation was then in a crushed condition. Although
Second Isaiah's prophecies came from the darkest hour
in Israel's history, they are filled with radiant hope.
This quality and his lyricism have resulted in inspiring
great cantatas, oratorios and other musical selections.

Second Isaiah's initial group of prophecies concerned the future of Israel. He began by comforting the
wounded nation.

> Comfort you, comfort you, my people, says your
> god. Speak consolingly to Jerusalem and an-
> nounce to her that her time of servitude is
> at an end, that her iniquity is pardoned, that
> she has received of Yahweh's hand double for
> all her sins (Isa. 40:1-2).

Since she had been punished twice as much as her sins
warranted, there was the implication that in recompense
Israel might be doubly rewarded. This ray of hope was
relayed as cheer to the devasted homeland.

> Get you up on a high mountain, and announce
> good tidings to Zion. Shout loudly with your
> voice. Announce good tidings to Jerusalem.

> Shout, don't be afraid. Proclaim to the cities
> of Judah, "Behold your god" (Isa. 40:9).

This prophet called upon the buried cities of Palestine
to rise from their graves, shake the dust from them, put
on their beautiful garments, and "break forth into joy"
and "sing together" because the moment of their redemption was at hand (Isa. 52:1-9).

All this was to be brought about by the Messiah
of the hour, Cyrus, the liberator.

> Thus says Yahweh to his Messiah, to Cyrus,
> whose right hand I have taken hold of, . . .
> he shall rebuild my city and shall let my ex-
> iles go free (Isa. 45:1-13).

Although this Persian invader had never heard of Yahweh
(vs. 4), Second Isaiah conceived that Israel's god was
guiding King Cyrus to conquer Babylon and liberate the
exiles.

Unable to think of taking the long way around the
Fertile Crescent to the north, Second Isaiah envisaged
returning by the most direct route, across the desert
to Jerusalem.

> Prepare in the wilderness the way of Yahweh,
> make straight in the desert a highway for our
> god (Isa. 40:3-5; cf. 35:5-10).

Far more important than his concerns about Israel's future were Second Isaiah's new thoughts about deity. These were four in number. Up to this point in the
present study the term *god* has been used for all deities,
including Yahweh, the chief divinity of Israel's worship. Even this prophet, in his four initial contributions, thought in terms of the god Yahweh. However, in
the course of time Second Isaiah came to realize that
there is only one deity in the entire universe. This
is God, with a capital G.

In line with this new perspective, it became evident to Second Isaiah that God had created the universe.
Previous mythologies had thought of creation, but in
terms of a co-operative effort among a pantheon of deities. Second Isaiah expressed his new insight best in
a series of rhetorical questions (Isa. 40:12).

Who has portioned out the waters in the hollow
of his hand? And measured the heavens with
the span? And dealt out the soil of the earth
with a measure? And weighed the mountains with
scales? And the hills with a balance?

Each of these queries was to be answered decisively by
the one word "GOD," who "stretched out the heavens as
a curtain, and spread them out as a tent in which to
dwell" (Isa. 40:22). This view regarding cosmic origins
flowered forth in the Bible's classic account of creation (Genesis 1), which probably was written by Second
Isaiah or some later poet whom he had inspired.

A correlative discovery was that God is the source
of all knowledge. This conclusion stemmed from another
set of rhetorical questions (Isa. 40:13-14).

Who has directed the spirit of Yahweh, or,
being his counselor, has taught him? With
whom did he take counsel, and who instructed
him, and taught him in the path of justice,
and taught him knowledge, and showed to him
the way of understanding?

The implied answer to all such questions was a decisive
"No one."

These new insights led Second Isaiah to the further
realization that God is the director of history.

He brings down princes to nothing; judges of
the earth he reduces to confusion . . . . He
gives power to the faint, and increases
strength to those who have no might (Isa.40:23,29).

With such words this prophet enunciated God's providence over all his creation.

Second Isaiah also was first in the Bible to conceive of God as "the good shepherd."

He will feed his flock like a shepherd, he will gather the lambs in his arms, and will carry them in his bosom (Isa. 40:11).

The two great Assyrian cherubim deities, which remain standing today with lambs in their arms at the palace gate of Calah along the upper Tigris, may well have suggested this good-shepherd concept of God to Second Isaiah. Since the Twenty-third Psalm contains the biblical flowering of this shepherd imagery, that classic of faith probably was not written until Second Isaiah's time, or later.

Such epochal additions to the concept of God necessitated certain subtractions from previous ideas of deity. Although animal sacrifice had been the most important religious rite up to that time, Second Isaiah called for discontinuance of all material sacrifices. The key to this conclusion is found in Isaiah 40:16 where God is shown so great that if all the animals in this world were to be used as a sacrifice, with all the trees in earth's forests for fuel, this would still be an inadequate sacrifice to place before such an exalted deity. Consequently, according to this prophet, every sacrifice was an insult to God's greatness. Except for the Jerusalem temple, where such rites continued until its destruction in A.D. 70, Second Isaiah was successful in removing material sacrifices from Israelite religion.

His other subtraction was to eliminate the making and worshiping of divine images. Using irony, Second Isaiah pointed out the absurdity of an individual's fashioning a god out of wood or metal and then kneeling and praying to it for health and prosperity. For a safe

journey people were imploring a god who was nailed down
and could not move (Isa. 40:18-20; 41:7; 44:9-17).

> Those who trust in graven images shall be
> turned back, they shall be put completely to
> shame, . . . Behold their works, all of them,
> are nothing and worthless, their molten images
> are wind and confusion (Isa. 42:17; 41:29).

In this crusade Second Isaiah was signally sucessful,
for imageless worship has been an essential of Judaism
ever since.

The crowning achievement of this prophet's creative
thought concerned the role of Israel in the divine
plan. How were his nation's grievous sufferings through
the centuries at the hands of neighboring peoples to
be explained? He came to see Israel as God's suffering
servant -- suffering vicariously for the sins of other
nations. This role is elaborated in the servant psalms
of Isaiah 41:8-10; 42:1-4; 44:1-4; 49:1-6; and 50:4-9,
with its best expression in 52:13-53:12. This climaxing
of the suffering-servant theme makes Isaiah 53 perhaps
the Old Testament's greatest chapter. It suggested to
Jesus the vocational choice of devoting his life in service to others, whatever the suffering and cost.

All of Second Isaiah's theological deductions are
summed up in the concept of monotheism. Pharaoh Akhenaten at 1380-1362 B.C. commonly has been regarded as the
world's first monotheist. However, he only tried to ban-
ish all other religions and unite Egypt in worship of
the sun-god Aton. He believed such achievement of uniform worship would be the key to real national unity.
In chapter 3 it was seen that Moses also was not a monotheist. Even the great pre-exilic prophets, from Amos
at 750 B.C. to the final exile at 586 B.C., saw no higher than Yahweh, the god of Palestine, the god of the
Hebrew people, while continuing to recognize the

national deities of neighboring countries. It remained
for Second Isaiah to make the epochal discovery that
there is only one God in the universe. This ultimate
concept of monotheism, with its fundamental scientific
belief in unity throughout time and space, has formed
the basis of all subsequent exalted religion.

INDIVIDUAL RESPONSIBILITY OF PERSONS AND NATIONS

From the Garden of Eden to 620 B.C. punishing the
innocent for sins of the guilty had been a blot on
Israel's history. Punishments for Adam's and Eve's sins
were construed as heaped almost wholly on their innocent
offspring to the end of time. Except for one family,
the innocent animals and people were drowned indiscriminately with the guilty in the flood story. The whole
sacrificial system had been constructed on the premise
that the only way a worshiper's sins might receive God's
pardon was by slashing the throat of an innocent animal,
pouring out its blood unto death, and burning the victim
to ashes on an altar. Punishing innocent children for
the sins committed by their parents or more remote an-
cestors also was in vogue. Exodus 20:5-6 and Deuteronomy
23:2-3 (3-4 in Hebrew) tell how children were to be punished for sins of their fathers to the third, fourth,
and even tenth generations.

It remained for the prophets to free Israel from
this moral perversion of punishing the innocent for the
guilty. In Deuteronomy 24:16, within a section likely
written by Jeremiah, that prophet reversed 23:2-3 and
enunciated his new doctrine by saying

> The fathers shall not be put to death for the
> children, nor shall the children be put to
> death for the fathers; every person shall be
> put to death for their own sin.

This was later restated by Jeremiah in his memoirs

(Jer. 31:29-30) and was copied into II Kings 14:6 and II Chronicles 25:4.

On this issue the prophet Ezekiel coined the terse and memorable statement, "The soul that sins, it shall die" in his chapter against punishing the innocent for the guilty (Ezek. 18:4, 20). Achieving this belief in individual responsibility marked an important stage in religious advance.

These prophets also swept aside the idea of favoritism in religion in all its forms. This included the belief that God had "a chosen people" whom he loved above all others and that he has "chosen individuals." Proclaiming the brotherhood of all mankind, these prophets showed that any individual or nation that obeys the divine will is a chosen person or people. Malachi even went so far as to assert that all the world's religions are acceptable to deity (Mal. 1:11).

THE IMMORTAL PROPHETIC HERITAGE

Surveying this panorama of prophetic development, one sees it pitted primarily against priestly religions which always have placed trust in rituals. They operate on the assumption that God delights in seeing rites performed meticulously according to directives and that he bestows his favours on individuals and nations that are scrupulous in such observances. With its backward look, priestly religion strives to obtain forgiveness for worshipers' already-committed sins through performance of approved rituals.

By contrast, the prophets developed a new type of religion, on a higher plane. They looked upon rituals as irrelevant to real religion and often an impediment to spiritual advance. With a forward look, and ethically concerned, the fundamental purpose of prophetic religion

was to inspire worthy conduct and prevent sin from occurring.

Until the prophetic age religion had been a circle
that moved about a center, which was ritualistic worship. The prophets changed this into an ellipse revolv-
ing around two foci, worship and ethics. Those spiritual
pioneers wedded these two phases of religion together
so completely that they have never since been thought
separable.

The prophets believed the voice of religion should
constantly be heard in governmental circles for wise
guidance, in the marketplace to insist that business
practices be conducted in an ethical manner, in the
courts to see that justice is administered impartially,
in financial circles to assure against exploitation of
the economically disadvantaged, and in the councils of
religion to make certain that worthy types are propagat-
ed. The fundamental duty of religion was thought to consist in transforming human life by having it lived in
conformity with divine will. This concern for the manifestation of religion in daily pursuits flowered forth
in the social gospel with its stress on action.

The major theological contributions made by these
men of spiritual vision lay in progressively expanding
the concept of deity. With regard to magnitude, the climax came when Second Isaiah transcended Yahweh, god of
Palestine and the Israelite people, by the monotheistic
discovery that there is only one God in the universe.

Comparable changes were made with respect to the
divine nature. Amos showed the absurdity of a deity act-
uated by caprice and favoritism as he proclaimed Yahweh
a god of justice and righteousness. Hosea advanced further by discovering forgiveness and long-suffering love
as the essence of deity. Micah replaced the vengeful
god, who delighted in punishing, with the deity who

> pardons iniquity, and passes over the trans-
> gressions . . . He does not retain his anger
> forever, because he delights in lovingkind-
> ness. He will again have compassion upon us;
> he will tread our iniquities under foot and
> . . . will cast all their sins into the depths
> of the sea (Mic. 7:18-19).

This whole development flowered forth in Joel's procla-
mation that God is "gracious and merciful, slow to
anger, and abundant in lovingkindness" (Joel 2:13).

A fitting benediction to this sixth religion of
the Old Testament is found in a daring expectation that
anticipates ultimate fulfillment of the human dream.
This is the vision of all nations joining in common worship, deserting their armaments, becoming truly civilized, and living together in harmony as

> they shall beat their swords into plowshares
> and their spears into pruning-hooks. Nation
> shall not lift up sword against nation, nor
> shall they learn war any more, but every per-
> son shall sit under their vine and under their
> fig tree, and no one shall make them afraid
> (Mic. 4:3-4).

By serving as a constant leavening influence for
six and a half centuries, these men of God gave to
Israel the finest hour in her religious history. Whatever values there would be in subsequent religions of
the Bible were destined to be based largely on those
fundamental spiritual principles which were discovered
by Israel's prophets.

CHAPTER 7

JUDAISM, WITH ITS ENDURING INSTITUTIONAL RELIGION

With respect to permanence, the Bible's seventh religion contrasts with the previous six as each of those was in prime for only a limited time. Judaism has become the first to endure throughout the ages as it continues to be one of the world's major living religions today.

As its name implies, Judaism is the religion which grew up in the tribe of Judah. *Theoretically*, that development began in 722 B.C. when the ten northern tribes of Israel were exiled to eastern lands. There, these "lost tribes" became assimilated into what are now Arab cultures and as such never were heard of again. Only the tribe of Judah was left in Palestine. Speaking *practically*, Judaism did not begin quite as early as 722 B.C. since the three and a half decades immediately thereafter witnessed a rather indecisive continuation of the Old Testament's fifth religion, the Canaanite-Hebrew.

Emerging Judaism must be viewed against the back-drop of a pagan age which lasted from 687 to 621 B.C. Manasseh and his son Amon, the worst kings in Hebrew history, were on the throne during most of that two-thirds of a century. That destructiveness continued through even the first eighteen years of the following monarch, King Josiah. After that prolonged period, during which the nation ostensibly was cleared of everything religious from the past, Judaism began to emerge at 621 B.C. into what was to become virtually a new religion.

The key person initiating that religious renais-
sance was Jeremiah. Although his important contributions
to the prophetic movement were cited in the previous
chapter, the ritualistic innovations he brought about
as the chief founder of Judaism belong in the present
chapter.

When a young man in his twenties, Jeremiah began
by searching Jerusalem to find "a righteous man," but
at first he found none (Jer. 5:1). However, in the
course of time he discovered several other prophetically
minded youth: Zephaniah, Huldah, and Uriah. These prophets were supplemented by a few kindred spirits from the
priestly-scribal coalition of the temple hierarchy:
Hilkiah, Shaphan, Ahikam, Achbor, and Asaiah (Zeph. 1:1;
Jer. 26:20-24; II Kings 22:3-20). Jeremiah conceived
the idea of confronting the corrupt opposition by organizing this small company into a righteous underground.

FIRST HOLY BOOK AND FIRST SACRED SCRIPTURE

While meeting in secret, this prophetic-priestly
group drew up an extensive program of national religious
reform. This document survives in the Bible under the
title of Deuteronomy. It is made up partly of sermons,
especially chapters 1-11, probably written in the main
by Jeremiah. The legal codes, interspersed among the
book's remaining twenty-three chapters, were supplied
by the priests and scribes in that editing group.

These new lawgivers found themselves puzzled over
how to get their program before the nation without themselves becoming known and killed. They evidently decided
to place this production in the collection box at the
temple entrance, since Hilkiah had the key. He would
"find" the scroll at a moment the group might think opportune. They hoped its impact would be strategic in

their effort to liberate King Josiah from subservience to the evil coalition which had placed him on the throne and had dictated his acts since he was eight years old.

The members of this group initiated their design by convincing King Josiah that the temple needed repairs. He authorized Hilkiah, the chief priest, to open the collection box, count the money, and issue it to the workmen (II Kings 22: 3-7). This is how Hilkiah "found the book of the law" in the collection box. Usually it has been assumed that this was an ancient scroll which was discovered while removing some temple walls. However, close examination of chapter 22 shows that it was "found" before the temple repairs were begun.

Hilkiah had Shallum, the royal officer, take the scroll at once to the palace and read it to the king. This young ruler shuddered at hearing the penalties listed for nonobservance of its edicts. He was a bit puzzled and wanted some warrant as to the book's authenticity. To that end he sent a committee of five to make inquiry of some prophet, not knowing he was dealing with the document's authors. They took it to Huldah, the prophetess, who told those representatives to assure King Josiah that this was a valid document and that its penalties would be exacted by Yahweh. However, divine favour would be extended to that monarch because of the receptive manner in which he was receiving the writing (II Kings 22:8-20).

The members of this reforming group pursued their religious coup d'etat by persuading the young king to assemble

> all the men of Judah, and all the inhabitants
> of Jerusalem with him, and the priests, and
> the prophets, and all the people, both small
> and great

to the temple. There the king read the entire scroll
to the asembled citizenry. As King Josiah stood by one
of the two pillars at the temple door, he

> made a covenant before Yahweh, to walk after
> Yahweh and to observe his commandments and
> his testimonies and his statutes, with all
> his heart and with all his soul, to perform
> the words of this covenant that were written
> in this book.

In response, the people stood as they made their covenant (II Kings 23:1-3). This was the Bible's first constitutional convention, when a program of reform was
presented to all the people and was adopted by popular
vote as the law of the land.

The thoroughgoing national reformation that ensued
began by removing all non-Israelite cult materials from
the temple. As these were burned in the Kidron Valley,
the sixty-six years of paganism went up in smoke. Offending shrines were then destroyed throughout the kingdom (II Kings 23:4-20). This was the most spectacular
religious reformation Jerusalem had ever seen.

Eliminating the paraphernalia of foreign cults was
fairly easy, but changing the patterns of Judaean religious thought was more difficult. These reformers responded to that challenge with equal vigor as they set
out to bring about a religious transformation of their
nation, following the directives in their new book,
Deuteronomy.

This writing was important as the first comprehen-
sive sacred Scripture in the Judaeo-Christian tradition.
It included the two prized older scriptural nuclei:
Moses' Decalogue in chapter 5 and the essentials of
Samuel's Code of the Covenant in the legal sections.
This composite book was the whole Bible as of 621 B.C.

What came to be called Judaism was largely a reorgani-
zation of the national life in accordance with religious
principles found in Deuteronomy.

ONE GOD AND ONE PLACE OF WORSHIP

Deuteronomy was significant as the last important
stage on the theological road leading toward monotheism.
Until that time, many local divinities had been worshiped at the high places. Even the national gods of neighboring nations had considerable vogue in Israel. Without denying the existence of such diverse deities,
these reformers turned their backs on the snycretisms
of past centuries by decreeing that henceforth only one
god should be worshiped in Judah. They marshaled their
whole national life around the one central focus of Yahweh, god of Palestine and the Judaean people.

Hand in hand with the Deuteronomic demand of one
god for Judah was the designation of Jerusalem as the
only legitimate place to carry on worship (Deut. 12:1ff.).
It was felt that ritualistic observances could be kept
under proper controls only in Solomon's temple. Since
the outlying "high places" were regarded as hopelessly
contaminated with pagan rites, all those worship shrines
were destroyed in Josiah's great reformation of 621-
620 B.C. (II Kings 23:1-20). This concentration of the
cult in Jerusalem greatly increased the temple's prestige as "one god" and "one altar" became the foundation
pillars on which the new religion was to be constructed.

Solomon's temple was destroyed with the city of
Jerusalem by the Babylonians in 586 B.C. and during the
ensuing seventy years of exile there was no temple. After an unsuccessful attempt by Haggai in 520 B.C.,
Zerubbabel succeeded in erecting a rather crude second
temple which was dedicated in 516 B.C. (Hag.; Zech.1-8).
Progressively remodeled during postexilic days, it was

completely rebuilt by Herod the Great (37-4 B.C.) into
a magnificent structure, commonly called Herod's temple.
It was destroyed by the Romans in A.D. 70 and since then
there has been no temple.

Luxurious synagogues called temples today are pre-
sumptuously named, for in true Judaism there can be only
one temple and that must be in Jerusalem. Even though
there has been no material structure since A.D. 70, the
temple has remained in existence, sentimentally. Now
that the State of Israel has come into existence, it
would seem that a third temple should be erected as the
focus of Judaism's religious glory. Such construction
is prevented since the site of Solomon's and Herod's
temples is occupied by the Dome of the Rock, the third
most sacred mosque in Islam. Only on that revered spot,
hallowed by Abraham's god-obedient willingness to sacrifice his son Isaac, could any valid third Jewish temple
be constructed.

The temple's location in the Judaean capital,
whether really or only ideologically, has made Jerusalem
the sacred city of Judaism during all these centuries.
If properly oriented, Jewish structures of worship,
wherever located, have faced toward that Holy City. Orthodox Jews continue to be buried facing Jerusalem.
Throughout the world they have prayed toward that holy
place three times each day, following the example of
Daniel (Dan. 6:10 [6:11 in the Hebrew Bible]). This
practice has inspired Muslims to face the holy city of
Mecca for their five daily prayers.

Judaism's most prized treasure, Moses' ark of the
covenant containing his tablets of the law, was destroyed with Solomon's temple by the Babylonian conquerors
in 586 B.C. However, a smaller reproduction was made
for the second temple. Instead of Solomon's seventeen-
foot-tall cherubim deities standing at each end of the

ark, two small golden cherubs were made to face each other on the ark lid. Yahweh was thought to dwell on the small "mercy seat" between these two protective cherubim. This second ark of the covenant, which became increasingly esteemed during postexilic times, was destroyed in turn with Herod's temple by the Romans in A.D. 70.

Judaism responded to that loss by constructing many arks. In the course of time it became the rule that every worship structure had to have as its central object a modified ark or Torah shrine containing the sacred scrolls. The Mosaic ark of the covenant has been adopted into liturgical Christian churches as the altar at the back center of the chancel, constituting, with the usual cross above it, the focal center of worship. In many Protestant churches the ark has become the communion table. The Torah shrine survives in Islam as the Mihrab, with its holy Qur'an.

PRIESTLY AND LEVITICAL HIERARCHIES

The basics of one god for Israel and one place of worship were accompanied by insistence on only "one" priesthood. In his Deuteronomic reformation King Josiah ordered that all priests be brought from the discontinued "high places" to Jerusalem and be joined to the temple personnel (II Kings 23:8). These newcomers were to perform menial temple tasks. The object of concentrating the priesthood in Jerusalem was to keep it pure by maintaining a close watch on all priestly acts.

During the Babylonian exile, with no temple, it was not possible to have a functioning priesthood. After the return, the priests were reintegrated into their officiating. During the course of postexilic centuries the priesthood achieved a prestige such as was scarcely anticipated in even the most prosperous days of

Solomon's temple. The office of High Priest was established, with its recognized esteem.

The main priestly duties consisted in offering multiple types of sacrifices as they evolved in Solomon's temple or were originated during postexilic time: burnt, sin, guilt, peace, thank, votive, free will, wave, heave, and meal offerings. Certain sacrifices were performed daily on a routine basis while others were presented at the request of individual worshipers. Priests ministered also at the table of showbread, giving communion to suppliants. Their administration of "the law" even gave them status as judges and medical authorities. During postexilic days this seventh Old Testament faith became basically the religion of priests and their devotees.

Israel's functioning priesthood came to an end with the destruction of the second temple in A.D. 70. However, individuals of priestly rank continue to treasure their genealogies and are recognized in orthodox services weekly by being the first ones invited into the pulpit to read Torah portions. If the temple were to be rebuilt, it would seem that the surviving priests would resume their prescribed duties in such a third temple.

An innovation of the Deuteronomic reform lay in focusing attention on the almost forgotten Levites. In the four books of I and II Samuel and I and II Kings, Levites are mentioned only three times (I Sam. 6:15; II Sam. 15:24; I Kings 8:4). As tribal descendants of Moses, who had constructed the ark, a few of them were given the honor of carrying it from place to place. After Solomon's temple was built and the ark was deposited permanently in the Holy of Holies, there was no further role for the Levites. Therefore they were never mentioned again in the Books of Kings. Since these people had obtained no geographical tribal territory when Canaan

was settled, during the more than five centuries between
that time and 621 B.C. the Levites became virtually
landless slaves to the tribe of Judah.

The Deuteronomists awakened to this situation and
sought to ameliorate the Levites' lot. They were to be
treated as family members or were to receive alms and
tithes along with widows, orphans, and the homeless
(Deut. 12:12, 18-19; 14:27-29; 16:11-14; 18:1; 26:11-13).
More important, to honor the descendants of Moses'
tribe, Levites were brought from outlying villages to
Jerusalem and were made priestly assistants in the temple, in charge of copying, reading, interpreting, and
teaching the new Deuteronomic law (17:9, 18; 18:6-8;
24:8; 27:9-26).

As the prestige of Moses skyrocketed during postexilic days, reverence for his fellow tribesmen, the
Levites, also mounted. Their importance is indicated
by thirty-five references to their duties in the legal
portion of Exodus, Leviticus, and Numbers. In rewriting
the exodus and conquest history the postexilic priestly editor introduced the Levites into the narrative account in forty-three places. The 158 references to them
in Chronicles, Ezra, and Nehemiah show what important
places the Levites occupied in postexilic times.

Although destruction of the second temple in A.D.70
brought a formal end also to the Levites' services,
they, as the priests, continue to treasure their lines
of descent. As a weekly reminder of their special role,
individuals of that group are called to the pulpit in
orthodox services to read their assignment of Sabbath
selections from the Torah. If the temple were rebuilt,
these Levites would resume their commanding position.

From 516 B.C. to A.D. 70 Judaism became a conglomerate of rites and rituals, focusing on the temple, ark
of the covenant, sacrifices, priests, and Levites. The

tithe, giving the tenth of all income or produce, became exacted of every Jew to support that elaborate ceremonial system.

INTRODUCTION OF THE PASSOVER

The Deuteronomists evidently speculated concerning how such reversions into paganism, as had been perpetrated by Kings Manasseh and Amon, might be avoided in the future. Toward that end these reformers devised the Passover. That annual spring evening festival, of special historical recollection, was named in memory of Israel's having been spared the tenth plague of terror in Egypt. By instituting this dramatic review of the exodus story around the Passover table, followed by seven days of eating only unleavened bread in memory of the escape from bondage, these reformers hoped the religious loyalty of all Israelites to the Mosaic tradition would be renewed each year (Deut. 16:1-7).

The record of that first Passover celebration in the eighteenth year of King Josiah, 621 B.C., is found in II Kings 23:21-23.

> Surely, no such Passover has been observed
> from the days of the judges who judged Israel,
> nor in all the days of the kings of Israel,
> nor of the kings of Judah.

These verses have generally been interpreted to mean that Passovers had been celebrated before this, but never with such meaning as upon this demise of the Manasseh-Amon paganism. However, since there is no mention or indication of Passover during the wilderness wanderings or in Judges, Samuel, and Kings up to this point, it appears likely that the passage means to describe this as the first Passover celebrated by the Hebrew people, and therefore a most significant event.

As with ritualistic worship, the Deuteronomists insisted that Passover be observed only at Jerusalem, i.e., "in the place where Yahweh shall choose, to cause his name to dwell there" (Deut. 16:2, 6, 7). This was feasible in 621 B.C., when the ten northern tribes already had vanished from the scene of history and only Judah remained. Since postexilic times found Jews settling over all Palestine, and surrounding nations in the diaspora, it became imprudent or impossible for most of them to keep Passover in Jerusalem because of the distances involved. Also, the Holy City would not have been able to accommodate so many pilgrims. In consequence, Passover gradually became a home celebration as the Deuteronomic requirement of observance in Jerusalem was ignored. This became completely true after the temple was destroyed in A.D. 70 and continues to this day.

According to Deuteronomy 16:1-7, and made more specific in Exodus 12:5-10, a year-old male lamb was to be "sacrificed" (killed), roasted, and served whole with even the viscera intact. Participants were to be gathered in family or community groups of a size that the entire animal could be consumed by morning in an all-night celebration. These regulations also were abandoned in time as Passover became only an evening commemorative meal, without any whole roasted "sacrifice."

It is difficult to overestimate the significance of this Passover which Jeremiah and his Deuteronomic associates brought into existence. Reliving annually that dramatic escape from slavery in Egypt has kept the Jewish people anchored firmly to their historic past through all these centuries. This has been an important factor in keeping Jews loyal to their religion in times of persecution and in Judaism's continuing as an important religion.

In the Christian world, Passover found itself transfused into Easter. In Muslim tradition it has become the feast of the Nebi Musa (the prophet Moses), celebrated annually at his supposed tomb near the northwest corner of the Dead Sea. Little could Jeremiah and his Deuteronomists have comprehended the annual galaxy of observances their first Passover would initiate throughout the world.

INTRODUCTION OF THE WEEKLY SABBATH

Introduction of the weekly Sabbath also was of great importance. As shown in chapter 5, by the time Deuteronomy was written, regularity in worship had evolved to the stage of celebrating two holy days per month, "new moon and sabbath." These observances were held on the first and fifteenth, when the moon first appeared and when it was full.

Jeremiah and his iconoclasts swept away those two evening and nighttime gatherings as pagan lunar festivals. Instead, these reformers substituted a series of daytime Sabbaths, with worship every seventh day. Assemblages on the first and fifteenth accordingly were replaced by this new set of meeting dates on the seventh, fourteenth, twenty-first, and twenty-eight of the month. This seventh-day Sabbath was to be used for rest, recreation, worship, and recalling Israel's liberation from slavery in Egypt (Deut. 5:12-15).

The Sabbath was a lifesaver for the Jewish people during the exile in Babylon. It provided for a type of weekly worship experience that could be entered into when away from the temple. As a bond of religious union it united the exiles and kept them yearning for the time when they would be liberated and could return to Jerusalem. If it had not been for the Sabbath, Judah might not have survived bondage in Babylon but would have perished as the ten tribes in their exile of 722 B.C.

During postexilic days the whole of Jewish religion came to revolve around the Sabbath when its role was expanded to include deeds of benevolence to the needy. As a derivative, special love for the number seven became a characteristic of this seventh Old Testament religion. Life became organized in groupings of sevens, including the sabbatical year and the year of jubilee.

The Sabbath was one of the religious fundamentals inherited by Christianity, which in time changed the day from Saturday to Sunday. Muhammad also adopted the sabbatical system, with observance shifted to Friday. The spectacular triumph of Islam in the Middle Ages, and of the Christian world in modern times, may be accounted for to considerable degree by the recreational and spiritual renewal which has come from this observance of a holy day each week. All this has been due to the vision of Jeremiah and his Deuteronomic reformers in establishing a day that has generated enduring values in these three religions.

SYNAGOGUE AND ASSOCIATED DEVELOPMENTS

Passover and Sabbath became supplemented by other innovations in worship which began to emerge in Judah during her final days before the exile. These developments were reactions against those portions of the Deuteronomic system which stressed ritual and decreed that religious observances could take place only in the temple. Since distance hindered many people from visiting Jerusalem to supply their weekly religious needs, residents in remote places resorted to alternate forms of worship which supplemented the Deuteronomic system. Because such outlying assemblies were not allowed to have altars, priests, or material sacrifices, these variant worshipers had to be content with religious fellowship, meditation, and their derivatives. This new coalition of religious practices eventually crystallized into what came to be called synagogues.

The Deuteronomic forms of Jerusalem-based ritualistic worship came to an end when the temple was destroyed in 586 B.C. and the Jews were removed from Palestine to an alien land. As those exiles became stranded in Babylonia they transferred wholly to the synagogue manner of worship with its less ritualistic procedures. Throughout postexilic times the synagogue gained such prestige that destruction of the second temple and its ritualistic system in A.D. 70 was not fatal to Judaism. Thereafter all worship was transferred to the synagogues which dotted every Jewish community, not only in Palestine but also in all nations to which Jews migrated. Through the Middle Ages the synagogue continued to grow in signficance and remains the bulwark of Judaism. In New Testament times the synagogue coalesced into the Christian church and in Islam into the mosque. Essential to all three is the "congregation," around which all religious life of the respective religious communities revolves.

The ritual of sacrifice was replaced in the synagogue by prayers offered up on their own behalf by worshipers without benefit of priests. The first hour of orthodox Sabbath-morning synagogue service usually has been devoted exclusively to prayer. In line with the precedent set by Daniel (Dan. 6:10 [6:11 in the Hebrew Bible]) it became customary to have three prayer sessions per day in the synagogue: one in the morning, one in late afternoon, and one after sunset, each about an hour in length. Islam has added two more cycles, making five series of prayers each day. The Jewish emphasis has also moved over into Christianity where extensive prayers survive in the liturgical portion of the service, with use of Orthodox, Catholic, Anglican, and other prayer books.

Reading Scripture also became an essential part of the synagogue service during postexilic time. In orthodox services an approximate hour is devoted to such activity, as the five "books of Moses" are read in their entirety each year. This practice also has been transmuted into Christianity's reading of select biblical passages in the liturgical portion of church services. In Islam the Jewish precedent survives in reading from the holy Qur'an.

With all deference to prayer and Scripture, a synagogue service reaches its climax in the sermon. A prelude to this development lay in the "oracles" delivered by the prophets at all types of public locations. However, it remained for Jeremiah to become the first "preacher" in the Bible as he originated the type of presentation which has since been called the sermon. He was the first to choose texts or object lessons and weave the ensuing remarks around a chosen theme. While some of his sermons may survive in Deuteronomy, scores of them in whole or part are preserved within the biblical book which bears his name. Especially notable are the drought, potter's vessel, bottle, palace, fig baskets, and temple sermons in chapters 14, 18, 19, 22, 24, and 26. Jeremiah's sermons were so critical of priests and prophets that he usually was not allowed to deliver them within sacred precincts. Nevertheless, his style and presentation eventually became the standard in synagogue services as the sermon came to form the concluding portion of Sabbath worship.

The sermon became adopted into Christianity and Islam as the post-liturgical portion of their services. It is difficult to comprehend what power the sermon has

had in our world through these three religions by way
of enlightenment, encouragement, inspiration, reproof,
and guidance.

The point of focus in the synagogue always has been
the pulpit in the front center of the platform. Prayers
are read from the pulpit by the leader or chanted by
the cantor. With the prized Torah reposing on its podi-
um, each Sabbath morning members of orthodox congregations are brought forward by invitation to read these
holy writings. Finally, from that same pulpit, the rabbi
concludes the service with his sermon, usually worded
with existential and social concern.

Christianity has inherited also the pulpit from
Judaism. Although in liturgical churches it is moved
to one side, to balance the lectern, in evangelical Protestantism the pulpit remains in center place. Because
of the mosque's frequent size, the minbar (pulpit) is
high, usually ascended by an imposing stair of steps,
often of marble. These three religions stand specially
indebted to Jeremiah for the spiritual power that has
proceeded from their pulpits through the centuries.

Another important role of the synagogue consisted
of its teaching function. Here the rabbi (teacher) e-
merged as the leading religious professional in Judaism,
gradually displacing in influence priests and Levites.
Psalm 119 portrays the devoted rabbi in his relentless
but joyful study of the Scriptures. Although the rabbi
has done the preaching in Judaism, he has been primarily
the teacher through all these centuries. This function
of instruction was exercised primarily on Sabbath after-
noons to interested groups and during the other six days
of the week as schools developed in connection with
synagogues.

In Christianity the rabbi became the minister,
whose educational function always has been important,

flowering in cathedral schools, Sunday Schools, and church-founded colleges. In Islam the rabbi became the imam, with his corresponding instructional role. The education function, begun by the rabbis, has been considerably responsible for the continuity and progress in these three great faiths.

The synagogue heritage -- with its pulpit, prayers, scripture reading, sermon, and religious instruction -- has been one of Judaism's greatest contributions to the religious world. It remains the light of Israel, as the church is the soul of Christianity, and the mosque is the source from which all Muslim blessings flow.

EMBARRASSING PERSISTENCE OF PRIMITIVE TABOOS

Up to this point the noble achievements of Judaism have been pointed out, as found in the prophetic portions of that religion's first sacred Scripture. However, to secure wider support, the Deuteronomic prophets allowed the priests to write part of the book. Unfortunately, priestly law codes in the latter half of Deuteronomy include primitivisms that have been a hindrance to the development of Judaism as a world religion.

One of these impediments is the regulation concerning foods, as found in Deuteronomy 14:3-20. This law divides the zoological creation into the artificial division of clean (edible) types on the one hand and unclean (inedible) species on the other. This division was made on the arbitrary basis of eating only animals that have cloven hoofs and also chew the cud. That law's prohibiting the eating of pork has caused Jews many heartaches, especially during Maccabean and Roman persecutions. Admittedly, among primitive tribes that ate meat raw, or when inadequately cooked, there has been the possibility of trichinosis in pork. However, beef, though acceptable, is subject to tuberculosis, anthrax, and hoof-and-mouth disease.

The real reason for abstinence from pork is that the pig was the sacred animal of Israel's eastern neighbors. When the Ammonites had their holy communion, the festal meal consisted of roast pork. The pig chapel excavated by Pere de Vaux, which one can see at Tirzeh, shows how the swine-god had invaded the territory west of the Jordan River. To keep Ammonite religion from making further inroads into Israelite practice, this most sacred animal east of the Jordan was declared taboo west of the Jordan. The holy animal of one people thus became the taboo animal of its neighbors.

Deuteronomy 14:9-10 decreed also, as observed in Orthodox Judaism through the ages, that only marine creatures with both fins and scales are edible. This rule admits the inexpensive Jewish favorite of carp -- basis of the gefülltefish served at Passover -- a fish that prefers to live in polluted waters on filth, and therefore will not be eaten by most non-Jews. Because of having skin rather than scales, this artificial division excludes from edibility the most cleanly and high-quality species such as swordfish, halibut, mackerel, and flounder. This rule also runs into the absurdity of eliminating all shellfish as unclean and inedible.

It is unfortunate that Judaism chose to follow the wrong passage concerning what meats are permitted for food. While Deuteronomy 14:1-20 divides species into edible and inedible, Deuteronomy 12:22 asserts that all God's animals, marine, and avian creation may be eaten.

Another food taboo is against eating milk and meat at the same meal. This is based on Deuteronomy 14:21, copied from Samuel's Code of the Covenant in Exodus 23:19, "You shall not seethe a kid in its mother's milk." Since nothing is intimated in either place as to the purpose of that law, in time the reason for such a directive became lost. As priests searched to recover the justification for this practice, they advanced the view that when meat and milk are mixed they become poisonous. In time that belief won general acceptance.

To prevent any possibility of such contamination, orthodox Jews concluded that separate groups of cooking utensils and dishes would be required. One set was to be used for milk meals, the other for meat meals, and the two never were to become mixed. To be absolutely safe, opulent homes, Jewish institutions, and Jewish agencies concluded it would be wise to have two kitchens, one for milk and its derivatives, the other for meat and meat products. Although one of the briefest laws, only five words in Hebrew, this prohibition has determined orthodox cooking for every meal throughout ensuing centuries.

Discovery of a Ras Shamra document (Birth of the Gods, 1:14) finally has supplied the lost reason for that regulation which, as misinterpreted, has been dietetically absurd. One of those clay tablets records that seething a kid in its mother's milk, and then gathering around to eat a festal meal, was the holy communion of the Canaanites, the counterpart to Jewish Passover. In light of Ras Shamra, that strange prescription in Exodus and Deuteronomy is now seen to mean nothing more than "Don't go to Canaanite communion." Loss of the real reason for that law has caused orthodox Jewish housewives to become enslaved through all these centuries into obeying a misinterpreted law by maintaining a divided diet and contending daily with two sets of kitchen and dining equipment.

Prohibition of drinking blood, or eating it with the meat, is another of these taboos (Deut. 12:16, 23). As stated in verse 23, this prohibition is based on the primitive belief that the life or soul is in the blood. To the degree that blood was taken into the body, it was thought the individual thereby assumed the soul of the animal, becoming a composite person, part animal. To avoid this danger, the orthodox Jewish housewife has had to carry out the elaborate koshering process, salting and kneading meat repeatedly to extract the last bit of blood. This heavy salting causes disintegrative effects in the circulatory system which shorten life, such as hardening of the arteries.

Circumcision is another primitivism that has survived from the early days of Judaism. This practice was observed widely among ancient people as a substitute for washing. That rite survived as an important element in Egyptian culture. When Abraham migrated to the land of Canaan and found himself in the Egyptian cultural orbit, for reason of relations with his neighbors he concluded his god thought it best that he and his whole tribe should become circumcised (Gen. 17:9-27). Also, in chapter 3 the observation was made that when Moses and his Midianite wife went to Egypt it was regarded as desirable to circumcise their son that they might not conflict with Egyptian mores in this regard (Exod. 4:24-26).

The rite of physical circumcision is not prescribed in Deuteronomy, but only "circumcision of the heart" (Deut. 10:16; 30:6). This would seem a virtual prohibition of physical circumcision. The laws "you shall not cut yourselves" and "neither shall they shave off the corners of their beards nor make any cuttings in their flesh" appear to prohibit circumcision the same as trimming the beard (Deut. 14:1; Lev. 21:5). Both practices were construed in these verses as insulting God's creative wisdom by marring the divine image in which man was formed.

Abraham's and Moses' compliance with Egyptian mores in this regard apparently was sufficient to fasten that primitive rite upon Israel's future (Lev. 12:3). It seems incongruous to picture God examining the penises of all males who appear before him on the judgment day, consigning the uncircumcised to perdition without further deliberation.

The taboos against women also have been notable. Orthodox Judaism, the only type until the nineteenth century, has been a man's religion. The few women attending synagogue services have been secreted behind screens or in balconies. Their attendance at daily prayers has been virtually precluded by the routine prayer of thankfulness for not having been born a woman.

Another group of taboos rests on the prohibition against things modern, sanctioning only primitive types for use in sacred rites and services. Two of these are carryovers from the stone-age prejudice against using metals. Extreme orthodox Jews accordingly refrain from utilizing metal knives in circumcision but continue with the flint knife, supposedly demanded by God, as employed by Zipporah in Exodus 4:25. Similarly, instead of easily blown loud metal trumpets, the ram's horn, whose weird and uncertain sound can be extracted only with great difficulty, continues to be required on Yom Kippur, the Day of Atonement.

Two taboos have grown up in connection with evolution of the synagogue service. One of these is a survival from the day in which all writing was done on the skins of animals, when newly invented paper and the book were regarded as taboo. Therefore, in recording the official Scriptures for reading in synagogues, only the hallowed leather scrolls are employed, in spite of their size, cumbersomeness, and much greater expense. Lastly, in all orthodox and some conservative synagogues men

wear the tallith (prayer shawl) and yarmulke (skull cap),
primitive garb originally intended to ward off demons.

By contrast with the many wonderful elements in
Judaism, of which all peoples and religions can be ap-
preciative, the surviving primitive taboos have created
frictions and enmities between Jews and Gentiles. Undue
attention to such practices has made it possible for
shallow Jews to conclude that the essence of religion
consists in wearing proper dress at services, practicing
circumcision, obeying the dietary laws of kosher, and
abstaining from eating unclean animals, unclean birds,
unclean fish, shellfish, blood, pork, meat and milk at
the same meal, etc. Although in its classic days Reform-
ed Judaism largely abandoned such practices, Orthodox
and, to a considerable extent, Conservative Judaism continue to observe the primitive taboos.

These observations suggest that when religiousness
comes to be tested by what individuals eat, what they
wear, or how they look physically, people are embracing
an ersatz religion that can bring only trouble.

THE STUMBLING BLOCK OF ANTIFOREIGNISM

Judaism's chief debit consisted in the antiforeignism that was endemic in that faith from its beginning.
In Deuteronomy it was prescribed that a Jew might not
eat an animal which dies of disease, but he might give
or sell it to a non-Jew (Deut. 14:21). Debts were to
be forgiven every seven years but were to be paid in
full by foreigners (15:1-3). In making loans, no interest was to be charged fellow Jews but it was permissible
to charge non-Jews interest (23:19-20). The law prohibiting any Ammonite or Moabite from entering Yahweh's
assembly to "the tenth generation . . . forever" must
have been construed as an insult to all Gentiles (23:3
[4 in Hebrew]). The rather lengthy prebenedictory sermon

in Deuteronomy 28 to 31 passes easily from hatred of
foreign gods to hatred of foreign nations who are regarded as "enemies" to be destroyed. That section pre-
dicted that all Israel's future ills would be caused
by softness toward foreigners and friendship with them.
The fact that this incipient hatred of Gentiles was
built into Deuteronomy, the founding scriptural document,
was ominous for the future of Judaism.

The bitter experiences of Jews at the hands of
their captors in the exiles of 597 and 586 B.C. accentuated this Deuteronomic attitude. The forty-eight ensuing
years of subjugation in Babylonia were difficult to bear.
Following 538 B.C. the returned Jews were menaced for
more than a century by neighboring peoples who tried
to prevent these expatriates from becoming re-established
in Palestine. The Books of Ezra and Nehemiah recount
a tragic story of enmities and counterenmities that went
out of control between 440 and 400 B.C. Plagued by
Samaritans, Ammonites, Edomites, and Arabians, the returned exiles were driven to distraction. In those days
the hatred of Jews for Samaritans and Samaritans for
Jews became eternalized, with neither having business
dealings or even speaking to a member of the other group.

The Jerusalem community went so far as to prohibit
marriage with foreigners and make all Jews divorce their
Gentile wives (Neh. 9:2; 10:28, 30; 13:30). Nehemiah
told how he confronted their husbands when he found Jewish children speaking the languages of their foreign
mothers. "I contended with them, and reviled them, and
beat up certain of them, and pulled out their hair" in
clearing Judah of all foreign wives (13:23-25).
Ezra rent his garments and his coat and tore the hair
from his head and beard in consternation over the way
Jewish men had married foreign women. He brought about
a decisive purge of all foreign blood (Ezra 9:3-10:44).

Since then both intermarriage and conversion of non-Jews to Judaism have been difficult and often impossible.

Hatred of foreigners became further accentuated in the Maccabean crisis during the second century B.C. At that time the Seleucid governors of Syria and Palestine tried to eliminate the Jews' adherence to the dietary laws, their revulsion against nakedness, and their refusal to worship emperors and other Greek gods. As a memorial to that struggle, the primitive December winter solstice observance was reinterpreted in terms of temple rededication and was renamed Hanukkah. This feast of lights, with giving presents, became the prototype of Christmas. Another cycle of hate occurred when the Romans subjugated Palestine, destroyed the temple in A.D. 70, and expelled all Jews from Jerusalem.

Persecution of Jews throughout the Middle Ages has left one of the greatest blots on Christianity. By denying civil rights to Jews, forcing them into ghettos, and killing them during Holy Week in eastern Europe each year, the Gentile-Jewish mutual antipathy triumphed on. This came to a climax with the Hitlerian incineration of some six million Jews in the gas furnaces.

All of this was aided and abetted by a boast which was developed by the postexilic priestly editors of Israel's early narratives. These writers interpolated into those documents the recurring assertion that Israel was God's "chosen people." Quite worthily, Israel had been "a choosing people" who, at the foot of Mount Sinai, had resolved to cast their lot with Yahweh. But warping this into the assertion that Jews were God's "chosen people" became the greatest religious insolence in the Hebrew Scriptures, an offense to all non-Jews.

This opinionated assertion was hallowed further by the doctrine that God had made a special covenant with Israel, the only people in the world with whom he

had deigned to do so. Israel had been an illustrious
spiritual pioneer, especially in the prophetic period.
However, to fossilize this into the assertion that Jews
were God's only covenant people not only tended to make
them arrogant but also invited resentment from all Gentile peoples.

In spite of all the good elements in the Israelite
heritage, this disdain for non-Jews, incorporated into
its founding Scripture of Deuteronomy, has been the
Achilles heel of Judaism. Because it forged ahead spiritually so far beyond other religions, Judaism was destined to be the religion of all humanity. However, it
forfeited this high opportunity by harboring the malignancy of antiforeignism. Lest one be too hard on Judaism
in this respect, there is the anomaly that on the issue
of race its successor, Christianity, has blundered into
the same pitfall.

THE RELIGION OF THE BOOK

By contrast with the spoken word of the prophets
and their orientation toward the future, from its beginning Judaism prized the written word, with devotion to
preserving the memory of Israel's past. In this way Judaism became a religion of historical research that
pioneered in literary endeavors. Deuteronomy, already
described as the founding Scripture of that religion
at 621 B.C., became the source from which was to proceed
an ensuing stream of canonical and other documents.

The next move in that direction came during the
final years of the monarchy when someone gathered together the available traditions and historical fragments
concerning Israel's origins and development. As a worthy historian, he wove his sources together without
modifying them. His own views appear only in the editorial transitional remarks by which he joined the basic

documents together. In these transitory observations
he passed judgment on most of the judges and kings. His
religiometer was whether they worshiped other gods and
whether or not they removed the high places. This Deuteronomic editor produced a five-volume master history of
Israel in the land of Canaan: Judges, I and II Samuel,
and I and II Kings.

The prophets had insisted that Judah's low morality
and unwise political policies of military alliance would
bring national annihilation by way of exile, the fate
customarily meted out to defeated peoples in that age.
Transport of Judah's population to the regions of Babylonia in 586 B.C. caused the exiles to recall the words
spoken by the prophets. The resultant increasing regard
for their utterances led to gathering into a nine-volume
collection the surviving writings and what people remembered from the public addresses given by the pre-exilic
prophets: Amos, Hosea, Isaiah, Micah, Zephaniah, Jeremiah, Nahum, Habakkuk, and Ezekiel.

Next in line was the work of the priestly editor
(or editors). At approximately 440 B.C. he assembled
and revised the early traditions of Israel, from creation until the conquest of Canaan, into the Books of
Genesis, Exodus, Leviticus, Numbers, and Joshua. These
five were combined with Deuteronomy to form what has
been called the Hexateuch. Leaving off the book of
Joshua, which seemed to spoil the theory of Mosaic auth-
orship for the whole, the other five became combined
into what later centuries were to call the Pentateuch,
the law of Moses, or the Torah. This collection was
canonized at approximately 400 B.C. by popular acclaim
as Ezra read the new Scripture to the assembled people
over an eight-day period (Neh. 8). This Torah still
holds priority over all later-devised Scripture and is
the chief portion read in synagogues on Sabbaths.

Since the Torah quickly became the most basic document in Judaism it is desirable to give some consideration to the editorial work in producing it. By contrast
with the Deuteronomic editor who transcribed the materials in Judges to II Kings without alteration, the opposite was true of the Babylonian Jew (or group of editors)
who produced the Torah.

The document which formed the basis of this work
was the Jehovistic history of Israel from creation to
the conquest of Canaan, a very authentic historical work
written probably during King Solomon's time around
925 B.C., by him or some nameless author. While re-
editing that five-century-old document at 440 B.C. into
the Torah, such extensive alterations and additions were
made that the exact bounds of the ancient classic are
difficult to determine. The changes were of four main
types.

An attempt was made to eliminate all traces of
polytheism in the prepatriarchal, patriarchal, and Mosaic stories. This type of revision was treated rather
extensively in chapters 1 to 3, showing however that
many primitivisms escaped editorial scrutiny. Only from
these places does one get a true picture of religious
allegiance during those early periods.

As the historical episodes in patriarchal and Mosaic life were not spectacular enough for this late
priestly editor, many of these were heightened into miracles, especially the dramatic events connected with
Moses' work. That editor could not find God working in
history but only miracles. The perverting of his sources
in this regard has been dealt with already in chapters
1 to 4.

Most late pre-exilic and postexilic theological
concepts and institutions of Judaism were retrojected
back, from their respective historical periods of origin,

to the time of Moses or creation. Solomon's temple, dedicated at 950 B.C., was retrojected back to Mount Sinai
(1225 B.C.) *via* the hypothetical movable prototype called the tabernacle or tent of meeting. The seventh-day
Sabbath, which began at 621 B.C., was carried back to
Moses and the week of creation. Monotheism, discovered
by Second Isaiah about 540 B.C., also was retrojected
back to Moses and Genesis 1. The official priesthood,
which began under David's reign and flowered in postexilic time, was brought back to Mount Sinai, making
Aaron and his sons the first priests. The Levites, who
became temple servants after 621 B.C., were retrojected
back to Moses' period. The annual feasts, begun by Samuel
and multiplied by Deuteronomy, were also attributed to
Moses as their supposed originator. The postexilic concept of the covenant was retrojected back as far as
Moses, Jacob, Isaac, and Abraham. Since all these, and
lesser retrojections, were incorporated into the historical portions of the Torah, those records of Israel's
remote past were made highly fictional and unreliable.

One retrojection is of such a major nature that
it deserves special consideration. The elaborate postexilic structure of priestly laws was brought back to
Moses' time and was ascribed to him. This Priest's Code,
extending through the last part of Exodus, all of Leviticus, and the first part of Numbers adds up to the total
equivalent of two whole biblical books. This spurious
forty per cent of the Torah, in so far as placement is
concerned, is a tragic intrusion into the Mosaic period.

These four types of changes and additions have made
the Torah a puzzling document from the historical point
of view. It is a complex mixture of truth and fiction,
mostly the latter. It seems strange that Judaism passed
by the highly truthful history from Judges to II Kings,

and the valid prophetic documents, and has given its chief loyalty to the Torah, which is untruthful in so many of its parts.

The recognition of Deuteronomy as sacred Scripture in 621 B.C. and the Torah at 400 B.C. led to further canonizations. Joshua and the aforementioned five-volume history of Israel's life in Palestine under the judges and kings was canonized, probably by popular consent, at approximately 300 B.C. as the Former Prophets:Joshua, Judges, I and II Samuel, and I and II Kings.

Canonization of these Former Prophets, but not the far greater Latter Prophets, called for rectification. To this end the nine-volume exilic collection of the pre-exilic prophets became supplemented by adding the six from postexilic time: Haggai, Zechariah, Obadiah, Malachi, Joel, and Jonah. This total fifteen-volume collection, called the Latter Prophets, was canonized at approximately 200 B.C. The Jewish Bible thereby became a collection in two parts, the Torah and the Prophets (including the Former and the Latter).

The Hebrew books that remained became gathered together and canonized by vote at the Council of Jamnia in A.D. 90, as the third body of Hebrew Scripture, called the Writings. Thus the Hebrew Bible, the Scripture of Judaism, in its tripartite arrangement of three separate volumes combined into one, was brought to completion. It continues to be called "The Torah, The Prophets, and The Writings."

Since Jews found chief expression of their genius in literature, further writings were produced but they never achieved canonical status. What have come to be called the *Apocrypha* and *Pseudepigrapha* are two extensive Jewish intertestament collections written mostly in Greek.

The classic decisions of the rabbis on traditional doctrines were gathered together during the first two centuries of the common era into the extensive collection called the Mishnah. During the following three centuries this was supplemented by further commentary called the Gemara. All this became assembled at approximately A.D. 500 into the monumental work called the Talmud, "the authority" in Judaism.

The fact that Judaism was so prolific in its writings stimulated Christianity in its first two centuries to produce its New Testament and become the second "religion of the book." Islam followed suit, and with its Qur'an became the third "religion of the book." These three bodies of Scripture have been of prime influence in bringing the worlds of Judaism, Christianity, and Islam to what heights they have attained of moral and religious excellence.

THE SPIRITUAL HERITAGE OF JUDAISM

While the sixteen remarkable young men of the prophetic movement were on their mountaintops of spiritual discovery, Judaism was the ongoing faith of the Israelite masses in the valleys below, relatively undisturbed by the vigorous prophetic demands.

Nevertheless, the enduring values in Judaism came to consist largely of certain fundamental ideas that filtered down from the heights of the prophetic movement and became adopted as integral parts of popular religion. This indebtedness was true especially with respect to the concept of deity. Completely devoted to belief in one God, as proclaimed by Second Isaiah, during post-exilic days Judaism became the world's first and greatest monotheistic religion.

The chief glory of Judaism has lain in sticking resolutely to that monotheistic course through the centuries, never stooping to worship any trinity, mother goddess, saints, or walis. Consequently, it remains today the world's truest monotheistic religion, refusing to revere any human being as deity, even its esteemed Moses.

Devotion to imageless worship also became an integral part of Judaism, which veered away from idolatry in all its forms. Through most of her history, Orthodox Judaism has taken the command against making a likeness of anything above, in, or beneath the earth as prohibiting even making pictures (Deut. 5:8). So great was reverence for the Creator's work that man must not run competition with God by indulging in any form of reproductive artistry or photography. Although this orthodox position has been extreme, it has saved Judaism since the Babylonian exile from all types of idolatry.

A third special genius of Judaism concerned the question of a heaven. To understand the attitude on this issue one must realize that through biblical centuries the Israelites were surrounded by religions whose main goal consisted in searching for a luxurious life hereafter. Subsequent generations could not forget how Moses' people had slaved in Egypt for Pharaohs and nobles who constructed luxurious tombs in expectation of a sensuous afterlife.

Reacting against this investing of wealth and effort in such determined pursuit of eternal bliss, Judaism set to the neglected task of reconstructing the moral and spiritual life of this world. The existential gearing of religion to this life, by concentrating on making it a sacrament of godly living, caused Judaism to forge ahead of all contemporary immortality-seeking religions in Old Testament days. Admittedly, Pharisaism and the modern reform movements departed from Orthodoxy by following the Daniel 12:2 late isolated expectation of resurrection, judgment day, Heaven, and Hell.

Nevertheless, even among these segments of Judaism such views have been kept in subordinate perspective so as not to interfere with the believer's proper performance of religious duties here and now.

Especially since destruction of the temple and the hierarchical priestly structure in A.D. 70, Judaism has been a democratic religion. With each congregation completely independent and wholly in control of all its affairs and beliefs, Judaism has proved uniquely fitted for functioning under democratic governments.

Judaism also is notable as the world's most enduring religion. In antiquity, cults came and went with the rise and fall of nations. By contrast, Judaism has survived the bitter persecutions of the centuries. In spite of the additional fact that for most of their existence the Jews have been deprived of national sovereignty and have had to live under other cultures and among more numerous religions, Judaism has persisted and grown because of the great hold that faith has had upon its adherents. That it has ministered to the souls of the Hebrew people from 722 B.C. to the present makes this the world's most enduring religion.

Perhaps the greatest service to the cause of world religion lies in Judaism's role as the mother of religions. Christianity may be described as but a re-adaptation of Judaism around the person, teachings, and memory of Jesus. In its origins the Islamic religon also was highly indebted to Judaism and remains deeply rooted in it. What moral and ethical triumph there has been in the portions of the world covered by these three faiths has been due largely to the spiritual heritage provided by the Jewish religion.

Judaism ultimately can be summarized in two of its most fundamental Scriptures. No synagogue worship can proceed without proclaiming the ultimate focus of Jewish religion, as stated in the Shema of Deuteronomy 6:4:

> Hear, O Israel, the Lord, our God is one Lord,
> and you shall love the Lord, your God, with
> all your heart, and with all your soul, and
> with all your might.

Companion to this are the words of Leviticus 19:18:

> And you shall love your neighbour as your-
> self.

CHAPTER 8

THE HUMANISTIC RELIGION OF POETS AND SCHOLARS

The final chapter in this series of evolving Israelite faiths was the result of a movement that refined
the best from the previous seven systems and combined
those select elements into another virtually new development. In their biblical order, the ten late canonical
books which belong to this terminal achievement are
Ruth, Esther, Job, Psalms, Proverbs, Ecclesiastes, Song
of Solomon, Lamentations, Daniel, and Jonah.

The authors of this eighth Old Testament religion
were the humanists and scholars of Israel. They had a
passionate concern for human values, believing that the
fundamental purpose of religion is to transform human
life by striving for the joy and possibilities that God
intends for it. Toward this end those writers expanded
the principles of law and order in Moses' Decalogue by
working to make its precepts universally operative in
Israelite life. Proverbs 7:2-3 states this goal by saying,

Keep my commandments, and live;

And my teachings, as the apple of your eye.

Bind them upon your fingers;

Write them upon the tablet of your heart.

The proponents of this new faith found chief expression in glorifying the spiritual heritage of the
Davidic and Solomonic traditions. This movement eventuated in attributing to those two authors most of the
song, philosophical, and proverbial literature -- the
chief types produced during the final Old Testament
period.

Although the high-powered drive of the prophets was not equaled by these wisdom writers, they strove to achieve in the life of Israel such prophetically desired goals as justice, righteousness, integrity, and regard for the poor. These innovators veered away from every inherited primitivism, taboo, antiforeignism, legalism, and exclusivism. By contrast, the constructive elements in mainline Judaism were retained. This selectivity made the faith of these humanists a religion that gathered together and gave to future generations the best in the Israelite heritage.

EMANCIPATION FROM ENSLAVEMENT TO RITUALISM

The prophetic disdain for rites and ceremonies, when not accompanied by ethical living, came to fruition with these new leaders, who became convinced that ritualistic observances have little or no place in spiritual religion. Since the literatures of Israel's seventh and eighth religions reveal their respective dominant interests, it is revealing to compare the ritualistic references in the ten humanist writings with similar occurrences in Chronicles, Ezra, and Nehemiah which are typical of Judaism, the Old Testament's seventh religion. These three books may therefore be referred to as "the trilogy" or "the Judaism trilogy."

The priesthood offers a prime example of the resulting contrasts. In the later Old Testament days the priests had become a burgeoning hierarchy that monopolized the temple worship and gained an increasing strangle hold on Judaism. Their prestige is shown by the fact that they are mentioned 188 times in Chronicles, Ezra, and Nehemiah. By contrast, similar references appear in the ten humanist books only eleven times. Six of these are in neutral routine historical reviews. One holds the degenerate prophets and priests responsible

for Israel's destruction (Lam. 4:13). Two cast aspersions upon the contemporary clerics by anticipating a
day when priests would be "clothed with righteousness"
(Ps. 132:9, 16). None of the eleven references show
any regard for these clerics. Eight of the ten humanist
books make no reference to priests. This silence speaks
volumes.

The Levites had become so important that in Chronicles, Ezra, and Nehemiah they appear 159 times. By contrast, these important associates of the priests in the
religion of Judaism did not receive a single mention
in the ten humanist books. The Levites were simply
ignored.

Sabbath, one of the most important institutions
in Judaism, is mentioned twenty-four times in the Judaism trilogy. By contrast, Sabbath appears only twice
in the texts of the ten humanist books, both times in
Lamentations which was the earliest in that group. Sabbath admittedly occurs in the heading to Psalm 92, but
that ascription was made by the later canonizer who
credited that orchestral psalm wrongly to Sabbath services rather than daily temple worship where instruments
were used. It is amazing that the Sabbath is not mentioned in the texts of any of the 150 psalms, the greatest religious classic in the Hebrew Scriptures. The
complete absence of any Sabbath reference in the other
eight humanist books is notable. Because the sensitivi-
ties of these late Old Testament people were increasingly annoyed by synagogue formality, they generally appear
to have avoided attending Sabbath services.

The importance of Passover, as a bulwark of official Judaism, is indicated by the mention of that feast
occurring twenty times in the trilogy. Surprisingly,
that term is never found in the ten humanist documents.

The ark of the covenant, the most sacred ritualistic object in Judaism because it was thought to be the earthly dwelling place of Yahweh, is referred to forty-seven times in Chronicles alone. By contrast, the ark is mentioned only once in the ten humanist books, Psalm 132:8. Most authors of those later writings evidently no longer believed in a Yahweh who could reside in that small wooden box.

The ritualization of giving by prescribing and collecting the tithe appears ten times in the Judaism trilogy but never in the humanist books.

Since the pages occupied in the Bible by the ten humanist writings are approximately twice those of the Judaism trilogy, the number of occurrences in the trilogy should be multiplied by two, thus doubling the already remarkable disparities between the two bodies of literature as just listed.

Absence in the ten books of other ritualistic basics of Judaism also is revealing. Censers, circumcision, dietary laws, and the multitude of legalistic prescriptions which occur with such profusion in legal portions of the Hebrew Scriptures are completely absent from the humanistic literature.

These observations should alert one to the fact that this humanistic faith of Israel's scholars was a virtually new noninstitutional religion. Its main achievement lay in emancipating itself from subservience to the complex and elaborate ritualistic system which had become characteristic of Judaism.

These spiritualistic pioneers did not waste their energies by attacking the rites and ceremonies that meant so much to their traditionally minded contemporaries. Usually these humanists simply ignored those types of observance and spent all available time advancing their own religion of heart, mind, and will.

RESPECT AND FRIENDSHIP FOR ALL PEOPLES

The greatest achievement of Israel's humanists lay in freeing themselves from bondage to the exclusivism which had become characteristic of contemporary Judaism. They shuddered at hearing proclaimed from altar and pulpit the arrogancy that Israel was God's chosen people whom he loved and supported while all other nationalities were inferior.

These wise people did not approach the malady of exclusivism negatively by making frontal attacks on offending contemporaries and denouncing their views. Instead, the new leaders in Israel proceeded in a positive manner to develop appreciation for all the peoples God has created. Although born under the clouds of prejudices and antiforeign hatreds that overshadowed postexilic days, the pioneers in this new movement were able to part those clouds and let the sunlight of wholesome human relations shine once more into their troubled land.

Chiefly responsible for this change was the nameless individual who set out to remove this malignancy from Israel by presenting a series of short stories about Ruth, Jonah, and Esther. Unfortunately, this trilogy has been split three ways in the Hebrew Scriptures. Ruth has been sandwiched into the early historical writings between Judges and I Samuel in the Former Prophets, Jonah has been placed in the Latter Prophets, and Esther has been located among the late Writings.

Probably the first of these three short stories to be written was the Book of Ruth. It was directed against hatred of Moabites. This antipathy had its origins a millennium and a half earlier when Lot's two daughters made their father drunk on successive nights and lay with him while he was intoxicated. In the course of time they gave birth to Moab and Ammon, progenitors of Israel's two eastern neighboring nations (Gen. 19:30-38).

Scorn for the peoples descended from those two il-
legitimate births became incorporated into Judaism's
founding Scripture in the statement that

A bastard shall not enter into Yahweh's assembly, even to the tenth generation none of his
(offspring) shall enter into Yahweh's assembly
(Deut. 23:2 [3 in Hebrew]).

Disdain for these two peoples was made specific in the
law that followed:

An Ammonite or a Moabite shall not enter into
Yahweh's assembly, even to the tenth generation none of them shall enter in Yahweh's assembly, forever.

This stigmatizing of Israel's two neighbors as bastard nations was unpardonably specific, especially rating them as ultrabastards by adding the "forever." Such
odious citation in the Hebrew Scriptures undoubtedly
made the blood of all Ammonites and Moabites boil. The
same must have been the result if a Moabite heard the
words of Psalm 60:6-8 (8-10 in Hebrew): "God has spoken
in his holiness, . . . 'Moab is my wash-pot.'"

By doing a little historical research this trilo-
gist found that David's great-grandmother was a Moabite
named Ruth. Seizing this opportunity, that author set
about to show how good a Moabite could be. The loyalty
of Ruth to her mother-in-law is portrayed as the ultimate in devotion. With Ruth the bonds of love and admiration took precedence over ties of family and national-
ity as she left her people and her country to be with
the one she so admired. Ruth spontaneously changed her
god and religion when passing over the boundary that
was thought to separate the domain of Chemosh from that
of Yahweh. In making that transition she uttered the
immortal words: "Your people shall be my people, and
your god, my god" (Ruth 1:16).

This author did not condemn hatred of Moabites and attack the purveyors thereof. Instead, it was shown how wonderful life can be when people of differing families, countries, cultures, and religions live together in mutual love and admiration. This author portrayed the people of all nations and religions as fundamentally good. The evident purpose in writing was to dissolve the corrosive hatreds of the time and leave the Israelite nation and religion freed from those blemishes.

There were two largely hidden barbs in the story. The first consisted in the subtle genealogical reminder that Israel's most esteemed King David, the "man after god's own heart," was part Moabite. The second barb involved David's ultimate successor, the hoped-for Messiah, who also would have that same Moabite blood in his veins.

While all characters in the Book of Ruth are good, the author tried the opposite technique in the Esther story by making all participants villains. Although it is commonly assumed that Esther was a wonderful heroine, closer examination reveals her as the most bloodthirsty woman in the Old Testament and Jews as the most bloodthirsty people in the story. After killing 500 Persians in the palace and perhaps 100,000 in the provinces, Esther requested another day of slaughter. On that second day the Jews killed 300 more in the palace and 75,000 more in the provinces. The name of God is wisely never used in that entire fictional story. It shows what happens when rival ethnic groups resort to intrigue and violence, each trying to get the upper hand, and how all eventually sink down into the caldron of mutual hatreds.

JONAH AND WORLD FRIENDSHIP

In a third short story this author showed how even the great prophetic movement had degenerated into a

travesty on religion. The plot features a would-be
prophet who was called by God to go and "preach" to the
Ninevites. Jonah was embarrassed by receiving such a
commission since he did not want to share his religion
with other peoples, especially such despised ones. He
therefore decided to take flight by sea in the opposite
direction. Since the sailors felt Jonah had caused the
ominous storm in which the ship was soon engulfed, he
was cast overboard and swallowed by a great fish. In
response to supposedly repentant prayer, after three
days and nights God ordered the fish to vomit him out
alive. Then the deity again directed that he "preach"
to the Ninevites. To avoid further tragedy, Jonah responded this time, but reluctantly. However, he could
not make himself "preach" to those Ninevites. Instead,
this supposed prophet announced to them: "Forty days
and Nineveh shall be destroyed."

Every Ninevite in the city repented upon learning
of those words. When God recognized their repentance
as valid and saved the city, this defaulting prophet
became so angry that he issued to the deity an ultimatum, either to destroy them or kill him. Jonah felt
there was nothing left in life to live for if he could
not see those more than a million Ninevites burn to
death. Such is the delusive mirage that is the end of
hate.

Although this story purports to recount but the
antics of a pretentious prophet, it is an allegory.
Jonah represents the supposed prophet nation. The first
part describes Israel's disdain for neighboring peoples
during pre-exilic times, refusing to share her religion
and spiritual heritage with them. Even after the disci-
plinary experience (exile) in Babylon (the fish's belly),
Israelites continued to regard religion as their monopoly
and clamored for the destruction of non-Jews.

The book concludes with a question: Would Jonah eventually see the light and get a more wholesome attitude toward the Ninevites? In reality the question was: Would Israel see the folly of her antiforeign attitudes and begin to move toward friendship with all peoples?

In an age of exclusivism and anti-foreignism, the Jonah story showed that all people are fundamentally good and responsive to new truth when it is given them. This author called upon Israel to share her religion with other peoples, even the most despised.

The character Jonah is represented as wanting a hard god who could ruthlessly incinerate whole cities and nations. By contrast, the book's author portrayed the highest concept of God's nature in the Old Testament:

> a God gracious and merciful, slow to anger and
> abundant in lovingkindness, and relenting when
> it comes to punishing (Jonah 4:2).

This is the God whom Jesus was to proclaim. Muhammad was inspired by Jonah 4:2 into beginning 113 of the 114 suras (chapters) in his Qur'an with "In the name of God, the Compassionate, the Merciful." Through the ages this immortal story has not ceased to offer its message of help toward bringing about a recreated humanity, a world of love and brotherhood in which prejudice, intergroup conflicts, and racial hatreds shall be no more.

RELIGION OF WOMEN'S LIBERATION

This trilogy on human relations may have been produced by a woman. Giving such prominent place to women, as observed in the Books of Ruth and Esther, and ending all three with the spotlight on infants, would have been unlikely from any male author at that time. Anonymity seemed necessary because she might have been executed as a "Moabite lover" after having issued the Book of

Ruth, probably her first production. If it had been known
that all three of those short stories were written by a
woman, few would have been the readers in that age.

Possibly only part of her writings have found their
way into the Bible. Other short stories by her could
have survived in Greek translation within the collection
called the *Old Testament Apocrypha*. The short story a-
bout Judith may have been produced by this same gifted
woman. That conclusion is suggested because the Judith
story is directed toward Israel's same Transjordanian
enemies, the Ammonites and Moabites, as in the Book of
Ruth. This authoress credits the Ammonite leader "Achior
and all the Moabites" as the people who tried to save
Israel (Judith 5:5-6:21; 11:9-11; 14:6-10). However,
as with the Esther plot, it finally took a woman to
liberate her country when the military defeat of Israel
seemed certain. With the women's - lib touch, Judith was
lauded in 13:18:

> Blessed are you, daughter, above all the women
> upon the earth in the sight of the Most High
> God.

The Book of Susanna also appears to be the work
of this distinguished woman author. That story should
have been included in the Bible, since it was the first
part of Daniel, but ostensibly was kept out because it
reflected on the male establishment. The Susanna narrative tells of two evil-minded Jewish elders who tried
to seduce a virtuous woman. After she refused their advances, they went to the local court and charged her
with immoral conduct. According to Jewish law, the test-
imony of two witnesses was sufficient to convict.
Susanna quickly was pronounced guilty and was being
led to her execution when Daniel appeared and demanded
that the two elders be cross-examined separately. Since
their witness did not agree, she was freed. This was

a massive protest against the common miscarriage of justice against women.

High tribute must be paid to that remarkable woman,
the greatest of her sex in Israel's biblical history.
She spearheaded the humanistic religion of her age into
several of its notable accomplishments by using the effective literary medium of the short story. Her productions played a strategic role in dissipating antifor-
eignisms and creating respect for the people of all nations. By having so many women characters in her productions, with the spotlight of attention focused on
most of them as heroines, this writer dignified the position of women. She was perhaps chiefly responsible
for trying to make the Old Testament's eighth and final
religion one in which women were equal with men.

Praise of The Worthy Woman in the final chapter
of Proverbs (31:10-31) is the supreme tribute to women
in the Bible. Also notable is the fact that wisdom, the
highest quality of life in the wisdom literature, is
always personalized as a young woman. Admittedly, condemnation is heaped on the prostitute in Proverbs, but
even that is pointed toward maintaining the honor of
women. The Song of Solomon portrays women on a parity
with men, glorifying the courtship routines and the sex
instinct in each.

Previous biblical religions had been largely of men,
by men, and for men. As part of the Old Testament's final development, the humanists sought to transform Israel's faith into a spiritual experience for women as
well as men.

RELIGION OF THE ECUMENICAL SPIRIT

The ecumenical spirit eventually found expression
at the Old Testament's close throughout the humanistic
portion of Israelite society. This accomplishment is

observed especially in the choice portions adopted from
the literatures of surrounding religions. Those borrowings served as a silent reproof to the innate antiforeignism of mainline Judaism with its millenium of antipathy toward other faiths and their adherents.

In spite of bondage under Pharaoh before the exodus,
and many subsequent invasions of Palestine by Egypt,
Israel's humanists were broad enough to recognize the
contributions from Egyptian sources. This achievement
found expression by incorporating into the Scriptures of
Israel's final Old Testament religion various selections
drawn from Egyptian religious literature.

One of these borrowings occurs in Psalm 19:1-6.
This adoration of the day sky is based on the Egyptian
Hymn to the Sun, composed around 1400 B.C.[1] The
figure of the sun as "a bridegroom coming out of his
chamber" and rejoicing "as a strong man to run his
course" is reminiscent of the sun-god's crossing the
zenith in the Egyptian hymn. However, the fifty-five
lines of the original text are reduced to fourteen in
the Bible.

Psalm 104 also is essentially an Egyptian psalm
composed by Pharaoh Akhenaten. This too was a hymn to
the sun-god, who was lauded as creator of all things.[2]
Eight similarities are observable between the Egyptian
and biblical versions with regard to length, stanza arrangement, and progression of thought. These parallels
indicate that some psalmist made a free rendition of
that masterful Egyptian poem. The presence of this
hymn to the sun-god in the Hebrew Scriptures is a tribute to the great Egyptian religious reformer and author,
and to the ecumenism of the Hebrew poet who adapted
that high-quality Egyptian story of creation to his
Israelite readers.

The first psalm also may be indebted to an Egyptian source. This introduction to the Psalter contrasts the righteous who are "like a tree plantd by the streams of water" with the wicked who are "like chaff which the wind drives away." This comparison seems to have come from chapter 4 in the *Instruction of Amen-em-Opet*.³

Another section from that same Egyptian classic appears to have been incorporated into Proverbs 22:17-24:22 under a new title, the Words of the Wise.⁴ Since the parallels are too extensive to describe here, Pritchard's summarization must suffice. His note 46 lists sixteen parallels between the two documents. Furthermore, in notes 9, 15, 21, 25-6, 28, 30, and 35-7 Pritchard cites thirteen passages in Amen-em-Opet's work that seem to be paraphrased in other collections within the Book of Proverbs.

The presence in Psalms and Proverbs of these borrowings from Egyptian religion shows that in late Old Testament times the ecumenical spirit finally triumphed over the enmity against all things Egyptian which had prevailed since the exodus.

BORROWINGS FROM OTHER RELIGIOUS CULTURES

The ecumenicity of the humanists is shown further by the fact that two more of the seven constituent collections in the Book of Proverbs were taken from other religious cultures: the Words of Agur, the Son of Jakeh in Proverbs 30 and the Words of King Lemuel, the Oracle which his Mother Taught Him in Proverbs 31. Since Agur and King Lemuel are unknown in Hebrew history, the best guess is that these copyings are from Edomite treatises, i.e., from the descendants of Esau who were famed for their wisdom. This borrowing may indicate that the millennium and a half of hatred between the descendants

of Esau and Jacob finally was transcended by the ecumenical spirit, at least among the proverbialists.

A borrowing from Greek religious literatures is
found in the quatrain of Proverbs 3:19-20 and the poem
in 8:22-31. These verses were derived from a primitive
hymn in which creation was construed as brought about
by the sexual union of the father and mother deities.
This physical act has become sublimated somewhat by the
biblical reviser into identifying the mother goddess
with Wisdom. Instead of being coequal, as in the original, she was now conceived as the firstborn of creation.
Nevertheless, Widsom remains the creator-god's consort,
applauding and praising each act of his workmanship.

The most extensive ecumenical importation into the
Old Testament is the Book of Job, which has been taken
over from the religions of Mesopotamia and Arabia. The
Job story had its beginning with a very ancient Sumerian
document translated by Samuel N. Kramer and entitled
Suffering and Submission: The First "Job". [5] This story
of a man plagued by multiple sufferings but finally rewarded with great blessings by his god has been rewrit-
ten by some Arabian writer into the prose drama of
Job 1:1-2:13 and 42:7-17. The geographical setting is
in central Arabia, the land of Uz, extending to Teman,
Sebea, and Chaldea -- the northwestern, southern, and
northeastern boundaries of Arabia.

Some later Arabian writer, seeing literary possibilities, elaborated the brief conversation between Job
and his three friends into the extensive quatrologue
of Job 3-31 and 38:1-42:6. In that masterpiece the abundance of quadriliteral roots, which often occur in
Arabic by contrast with the triliteral roots in Hebrew,
indicates those chapters were written by a proto-Arabic
poet. The Arabic origin is revealed also in the

non-Israelite thought such as accusing God of being a-
moral, immoral, and sadistic in 9:22-31. Including in
the Hebrew Scriptures both the Arabian prose drama and
the great philosophical poem of Arabian religion is perhaps the highest tribute to the ecumenism of these humanists.

The Jonah story is another example. In searching
for an appropriate means of disciplining the villain
in her plot, that author appropriated the ancient Poly-
nesian religious myth of the sun being swallowed each
evening in the west by the huge seamonster and disgorged
in the east the following morning, as modified into the
universal story of a sinful man swallowed by a monster
and vomited out alive after repentance.

Although revised to a Palestinian setting, the Song
of Solomon is so different from anything else in the
Israelite tradition that one may suspect it is basically
another foreign importation. With its stress on exotic
gardens and eroticism, this may be an adaptation from
Tammuz worship as carried on among the North Semites
and in Persia.

Although consideration has been given here to major
importations into the final Old Testament books from
other religious traditions, Pritchard's monumental work
suggests a multitude of minor borrowings.

Ecumenism is a characteristic of mature religion,
emancipated from the dogmatism that one's own is the
only "right" religion. By contrast with the venomous
attitudes toward other faiths and their worshipers that
was characteristic of contemporary Judaism, the humanists did not hesitate to recognize the good aspects of
other religions and appropriate the best elements from
those faiths to themselves. In this way they were
achieving the makings of a universal religion.

ADVENTURES INTO RELIGIOUS EDUCATION

Although education had been initiated by King Solomon, a higher type of religious instruction was developed by the humanists. With these wise people, simple principles of living replaced complex laws, precepts, and prescriptions.

The Book of Proverbs contains the religious curriculum materials used in those days when education consisted in teaching and memorizing gems of wisdom. Most proverbs consist of an important truth, usually concentrated into a memorable couplet. Others are larger, even to the size of short essays. Wise men taught proverbs to the children and youth who gathered about them. More often such education was carried on in the home, often couched in the form of a father's instruction to his children.

The religion of these humanists was conservative in the truest sense of that term, i.e., conserving humanity's spiritual heritage from the past and transmitting it untarnished from generation to generation. That system of religious education was based on the belief that there is a science of human life. Certain modes of living were recognized to be in harmony with the spiritual laws of the universe, and that a person departs from them to one's sorrow. The results of human experience through the ages were coined into the form of proverbs presented to each rising generation as wise sayings.

Prime stress was placed upon wisdom as the most important acquisition in this world, to be prized above all material treasures (Prov. 3:13-15).

Happy is the person who finds wisdom, . . .

For the gaining of it is better than the gaining of silver,

And its value, than pure gold.

She is more precious than rubies,
   And nothing you can desire is comparable
   to her.

The passage then goes on to say that the individual who achieves wisdom is likely to be rewarded also with health, long life, riches, honor, pleasantness, and peace. Wisdom was conceived of as very comprehensive, including knowledge, understanding, discretion, discernment, good judgment, and prudence. Wisdom's impassioned invitation for followers constitutes the most moving poetry in Proverbs (1:20-33; 8:1-9:6).

A large per cent of the couplet proverbs contrast the way of righteousness with the way of wickedness. Although the evil manner of life might "seem right to a person," it was stressed that "the end thereof is the way of death" (Prov. 14:12; 16:25). By contrast, the reward of those who follow in the way of righteousness is summarized in Proverbs 4:18.

But the path of the righteous is as the dawn-
   ing light,
   That shines more and more until the perfect
   day.

Extended treatment was given to the pitfall concerning which young men were thought to need special warning. The ultimate in fatherly advice was directed against becoming involved in prostitution and adultery (Prov. 2:16-19; 5:1-23; 6:24-7:27; 9:13-18). One who indulges in such relations is likened to "an ox going to the slaughter, or as . . . a bird flying into a trap" (7:22-23).

Strong admonitions against becoming addicted to liquor are found in Proverbs 23:19-35 and 31:4-7. Many couplets, such as 20:1, add their words of caution:

Wine is a mocker, strong drink a brawler;
   and whoever errs thereby is not wise.

Young people were warned also against the deceit-
fulness of riches and making pursuit of wealth the major
goal in life:

Better is little, with reverence for the Lord,

than great wealth and trouble therewith (Prov.

15:16; cf. 16:8).

The economic golden mean was counseled lest a person be
poor, and tempted to steal; or rich and forgetful of God
(30:8-9).

Industriousness was advocated as one of life's
highest qualities. Here Benjamin Franklin obtained his
favorite proverb:

Do you see a man diligent in his business?

He shall stand before kings, he shall not

stand before obscure men (Prov. 22:29).

Three poems on "The Sluggard" present graphic cautions
against laziness (6:6-11; 24:30-34; 26:13-16).

Many passages stress the value of reproof, and advise youth to accept correction without resentment.

The ear that listens to the reproof of life

shall abide among the wise.

He who refuses correction despises his own

soul (Prov. 15:31-32).

Train up a child in the way he should go,

and even when he is old he will not depart

from it (22:6).

The rewards of the disciplined life to the person who
achieves it are expressed in the words:

He who is slow to anger is better than the

mighty;

and he who rules his own spirit, than the one

who takes a city (16:32).

The ultimate test of any religion is found in its
attitudes toward enemies. In this crucial area the wisdom writers rank high.

When a man's ways please the Lord, he makes
even his enemies to be at peace with him.
(Prov. 16:7).

Rejoice not when your enemy falls, and let
your heart not be glad when he is overthrown;
. . . Do not say "I will do to him as he has
done to me, I will render to the man according
to his doings" (24:17, 29).

If your enemy is hungry, give him bread to
eat; and if he is thirsty, give him water to
drink, . . . and the Lord will reward you (25:
21-22).

The Book of Proverbs is the jewel box of the Bible.
These concentrated utterances are like diamonds, to be
appreciated one at a time when mounted in the setting
of a person's consideration. Such a wise saying had to
be sufficiently brilliant that it would remain in
thought until its life-transforming role was accomplished. Since the prime motive power for the wisdom era came
from its myriads of proverbs, their total impact was
significant.

THE WISDOM OF JESUS, THE SON OF SIRACH

The ecumenical spirit of the humanists manifested
itself in respect to the language in which their religion was expressed as well as in their relationships
with non-Israelite cults. By reason of commercial expansion, or avoidance of Maccabean persecutions, numbers
of enterprising Jews came to live in various countries
of the Hellenistic world, notably Asia Minor, Greece,
Italy, and especially Egypt, where Alexandria had more
Jews than Jerusalem. By reason of their lack of prejudice, most of these emigrants adopted the vernacular
of that world, the Greek language. This was particularly

true of Alexandria, which became the center of Jewish scholarship written in Greek.

The official Hebrew-based Judaism of Jerusalem did not approve of this linguistic departure. Since members of the establishment were certain that God speaks only Hebrew, they were convinced that no books written in any other language could have been divinely dictated or inspired. Consequently, books written in Greek, even though by Jews, became looked on with contempt. When the Council of Jamnia met in A.D. 90 to close the bounds of the Old Testament, it was decreed that no books written in Greek should be included.

This decision kept out of the Bible some of the most important religious literature produced by Israel's humanists. Some thirty excluded productions have been collected into what is commonly called the *Apocrypha* and *Pseudepigrapha*. Since the canonizers gave no attention to literary and religious values, one finds many of these so-called intertestament writings superior to certain Old Testament books.

The best of these so-called apocryphal books is the Wisdom of Jesus, the Son of Sirach. By the Greeks it was called Ecclesiasticus (Churchbook) because it was read as a favorite Scripture in Christian churches until the fourth century A.D. Ben Sirach's work is an encyclopedic collection of proverbs, poems, and small essays on life and ethical conduct, with shrewd observations and strong religious emphasis throughout. Ecclesiasticus is similar in subject matter and religious tone to the biblical Book of Proverbs, but is almost twice as long.

This classic of the wisdom movement begins with the ultimate statement: "All wisdom comes from the Lord." While Genesis 1:3 asserts that the first glimmer of creation was when God said, "Let there be light," according

to Jesus ben Sirach 1:4-10 God's prior creative command
was presumably "Let there be wisdom." The firm religious foundation upon which that wisdom book is based
found further expression in the ensuing verse:

> Reverence for the Lord brings glory, and exul-
> tation, and gladness, and a crown of rejoicing.

This is the God who "is full of compassion, and mercy,
and who forgives" (2:11).

Jesus ben Sirach was noted for his groupings of
proverbs on particular subjects. A good example is the
collection on gossip in 19:7-10:

> Never repeat what is told you, and you shall
> fare never the worse. Whether it be of friend
> or foe, tell it not; . . . Have you heard a
> word? Let it die with you. Hold out, it will
> not burst you.

In contrast with the previous seven religions of
the Old Testament, which placed a premium on the number
of children, the son of Sirach was a pioneer in population limitation. He proceeded not from the demographical
point of view but from moral considerations. He inveigh-
ed against bringing into the world multitudes of children and then not giving regard to their manner of life:

> Desire not a multitude of good-for-nothing
> children, . . . If they multiply, delight not
> in them unless reverence for the Lord is with
> them. . . . For one is better than a thousand;
> and to die childless, than to have ungodly
> children (16:1-3).

A choice contribution is on the subject of friendship. This Jesus spoke of fair-weather friends and
pointed out that those who remain through times of adversity are few in number. The following are several
lines from this noted production:

If you would get yourself a friend, get him in
the time of trial, and be not in a hurry to
trust him. For there is a friend who is so
for his own advantage, and will not continue
in the day of your adversity . . . . A faithful friend is a strong defense, and he who
has found such has found a treasure. There
is nothing that can be taken in exchange for
a faithful friend, for his excellence is beyond price (6:5-17).

Ben Sirach penned a superb passage in 28:12-26 on
the deadliness of the tongue and need for its discipline,
of which the following six lines must suffice:

The stroke of a whip makes a mark in the flesh,
but the stroke of a tongue will break bones.
Many have fallen by the edge of the sword,
but not so many as those who have fallen because of the tongue . . . . Weigh your words
with a scale, and make a door and a bar for
your mouth.

Of the essays produced by this Jesus, two stand
out with distinction. The first compares the crafts with
the professions, distinguishing its author as one of the
world's first proletarians. Successive stanzas are devoted to the farmer, the engraver, the smith, and the
potter. Ben Sirach tells how each of these becomes master of his trade and, when unable to sleep at night,
gives thought to how he can improve his craftsmanship.
Then comes the grand conclusion:

Without these no city could be inhabited,
. . . They shall not be sought for in the
councils of the people, . . . They shall not
sit on the seat of the judge, . . . and where
parables are they shall not be found. But they

maintain the fabric of the world, and in the handiwork of their crafts is their prayer (38:24-34).

The most-quoted passage from Ben Sirach's writing is in chapter 44. Its Praise of Famous Men is a declaration stressing the immortality of personal influence. After the initial words "Let us now praise famous men, even our fathers who begat us," the contributions of the great leaders in Israelite history are summarized. Parts of the concluding encomium are as follows:

But these were men of mercy, whose righteous deeds have not been forgotten . . . . Their seed shall remain forever, and their glory shall not be blotted out. Their bodies are buried in peace, and their names will live for evermore. Peoples will declare their wisdom, and the congregation will tell forth their praise.

Although this work by the first Jesus was written in Hebrew, it became so popular in its translated Greek form that at the time of canonization no Hebrew text was available. Because of the dogma that regarded only Hebrew as a sacred language, and all others as profane, this valuable writing by one of Israel's greatest wise men was kept out of the Old Testament.

ACHIEVEMENT OF BELIEF IN IMMORTALITY

The fate of being relegated to the forbidden *Apocrypha* was shared by another illustrious treatise on ethics, the Book of Wisdom, produced between 50 B.C. and A.D. 40. Written in the name of King Solomon, who ruled almost nine centuries earlier, that publication commonly has been called the Wisdom of Solomon. Its greatest achievement lay in making a strong case for belief in personal immortality.

The standard Old Testament view had been that at death all people, good as well as bad, went into the dark underworld of Sheol, where they would lapse into a somewhat painful eternal semisleep, unless awakened for a moment by a necromancer. Job speculated about more satisfactory ways of life survival, but dismissed them as wishful thinking (Job. 14:7-22). Ecclesiastes contains the certainty in 3:18-22 that man is no different from the animals, dying and returning to dust exactly as they. It remained for three books of the wisdom period to advance the belief that man is immortal -- Daniel 12:1-2, Wisdom, and II Maccabees, but the greatest of these is the Book of Wisdom.

Following the lead of Jesus, son of Sirach, the Book of Wisdom describes the immortality of individual influence in even more classical form:

> For righteousness is immortal:. . . For in the
> memory of virtue is immortality, because it is
> recognized both before God and before men. . . .
> And throughout all time it marches crowned in
> triumph, victorious in the strife for the
> prizes that are undefiled (Wis. 1:15; 4:1-2).

In Wisdom 3:1-9 this author went further by advancing the belief in personal immortality:

> But the souls of the righteous are in the hand
> of God, and no torment shall touch them. In
> the eyes of the foolish they seem to have died;
> . . . but they are in peace. . . . Their hope
> is full of immortality.

The vicissitudes of life are construed as God's chastening, to make people deserving of survival:

> And having borne a little chastening, they
> shall be greatly rewarded; because God made
> trial of them, and found them worthy for

himself. As gold in the furnace he refined
them, and as a whole burnt offering he received them.
Then comes the eventual triumph in regions immortal:
And in the time of their visitation they shall
shine forth, . . . And the Lord shall reign
over them for evermore (Wis. 3:5-8).

The triumph of that author's belief in immortality
is found in Wisdom 5:15-17:

But the righteous live forever, and with the
Lord is their reward, and the care of them
is with the Most High. Therefore they shall
receive the crown of royal dignity and the
diadem of beauty from the Lord's hand, for
with his right hand he shall shield them, and
with his arm he shall protect them.

Understandably, at funerals and memorial services
today resort is freely made to the wisdom writings of
Israel's humanists -- especially, Ben Sirach's Praise
of Famous Men and the assurances in the Book of Wisdom
concerning life hereafter.

A RELIGION OF SCIENCE AND ECOLOGY

The pioneering work of King Solomon, in observing
nature and in scientific study, came to fruition in this
eighth Israelite religion. High industrial development
is shown in a wisdom supplement (28:1-11) to the Book
of Job. That chapter tells how mining operations were
carried on for silver, gold, iron, and copper in late
Old Testament days. Verse 9 shows strip mining already
in vogue: "He overturns the mountains by the roots."
Verse 4 describes the more common shaft mining with the
cage "swinging to and fro" in the "open shaft" while
being lowered and raised from the tipple. Energy for
such operations was supplied by water power from dams

constructed to "bind the streams that they flow not"
(vs. 11).

Description then follows of the tunnels as the
miner "puts forth his hand upon the flinty rock" and
"cuts out corridors among the rocks" (Job. 28:9-10). In
those underground passageways man "sets an end to darkness and, to the furthermost bound, searches out the
stones of obscurity and dense darkness" as "his eye discovers every precious thing" (vss. 3, 10). That type
of underground operation

> no bird of prey knows of, nor has the fal-
> con's eye seen it: the proud beasts have not
> trodden it, nor has the fierce lion passed
> thereby (vss. 7-8).

After recounting how the valued metals were recovered, the poem goes on to tell how precious stones and
gems were being mined: onyx, sapphire, volcanic glass,
crystal, and topaz. But more precious than all these
is wisdom, and where can it be found? The answer is that
God alone "is aware of the way" that leads to it and
"knows the place" of it (Job 28:23).

> And unto man he said, "Behold, reverence for
> the Lord, that is wisdom; and to depart from
> evil is understanding " (vs. 28).

That distinctive chapter shows how science, industry,
and religion are all interlocked.

The greatest scientific treatise of the wisdom age,
The Book of the Heavenly Luminaries, survives as chapters 72-81 in the pseudepigraphic Book of Enoch. That
section describes the natural laws governing the succession of days, months, and years, plus the interrelation-
ships and movements of the heavenly bodies. The length-
ening and shortening of days is accounted for and the
supposed movement of the sun from south to north and
return, as well as the fractional day at year's end

which makes construction of a satisfactory calendar difficult. The differences between the lunar and solar
years are treated, and the systems by which each can
be brought into harmony with the real year. That auth-
or's manner of dealing with the waxing and waning of
the moon indicates he already knew that this planet dispensed only reflected light. This document is one of
the world's earliest examples of pure science, with no
religious or philosophical presuppositions mixed into
the astronomical observations, even though the author
was a deeply religious person.

RELIGION THAT FINDS GOD THROUGH NATURE

Most nature psalms were late, penned by writers in
this eighth religion. These humanists did not find the
deity so much by reading their Scriptures as by observing the created world about them. Nature was looked upon
as the great stage upon which God acts. In 8:1-4 a psalmist proclaimed God's revelation to all mankind through
the celestial wonders:

How wonderful is your name in all the earth,
Who has set your glory upon the heavens! . . .
When I consider your heavens, the work of your
    fingers,
The moon and the stars which you have ordained;
What is man that you are mindful of him?
God also has made everything under the heavens.
In his hands are the deep places of the earth,
The heights of the mountains are his also;
The sea is his, for he made it,
And his hands formed the dry land (Ps.95:4-5).
These nature lovers found God even in the storm with its
thunder and lightning.
The voice of the Lord is powerful,
The voice of the Lord is full of majesty,

> The voice of the Lord breaks the cedars, . . .
> The voice of the Lord cleaves the flames of
>   fire,
> The voice of the Lord shakes the wilderness,
> The Lord shakes the wilderness of Kadesh (Ps.
>   29:4-8).

The Song of Solomon abounds in descriptions of exotic
gardens in the Near East at springtime when

> The flowers appear on the earth; . . .
> And the song of the turtledove is heard in
>   our land;
> The fig-tree ripens her green figs,
> And the vines are in blossom (Song of Sol.
>   2:12-13).

Proverbs has nature descriptions throughout, but especially in chapter 30, where many animals, birds, and
insects are featured. In verse 19 the four wonders of
the world are listed as

> The way of an eagle in the air,
> The way of a serpent upon a rock,
> The way of a ship in the midst of the sea,
> And the way of a man with a maiden.

Four marvels of nature are cited:

> The ants are a colony not strong,
>   Yet they store their food in the summer;
> The rabbits are but a powerless species,
>   Yet they make their homes in the rocks;
> The locusts have no king,
>   Yet they march forth, all of them, in ranks;
> You can seize the lizard with your hands,
>   Yet she is in king's palaces (Prov.30:25-28).

Delight in God's animal, bird, and marine creation came
to its highest level in the thirteen portrayals of Job
38:39-41:34. Poetic renditions on the lioness, raven,
wild goat, deer, wild ass, wild ox, and hawk regrettably

must be passed over with these slight mentionings. Four
selected lines each from the other six poems must suffice.

> The wings of the *ostrich* wave proudly,
>> But are they the pinions and plumage of love?
> For she leaves her eggs on the ground, . . .
>> And forgets that the foot may crush them. . . .
> Have you given the *horse* his might?
>> Have you clothed his neck with the quiver-
>> ing mane?
> Have you made him to leap as a locust?
>> The power of his snorting is frightening. . . .
> Is it by your command that the *eagle* mounts up,
>> And makes her nest on high? . . .
> From there she spies out the prey,
>> Her eyes behold it afar off. . . .
> Behold now the *hippopotamus*, which I made as
>> well as you,
>> He eats grass as an ox. . . .
> His bones are like tubes of brass,
>> His ribs are like bars of iron. . . .
> Can you catch the *whale* with a fishhook? . . .
>> Can you pierce his skin with harpoons?
> Or his head with fish spears? . . .
>> No one is so mighty that he dare stir him up. . . .
> I will not keep silence concerning his (*croco-
> dile*) limbs, . . .
>> Who can open the doors of his face?
> Round about his teeth is terror,
>> His courses of scales are his pride.

As these passages have shown, a chief characteristic of this terminal Old Testament religion was its high
regard for the wild life of land, air, and water. Nature's
creatures, of diverse appearances and insticntive ways,
were reverenced as the work of God and part of the

creative design. Those scientifically minded people began to comprehend the amplitude of divine wisdom by ap-
preciatively observing wildlife ways. This was the ecological movement in full swing, recognizing the interde-
pendence of the human and animal creation as one world
and including all within the bounds of ethical concern.

These humanists regarded both the material and sentient worlds as an expression of the spiritual and saw
no opposition between science and religion. They gloried
in all creation as God's handiwork and credited him with
the ongoing laws by which the infinite number of its
parts operate from day to day. According to that perspective, humanity, the material creation, and the natural world find their unity in God.

OVERPOWERING SENSE OF GOD'S REALITY

Even though mention of "religion" never occurs in
the Old Testament, its constituent elements became well
formed in the humanist period. The nearest biblical e-
quivalent to the term "religion" was "the fear of the
Lord." Because of the bad connotation carried by the
word "fear" today, this most frequently recurring phrase
in the wisdom and psalm literature may best be paraphrased as "reverence before God."

In Israel's religious quest the Psalter constitutes
the greatest achievement of this eighth Old Testament
religion. Although certain psalms were of pre-exilic
and exilic origin, even these did not come to be treasured until in the later postexilic centuries. The fact
that the Psalter did not get canonized into the Hebrew
Scriptures until the latest date, at A.D. 90, indicates
that the majority of psalms came from the final Old
Testament period.

As a mature religion that found expression in joy
and song, most of the humanist writings were expressed

in poetry. Introductions to the psalms indicate the number and significance of the temple choirs. Psalms 33:1-3,
47:5-7, and 150 show the important role of song in worship and describe the types of orchestral accompaniment
offered by the temple musicians as instrumentalists
joined vocalists in praise to God.

This song literature flowered forth in tributes
to God and in expositions concerning the indebtedness
of earth's inhabitants to him. Psalm 139:7-12 shows that
there is no escape from God's jurisdiction.

> Where can I escape from your spirit?
>> Or where can I flee from your presence?
> If I ascend up into Heaven, you are there.
>> If I make my bed in Sheol, behold, you are
>> there.
> If I take the wings of the morning
>> And sail to the uttermost parts of the sea;
> Even there your hand shall lead me,
>> And your right hand shall hold me.
> If I say "Surely the darkness shall cover me,
>> And the light about me shall be night;"
> Even the darkness does not hide from you,
>> But the night shines as the day,
>> The darkness and the light are both alike
>> to you.

The powerfulness of God is stressed especially in Job
9:5-10:

> He who removes the mountains, and they know
> it not;
>> When he overturns them in anger;
> Who shakes the earth out of its place,
>> And the pillars thereof tremble;
> Who commands the sun and it rises not,
>> And seals up the stars;
> Who alone stretched out the heavens,

And treads upon the waves of the sea;
Who has made the Bear, Orion, and the Pleiades,
And the chambers of the south;
Who does great things past finding out,
Yes, marvelous things without number.

In spite of his power as creator and sustainer of
the universe, these humanists saw God tender "as a father" who "has compassion for his children" (Ps.103:9-12).

He will not always chide,
Nor will he keep his anger forever.
He has not dealt with us according to our sins,
Nor punished us according to our iniquities;
For as the heavens are high above the earth,
So great is his lovingkindness toward those
who reverence him;
As far as the east is from the west,
So far has he removed our transgressions
from us.

The Book of Ecclesiastes was written by an individual who had pursued successive interests: education,
sensual pleasures, material wealth, investments, and
finally the unsought quest of old age. Disillusioned,
he at last found himself facing death with the belated
realization that he had accomplished nothing really
worthwhile during his entire life. Even this seemingly
destructive writer ended his book by advising readers
to avoid the colossal mistake he had made in shunning
religion. That gentle cynic accordingly has left as his
constructive benediction,

Remember your creator in the days of your youth,
Before the days of adversity come, . . .
Revere God and keep his commandments,
For this is the whole duty of man (Eccl. 12:1,
13).

A RELIGION OF MATURITY FOR FREE MINDS

This final religion of the Old Testament was quite different from the seven preceding ones. It was a multi-faceted practical faith that dealt with every problem and phase of human life. No distinction was made between sacred and secular, for the whole creation was regarded as sacred. These writers did not complain about life, but found it very good as they dwelt on the ennobling possibilities of human existence. Reliance upon God was the motive power behind their effort to transform the life of mankind.

These humanists had little regard for the cramping and hairsplitting theologies of orthodoxy that were untrue. In the person of his three friends, Job (13:7) chided religious people for lying in order to defend God. These wisdom devotees of Israel were dedicated to searching for spiritual reality in order to establish their faith on a firm foundation of truth.

Of all eight Old Testament religions, this one attained the broadest scope and gained considerable momentum as an ongoing movement during the three centuries from 200 B.C. to A.D. 100. This type of religion prevailed especially among those many Jews who were scattered throughout the Greek world. These dispersed ones were geographically isolated from the ritualisms and dogmatisms that clustered around the Jerusalem temple. Broadening of perspectives was aided by contacts with Hellenistic cultures.

These humanists initiated the first attempt at establishing a reform Judaism that had prospects of becoming a universal religion for all mankind. This achievement might have endured if its inheritors had appreciated the profundities of a free and undogmatic approach to religion. With respect to survival possibilities, this humanistic faith had several fatal deficiencies.

As the work of Israel's scholars and wise men, this approach to religion was too intellectual for the masses who prefer more shallow types of religion. Also, this final Old Testament religion did not insure its permanence by institutionalizing itself with an array of rituals, which seems a necessary evil if a religion is to last for any extended period of time. In the absence of such provision, this religion became swallowed up by scribalism, legalism, Pharisaism, orthodoxy, and Talmudism. Such was the fate of the Old Testament's final and most worthy religion.

Nevertheless, the ten humanistic writings in the Hebrew Scriptures, with certain associated books in the *Old Testament Apocrypha* and the *Pseudepigrapha*, remain a literary monument to an age of creative spiritual discovery. Strange as it may seem, except for some thirty of the psalms, this rich treasure chest of the Bible is largely ignored. While Jews now magnify the Torah and Christians treasure the prophecies, one may look forward to the day when the rich humanist writings will again receive the attention they deserve. As only deep water flows without ripples, so it is with mankind's faiths. This religion of outreach toward God was at home in the quiet depths of the human soul.

NOTES TO CHAPTER 8

1. Pritchard, *Op. cit.*, pp. 367-368.

2. *Ibid.*, pp. 369-371.

3. *Ibid.*, p. 422, note 11.

4. *Ibid.*, pp. 421-425.

5. Kramer, *Tablets of Sumer*, pp. 147-151.

ILLUSTRATIONS OF BIBLICAL THEMES

BY
DIANE KRUEGER

CHAPTER 9

THE MANDAEAN RELIGION OF JOHN THE BAPTIST

Almost two centuries intervened between the last Old Testament book and the public ministry of John the Baptist. Those intertestament years marked the decades when the Roman Empire gained its strangle hold on the world. That government's oppressions caused the persecuted to place their hope in eschatological expectation. It was anticipated that God himself would come to earth, vanquish Rome, take over the government of the world, and exalt the oppressed. John found himself born into that milieu of expectations regarding the end of the age and the dawn of a new righteous era.

This most colorful character in the New Testament inaugurated the Bible's ninth religion, the first in the New Testament. Since baptism by immersion in water was the central rite of his ministry, he is usually called John the Baptist. He so captured the attention of the gospel writers that almost as much attention is given to his conception and birth as to the conception and birth of Jesus, and John's is portrayed almost as miraculous. Widespread interest in the Baptist is seen in the many supposed heads of that evangelist that continue to be treasured as relics today in the churches, mosques, and small museums of Mediterranean lands and the Middle East.

Authentic information regarding John the Baptist is found in Luke 1 and 3, Mark 1, Matthew 3, and a few scattered references in those gospels. It is amazing how carelessly these materials have been interpreted. The authentic facts have been overclouded by the

unwarranted stereotype that this innovator's main purpose was to be the herald of Christianity, preparing
the way for Jesus and announcing his coming. Exegetive
eyes have been largely blinded to the real John as described in Mark's and Luke's gospels.

Careful examination of the documents shows John
to have been the founder of a new religion, Mandaeanism,
the Bible's ninth faith which continues in the Middle
East today. To understand that development it is necessary to explore into John's origins and manner of life.

Until the Dead Sea scrolls were discovered in 1947,
and throughout the following decade, it was virtually
impossible to appreciate the Baptist's significance.
With the newly available knowledge concerning the scroll
people it became apparent that the Gospel of Luke has
been stating for nineteen centuries that John was born
into an Essene home and was brought up in that sect.

Since John's father, Zacharias, was a priest, it
formerly had been assumed that such priestly service
was rendered at the temple in Jerusalem. However, the
Greek word in Luke 1:9 and 21 is *naos* (sanctuary) -- not
'ieron (temple) as the Jerusalem structure usually was
termed. This indicates that Zacharias' priestly duties
were probably rendered at the small sanctuary in the
Essene monastic settlement near the northwest corner
of the Dead Sea at Qumran.

That locale may be suggested also by the fact that
Zacharias is credited only with "burning incense" at
"the hour of incense" at "the altar of incense" (Luke
1:9-11). By contrast, presenting animals on the altar
of burnt sacrifice was the main priestly duty in Jersa-
lem, the only place where offering of animals was allowed.

Since Zacharias was married, as were many Essenes,
he lived at his home "in the hill country of Judaea"
(Luke 1:65). He likely went to nearby Qumran only when

his turn for service came to "execute the priest's office before God . . . in the order of his course" when
"his lot was to enter into the sanctuary of the Lord"
(Luke 1:8-9). The description of his wife Elisabeth in
Luke 1:5 as "of the daughters of Aaron" indicates she
was from an Essene family, since that was a favorite
way of designating them.

As Elisabeth had been barren for some years, according to Luke 1:7, the conception of her child, John,
was regarded as a miracle. In thankfulness for this gift
the parents evidently decided to follow the example of
Hannah to whom a similar conception was ascribed a millennium earlier. After Samuel was weaned, Hannah took
this miracle child of her barrenness to the temple in
Shiloh that he might be reared by the priests as a temple attendant. The boy Samuel thereby was given back
to God in token manner. Luke 1:80 states that John "was
in the deserts until the day of his showing to Israel."
This statement suggests that, duplicating the Samuel
precedent, John was raised by the Essene priests, either
in the monastery at Qumran or in the surrounding desert
caves.

AN UNCONVENTIONAL EVANGELIST
When approximately thirty years of age, John left
the Essene community and went out on his own as an unconventional evangelist. His break with the Essenes was
most evident in his manner of dress. Orthodox Judaism
and Essenism were ultrastrict in this matter, prohibiting all bodily exposure except for minimal portions of
feet, hands, and face. In his disgust with the Essene
system John went to the opposite extreme, going about
virtually naked. If translated properly, Matthew 3:4
tells that John wore as clothing only the hairy pelt
of a camel and a leather strap. The camel's pelt

evidently was thrown over his body only at night and
on cold days. Since weather in the Jericho area usually
is torrid, even in winter, John likely wore only his
leather loinstrap most of the time. This made him a sensation and accounts for Jesus' statement in Matthew 11:7-8,

> What did you go out to see in the desert? A
> reed shaken with the wind? But what did you
> go out to see? A man clothed in soft garments?

In this failure to wear conventional clothing John
was following the example of Micah in journeying "barefoot and naked" from Jerusalem southwest into the
Shephelah lowlands, announcing to all cities and villages that enemy armies were about to attack (Mic. 1:8).
By example Micah was warning residents along the way
that soon they would be as "barefoot and naked" as he.
Similarly, by lack of clothing John was warning all people that they were about to stand with naked souls before the judgment day of God.

John was sensational also in his diet. He abstained
from prepared and cooked foods and existed on what was
found in the wild, especially locusts and wild honey
(Mark 1:6). This man of the deserts must have astonished
that whole generation with his unorthodox diet as he
bypassed the requirements of eating only kosher food.

The annunciation statement to Zacharias included
"he shall drink no wine nor strong drink" (Luke 1:15).
Since this was part of the Nazarite vow, the conclusion
"and no razor shall come upon his head" (Judg. 13:5)
was implied.

Long hair, untrimmed beard, naked except for loinstrap, presumed hairy body, and eating unconventional
food combined to make this unkempt wild man of the deserts appear as a sensation. It was little wonder that
multitudes of people came to see and hear this strange
specimen of humanity. In typical Oriental exaggeration

Mark 1:5 records: "And there went out unto him all the country of Judaea and all they of Jerusalem."

The Essene community must have been scandalized over this son of their own monastic life who had become a renegade preacher, disobeying much of what they had taught him, displaying what they regarded as disgraceful personal habits, and organizing a distasteful rival religious movement in their own back yard at Jericho.

THE HERALD OF GOD'S IMMEDIATE COMING

This ex-Essene was announcing that the time finally had arrived when the expectation expressed in Isaiah 40:3-5 would be fulfilled as he shouted, "The voice of one who cries in the wilderness: 'Prepare you the way of the Lord'" (Mark 1:3; Luke 3:4; Matt.3:3). That passage convinced John that God was so disgusted with the manner of life in that day that he was about to descend from Heaven and set matters right on earth. To that end John considered it his divinely appointed mission to announce this impending world-shaking event of God's coming and prepare people for it.

John anticipated that, upon arrival, God would begin his work by reconditioning the earth physically. Since Palestinians were plagued by their rock-strewn mountains and eroded wadis, John proclaimed in Luke 3:5-6 that the first act of God would be to bring down the hills and mountains, fill the forbidding valleys, and turn the entire earth into a productive plain.

> Every valley shall be filled,
>> And every mountain and hill shall be brought low;
> And the crooked shall become straight,
>> And the rough ways smooth;
> And all flesh shall see the deliverance of God.

God then would turn to reconditioning the human
race. The deity was pictured in Matthew 3:10 as a horti-
culturist, the earth as his orchard, and its fruit trees
as his people. According to John, God was about to burn
up all evil people on earth with fire, as an orchardman
cuts down all unproductive trees and burns them to ashes
in a great bonfire. John stated that the trunks of the
doomed trees already were being marked by axe blazes
for destruction. This indicated the immediacy with which
God was ready to execute his judgment.

> Even now, the axe also is laid at the trunk of
>   the trees,
> Every tree, therefore, that does not bring
>   forth good fruit will be hewn down and cast
>   into the fire.

This fiery preacher then varied his presentation by
using the parallel figure of God as a farmer, and the
earth as his threshing-floor. John said,

> He shall baptize you in the holy spirit and
> in fire; whose fan is in his hand, thoroughly
> to cleanse his threshing-floor and gather the
> wheat into his garner, but the chaff he will
> burn up with unquenchable fire (Luke 3:16-17).

These verses pictured God ready for his judgment
day, time of harvest and threshing. In his venomousness
against evil the deity would see to it that every bit
of chaff (the evil people in his world) would be burned
up. This was not any hellfire of eternal punishment to
which they would be consigned. It would be terribly immediate. God was not going to allow that fire to be put
out until the last evil person would be removed from
the earth.

John made the people shudder as he called them but
a bunch of snakes (Luke 3:7). "You offspring of vipers
-- who warned you to flee from the coming wrath?" With

his frightening words this evangelist was impressing upon his audiences how furiously angry God would be with sinful mankind when he would come to usher in the judgment day.

Luke 3:18 says, "With many other exhortations therefore he preached good news to the people." John's message was "good news" only to the good people who he thought were about to take over the earth. With all wicked individuals removed from this planet, it henceforth would be a place of perfect righteousness, with no more annoyance from evil.

A VIGOROUS PROGRAM OF ETHICAL CONDUCT

As the multitudes cowered in fear before this sensational prophet, he revealed what he thought to be God's requirements with respect to ethical conduct.

Bring forth therefore fruits worthy of your
repentance,
And do not begin to say within yourselves,
We have Abraham as our father, for I say unto
you
That God is able of these stones to raise
up children to Abraham (Luke 3:8).

Listeners could not expect to be exempted from impending punishment by reminding God that they were "children of Abraham." John shattered such false hopes by asserting that ancestral genealogies and boasts of being "the chosen people" would not rate before God when he would come in his anger. As such fiery preaching curdled the blood of those who heard it, the people in his audience cried out in terror (Luke 3:10), "What then must we do?" John answered,

He who has two coats,
Let him share with him who has none;

And he who has food,

    Let him do likewise (Luke 3:11).

John proclaimed a hard gospel. His demands upon the masses were summed up in one word -- sharing. He was insisting upon an equalitarian society in which there would be neither wealth nor poverty.

The politicians who came to his preaching also shuddered at the judgments that flamed from his lips. These supposed public servants cried out, "Teacher, what must we do?" They were mostly the hated tax gatherers who lined their pockets by over-collecting as much as possible. John's command to these exploiters was simple: "Extort no more than that which is appointed to you" (Luke 3:12-13). This all boiled down to honesty in public office and abstinence from graft. In any age, this is an unwelcome gospel for public officials who work where the money is and are tempted to feather their nests.

Even soldiers who came to John's preaching were mellowed by his forcefulness, and cried out, "And we, what must we do?" These were what now are called policemen. In those days there was no police class, since the task of preserving domestic order was entrusted to "soldiers." On them John weighed a triple charge. "Extort from no man by violence, neither accuse wrongfully, and be content with your wages" (Luke 3:14). By this triple ultimatum he charged them to abstain from the common offenses of such officials: police brutality, graft, unjust accusation, and striking for higher wages.

Were these requirements for civil and governmental life only an interim ethic, applicable until God should come to earth and use them as criteria for separating the evil from the good on his judgment day? Presumably John regarded these principles of conduct also as keys

to the new age of righteousness that soon was to follow
and would endure for all future time.

BAPTISM UNTO REMISSION OF SINS

An important element in Essene religion was the
practice of baptisms (usually called lustrations) by
each individual several times a day. Even though John
repudiated most of the Essene system, this rite of abso-
lution by water meant much to him. He therefore retained
it as the heart of his system. Only, instead of remaining a daily practice, he modified baptism into becoming
a once-in-a-lifetime observance.

As indicated in Luke 3:3, there were two phases
to John's baptism:

And he came into all the region round about
the Jordan, preaching the baptism of repentance unto the remission of sins.

Proper qualification for baptism, by way of repentance,
was the prerequisite. All such repentant ones presented
themselves to John who immersed these applicants in the
Jordan River. This ritual was believed to purify
the individual by bringing remission from all past
sins.

The ultimate purpose was to prepare these recipi-
ents for the impending judgment day of God. By having
a clean slate of sinlessness, the baptized could survive in that coming great day of decision. Therefore,
to be baptized or not was a matter of life or death.
It is understandable why people flocked in masses to
his baptism -- so they might survive when God was about
to come and purge his world of evil.

Since baptism played such a pivotal role as the
all-important and virtually only rite in John's
religion, wherever his influence has gone baptism has
remained central.

THE RELATIONSHIP BETWEEN JOHN THE BAPTIST AND JESUS

Of John's many converts, Jesus was to become the most famous. While Christian theology has revered John as having the one purpose of preparing the way for Jesus' ministry, Jesus in no way fitted that evangelist's description of the role to be played by the "coming one." Jesus did not descend from Heaven. He did not begin in a dramatic manner by bringing down hills, filling valleys, and converting the earth into a fertile plain. Jesus found all people basically righteous and did not pronounce doom on any people or inaugurate any judgment day. He did not burn all wicked people from the earth with unquenchable fire. He did not bring in a spectacularly new era in earth's history. From these negatives it is apparent that the work of Jesus did not fulfill John's predictions. The Baptist had no intention of "preparing the way" for his cousin Jesus.

John's shoe-untying statement also is pivotal. "But there is coming one who is mightier than I, the laces of whose shoes I am not worthy to untie" (Luke 3:16). John certainly would not have hesitated to tie or untie the laces of his cousin's sandals. However, to do this for God would have been quite a different matter since the Jewish Scriptures taught that to look upon the face of God would mean certain death. Touching God's sandals might not have been quite so dangerous as looking at his face, but almost as hazardous. This sandal-untying statement offers further evidence that John's description of the one who was about to come did not fit Jesus.

What would Jesus do after his baptism? In light of their blood relationship it might have been expected that this new convert would remain with the Baptist and assist in carrying on this ministry. Although John was powerful enough to bring his cousin to baptism, Jesus apparently reacted against "the baptizer" in several

ways. (1) In the next chapter it will be shown that
Jesus reacted against the crudity of water baptism as
an initiatory religious rite. (2) John was too sensational and spectacular for Jesus. (3) From Jesus'
preaching it is evident that he did not follow John's
central belief that God was about to descend from Heaven
and bring "this age" to an end. These three barriers
were to separate into segregated movements the subsequent efforts of these two cousins.

As time went on, John became more daring in his
preaching. By recklessly following the policy of let-
ting the chips fall where they would, and denouncing
evil in high places as well as low, he soon met his
Waterloo. It was too much for royalty to tolerate when
John became so emboldened as to bring public denuncia-
tion upon the king for the immorality of living with
his brother's wife.

Herod Antipas had John arrested and placed within
the dungeon in the middle of the small mountain under
the winter royal palace at Machaerus, east of the Dead
Sea. One can enter this prison today and see the irons
to which prisoners were chained. The king feared John,
had no intent of bringing about his death, but meant
only to restrain this over-daring preacher (Luke 3:19-20).

Following his baptism Jesus had gone into the wilderness to consider the possibilities of appropriate
service. On approximately the fortieth day of those
questionings someone came to him with the information
that John had been imprisoned. This news crystallized
Jesus' accumulating resolves and sent him forth to begin
his own ministry (Mark 1:14).

John's disciples evidently felt that if Jesus wanted to carry on a ministry while their leader was in prison, it should have been done in furtherance of John's
movement. Because of not taking that course, Jesus began

to be looked upon by John's followers as carrying on an opposition ministry.

While in prison John heard about the popular excitement over the beginnings of Jesus' movement and sent two of his disciples to Jesus, asking "Are you the one who is to come, or do we look for another?" Jesus gave no direct answer. He suggested only that these investigators tell John what they had seen and heard, and beg him not to be offended at what was transpiring (Luke 7:18-23).

After John's disciples left, Jesus explained to the audience his relationship to John. Jesus credited the Baptist with being the greatest in the old order but declared that those who were only beginning to achieve something of the higher spiritual potential evident in his own movement were greater than John (Luke 7:24-29). When John's followers heard of those remarks they must have felt insulted at Jesus' disparagement of their leader.

Herodias continued to have venemous thoughts toward John for denouncing her before the nation as an immoral woman. Her opportunity came at Herod's birthday party when hilarity was rife. Herodias had her daughter Salome perform an erotic dance. The presumably intoxicated king was so jubilant over this performance that he promised Salome anything she might wish, up to half the kingdom. She consulted her mother and requested the head of John the Baptist, served up on a platter. Since Herod did not wish to be disgraced before his guests for breaking his promise, the king ordered John decapitated in the dungeon below. The Baptist's bleeding head was soon delivered before the dancer on the designated platter.

JOHN'S ONGOING MANDAEAN RELIGION
It would have seemed that the martyrdom of their leader might have brought an end to John's distinctive religion, but this did not occur. Here, as so often

throughout history, the blood of a martyr became the seed of an ongoing movement.

The nine mentionings of John the Baptist's name in Acts shows that his religion was a force with which early Christianity constantly had to reckon. Acts 19:3-4a indicates that John's Mandaeanism had become established in the great city of Ephesus before Paul arrived there. The nineteen references to John the Baptist in the first ten chapters of the Fourth Gospel suggest that Mandaeanism and Christianity were rivals in that religious center as late as A.D. 100.

Jesus admittedly had been cool toward John and had not visited him in prison. To what degree John may have felt enmity toward Jesus is unknown. At any rate, antagonism of Mandaeans toward Christians became increasingly pronounced. The flames of this antipathy were fanned as overzealous early Christian evangelists attempted to terminate the Mandaean movement by placing false directives on the lips of John the Baptist. In those statements John was made to disavow any attempt at developing a personal following for his own purposes. He was made to assume the role of announcing Christ's coming and gathering a following to greet him upon arrival. The mission was to end with John's turning over all his followers to Christ and Christianity. Three good illustrations of this evangelism that overstepped the bounds of truthfulness are observable in the gospels and Acts.

(1) At Ephesus Paul won over John's followers by telling them that when "John baptized" he said "to the people that they should believe on him who should come after him, that is, on Jesus" (Acts 19:4b).

(2) Matthew, at approximately 85 A.D., interrupted his summarizing of Mark's and Luke's truthful portrayals of John by inserting a statement of reluctance about baptizing this one whom he is represented to have greeted

as a heavenly visitant.

> But John would have hindered him, saying, "I
> have need to be baptized of you, and you come
> to me?" But Jesus, answering, said to him,
> "Grant me now, for thus it is proper for us
> to fulfill all righteousness" (Matt. 3:14-15).

(3) One purpose leading John the Elder of Ephesus to write the Fourth Gospel was to terminate the Mandaean religion by directing all followers of John into the Christian fold. This was done through the travesty of beginning his "gospel of truth" by falsifying the mission of John through chronicling the Baptist's supposed witness to Jesus in John 1:1-40 and 3:22-30. When John first saw Jesus coming to the Jordan River, the Baptist is represented as proclaiming to the multitude, "Behold the Lamb of God who will take away the sin of the world" (John 1:29). Since the Fourth Gospel's author regarded Jesus as a visitant from Heaven, and that to subject him to baptism would have been a travesty, there is no baptism of Christ in that gospel. According to that theology, after serving his role of bearing witness to the appearance of Christ on earth, John's work was completed. He therefore is represented as turning over all his disciples to Jesus. Toward this end the final words placed on the Baptist's lips were, "He must increase, but I must decrease" (John 3:30).

The Baptist's followers saw through this scheme and became bitterly offended. However, they had no great leader who could compete with the vigor of Paul in extending Christianity. The forged tributes of the Baptist to Jesus assisted materially in extinguishing John's movement in time from the Christian world.

However, John's Mandaean religion has survived beyond the eastern periphery and lives on in Iraq and Iran, especially along the Tigris River. Eric Pace tells

how that "Ancient Mandaean Sect Thrives in Iraq" today
(New York Times, Jan. 8, 1971, p. 60). Some 40,000 adherents remain in that country, living mostly in Baghdad
and Basra. Traditionally, most Mandaeans have been gold-
smiths and silversmiths but stress on education in recent years has enabled many to become engineers, doctors,
and governmental officials. These Mandaeans continue
the bitterness of the centuries, contending that "Jesus
was a false messiah whom John baptized by mistake" after
"Jesus feigned humility."

Such is the tragic fruitage of a Pauline, Matthean,
and Johannine evangelism that by misrepresentation attempted to steal a whole religious movement and use it
to advance Christian evangelism.

CHAPTER 10

THE SPIRITUAL RELIGION OF JESUS OF NAZARETH

The Bible's tenth religion was developed by a peasant boy named Jesus. He was born to Joseph the carpenter and his wife Mary who resided in Nazareth. That small town was located in the extreme northern part of Palestine in the province called Galilee. Away from the oppressive bureaucracies that thrived in Jerusalem, remote Galilee was a place of political freedom and religious liberalism.

Observation of Jesus' developing religion begins with the earliest boyhood glimpse of him and ends at 3 P.M. on Good Friday when his public ministry came to a close with his last breath on the cross. The Synoptic Gospels indicate that this period of work was brief but intense, beginning at one Passover and ending at the next. Yet in that short time he was able to offer mankind a relatively new religion of spiritual maturity and intensity.

In approaching this tenth religion of the Bible, the matter of valid documents is important. With the four gospels at one's disposal, describing Jesus' religion would seem to be an easy task. However, the virtual opposite is true since even the earliest surviving gospel did not come into existence until at least three and a half decades after Calvary. During that prolonged period of unwritten transmission it was rather easy to lose, change, or add to the oral traditions. As a result, the gospels are sufficiently interfused with spurious statements which the early Church placed on Jesus'lips that it is not easy to tell exactly what he thought and

said on some subjects. The task is to determine which,
of inconsistent or opposing statements, represent the
actual words of Jesus. Usually, the earlier the gospel,
the more historically authentic it is.

For appraising Jesus and his religion one is de-
pendent primarily on two early sources: (1) the teachings of Jesus as recorded in the now-lost early Q
(Quelle) gospel and (2) the life of Jesus as presented
at approximately A.D. 67 in Mark's gospel. Although both
Luke and Matthew added some new material, their main
service lay in combining most of Q and Mark into complete gospels. Because of being so similar, Mark, Luke
(written at A.D. 75?), and Matthew (written at A.D. 85?)
are called the three Synoptic Gospels. The Gospel of
John (written at A.D. 100?) is so remote in both time
and veracity as to make it historically almost negligi-
ble. The present study is based on the conclusion that
the approximate per cent of authenticity is Q 100%;
Mark 95%; Luke 95%; Matthew 80%; and John 15%.

To superficial view Matthew's gospel appears to
be the best of the Synoptics. He ordinarily copied materials from the Q and Marcan gospels accurately and
more fully than did Luke. However, where Jesus conflict-
ed with Matthew's prejudices, that gospel writer felt
free to reverse, change, or remove those portions from
the Gospel. As will be seen, this tactic resulted in
Matthew's eliminating from his gospel a number of the
more important elements in Jesus' religion.

Valid information regarding Jesus' emerging religion therefore is found primarily in the Gospels of Mark
and Luke, including such portions of Q as have been salvaged by Luke and Matthew.

IN THE TEMPLE AT TWELVE

The earliest insight into Jesus' religion is gained
from Luke 2:41-51 when Joseph and Mary took him with
them at the age of twelve to observe Passover in Jerusalem. It seems inconceivable, according to the usual explanation, that these parents could have been so negli-
gent as to start home without him and not miss their
son until they had gone a day's journey on their return
trip to Nazareth.

A more careful look suggests that Jesus had become
infatuated with temple life and was determined to remain
there but was forced to return with his parents. Since
pilgrim groups reintegrated as families at meal times,
Jesus must have been with his parents at noon on the
first day out. After lunch he apparently slipped unnoticed from the company and returned to Jerusalem where
he was welcomed by the priests in his resolve to remain
with them as a temple attendant. The parents did not
miss him until at the evening meal. They suspected what
had happened and returned to Jerusalem. They expected
to find him in the temple but were "astonished" to see
him "sitting in the midst of the teachers, both hearing
them and asking them questions" and that "all who heard
him were amazed at his understanding and at his answers."

Mary reproved Jesus: "Son, why have you dealt so
with us? Behold your father and I sought you sorrowing."
Jesus replied, "How is it that you searched for me?
Didn't you understand that I must be in the things of
my Father?"

The parents shattered Jesus' hopes for a *religious*
life by making him return with them to Nazareth where
they probably were stringent as they made him "subject
to them" (Luke 2:51). Nevertheless, in spite of the virtually captive years in the carpenter shop, he continued
to dream about some form of spiritual mission.

The only other insight into the early religious development of Jesus is found in Luke's conclusion regarding the "unknown" years from twelve to thirty: "And Jesus advanced in wisdom and in stature, and in favor with God and man" (Luke 2:52). This statement indicates that Jesus developed a well-rounded religion of the fourfold life -- mental, physical, spiritual and social -- all blended into one unfolding personality.

CALLED OF GOD TO MINISTRY

At the age of thirty Jesus decided that the family members, whom he had supported since Joseph's death, were old enough to take care of themselves. He therefore concluded that the time had come for larger service. Although Jesus undoubtedly went first to the temple in Jerusalem, it affected him differently from eighteen years earlier. This time he was repulsed by its rituals and left quickly for Jericho to observe John's spectacular preaching and was much impressed.

Jesus submitted himself for baptism to John, evidently as a sinful person confessing his transgressions and wishing to have them remitted through that rite. While coming out of the water he had an overpowering religious experience as he felt the spirit of God descend upon him. It was as real as if a dove had flown down from Heaven and had alighted upon him. At the same time he seemed to hear God saying to him, "You are my loved son, I am much pleased with you" (Luke 3:22). This did not mean that Jesus was God's *only* son. In the idiom as used here, a son of God is a godly person. Jesus felt that God was pleased with the move that had been taken. This belief strengthened Jesus' resolve to spend the remainder of his life in some special religious work, but he questioned as to what exact form that service might take.

In choosing the type of ministry he would follow, Jesus' mind appears to have centered on that famed Essene "teacher of righteousness" who had made an indelible impression on the people of Palestine. Since memory of that teacher's work remained vivid after the passing of several centuries, Jesus resolved to become a second teacher of righteousness, not to a cloistered monastic group but to all humanity. Isaiah 53 provided the other pole of ministry, to accept persecution for his cause and become a suffering servant of God. With these two objectives in mind, Jesus went forth to work for higher concepts in religion.

A SIMPLE NONECCLESIASTICAL RELIGION

The religion of Jesus was very simple and informal. It was a noninstitutional faith, with none of the ceremonies and paraphernalia that usually are thought fundamental to religion. He had no place for any semblance of ecclesiasticism or the rituals and vestments commonly associated therewith. Since he believed all persons have free access to God, there was no room in his religion for intermediary priests.

Although his was an aggressive religion, it was not evangelistic in the conventional sense of making converts. He was content for his followers to remain a free association of seekers after God. He did not organize them into congregations and he had no membership lists. He drew up no catechism or creed for his devotees to repeat or master.

Jesus never asked anyone to accept him as their *personal savior.* In the Synoptic Gospels he objected to *witnessing* concerning what *he* had done for them. Rather, he asked people to tell abroad how God had transformed their lives (Luke 8:39). Jesus did not even want to be called "good" and reproved the rich ruler who so

addressed him, "Why do you call me good? None is good
except one, God" (Mark 10:18; Luke 18:19).

Jesus' only semblance of conventionality related
to the synagogue. He began his first day of ministry
in the Capernaum synagogue with startling success (Mark
1:21-34). However, when he returned to that presumed
same synagogue on a later Sabbath the authorities "took
counsel against him, how they might destroy him" (3:6).
Upon his only return to Nazareth, and speaking in that,
synagogue, the attendants

> were all filled with wrath in the synagogue
> as they heard these things; and they rose up
> and cast him forth out of the city and led
> him to the precipice of the hill on which
> their city was built, that they might throw
> him down headlong (Luke 4:28-29).

In the only other specific instance of synagogue attendance he also became involved in trouble as "the ruler of
the synagogue was moved with indignation" at him
(Luke 13:10-14).

Even though Jesus may have hoped to carry on his
work in the synagogues of Galilee, those three disheart-
ening experiences apparently caused him to conclude that
the synagogue could play no compatible part in his ongoing movement. Accordingly, his ministry thereafter was
carried on along the lakeside, in homes, in the fields,
at marketplaces, and on the hilltops -- wherever inquir-
ing listeners assembled for teaching. In stating that
"Jesus went about in all the cities and the villages
teaching in their synagogues", Matthew in 9:35 was improperly paraphrasing Mark 6:6 "And he went round the villages teaching."

Since most synagogues were controlled by scribal
Pharisaic legalists, their influence pursued and plagued
Jesus' work in virtually every community where he tried

to minister. His alienation from the synagogue reached the point that he ridiculed the long-robed scribes and called the attendants "hypocrites" and "lovers of the chief seats" (Mark 12:39; Luke 11:43; 13:15; 20:46; Matt. 23:6). He warned his disciples that they were likely to "be beaten" if they entered synagogues (Mark 13:9).

Even the institutional Sabbath came to mean little for Jesus. His disregard of the meticulous scribal regulations concerning its observance was looked upon by the religious establishment as scandalous. He never urged his disciples, or people in his audiences, to assemble together and keep the Sabbath. After the first few weeks there is no evidence that he observed the Sabbath in any manner different from other days, as all days to him became Sabbaths, days devoted fully to doing good.

All these events conspired to drive Jesus into a nonconformist ministry, away from the conventionalities that usually attach themselves to organized religion. He was left with only the unobstructed access of his soul to God, and its outworkings in individual integrity and social conduct.

JESUS AS A MAN OF PRAYER

If most of the popularly construed essential accompaniments were lacking in Jesus' religion, what then was there of value in it? It is fitting that first consideration be given to Jesus' chief resource -- the spiritual vision and power that came to him as he prayed for guidance and strength.

Luke 3:21 records that Jesus was praying when he came up out of the water at his baptism, followed by forty days of prayer in the wilderness, trying to decide what specific form of service to follow. After the first day of ministry miscarried so completely from what was

intended, this troubled sleepless teacher sought divine
guidance on this problem:

> And in the morning, a great while before day,
> he rose up and went out, and departed into a
> deserted place, and there prayed (Mark 1:35).

When his teaching ministry was menaced by unwieldy mobs,
a day or so later, he "withdrew himself into the desert
places and prayed" (Luke 5:16).

Before choosing the twelve, and delivering the
Sermon on the Mount, Jesus "went out into the mountain
to pray, and he continued all night in prayer to God"
(Luke 6:12). When he took the twelve on a retreat to
Caesarea Philippi he prepared for it by "praying apart"
(9:18). The transfiguration experience occurred when
Jesus "went up into the mountain to pray," and giving
the so-called Lord's Prayer followed a time of private
prayer (9:28-36; 11:1). His motive in cleansing the
temple on Monday of Holy Week was to restore that famed
place of worship as "a house of prayer for all the
nations" (Mark 11:17). On Maundy Thursday night he
wrestled in prayer during those fateful hours in Gethsemane (14:32-42).

Three of Jesus' recorded "last words" from the
cross were words of prayer. Concern for his crucifiers
triumphed over his death throes as he said, "Father forgive them, for they know not what they are doing" (Luke
23:34). He cried out in despair as he thought of how
God had allowed this ministry to end in such a tragic
manner (Mark 15:34), "My God, my God, why have you for-
saken me?" In those final moments, "crying out with a
loud voice," Jesus said, "'Father, into your hands I
commit my spirit,' and, having said this, he expired"
(Luke 23:46). As Jesus began his ministry with prayer at
his baptism, he fittingly ended it in the same way on
the cross.

DIRECTIVES FOR EFFECTIVE PRAYER

Since prayer was to Jesus a very demanding but most rewarding medium of spiritual experience, he gave to his followers certain directives for prayer which he had found effective (Matt. 6:5-8).

(1)   Prayer must not be for show, else it becomes valueless and offensive in the sight of both God and man.

(2)   To be most effective, prayer should be private.

And you, when you pray, go into your back
room and, having shut the door, pray to your
Father who is in secret and your Father who
sees in secret shall reward you (Matt. 6:6).

Except in his desperation on the cross, there is no evidence in the Synoptic Gospels that Jesus ever prayed in public. Even when he took the twelve, or his three most trusted disciples with him to a place of prayer, Gethsemane may be typical of his withdrawing a distance to be apart by himself. He evidently felt that real prayer can be only when the individual is alone in intimacy with God.

(3)   Prayers ought to be spontaneous. There was no place in Jesus' religion for using the prayers made by others. He felt that prayers must express the special needs of the particular moment and therefore never can be prayed again at a later date with full effectiveness. Reading the prayers of others may have beneficial effect upon one's self, but that is not praying.

(4)   Jesus regarded repetitive prayers as relatively useless. He ridiculed the synagogue prayers of his day as "vain repetition." He would have been astounded at the way these were to develop into three almost identical cycles of hour-long daily prayers, five uniform daily cycles in Islam, and the medieval Christian liturgies. What would he have said if he had known that

his supposed Lord's Prayer would succumb to the same
type of repetitive fate?

Christians speak thoughtlessly of "The Lord's Prayer" and introduce it with such statements as, "the prayer which our Lord taught us to pray." It is doubtful
if the words in Matthew 6:9-13 were spoken as a prayer
that Jesus prayed and intended his disciples or later
followers to pray. Rather, in those five verses he presented a set of directives for prayer -- a list of typical concerns to which people might address themselves in
prayer.   .

(a)   Recognition of God always fittingly comes
first in words comparable to "Our Father, you who are
in Heaven, hallowed be your name."

(b)   Thoughts about advancing God's "kingdom" by
b ringing his rule more fully into human life through
a transformed society.

(c)   The need of food for one's self and for starving humanity in days when hunger is a pressing problem.

(d)   The matter of securing God's forgiveness for
one's shortcomings and transgressions, and forgiving
others.

(e)   For strength to withstand evil in a world
where temptation is everywhere present. Instead of making God the tempter, as in the usual translation, Jesus
spoke this petition in the sense of "Let us not succumb
to temptation."

(f)   To be saved from earthquake, flood, fire, tor-
nado, theft, and a thousand other misfortunes that are
daily potential perils. This final directive encounters
the dual meaning of the Aramaic ra' (both evil and misfortune). Standard translation chooses the former "Deliver us from evil," but that virtually duplicates the
previous concern. Jesus probably intended the final
prayer suggestion to read "Deliver us from misfortune."

That this so-called Lord's Prayer is only a sample list of prayer themes is confirmed by the fact that "Deliver us from misfortune" is hardly the conclusion to a prayer. The early Church attempted to make those verses into a prayer by adding, in several late Greek manuscripts of Matthew, "for thine is the kingdom, and the power, and the glory, forever. Amen."

In addition to moments of withdrawal and worded prayers, from the Synoptic Gospels one may judge that Jesus lived every hour of every day in a prayerful mood and expected the same from his followers.

THE DAWNING OF GOD'S KINGDOM

Jesus' religion is summed up in his concept concerning the "kingdom of God." The purpose in his preaching and teaching was to bring the "kingdom" to reality and power by getting people to enter it (Mark 1:15; 9:47; Luke 4:43; 8:1; and scores of other passages).

But what exactly was the "kingdom"? At this point there is confusion because several concepts of the "kingdom" were in circulation during that day. Many people, including John the Baptist, assumed that God was about to descend from Heaven, take over the government of the world, and establish an earthly reign of righteousness with himself as king. Others, such as Matthew, believed that the "kingdom of God" would be in Heaven and they looked forward to arriving there and entering it. Although Jesus used the same phrase, "kingdom of God," he conceived of it quite differently. By that term he meant the rule of God in the lives of people, i.e., the spiritual kingship of God.

Jesus recognized that all people need to be controlled. Most individuals must be controlled from without by governments, laws, courts, police, public opinion, etc. Reliance on such outer controls tends to result

in more courts, more attorneys, more jails, and eventually a policeman on every corner. He could see that such
pyramiding of outer controls can become so costly that
societies collapse under the burden and are left both
morally and economically bankrupt. By teaching people to
live under the guidance of God, Jesus was building a
more worthy society of persons dedicated to doing what
is right. Such people have no need of police, criminal
courts, jails, or the restraining hand of government.

The importance Jesus attached to his teaching about
the "kingdom of God" is shown by making the first petition in this so-called Lord's Prayer "Your kingdom come,
your will be done on earth as it is in Heaven" (Matt.
6:10). Jesus further stressed this expectation by offering a group of parables concerning the kingdom. That
largest body of teaching material includes such titles
as the Mustard Seed, Seed Growing by Itself, Leaven,
Hidden Treasure, Pearl of Great Price, Soils, Tares, and
Dragnet. Such parables show the value of the kingdom and
how religion can best be spread, not in formal ways but
from person to person quietly by way of spiritual conta-
gion.

Matthew made a vitiating alteration in this important teaching by changing, in most instances, the "kingdom of God" as found in the Q, Marcan, and Lucan gospels, into the "Kingdom of Heaven." This change removed
the kingdom not only from earth to Heaven but also made
it to be obtainable only at death or in some future eschatological age.

By contrast, Jesus saw that the rule of God in
the lives of people was becoming an increasing reality
all about him. He therefore could say, "The kingdom of
God is in the midst of you" (Luke 17:21). What was begun
in a small way on the Capernaum lakeshore was destined
to become a great religious movement (Mark 4:26-32). The

changed persons in his audiences, and their enthusiasm
for higher modes of living, caused him to say,

> There are some of those who are standing here
> who shall in no wise taste of death until they
> see the kingdom of God come with power (Mark
> 9:1).

That is, he believed his movement for godly living would
gain such wide support that, before they die, the younger people in his audience would see this movement for
God-directed living become a tremendous power.

Permeating all Jesus' religion was this feeling
that the hope of the future lay in developing a society
of people with integrity, directed from within by godly
principles, and devoted without compulsion to the common
welfare. Of such was Jesus' much-heralded "kingdom of
God."

RESPECT AND FRIENDSHIP TOWARD FOREIGNERS

In his religious outreach Jesus gave attention to
four special problems of his day. Foremost among these
areas of concern was antiforeignism, the greatest blot
on most of the Old Testament and the religion of Jesus'
day. It was customary to scorn non-Jews in Palestine and
the peoples of other nations. The only redeeming aspect
lay in a minority strand of the Hebrew Scriptures that
recognized religious duty to "the stranger within your
gates," i.e., the foreigner traveling or living within
Israel. Jesus developed that small beginning into a major stream of religious concern, issuing forth in wholesome attitudes toward all peoples.

Of all hatreds in Jesus' day, the most virulent was
directed against the Samaritans. Jews could not forget
the Ezra-Nehemiah times when Manasseh, of Israel's high-
priestly family, married a Samaritan woman, Nikaso. When
he was pressed to divorce her, he fled with her to

the Samaritan community. To make matters worse, his
father-in-law, Sanballat, built for him on Mount Gerizim
a temple that operated in opposition to the Jerusalem
temple. As Judaism and Samaritanism became rival religions, Jews were supposed to have no contacts with
Samaritans, or even speak to them.

Jesus tried to replace that enmity with proper religious attitudes toward the Samaritan people. He did
this especially by presenting three portraits of worthy
Samaritans. First was the parable of the Good Samaritan
(Luke 10:30-37). That parable gave silent reproof to
the priest and the Levite, supposed examples of religious rectitude, for their callousness and lack of sym-
pathy as they "passed by on the other side" when they
saw the robbed man was stripped, wounded, and half dead.
By contrast, this Samaritan

> was moved by compassion, and came to him and
> bound up his wounds, pouring on oil and wine.
> And he set him on his own beast and brought
> him to an inn, and took care of him. And on
> the following day he took out two shillings
> and gave them to the host and said, "Take care
> of him, and whatever you spend more, I, when
> I return again, will repay you."

He was the Good Samaritan.

Luke 17:11-19 tells of "journeying through the borders of Samaria and Galilee" where Jesus healed a group
of ten lepers. He counseled all ten that they should
report to a priest for health certification, but only
one returned to thank Jesus for the cure.

> And one of them, when he saw that he was heal-
> ed, returned, with a loud voice glorifying
> God, and he fell upon his face at his feet,
> giving him thanks, and he was a Samaritan.

This was the Thankful Samaritan.

John 4:3-42 records the episode of Jesus sitting on the curb of Jacob's well, conversing with a Samaritan woman who was particularly keen in her perception of spiritual values. It took her only a few moments to comprehend the significance of Jesus' message. She became at once the greatest missionary Jesus ever had. "And from that city many of the Samaritans believed on him because of the word of the woman who testified." She was the Receptive Samaritan.

These three parables must have cost Jesus a considerable portion of his following as he henceforth was labeled a Samaritan lover. Even the disciples were afflicted with anti-Samaritanism, as shown when Jesus and the twelve were denied lodging in a Samaritan village. The enraged disciples asked Jesus to permit that they "bid fire to come down from Heaven and consume them." Since Jesus was amazed at such continuing antiforeignism among the twelve, he "turned and rebuked them" (Luke 9:52-55). One wishes that what was said to them might have been preserved.

Only slightly less intense than hatred for Samaritans was Galilean antipathy toward the Syrian and Phoenician neighbors to the northeast and north. Jesus delighted to get out of the hate orbit of his people by going into those foreign areas, and he was well received there.

While in the regions of Tyre and Sidon a Syrophoenician woman requested that Jesus cast the demon out of her daughter (Mark 7:24-30). He replied, "Let the children first be filled, for it is not proper to take the children's bread and throw it to the dogs." This must be understood in the sense, "How can you ask this of me when you know my people regard you as a foreign dog?" She was a clever woman and, sensing how he meant it replied, "Yes, Lord! Even the dogs under the table eat the children's crumbs."

When Jesus returned to his home town of Nazareth, went to the synagogue service and spoke, he addressed himself to what apparently was regarded by him as the greatest religious deficiency of those people, their antiforeignism (Luke 4:16-30). He declared that the religion of foreigners often was more acceptable in God's sight than worship offered by self-satisfied Israelites who were claiming to be God's only chosen people.

> There were many widows in Israel during the days of Elijah, . . . when there came a great famine over all the land, and Elijah was sent unto none of them but only to Zarephath, in the regions of Sidon, to a woman who was a widow. And there were many lepers in Israel during the time of Elisha the prophet, and none of them was cleansed, but only Naaman the Syrian.

These words, so favorable to foreigners, created a riot that broke up the synagogue service. They took him out of the village to the top of the ledge and were about to cast him over the cliff to his death. Such was the Nazareth penalty for loving foreigners.

Especially delightful was Jesus' contact with the Roman centurion who built the Capernaum synagogue and had charge of maintaining law and order in that area (Luke 7:1-10). In connection with the curing of that officer's servant Jesus said to the multitude, "I have not found such great faith, no, not in Israel." This rating of a foreigner's faith above any Jesus found in Israel undoubtedly caused great offense. Consternation must have reigned when Jesus asserted that Tyre, Sidon, and wicked Sodom would have been more responsive to his message and would fare better in the judgment day than

Capernaum, Bethsaida, and Chorazin -- the Israelite villages in which most of his teaching had been done (Luke
10:13-15).

One reason Matthew wrote his gospel was to counter-
act what he regarded as the many regrettable influences
of Jesus. Since Matthew hated foreigners, he eliminated
from his expurgated gospel such supposedly pernicious
passages as the Good Samaritan, the Thankful Samaritan,
the Responsive Samaritan, verses favoring foreigners
in the Nazareth synagogue sermon, and Jesus' reproof
of the disciples for wanting to call fire from Heaven
and destroy the Samaritan village. The story of the
Syrophoenician woman was retained because in it Jesus
ostensibly called all foreigners dogs.

Matthew was not satisfied with omitting objection-
able material. He further changed Mark's and Luke's portrait of Jesus as a friend of all people by turning him
into an ethnic bigot. This end was achieved by taking
the liberty to place on the lips of Jesus revisionary
statements that were pleasing to Matthew. For instance,
when sending the disciples out on their mission journey
Matthew had Jesus say to them,

> Go not into any way of the Gentiles, and enter
> not into any city of the Samaritans, but go
> rather to the lost sheep of the house of
> Israel (Matt. 10:5-6).

Another similar addition by Matthew occurs in 15:24,
"But he answered and said, 'I was not sent but to the
lost sheep of the house of Israel.'"

The most terrible antiforeign statement placed on
the lips of Jesus was interpolated into none other than
the Sermon on the Mount where Matthew, in 7:6, made
Jesus say,

> Give not that which is holy unto the dogs,
> nor cast your pearls before the swine, lest

perchance they trample them under their feet,
and turn and attack you.
The import of Matthew's admonition would have been well
understood in that day when Palestinians commonly expressed their hate of foreigners by calling them "dogs"
and "swine."

Jesus met head-on not only the general antiforeignism that was characteristic of his day but also the related discrimination because of national origins and
race. He regarded it as a fundamental of religion that
the people of all nations and races are one in the sight
of God, and therefore deserve respect.

CONSIDERATION FOR THE WELFARE OF WOMEN

The second major outreach in Jesus' religion was
for the welfare of women. This basic concern should be
viewed against the background of environing Judaism in
that day, a religion of men, by men, and for men. Since
most of his teaching was done away from the synagogues
and their scribal restraints, women flocked to his ministry.

It is significant that the first physical healing
attributed to Jesus was of a woman, Simon's mother-in-
law (Mark 1:29-31). Once on a Sabbath, when he noticed
a crippled woman in the congregation, Jesus interrupted
his teaching by calling this "daughter of Abraham" to
him and ministering to her infirmity (Luke 13:10-17).
Even though surrounded by multitudes, Jesus diverted
his work on three occasions that he might give attention
to the respective needs of women: Jarius' daughter, a
woman with an issue of blood, and the widow of Nain
(Mark 5:21-43; Luke 7:11-17). When on a quiet retreat
into the regions of Tyre and Sidon, Jesus was besieged
by a Greek woman who asked him to cure her epileptic
daughter (Mark 7:24-30). Again, he showed no resentment

at being disturbed, listened to her earnest plea for help, and cheerfully gave attention to her request.

Luke 7:36-50 records the chief instance where it might have been expected that Jesus would show resentment over a woman's approaches. One of the Pharisees had invited him to an evening meal and, while the guests were reclining and eating, a street woman came in uninvited

> and standing behind at his feet, weeping, she
> began to wash his feet with her tears, and
> wiped them with the hair of her head, and kis-
> sed his feet much, and anointed them with the
> ointment.

Jesus well knew how the host and other guests had been scandalized by the actions of that woman, even though repentant. Nevertheless, he took that intrusion in stride even though it may have spoiled the hope of bringing that somewhat receptive Pharisee into the movement. He responded by calmly saying to the gathering, "Her sins, which have been many, are forgiven," and to her he said, "Your faith has saved you, go in peace."

Mark 14:3-9 records a similar episode during Holy Week when Jesus was having a meal at the home of Simon the leper. A repentant street woman entered and anointed Jesus' head with "an alabaster cruse of ointment of pure liquid nard, very costly." When others at the table showed "indignation" and "murmured against her," Jesus defended the woman, saying,

> Let her alone. Why should you trouble her?
> She has wrought a good work on me. . . . She
> has done what she could . . . . Wherever the
> Gospel shall be preached . . . that also which
> this woman has done shall be spoken of as a
> memorial to her.

Jesus recognized that women were treated as under-
dogs in the society of that day. He understood how the
hardness of life tended to force disadvantaged widows
and divorced women into prostitution, and he had sym-
pathy for them. This is shown especially in John 8:1-
11 where a woman taken in the act of adultery was about
to be stoned to death. When the accusing mob tried to
force Jesus into concurring in that judgment, he said,

> "He who is without sin among you, let him cast
> the first stone at her" . . . . And they, when
> they heard it, went away one by one, . . .
> And Jesus . . . said to her, "Woman, where
> are they? Did no man condemn you?" And she
> said, "No man, Lord." And Jesus said, "Neither
> do I condemn you. Go your way. From henceforth
> sin no more."

This episode pinpointed the unfair treatment of women.
In situations such as this, where the two were caught
in the act, the man would go free with no blame while
the woman would be stoned to death.

Even the twelve disciples were outraged when they
returned from a shopping trip and found Jesus conversing
with a woman of Samaria at Jacob's well in John 4. This
episode shows how he talked freely with women and treated them as equals, even sinful women. He believed women
with moral deficiencies had more need of the Gospel than
upright women.

Luke 15:8-10 records Jesus' parable of the woman
who had lost one of her ten silver coins. He paid tribute to women's thrift and industry as he asked, "What
woman . . . does not light a lamp, and sweep the house,
and search diligently until she finds it?"

Although in the early days of his ministry Jesus
chose twelve men as disciples, women soon became a

welcomed part of the movement. The most significant no-
tation regarding them is found in Luke 8:1-3. It records
that Jesus was accompanied on a preaching tour by

> the twelve and certain women who had been
> healed of evil spirits and infirmities: Mary,
> who was called Magdalene, from whom seven de-
> mons had gone out; and Joanna, the wife of
> Chuzas, Herod's steward; and Susanna, and many
> others who ministered to them of their sub-
> stance.

Entrance of these women into the movement, and the wel-
come Jesus gave them, constituted one of the brightest
spots in his religion. The aid and encouragement supplied by them became a significant element in his ministry. On the other hand, this attending group of women
must have thrown Jesus and his disciples open to the
charge of grave immorality.

Jesus gained satisfaction from wholesome association with women, as illustrated by his delight at being
in the home of Mary, Martha, and Lazarus in Bethany
(Luke 10:38-42). He appreciated especially Mary's interest in his teaching as she "sat at the Lord's feet, and
heard his words." He did not want women to be house
slaves, and so reproved Martha for being "distracted
about much serving."

During Passion Week, when watching the procession
of worshipers placing their contributions in the temple
collection box, Jesus' admiration was attracted by a
poor widow as the ultimate example of sacrificial giving.
He was so impressed by her devotion that

> he called his disciples to him and said to
> them, "Indeed I say to you, this poor widow
> cast in more than all those who are casting
> into the treasury, for they all cast in of

their abundance, but she of her want cast in
everything which she had -- all her living"
(Mark 12:41-44).

As Jesus was taken from the judgment hall to Calvary, Luke 23:27-28 records that

a great multitude of the people followed him,
and of women who bewailed and lamented him.
Turning to them, Jesus said, "Daughters of
Jerusalem, do not weep for me, but weep for
yourselves and for your children."

The women who followed Jesus remained loyal to the
end. Although the last of the disciples had vanished
into hiding by early morning of Good Friday, "the women
who had followed with him from Galilee" were near at
the crucifixion (Luke 23:49).

Mary Magdalene and Mary the mother of John
observed where he was entombed. And when the
Sabbath was past, Mary Magdalene, and Mary
the mother of James, and Salome bought spices,
that they might come and anoint him (Mark 15:
47-16:1).

Mark 16:2-8 describes the Easter morning experiences of the three women at the empty tomb. When they
went to the eleven and told what they had seen, the disciples did not believe the reports. The women succeeded
in getting only Peter to visit the tomb, and he was puzzled (Luke 24:11-12). The Easter evening gathering, like
the Last Supper, probably was in the upper room of Mary
Magdalene's and her son Mark's house. This may indicate
that the women got the disciples out of their hiding
by Easter evening to rehearse the experiences of that
day. Even when Jesus entered the room the disciples
still "disbelieved." To save their reputation, some an-
notator evidently added the absurdity that the disciples
disbelieved "for joy" (Luke 24:41).

If the women had not stood their ground, observed the happenings from Friday to Sunday, provided an ongoing continuity, gathered the disciples together, and re-enervated them, Calvary might have marked the end of Jesus' movement and Christianity might never have come into being. The women cannot be praised too highly for the service they rendered on that strategic weekend when the eleven had decided to close up shop and quit.

Matthew was a man's man who believed women should be kept in their place, the home. As such, he deplored the attitudes Jesus had shown toward them. He therefore regarded Jesus' treatment of women as another place the record needed expurgation. To that end Matthew excluded from his gospel twelve of the more significant scenes about women described in these preceding pages. He retained only the more routine references, and usually greatly abbreviated them. By contrast, Luke, Mark, and even John deserve credit for keeping the record straight and preserving for posterity this distinctive contribution of Jesus.

Jesus suffered great criticism for his benevolent treatment of women, especially the downtrodden. Nevertheless, he continued through his teaching and daily life to stress, as an essential in religion, that women should be treated with respect as equals. He saw the world made up not of men and women, but only children of God.

APPRECIATION OF CHILDREN AND THEIR QUALITIES

The third major outreach in Jesus' religion lay in developing desirable attitudes toward children. He showed high regard for them in an age when it was almost wholly an adult's world. In a supposed "humanity," where children all too often have been but the unsought and

neglected products of lust, Jesus placed the child at
the center of attention.

Children reciprocated by following him, and were
present when the five and four thousand were fed (Matt.
14:21; 15:38). His readiness to leave the multitudes,
and on four occasions respond when the needs of children
were brought to his attention, showed his concern for
them: a "little daughter at the point of death," a supposedly dead son, the "little daughter with an unclean
spirit," and the boy with the "dumb spirit" (Mark 5:21-
43; 7:24-30; 9:14-29; Luke 7:11-17).

When the twelve disciples were arguing about which
of them was the greatest, Jesus "took a little child and
set him in the midst of them, and taking him in his arms,
he said to them,

> Whoever shall receive one of such little
> children in my name, receives me: and whoever
> receives me, receives not me but him who sent
> me (Mark 9:34-37).

Jesus' highest tribute to children is found in Mark
10:13-16.

> And they were bringing little children to him
> that he might touch them, but the disciples
> rebuked them. But when Jesus saw it, he was
> moved with indignation and said to them, "Per-
> mit the little children to come to me. Do not
> forbid them, for to such belongs the kingdom
> of God. I truly say to you, Whosoever shall
> not receive the kingdom of God as a little
> child -- he shall in no wise enter therein."
> And he took them in his arms and blessed them,
> laying his hands upon them.

On another occasion Jesus is quoted as having said,
restoring the presumed original kingdom of God,

I indeed say to you, Except you repent and
become as little children, you shall in no
wise enter into the kingdom of God. Whoever
therefore shall humble himself as this little
child, the same is the greater in the kingdom
of God . . . . See that you do not despise
one of these little ones . . . for it is the
will of your Father who is in Heaven that not
one of these little ones should perish (Matt.
18:3-14).

Children formed a large portion of the applauding
crowd when Jesus cleansed the temple:

But when the chief priests and the scribes
saw . . . the children who were shouting in
the temple and saying, "Hosanna to the son
of David," they were moved with indignation
and said to him, "Do you hear what these are
saying?" And Jesus said to them, "Yes! Did
you never read, Out of the mouths of babes
and sucklings you have perfected praise?"

That scene illustrates how children responded to
the love and admiration Jesus showed them (Matt. 21:15-
16).

Jesus delighted to observe boys and girls playing
their games in the marketplaces (Luke 7:32). In children
he saw many valuable qualities which tend to become
lost in the process of growing into adulthood: humility,
teachableness, receptivity, quickness of response, the
thrill at encountering what is new, eagerness in following the lure of accomplishment, and cheerfulness. Jesus
reminded his generation that children also are *people*,
that they have rights, and that any worthy religion must
minister meaningfully to them.

CONCERN FOR THE POOR AND NEEDY

Last in this quartet of major outreaches in Jesus' religion was his regard for the poor and needy. Here he was indebted to the Old Testament prophets, beginning with Amos, who were concerned for the welfare of all disadvantaged people, especially widows and orphans.

The text around which Jesus wove the strong social message he delivered in the Nazareth synagogue expressed his dominant purpose as ministering to the poor and downtrodden.

> The spirit of the Lord is upon me, wherefore he has anointed me to preach good news to the poor. He has sent me to proclaim release to the captives, and recovering of sight to the blind; to set at liberty those who are bruis- ed, to proclaim the acceptable year of the Lord (Luke 4:18-19).

"The acceptable year of the Lord" was *now*, the time for those overdue liberations to be brought about.

Jesus' parable of the last judgment in Matthew 25:31-46 lists ministries to the disadvantaged as the religious action that must have positive checkoff in any passport to Heaven.

> Then the King shall say to those on his right hand, "Come, you blessed of my Father, inherit the kingdom prepared for you from the founda- tion of the world: for I was hungry, and you gave me to eat; I was thirsty, and you gave me drink; I was a stranger, and you took me in; naked, and you clothed me; I was sick, and you visited me; I was in prison, and you came to me."

When the righteous reply that they recall no such ser- vices ever rendered to him, "the King shall answer . . . . 'Inasmuch as you did it to one of . . . even these least,

you did it unto me.'" According to that parable, ministries to the hungry, thirsty, homeless, naked, sick,
and imprisoned were proclaimed by Jesus as priorities in
God's sight.

The same conclusion is drawn in Jesus' parable of
the Rich Man and Lazarus (Luke 16:19-31). That man of
wealth was "living in mirth and splendor every day" in
contrast with the beggar who was "full of sores and de-
siring to be fed with the crumbs that fell from the rich
man's table." By ignoring the beggar at his gate this
rich man made himself lower than a dog, for "even the
dogs came and licked his sores." Such callous disregard
of the beggar's needs was sufficient to land the rich
man in Hades, in torment and anguish among its flames.
By contrast, the poor beggar at death "was carried away
by the angels into Abraham's bosom" in Paradise.

Jesus suggested that "When you make a dinner or
a supper, . . . invite the poor, the maimed, the lame,
the blind, and you shall be blessed; because they do
not have wherewith to pay you back, for you shall be
paid back in the resurrection of the just" (Luke 14:12-
14). This advice was driven home further by Jesus' parable of the Great Supper in Luke 14:16-24. That parable
ends with the master of the house saying

          to his servant, "Go out quickly into the
          streets and alleys of the city, and bring in
          here the poor and maimed and blind and lame."

An earnest rich man once came to Jesus and asked,
"What shall I do that I may inherit eternal life?" When
Jesus cited the Decalogue, the man said,

          "Teacher, all these things I have observed
          from my youth." And Jesus, looking upon him,
          loved him, and said to him, "You lack one
          thing -- go, sell whatever you have, and give
          to the poor, and you shall have treasure in

Heaven: and come, follow me." But his countenance fell at the saying and he went away sor-
rowful, for he was one who had great possessions.

Then Jesus looked round about, and said to
his disciples, "How hardly shall those who
have riches enter into the kingdom of God!"
And the disciples were amazed at his words.
But Jesus answered again and said to them,
. . . "It is easier for a rope to go through
a needle's eye than for a rich man to enter
into the kingdom of God" (Mark 10:17-25).

The Greek mistranslation "camel" has resulted from
the confusion of two similarly sounding Aramaic nouns.
The original reading of "rope" survives in the writings
of   Cyril   of   Alexandria,   some   Greek   manuscripts,   and
the Armenian version. The translation "rope" heightens
Jesus' literary ability by saving him from using a split
figure. While no one would try to thread a needle with
a   camel,   someone   conceivably   might   try   to   thread   a
needle with a rope.

Exegetes have tampered with this metaphor by referring it to the supposed small door, in city gates, used
by pedestrians at night when the gates are shut. Even
such mini-entrances would be too small for any camel
to shuffle through on its knees, if such were possible,
although relieved of its load. Whether "rope" or "camel,"
the element of impossibility remains unchanged. Lack
of   response   from   the   rich   convinced   Jesus   that   they
could not enter into "the kingdom of God" (the company
of God-guided individuals) since he had observed that
their wealth almost always held them back. They did not
need God or the Gospel since money was the god that supplied their material wants and they were insensitive
to spiritual needs.

Here, again, Matthew's views clashed with those of Jesus. This gospel writer scorned the poor, evidently feeling poverty was their own fault and that they deserved to live in it. To this end he felt it his duty to expunge from his gospel the parable of the Rich Man and Lazarus, the Great Supper, the Nazareth sermon, and Luke 14:12-14 urging dinner invitations to the poor and outcasts.

Jesus recognized that poverty is an eternal problem as he said, "you always have the poor with you" (Mark 14:7). Nevertheless, he felt that persistence of this ageless blot on society must not deter religious people from accepting the mandate to eliminate poverty as completely as possible.

CONDEMNATION OF ACCUMULATED WEALTH

In contrast with Jesus' respect and solicitude for the poor and needy, the other side of that coin was his concern about the wealthy. The parable of the Rich Fool tells how "a certain rich man whose ground produced plentifully" was about to pull down his barns and build larger. He said to himself,

"Soul, you have much goods laid up for many years -- take your ease, eat, drink, be merry." But God said to him, "You foolish one, this night your life will be required of you; and the things which you have accumulated -- whose shall they be?" So is he who lays up treasure for himself and is not rich toward God (Luke 12:16-21).

When Jesus was going through Jericho his attention was attracted to a rich man by the name of Zacchaeus. Jesus apparently heard the crowd hurling such jibes as "rich crook" at that short-statured man who had climbed the sycamore tree to see the passing procession. The master stopped short and invited himself to Zacchaeus' home. None of Jesus' words to that man of wealth have survived, but only the response to them.

> Zacchaeus stood and said to the Lord, "Behold,
> Lord, to the poor I will give the half of my
> wealth; and if I have wrongfully exacted any-
> thing of any person, I will restore fourfold."
> And Jesus said to him, "Today, salvation has
> come to this house" (Luke 19:1-10).

Jesus noted that people divide themselves into two types. One group is interested in pursuing material goals -- accumulation of wealth and the comforts it provides. Another portion of society is absorbed with immaterial interests -- literature, art, music, educa- tion, and religion with its social and humanitarian con- cerns. Either consciously or unconsciously, most persons cast their lot in one camp or the other. Since Jesus saw that it is almost impossible to steer a middle course between these two extremes, he concluded that

> No man can serve two masters: for either he
> will hate the one and love the other, or else
> he will hold to one and despise the other.

Then he added the words which were to become a stumbling block to the capitalistic world: "You cannot serve God and mammon" (Matt. 6:24).

The thoughts in Matthew 6:19-21 offer what might be called Jesus' summation regarding the accumulation of wealth and material goods.

> Lay not up for yourselves treasures upon the
> earth, where moth and rust consume, and where
> thieves break through and steal; but lay up
> for yourselves treasures in Heaven, where
> neither moth nor rust do consume, and where
> thieves do not break through nor steal: for

where your treasure is, there your heart will
be also.

In an age when there were for the most part only
the extremes of great wealth held by a privileged few
on the one hand and, on the other, the vast sea of
poverty in which the dispossessed multitudes lived,
Jesus was the prophet of the middle class which had not
yet emerged. He felt that a wholesome life can develop
only where the extremes of wealth and poverty are eliminated from society.

REDEEMING THE LOST SEGMENTS OF HUMANITY

Passion for seeking and saving the lost individuals and segments of society was a major objective in
Jesus' religion. That mandate was given forceful expression in the three parables of Luke 15 -- the Lost
Sheep, the Lost Coin, and the Lost Son.

What man of you, having a hundred sheep and
having lost one of them, does not leave the
ninety and nine in the wilderness, and go after the one that is lost, until he finds it?
. . . I say to you, that similarly, there
shall be more joy in Heaven over one sinner
who repents than over ninety and nine righteous persons who need no repentance (Luke 15:3-
7).

The companion parable tells how a woman who has
lost one of her ten coins rejoices when she finds it.
The overtone states that there is similar "joy in the
company of God's angels over one sinner who repents"
(Luke 15:8-10).

The parable of the Lost Son, which brings this trio
to a climax, is the story of a young man who went into
"a far country" and squandered all his inheritance "in
riotous living." After sinking into the depths of

privation and hunger, even envying the pigs the food they
ate, this wretched young man finally "came to himself"
and resolved to return home.

> But while he was yet far distant, his father
> saw him, and was moved with compassion, and
> ran, and fell on his neck, and kissed him much.
> And . . . the father said to his servants,
> "Bring forth quickly the best robe, and put
> it on him; and put a ring on his hand, and
> shoes on his feet; and bring the fatted calf,
> kill it, and let us eat and make merry; for
> this my son was dead, and is alive again; he
> was lost, and is found" (Luke 15:11-32).

The charge that Jesus received outcasts and sinners
plagued him from the earliest days of his ministry. That
scandal arose when he chose the despised taxgatherer,
Levi, as the fifth disciple and attended a banquet at
his home, with many other community outcasts who became
"followers" of Jesus (Mark 2:13-16).

> And when the scribes of the Pharisees saw that
> he was eating with the sinners and publicans,
> they said to his disciples, "How can it be
> that he eats and drinks with publicans and
> sinners?"

On another occasion

> all the publicans and sinners were drawing
> near unto him to hear him. And both the Phari-
> sees and the scribes murmured, saying, "This
> man receives sinners, and eats with them"
> (Luke 15:1-2).

By recruiting so many of his earlier followers from the
Capernaum underworld, the respectable people in that village must have turned against him.

Wherever Jesus went in Galilee his concern for outcasts scandalized the "good" people as they saw him

giving attention to prostitutes, publicans, sinners, and other riffraff of society. Since people even in that day believed individuals are known by the company they keep, few *upright* persons would have wanted to be caught in Jesus' audiences. Far less would they have allowed a son or daughter to attend the preaching of such a shady character.

Jesus paid a high price for giving so much of his attention to people of ill repute. However, he justified bringing *that element* into his movement by saying,

Those who are well have no need of a physician, but those who are ill. I came not to call the righteous, but sinners" (Mark 2:17).

Matthew in particular was embarrassed by Jesus at this point, and accordingly eliminated from his gospel the parable of the Lost Coin, the story of Zacchaeus' redemption, and the episode (Luke 15:1-2) of Jesus "receiving sinners and eating with them." He expunged even the classical parable of the Lost Son, who to him probably was the good-for-nothing son.

Ministering to the unfortunate was one of the most glorious phases of Jesus' work. He believed it is a prime duty of religion to redeem the lost segments of humanity, not basically for a distant heavenly existence but for life here and now. He found it rather futile to build costly religious structures that isolate worshipers from the world, and for like-minded *good* people to gather in them to praise God, read prayers, and sing hymns. He believed that real religion should drive one out for service to the unfortunates across the tracks, in slums, ghettos, and at all places where the downtrodden and prodigals are found. In Luke 19:10 Jesus said he "came to seek and to save those who were lost," and that is a basic task of all worthy religions.

THE MAGNA CARTA FOR THE COMMON MAN

If Jesus' teachings are like a range of mountains, the Beatitudes constitute some of the highest peaks. These imperatives to religion deal with the age-old class struggle of group against group, the haves against the have-nots. The Beatitudes may well be called "The Magna Carta for the Common Man."

To understand these "blesseds" one must realize most of the people who formed the responsive multitudes that came to Jesus' teachings were from the lower ninety per cent of society. Jesus expressed admiration for those underprivileged people as he said, "Blessed are you poor, for yours is the kingdom of God" (Luke 6:20). Since they had little financial resources on which to rely, their main hope lay in God's providence. Jesus found these needy people eager for spiritual sustenance and attentive to his message. When he said "yours is the kingdom of God" he was complimenting them on being the religious people, i.e., those who recognize the kingship of God by allowing him to rule in their lives.

Luke's second beatitude concerns the hunger that by force of circumstances these submerged poor had been made to endure. He regarded elimination of hunger as a minimum requirement of religion and said, "Blessed are you who hunger now, for you shall be filled" (Luke 6:21).

The third Beatitude Luke listed was in line with the other two: "Blessed are you who weep now, for you shall laugh" (Luke 6:21). Jesus again was talking to those ninety per cent of Palestinian people who were leading a mournful existence. He announced that there must no longer be this weeping from day to day over the hard economic blows and pressures by which they were being victimized. That rectification, as with elimination of hunger, was not to be at some future day or in Heaven but during the lifetimes of the people in his audience.

To assure that no one could escape the import of these three Beatitudes, Jesus gave them also in reverse by heaping "woes" upon all who resisted such equalitarian change.

> But woe unto you who are rich,
>> For you have received your consolation.
> Woe unto you, you who are full now,
>> For you shall hunger.
> Woe unto you who laugh now,
>> For you shall mourn and weep (Luke 6:24-25).

The strong medicine in these two verses has been ignored by Jesus' followers. Such incisive words are neither read from pulpits nor included in curriculum materials.

Matthew evidently was scandalized by these statements in the Q Gospel he was copying, in their positive (blesseds) as well as negative (woes) renditions. He therefore chose to exclude from his new gospel the three maledictions (with their "woes") and change the three Beatitudes (with their "blesseds") rather radically. As an individual of presumed wealth, he was especially offended by the first beatitude and set about to alter it completely by changing "Blessed are you poor, for yours is the kingdom of God" of the Q and Luke Gospels into "Blessed are the poor in spirit, for theirs is the Kingdom of Heaven" (Matt. 5:3).

This seemingly trivial modification entailed three major innovations. (1) While Jesus spoke directly *to* the individuals before him in his audiences, Matthew vitiated that directness by having Jesus speak *about* people. (2) Matthew changed "poor" into "the poor in spirit," i.e., the humble. Thereby Jesus' purpose in giving this Beatitude was entirely diverted. (3) While

Jesus was declaring God's favor on the poor as a *present reality*, Matthew made his "poor in spirit" to wait until a future in Heaven for their reward.

Similarly, "Blessed are you who hunger now, for you shall be filled" was changed by Matthew into "Blessed are they who hunger and thirst after righteousness, for they shall be filled" (Matt. 5:6). No one can object to "hungering and thirsting after righteousness" but that was not what Jesus said.

"Blessed are you who weep now, for you shall laugh" was diverted from the mournful daily existence of the submerged masses into the bereavement pattern at funerals as Matthew changed this Beatitude into "Blessed are those who mourn, for they shall be comforted"(Matt. 5:4).

Only Matthew copied from the Q Gospel the remaining five Beatitudes. Since they did not clash so sharply with his prejudices, he appears to have copied these correctly.

"Blessed are the meek, for they shall inherit the land" is the fourth Beatitude. By "the meek" Jesus was referring to the downtrodden who were accustomed to endure their hardships and sufferings with equanimity and without resorting to violent protest. Jesus saw that impoverished masses, aided by their higher birthrate, eventually were likely to take over the land of Palestine. He was speaking of the inevitable overturn in disparate societies when the victimized masses come up and their exploiters go down.

While the first four Beatitudes were spoken to the oppressed, the last four were addressed to the wealthy and privileged who either inadvertently or intentionally kept the ninety per cent down. In saying "Blessed are the merciful, for they shall obtain mercy" (Matt. 5:7) Jesus called on those in power to show mercy toward the inarticulate masses. Then, if a violent overturn were to occur, the new wielders of power might reciprocate by treating their former overlords mercifully.

"Blessed are the pure in heart, for they shall see God" (Matt. 5:8) likely refers to those individuals of power who have no evil designs of an exploitive nature. These people God loves especially.

"Blessed are the peacemakers, for they shall be called the sons of God" (Matt. 5:9) is not concerned with war and peace in international perspective. It applies to those who make peace between class and class, and thus prevent intergroup conflicts and violence.

"Blessed are they who have been persecuted for righteousness sake, for theirs is the kingdom of God" (Matt. 5:10) may well have reference to those overlord people who treat their subjects well. Such benevolent ones often are discriminated against and presecuted by malevolent members of the upper classes who resent any move toward weakening their strangle hold on the populace. This kind of persecution can be the most wicked of all types. As in the first Beatitudes, Jesus undoubtedly said "theirs is the kingdom of God" but Matthew changed it to "theirs is the Kingdom of Heaven." Again this gospel writer was postponing any reorienting of society until the next life in Heaven. By contrast, Jesus was encouraging such persecuted doers of right by assuring them that they were doing what God desires.

Jesus was a social and economic revolutionary. But there are two types of revolutionaries: those who devote themselves to peaceful change and those who choose the path of violence. Jesus was of the former type. He had the foresight to envision the class conflict in all its viciousness. He could see that if greater equalizing of society is not attained peacefully, and the disparity between wealth and poverty becomes too wide, violent

revolutions are likely to occur, and at much pain and
tragedy to the so-called upper classes.

Jesus enunciated his program of peaceful change by
showing that the creation of a more equitable society
is one of the essentials in religion. In this instance
he was far ahead of his time, predating Karl Marx by
almost two thousand years. If the Church had followed
these beatitude teachings, the great proletarian revolutions of Europe might have been avoided and communism
might never have been born.

FILLING FULL THE LAW AND THE PROPHETS

The charge was being brought against Jesus that
he was destroying the Scriptures. In reply he said,

    Think not that I came to destroy the law or
    the prophets: I came not to destroy but to
    fulfill (Matt. 5:17).

This common translation of that last word misses the
point of Jesus' remark. Such rendition throws one into
thinking about supposed predictions of Jesus' coming,
and that by his presence in Galilee he was "fulfilling"
them. By turning the word end for end one achieves the
meaning Jesus intended: "Think not that I came to destroy the law or the prophets: I came not to destroy
but to fill full."

Jesus used the "law and the prophets" as the foundation upon which to erect his structure of higher spiritual upreach and broadened ethical concern. Far from
destroying those Scriptures, he was extending their religious horizons. The Sermon on the Mount contains a
series of teachings that show how Jesus "filled full" or
"filled out" the Bible of his day.

The first example is the law against murder as
found in Moses' Decalogue. Jesus said,

You have heard that it was said to them of old time, "You shall not kill," and whoever kills shall be in danger of the judgment, but I say to you that everyone who is angry with his brother shall be in danger of the judgment " (Matt. 5:21-22).

Inasmuch as murder usually is the product of anger, Jesus pointed out that if people do not allow themselves to become angry, murder will not likely be within the range of possibility.

Not satisfied with this, Jesus went on to give a further expansion of the law against murder: "and whoever says to his brother *raca* shall be in danger of the council." *Raca* was an insulting term that is difficult to translate. Here Jesus expanded the murder law to include the causes of anger, in this case personal insults. By refraining from provocations which arouse anger, murder becomes even more remote.

However, Jesus proceeded to make a third expansion of the law against murder by advising that individuals should not use even mildly disparaging names such as sap, dummy, idiot, and thousands of others that are commonly used in daily speech: "and whoever says 'You fool' shall be in danger of the Gehenna of fire." Most Bibles are absurd at this point by prescribing the most severe punishment for the slightest offense by mistranslating as "Hell" or "Hell fire." Gehenna was the Jerusalem dump into which all that city's worthless refuse was cast. Punishment here was not by court "judgment," as with murder or anger that comes to blows, or even reproof by elders in the community "council." The only punishment for using such demeaning names is self-inflicted, consisting in the name-caller's reducing him or her self to worthless rubbish to the extent such names are employed. Although Jesus realized that such quips have a

concealed sting, he was more concerned over what effect
their usage has upon the person who speaks them. He
could see that uttering such seeming innocuous names
can lead to using vile names, which in turn produce anger that may lead to murder. By not starting up the ladder of violence, Jesus was assuring that those who heed
his words will never arrive at the murderous top.

By this triple expansion of the law against murder
Jesus was getting down to the roots of murder and removing them. Rather than dealing with offenses after they
have been committed, this was preventive religion which
halts undesirable trends before they eventuate in overt
acts. In this way Jesus "filled full" the Decalogue command "You shall not kill."

Another of the ten commandments drew Jesus' similar
attention in Matthew 5:27-29:

> You have heard that it was said, "You shall
> not commit adultery," but I say to you that
> everyone who looks on a woman to lust after
> her has committed adultery with her already in
> his heart.

By dealing with adultery at the source, in the
realm of thought, Jesus was removing the act of adultery
into unthreatening remoteness. He went on to say further,

> And if your right eye causes you to stumble,
> pluck it out and cast it from you, for it is
> better for you that one of your members should
> perish, and not your whole body be cast into
> Gehenna.

If a person can use the eyes only to look with lust and
animality upon a person of the opposite sex it would
be advisable to cut out the offending eye and throw it
into the rubbish heap.

The greatest area in which Jesus "filled full" the law and the prophets was in regard to attitudes toward enemies.

> You have heard that it was said, "You shall love your neighbor and hate your enemy," but I say to you, Love your enemies, and pray for those who persecute you, that you may be sons of your Father who is in Heaven, for he makes his sun to rise on the evil as well as the good, and sends rain on the unjust as well as the just.
>
> For if you love those who love you, what thanks do you have? -- for even sinners love those who love them . . . . But love your ene-mies, and do them good, . . . and your reward shall be great, and you shall be sons of the Most High, for he is kind toward the unthank-ful and the evil (Matt. 5:43-45;Luke 6:32-35).

"Love your enemies" is one of the most difficult demands Jesus made of himself and his followers, but it is im-portant, for it leads to a world of love in which enmity shall be no more.

These are only three of the many areas in which Jesus "filled full" the law and the prophets by advanc-ing religion to its frontiers of dealing with thoughts and motives. Far from destroying the Bible, as he was accused of doing, he was expanding it and filling it full. By purifying the wellsprings of thought, and giv-ing inspiration for spiritual living, Jesus found reli-gion's unique service to life.

THE FINE ART OF FORGIVING AND FORGETTING

Another way in which Jesus filled full the law and the prophets was with respect to discovering the power of forgiveness in establishing wholesome relations between person and person, as well as between God and mankind. In both instances forgiveness is the ultimate step that brings injurer and injured into harmony.

Jesus was certain that there is no problem with respect to God's part, since the deity always is ready to forgive. However, even God is powerless to forgive unless wrongdoers bring themselves into the orbit of forgiveness by taking two initiatory steps. (1) Offenders must make confession and, if possible, make restitution. (2) The person craving divine forgiveness must have a clear record with respect to having forgiven fellow persons for offenses they have committed against the petitioner.

This latter requirement was included by Jesus among the six basic prayer suggestions outlined in what is known as the Lord's Prayer. "And forgive us our trespasses as we in turn have forgiven those who have transgressed against us" (Matt. 6:12). Forgiveness is the only one of those six prayer concerns upon which Jesus elaborated:

> For if you forgive men their trespasses your
> heavenly Father will also forgive you, but
> if you do not forgive men their trespasses,
> neither will your Father forgive your trespas-
> ses" (vss. 14-15).

This two-verse elaboration on forgiveness suggests how important Jesus considered it is in religion to have a forgiving spirit.

Since God's forgiveness is always ready and waiting, Jesus could say to the repentant paralayzed man, "your sins are forgiven" (Mark 2:5, 9). In Luke 7:47-48 Jesus remarked similarly to the assembled group, concerning the repentant street woman who had washed his feet with her tears and anointed them with ointment,

"Her sins, which have been many, are forgiven;"
. . . And he said to her, "Your sins are forgiven."

Jesus had no regard for priesthoods that make a
financial monopoly out of supposedly securing divine
forgiveness for sins. When Jesus was saying in Mark 2:10
that "the son of man has authority on earth to forgive
sins" he was saying that ordinary man has that power.
In such passages Jesus used the term "son of man" in
the Old Testament sense as a poetic variant to "man";
as "sons of the prophets" was a poetic term for prophets; "sons of Israel," a poetic term for Israelites;
etc. To capitalize the S, and thereby make a supernatural Son of Man the only individual who can dispense forgiveness, misses Jesus' doctrine concerning the priesthood of all believers.

Reciprocity in forgiveness is illustrated in Jesus'
parable of the king who "made a reckoning with his servants" (Matt. 18:23-35). The parable focuses on a servant
who owed an enormous debt.

But inasmuch as he had nothing with which
to pay, his lord ordered him and his wife and
children and all that he owned be sold and
payment be made. Thereupon, the servant fell
down and implored him, saying, "Lord, have
patience with me and I will pay you all." And
the lord of that servant, being moved with
compassion, released him and forgave him the
debt.

But that servant went out and found one of
his fellow-servants who owed him a hundred
dinars (seventeen cents), and he laid hold
on him and took him by the throat, saying,
"Pay what you owe." Similarly, his fellow-
servant fell down and pled with him, saying,

"Have patience with me and I will pay you."
But he would not, and went and cast him into
prison until he should pay that which was due."
When the king learned what had happened, he summoned
the offender and said,

"You wicked servant. I forgave you all that
debt because you begged me. Should you not
also have had mercy on your fellow-servant,
even as I had mercy on you?" And the lord was
angry and delivered him to the tormentors until he should pay all that was due.

The parable of the Prodigal Son (Luke 15:11-32)
might more appropriately have been called the parable
of the Forgiving Father and the Unforgiving Son. That
father did not hesitate a moment in bestowing bountiful
forgiveness upon the repentant son and in forgetting
all the past. By contrast, the older son could neither
forgive nor forget. The ensuing happiness of the forgiving father and the forgiven son contrasts with the sulk-
ing older brother who had shut the door on forgiveness.

The question arose as to how often one should forgive.

Then Peter came and said to him, "Lord, how
often shall my brother sin against me, and
I forgive him? Until seven times?"

Peter probably expected Jesus to say something like,
"Oh, not that much. Three times will be plenty." This
lead apostle must have been taken by surprise when Jesus
replied, "I say to you, not until seven times, but until seventy and seven times" (Matt. 18:21-22). This
meant that forgiveness must be without limit. On another
occasion Jesus said,

If your brother sins, rebuke him; and if he
repents, forgive him. And if he sins against
you seven times in one day, and seven times

turns again to you, saying, "I repent;" you
shall forgive him (Luke 17:3-4).

Jesus' commitment to the way of forgiveness is evi-
denced by continuing it even to the end as two of his
four synoptic "words" from the cross were statements
of forgiveness (Luke 23:34, 42-43). According to Luke,
as Jesus looked down from the cross upon those who had
crucified and mocked him he prayed, "Father, forgive
them, for they know not what they do." In response to
the repentant criminal who cried out, "Jesus, remember
me when you come into your kingdom," Jesus assured him
of forgiveness by saying, "I indeed say to you, Today
you shall be with me in Paradise."

Matthew showed coolness to the idea of forgiveness
by not including in his gospel the parable of the Forgiving Father and the Unforgiving Son, the teaching a-
bout forgiving the same person seven times in one day,
and Jesus' two "words" of forgiveness from the cross.
Instead, Matthew inserted a section from the presumed
manual of discipline as devised by the Jerusalem church:

And if your brother sins against you, go show
him his fault between you and him alone. If
he hears you, you have gained your brother.
But if he does not hear, take with you one
or two more, that at the mouth of two or three
witnesses every word may be established. And
if he refuses to hear them, tell it to the
church, and if he refuses to hear the church
also, let him be to you as the Gentile and
the publican (Matt. 18:15-17).

This discipline statute intruded normative Palestinian practice into the Jerusalem church. It goes contrary to Jesus' teaching regarding forgiveness by reducing the options from seventy-seven, or seven in one day,

to a total of three, followed by the satanic practice of shunning the unrepentant.

By contrast, the authentic teachings of Jesus show that he regarded forgiveness as one of the master keys to the spiritual life. This was one of his unique contributions since forgiveness was a religious quality almost unknown in the Old Testament.

GEMS IN THE RELIGION OF JESUS

Scattered throughout the gospels are a number of gems that merit special attention in Jesus' religion. Most notable of these is the Golden Rule.

All things therefore whatever you would that
people should do to you, you should do likewise also to them, for this is the law and
the prophets (Matt. 7:12).

If this Golden Rule were the only prescription in religion, and it were followed, further guidelines would hardly be needed.

Another summarization of the Old Testament was made when a scribe came to Jesus and asked, "What commandment is the most important of all?" Jesus answered,

The first is, Hear, Oh Israel! The Lord our
God, the Lord is one, and you shall love the
Lord your God with all your heart, and with
all your soul, and with all your mind, and
with all your strength. The second is this,
You shall love your neighbor as yourself. There
is no other commandment greater than these
(Mark 12:28-31).

Most readers of the gospels are not aware that in this statement Jesus was quoting from the Old Testament. The first part came from Deuteronomy 6:4 which is repeated at least once in every Jewish service. The latter portion was taken from Leviticus 19:18. This also

is a masterful summarization, for if an individual has
love toward God and love toward fellow men, that person
cannot go far wrong.

   One of Jesus' most terse but yet most important
commands was, "Judge not that you be not judged" (Matt.
7:1). For the most part, Jesus' religion did not consist
in seeking out the faults of people and criticizing
(judging) them. What criticism a person indulges in,
should be spent on one's self. If sufficient attention
is given to detecting and eliminating one's own failings, usually little time is left to judge other people.
To this end he cited the parablette of the man with the
beam in his own eye, determined to remove the splinter
from his neighbor's eye. To all who spend their time
maximizing the faults of others, Jesus left as his concluding words,

   You hypocrite, remove first the beam from your
   own eye, and then you may see clearly to remove the splinter from your brother's eye"
   (Matt. 7:2-5).

   In the finest sense of the term, Jesus had a very
selfish religion. That is, he laid upon each individual
the obligation to look within and spend most time developing his or her own self, by forming attitudes that
are acceptable in the sight of God. To this end the Sermon on the Mount in particular was given by Jesus as
his program for soul culture in the spiritual realities
of life.

TROUBLESOME ISSUES OF PERFECTIONISM AND NONRESISTANCE

   While it has been valuable to determine what Jesus'
religion *was* , it is almost equally important to know
what it *was not*. For this distinction, attention should
be directed to certain mis-statements in the gospels.

One of the great illusions is that Jesus demanded
perfection. This misconception is based on two incorrect
Matthean renditions. Matthew 5:48 has Jesus say, "You
therefore shall be perfect, as your heavenly Father is
perfect." Selfevidently, it is ridiculous to say that
a human person must be perfect as God. In this instance
Matthew changed the wording he obtained from the Q Gospel. By contrast, Luke has translated correctly from
the Aramaic into the Greek: "You shall be merciful, even
as your Father is merciful" (Luke 6:36). The other erroneous statement is in Jesus' words to the rich man.
"You lack one thing" of Mark 10:21 and Luke 18:22 was
changed by Matthew (19:21) into "If you would be perfect." By these two changes Matthew has made Jesus enun-
ciate the absurdity that all who follow his religion
must be perfect. In this way Matthew gave warrant for
illusory perfectionist individuals and sects.

Striving for perfection in religion leads to a dead
end. When people come to the point of feeling that their
religion is perfect, they usually have become bigots
and have ceased to have any real religion. Jesus had
only scorn for the Pharisees' striving for perfection.
To this end he spoke his parable of the Pharisee who
boasted that he was perfect, and the humble publican
who beat his breast, realized how far he fell short of
the divine will, and prayed "God, be merciful to me,
the sinner" (Luke 18:9-14). Since Matthew lauded per-
fectionism, it is understandable why he omitted this
parable from his gospel, with his discarded chain of
other distasteful passages.

Jesus gave the Sermon on the Mount, with its vigorous principles, as a program for experimentation. While
no mortal can come within range of perfection in following the demanding calls to higher life there enunciated,
that choice body of teaching issues the challenge for

people to go as far as possible into higher realms of
spiritual living.

A second type of damage to Jesus' Gospel was inflicted by Matthew in 5:39 on the matter of nonresis-
tance. In this instance loss was incurred through incom-
plete copying by recording only "Resist not evil." That
partial statement has contributed to ivory-towered religion of aloofness that takes no part in meeting the e-
vils of the day but allows them to thrive. Fortunately
Paul, in Romans 12:21, has salvaged the lost conclusion,
"but overcome evil with good." Jesus realized that if
evil is resisted directly, one almost invariably must
resort to evil's methods to put it down, as in the case
of war. Although overcoming evil with good may be slower
in achieving results, it is the more certain method.

The attitude of Jesus toward armed might also has
been misrepresented. Luke, copying from the Q Gospel,
recorded Jesus' words as, "Do you think that I have come
to bring peace in the land? I tell you, No, but rather,
division" (Luke 12:51). This statement must be understood as not expressing his intent but stating the facts
of how families were becoming divided when some member
or members joined his movement and others set up opposition. This was an especially sore point with him since
his own family and the people of his home town of Nazareth had reacted so violently against him.

Inconceivable as it may seem, Matthew in 10:34 took
the unpardonable liberty of changing Jesus' wording
to "Think not that I came to send peace on the earth. I
came not to send peace, but a sword." By ignoring the
context, and taking these words as a simple proof-text,
militarists have seized on this statement as evidence
that Jesus supported war. When one sees how Matthew has
perverted Jesus' statement, such supposed hallowing of
violence in that passage vanishes.

Jesus' cleansing the temple also is commonly cited in justifying use of physical force, quoting John 2:15 where "he made a scourge of cords, and cast all out of the temple, both the sheep and the oxen." Even here the statement does not indicate that he used the scourge against the money-changers and sales people. The historical Synoptic Gospels make no mention of any such scourge of cords.

In spite of Luke's extreme accuracy as a researcher, a confused and manifestly spurious passage on the subject of resistance intruded itself even into his gospel in 22:35-38, probably at the hands of an interpolator. The remark occurs in a supposed conversation between Jesus and the disciples following the Last Supper.

"But now, he who has a purse, let him take it and, likewise, a wallet; and he who has none, let him sell his cloak and buy a sword." . . .

And they said, "Lord, behold, here are two swords." And he said to them, "It is enough."

This passage would indicate that Jesus was preparing to have the disciples resist with arms any mob that might come to take him.

This statement in Luke is proved false by (1) Jesus' offering no resistance to the arresting mob and (2) by his reproof of the individual who struck the high priest's servant and sliced off his ear. Jesus said to that violent one, "Put up again your sword into its place, for all they who take up the sword shall perish by the sword" (Matt. 26:52). That immortal statement should settle the matter, together with (1) Jesus' refusal to give or suggest physical resistance at any other place in the gospels and (2) in light of his special blessing invoked on the peacemakers in the Beatitudes.

As a man devoted wholly to peace, it would have been incongruous to think of him sanctioning physical

force or militarism in any form. He is rightly called
the prince of peace, since his was a religion of "Glory
to God in the highest, and on earth, peace, goodwill
toward men" (Luke 2:14).

FURTHER MISUNDERSTANDINGS OF JESUS' RELIGION

The religion of Jesus has been the victim of multiple misunderstandings which have occasioned many untrue
views regarding what he believed and taught.

What about sacraments? The medieval Church developed seven of these and Protestantism has retained two.
By contrast, Jesus had a religion without the supposed
essentials called sacraments, since sacramentalism in
all its forms was repulsive to him.

Jesus admittedly had been baptized and, as has been
observed, had obtained a significant religious experience
therefrom. However, he evidently came to regard water
baptism as rather crude. The rite came from primitive
people's paying tribute to supposed water gods that generally were believed to inhabit springs, lakes, and rivers. Immersion in the supposed purifying waters of those
aquatic deities, as in India today, has survived
through the ages.

The spurious late ending to Mark's gospel in 16:9-20
(not in early manuscripts) places on Jesus' lips the
statement (vs. 16), "He who believes and is baptized
shall be saved." The unauthenticity of this statement is
indicated by its association with the supposed warrant
Jesus gave to tongue speaking, snake handling, and ordeal by poison as tests of spirituality and truthfulness
(vss. 17-18). Contrary to Mark 16:16 and the Fourth Gospel, Jesus evidently discarded the sacrament of baptism
as a materialism that has no place in spiritual religion. It is significant that in Mark, Luke, and Matthew

neither Jesus nor his disciples are ever recorded as having baptized during his ministry.

Jesus also presumably did not intend that the Last Supper should be turned into a formal sacrament, that by partaking of a bite of bread and a swallow of wine at church services the communicant would be assured of immortality. This was too much like primitive man's belief that you become religious by what you eat. The "Last Supper" was simply an ordinary bread-and-wine meal of the Palestinian poor, made sacred by the memorable occasion and the symbolism Jesus interpreted into it. He virtually said to the disciples, "Whenever you sit down or recline to eat your bread and drink wine at your daily meals, remember this sacred hour." If the term must be used, then every meal of his followers thereafter was to be a sacrament of remembrance of Jesus and his imperatives for spreading the gospel of the higher spiritual life.

Matthew has been the offender in attributing to Jesus the founding of the Church. That Jesus never used the term church is confirmed by the fact that it never occurs in the other three gospels. Ekklesia (church) is a Greek term. Jesus spoke Aramaic. Even Matthew's gospel speaks of "church" at only two locations.

In Matthew 18:17 "church" occurs twice, apparently in a later insertion from the bylaws of the Jerusalem church:

> . . . tell it to the church, and if he refuses
> to hear the church also, let him be to you
> as the Gentile and the publican.

That whole section (vss. 15-18) runs counter to the spirit of Jesus (1) in excommunicating those who disobey the church and (2) in proclaiming the power of the priesthood, with Heaven doing only the rubberstamping and filing. This heavenly abdication to the earthly priesthood is implicit in the promise that whatever the priests "bind on earth shall be bound in Heaven" and what they "loose on earth shall be loosed in Heaven." In other words, all confessional prescriptions for forgiving sins are validated in Heaven.

The other occurrence of the word "church" in Matthew (16:17-19) is even more startling.

> And I also say to you that you are Peter (Petros) and upon this rock (petra) I will build my church, and the gates of Hades shall not prevail against it. And I will give to you the keys to the Kingdom of Heaven, and whatever you shall bind on earth shall be bound in Heaven, and whatever you shall loose on earth shall be loosed in Heaven.

Several factors militate against the authenticity of these supposed words of Jesus. (1) They are missing in Mark's gospel, which Matthew apparently was copying at this point. (2) They are missing in Luke, who also was copying Mark. (3) This advanced doctrine of the primacy of Peter and his papal successors to whom Jesus supposedly "gave the keys to the Kingdom of Heaven" represents a late development that was not yet on the ecclesiastical horizon in Jesus' day. (4) The fullblown confessional here, as in Matthew 18, also indicates church lateness. (5) If Jesus had spoken such words, they hardly would have been ignored by the entire later New Testament but probably would have been dwelt upon as perhaps the most important verse, ecclesiastically, in the Christian Scriptures. (6) The most decisive evidence against the authenticity of these two verses that boost Peter to the skies is the fact that four verses later Matthew has the authentic words of Jesus to Peter,

Get you behind me, Satan -- You are a stumbling block to me, for you do not mind the
things of God but the things of men (Matt.
16:23).

Matthew should not be held responsible for this
misrepresentation of Jesus since 16:17-19 and 18:15-18
were clearly interpolated into that gospel later, after
Catholicism was well formed. Jesus was not a churchman
and probably had no intention of creating any ecclesiastical structure. His disillusionment with the synagogue may have led him to feel that he had seen enough
of religious institutionalism. He was interested only in
helping to create a more worthy spiritual climate.

A major misunderstanding of Jesus resulted from
misconstruing the meaning of the term "son of God."
In the Synoptic Gospels "son of God" was an idomatic
designation for "a godly person." A good illustration of
this usage occurred at the foot of the cross when the
centurion saw how Jesus took his suffering and spoke
his last words. That soldier said, if translated properly, "Surely, this man was a son of God" (Mark 15:39).
Since Luke was aware that this idiomatic term already
was being misinterpreted at the time of his writing,
that gospel writer wisely and quite properly paraphrased
it as, "Certainly this was a righteous man" (Luke 23:47).
The humble synoptic Jesus did not prate himself before
people as "The Only Son of God." Rather, he devoted his
ministry to making himself and all persons into "sons
of God," i.e., into religious people (Luke 6:35;
Matt. 5:9, 45).

One of the greatest misunderstandings of Jesus consisted in believing that he was the promised Messiah who
would take over the government of Palestine and win independence from Rome. This was the great illusion
of the disciples who increasingly felt that they had

been chosen to be his cabinet officers. They came to
believe he was concealing this role from them until such
time as it would appear psychologically opportune to
make such declaration. On entering Jerusalem they concluded that the time had arrived to go public. Although
all gospels portray that event as engineered by Jesus,
Luke 19:35 appears to preserve the remnant of a variant
view, that the disciples arranged the coronation procession. That strategic verse may contain the key to the
real "triumphal entry" by indicating that the disciples
"set" Jesus on the donkey and paraded him into that capital city as king, to fulfill the Messianic prophecy
of Zechariah 9:9. By this act they unknowingly made it
inevitable that he would be crucified by the Roman government. The supposed "triumphal entry" was really the
act of betrayal on the part of all twelve disciples,
who conceived of Jesus as Messiah, and only political
Messiah.

Mark 14:62 is one of the few places where that gospel is in error as it records Jesus' supposed assertion
that he was the Messiah. This verse is shown invalid
by the other five places (Matt. 26:64; 27:11; Mark 15:2;
Luke 22:70; 23:3) where the question of Messiahship was
put to Jesus and he evidently denied it by replying,
"You say," in the sense of "That's what you say." By
insisting that he was Messiah and only Messiah, the
twelve disciples largely missed the spiritual import
of his work.

The most damaging misunderstanding of Jesus, with
respect to his teaching ministry, was the popular misconception of the multitudes that he was a healer and
only a healer. Jesus was powerless to stifle his deep
compassion that went out to all suffering people. Nevertheless, he felt that his unique ministry was to sick
souls rather than to sick bodies.

The mania for healing sidetracked Jesus' ministry even on the first day in Capernaum (Mark 1:21-34). He apparently was so distressed over what had happened that he was unable to sleep and went out to a lonely place and prayed (vs. 35). When he was found the next morning and was urged to come and give attention to the mass of ill people who had come for healing, he refused, saying, "Let us go elsewhere into the next towns that I may preach there also, for to this end I came forth" (vss. 37-38). Tragically, the same miscarrying of his ministry into the groove of healing occurred in every Galilean village that he entered.

Since the multitudes insisted on making Jesus a healer, and only a healer, the cures proved to be a parasitical growth that sucked the life out of his Galilean mission. Consequently, after about nine months, he felt compelled to write off his work in Galilee as a failure. When Jesus left he pronounced curses upon the three villages in which most of his healings had taken place.

> Woe to you, Chorazin! Woe to you, Bethsaida!
> for if the mighty works which were done in
> you had been done in Tyre and Sidon, they
> would have repented long ago, sitting in sack-
> cloth and ashes, but it shall be more toler-
> able for Tyre and Sidon in the judgment than
> for you. And you, Capernaum, shall you be ex-
> alted unto Heaven? You shall be brought down
> to Hades (Luke 10:13-15).

In light of all the work Jesus did in his Galilean ministry, it is significant that not one church was formed there.

Jesus proposed to avoid the tragedy of his Galilean mission by making a new start in the south were he hoped to devote all attention to teaching. In this resolve he was successful for, according to the Synoptic Gospels, healing never got started in Jerusalem. However, he faced the fate there of having his new teaching ministry stopped by crucifixion. Nevertheless, three days devoted to uninterrupted teaching (Monday, Tuesday, and Wednesday of Holy Week) sufficed to bring into existence a Jerusalem church, the mother church of Christendom.

When these major mistranslations and misunderstandings of Jesus are combined with the myriad of lesser false views regarding him, it gives a bewildering maze of distortions. It seems inconceivable that his person and religion could have been so tragically misconstrued. As an even greater marvel, all those erroneous conceptions continue to persist today.

JESUS AND LIFE HEREAFTER

That Jesus believed in life after death is certain. However, two questions regarding the specifics in his concept of the hereafter are not so easily determined. When does that coveted existence begin? What is the exact nature of that second life?

Here one encounters the mutually exclusive concepts of immortality and resurrection. According to immortality the individual is a dual being of body and soul. At so-called death only the body dies while the soul lives on, transported to other spheres. By contrast, resurrection assumes a unit being, with the total person dying and disintegrating at death. However, on the distant day of resurrection each person will be restored fully, as in this life.

It would appear that Jesus believed in immortality rather than resurrection. According to the immortality concept there will not be a great judgment day when all people who have lived on earth will be judged. Rather, according to that belief, the day of one's death is the day of one's individualized judgment. This immediate

resolution of the future state is implied in the parable
of the Rich Man and Lazarus in Luke 16:19-31. These two
men already were in their respective places of final
disposition: Lazarus in Abraham's bosom in Paradise and
the rich man in his "place of torment."

Transition of the immaterial person to Heaven at
the moment of physical death is implicit also in the
Transfiguration narrative which relates that Moses and
Elijah came down and conversed with Jesus on the mountaintop (Mark 9:2-13). According to that account, these
two, plus probably the other righteous ones from Old
Testament times, were thought of as enjoying an immortal
existence.

In Mark 12:24-27 Jesus refuted the belief in a resurrection of the dead.

> But as touching the dead, that they are rais-
> ed -- have you not read in the book of Moses,
> how God spoke to him at the bush, saying, "I
> am the God of Abraham, and the God of Isaac,
> and the God of Jacob?" He is not the God of
> the dead, but of the living. You do err griev-
> ously.

This statement indicates that he believed God already
had bestowed immortality upon the worthy people of past
ages. Jesus said "they shall rise from the dead" and
"they are raised" presumably in the sense that the soul
rises from the inert body at the moment of death (vss.
25,   26). In rewriting this Marcan passage Luke and
Matthew both changed Jesus from an opponent of resurrection into a supporter of it (Luke 20:35-36; Matt.
22:30-31).

Two of Jesus' "words" from the cross also indicate
that he believed in immortality rather than resurrection. Luke 23:43 records Jesus saying to the repentant
thief on the cross, "Today you shall be with me in

Paradise." He did not say, "Three days from now when
I am resurrected you shall be with me in Paradise." The
"word" in verse 46 also seems to express the immediacy
of immortality: "And Jesus, crying with a loud voice,
said, 'Father, into your hands I commit my spirit.'"
This implies Jesus felt that his soul was at the point
of returning to God at that moment.

Jesus advised people to "lay up for yourselves
treasures in Heaven" (Mark 10:21; Matt. 6:20). His only
intimation regarding the immortal state is found in Mark
12:25 where he is quoted as having said, "they neither
marry nor are given in marriage, but are as angels in
Heaven." His greatest certainty was that people who hold
the *right* theological beliefs, observe the *proper* rituals, and are *certain* of going to Heaven, are not likely
to arrive there. Conversely, he anticipated that Heaven
will be inhabited to an amazing degree by repentant
individuals who on earth had been regarded as "sinners" and the riffraff of society (Luke 14:15-24; Matt.
25:31-46).

Although Jesus believed in an immortal afterlife,
he said little about it. He was so interested in getting
people to do God's will "on earth" that he had little
time to dwell on either the nature or desirability of
a life hereafter. He apparently felt that if this life
is carried on in accordance with divine principles,
whatever afterlife there is will take care of itself. He
saw the fundamental purpose of religion as not to get
people to Heaven but to spiritualize this life by transforming it into a meaningful and sacramental heavenly
experience here and now.

RELIGION OF UPREACH, SPIRITUAL RENEWAL, AND OUTREACH

Jesus brought to full fruition the religion of Israel's prophets, sages, and humanists. He synthesized

the best elements of the Old Testament into what might
be called "the essence of Judaism." He apparently never
thought of starting a new religion but was content to
inaugurate a reform movement in the Judaism of his day.

The religion of Jesus avoided theological complexi-
ties and was very simple. It consisted in upreach toward
God, inner-reach into the self by way of spiritual renewal, and outreach toward fellow persons. This reducing
of religion to its three most elemental quests appealed
to the common people who were theologically illiterate.
This was the religion of a powerful personality who so
inspired the multitudes that on one occasion thousands
remained attentive to his teaching for three days in
a desert place (Mark 8:2).

The simplicity of Jesus' religion was observed also
in his ignoring the myriads of laws and hairsplitting
rules of conduct as devised by the Pharisees and their
scribes. In the place of such meticulous regulations
he enunciated the fundamentals of religious conduct as
contained in the Sermon on the Mount. These principles
found their summary in love to God and man, the Golden
Rule, and passion to redeem the lost segments of humanity.

In addition to being profound, yet simple, Jesus'
religion was very inclusive. He believed that women,
children, outcasts, the poor, and foreigners are part
of God's creation. This was a hard Gospel for his hear-
ers to accept. Nevertheless, he kept to his consistent
course by proclaiming friendship for all people.

Religion was demanding and took priority over all
other interests in Jesus' life and he expected that same
devotion to it among his followers. To the man fulfilling the orthodox requirement of attending synagogue
prayers daily for a year following a death in the family
Jesus said, "Leave the dead to bury their own dead, but

go and proclaim abroad the kingdom of God" (Luke 9:60). If following this higher religion was leading to broken relations with an antagonistic family, he insisted that the person continue following the spiritual gleam (Matt. 19:29). This was a religion of forward movement into ever-new spiritual frontiers, and there was no turning back: "No man, having put his hand to the plow, and looking back, is fit for the kingdom of God" (Luke 9:62).

The religion of Jesus was characterized by humility. He did not wish that any attention be attracted to himself. He took no credit for the "mighty works" that flowed from his ministry but gave all credit to God (Luke 8:39). He objected to being called "Lord" since he regarded himself as "servant."

> You know that those who are expected to rule over the nations lord it over them; and their great ones exercise authority over them. But it should not be so among you, for whoever would become great among you shall be your minister, and whoever would be first among you shall be servant of all, for the son of man also came not to be ministered unto, but to minister, . . .   (Mark 10:42-45).

This was a modest and unpretentious religion of unspectacular everyday living, a steady attempt to do God's will. The whole of the so-called Lord's Prayer was laid forth in the words, "Your will be done, as in Heaven, so on earth" (Matt. 6:10). Jesus conceived that neither himself nor his followers would be judged by the rituals they performed or by what they wore, said, professed, or believed, but only by what an individual does. The standard of measurement was "By their fruits you shall know them" (Matt. 7:16). His conclusion to the Sermon on the Mount gave his final stress on religious living (Matt. 7:24-25).

Every one therefore who hears these sayings
of mine, and does them, shall be likened unto
a wise man who built his house upon the rock;
. . .

Largely lost among the medley of misconceptions
about him, the religion of this spiritual pioneer virtually died with him on Calvary. His religion is so ethically demanding that the Church has been afraid of
it and is uncomfortable when the Gospel is read from
the pulpit. Even the so-called Apostle's Creed dodges
the life and religion of Jesus completely as it proceeds from "born of the Virgin Mary" directly to "suffered under Pontius Pilate." The fact that few sermons,
and almost no tract quotations, are devoted to the life
and synoptic words of Jesus shows that the supposed
Christian Church has little time for his religion. When
read, the Gospel is regarded as a glimpse of life in
Heaven rather than a program for spiritually transforming life here and now. By reason of this benign neglect,
the religion of Jesus remains perhaps the world's
greatest relatively untapped spiritual resource.

CHAPTER 11

PAUL'S MYSTICAL RELIGION OF THE INDWELLING CHRIST

The New Testament consists largely of the shadows cast by Jesus of Nazareth and Paul of Tarsus, two quite different personalities. While Jesus was a relatively untrained small-town young man, Paul was highly educated. Jesus spoke in everyday Aramaic to common people, but Paul used Greek philosophical terminology, with sentences that often were long and involved. In contrast with Jesus' brief public life of one year, indicated by the Synoptic Gospels, Paul's year at Antioch, three missionary journeys, and final trip to Rome covered fifteen to eighteen years. Jesus never gave himself to writing, but Paul was a prolific producer of letters. While Jesus was devoted to practical religion, which he made very simple, Paul was absorbed in theology, whose theoretical speculations could become extremely complex. In most other respects the differences between these two leaders were equally pronounced.

Thirteen New Testament epistles are ascribed to Paul: two each to the Corinthians, Thessalonians, and Timothy; and one each to the Romans, Galatians, Ephesians, Philippians, Colossians, Titus, and Philemon. Some scholars think Ephesians, at least parts of Colossians, and conceivably II Thessalonians were written by one or another of Paul's devoted followers. Without spending time on this problem, the term Pauline is employed in this chapter to include the work of both the apostle and the circle of missioners who were associated with him.

Most writings assert that Saul and Paul were his respective Jewish and Christian names. This distinction is not quite correct, for no such change took place at his conversion. Rather, Saul was his name in Hebrew and Aramaic, and Paul, his name in Greek. Except in quotations, the name Paul will be used here throughout.

In contrast with Jesus' consistency in pursuing a single goal of fostering spiritual renewal, Paul was a flighty person of varying moods, going off on a succession of tangents with their respective extremes. By reason of this inconstancy, the first half of his public life displays a succession of six different Pauls.

JEWISH SCHOLAR, VIGILANTE, CHRIST EVANGELIST

First was Paul the ultraorthodox Pharisaic Jew (Acts 22:3; 23:6; 26:5; Phil. 3:5-6). Since his brilliance in studying the Jewish Scriptures attracted attention, he was sent to Jerusalem where he was privileged to study under the great Rabbi Gamaliel (Acts 5:34; 22:3). This was the Paul who was in training to become one of the leading rabbinic theologians of that day.

Second was Paul the vigilante. This new vocation began at the death of Stephen when the student from Tarsus held the garments of those who hurled the stones. Paul "was consenting unto" Stephen's death and quickly decided that he would devote his efforts toward purging Palestine of such menacing people. A young man of action, he set himself to this chosen task with vigor as the persecutor of Jesus' followers. In this role Paul "laid waste the church, entering into every house, and dragging men and women committed them to prison" (Acts 7:58-8:3).

In making this riddance complete, Paul set out to pursue and capture the refugees who had fled for safety to neighboring countries.

But Saul, yet breathing threatening and slaughter against the disciples of the Lord, went to

the high priest and requested of him letters
to Damascus, to the synagogues, that if he
found any who were of the Way, whether men
or women, he might bring them bound to Jerusalem (Acts 9:1-2).

This was Paul, the Hitler of that day, who concluded
that everything connected with Jesus and his followers
was bad, that those people had to be exterminated, and
that he was God's divinely appointed agent to accomplish
that achievement.

Paul the vigilante persecutor of "the Way" came
to a sudden halt on the Damascus road with advent of
the third Paul, evangelist for the immortal Christ. According to Acts 9:3-5 this zealot was certain that he
had been struck down by the heavenly Christ who said,
"Saul, Saul, why do you persecute me?" Three days of
psychic blindness followed, after which Ananias brought
about Paul's baptism (9:6-19). This was conversion in
its most sudden and dramatic form, bringing an almost
instantaneous and complete reversal of goals. After some
days of instruction, Paul threw himself into proclaiming
Jesus as "the Son of God" with as much vigor as he previously had opposed the followers of Jesus. In the synagogues of Damascus this neophyte carried on such a
whirlwind mininstry that he became at once the spectacular apostle of the Christ (9:19-22).

FLIGHT INTO ARABIA FOR THREE YEARS

The outraged orthodox Jews of Damascus quickly
formed a plot to kill the new apostle, and this became
known to him. To save his life, Paul's newly formed
friends "took him by night, and let him down through the
wall, lowering him in a basket" (Acts 9:23-25; II Cor.
11:32-33). Acts does not say where this new convert fled
on that fateful night, but Galatians 1:17-18 gives the

answer. Although the clauses are a bit confused, Paul
apparently meant to say that he "went away into Arabia"
and stayed there "three years" before returning through
Damascus on his way to Jerusalem. Regrettably, no information is found in the entire New Testament as to
how or exactly where that time in Arabia was spent.
Until recently, those three years have been shrouded
in mystery.

Discovery of the Dead Sea Scrolls, and excavation
of the Essene monastery at Qumran, in the mid-twentieth
century have cast new light on those lost years. When
the Essenes were driven from Qumran they fled to the
regions of Damascus. Attention becomes focused on that
Essene monastery which in Paul's time was located in
the Arabian Desert. A document from that Essene monastery has been published by R.H. Charles, *Apocrypha and
Pseudepigrapha*, Vol. II, *Pseudepigrapha* , 1913, pp. 785-
834. That Damascus Fragment tells how these refugees
"went forth out of the land of Judah and sojourned in
the land of Damascus" (8:6, p. 812).

It now appears likely that when Paul fled from
Damascus "into Arabia," he escaped to that Essene monastery, where he found refuge and remained for three
years. The length of his stay there may be significant.
Three years was the probationary period in Essene monasteries. This means that Paul stayed the time limit as
a probationist. Why did he remain until the end of that
period and then leave?

When the deadline for choice drew near, Paul may
have felt that he could not become a permanent member
of the movement, and therefore may have withdrawn volun-
tarily from the monastery. Against this option is the
probability that, if he had disliked Essene life, he
likely would not have remained with those monks for such
an extensive period of time as the full three years.

His stay for the entire length of the probationary period would suggest that, when Paul became a candidate for full membership, he was blackballed. Since he was an extremely aggressive person, who had to be first in any movement of which he was a part, the other monastics probably looked upon him as a discordant person who was disrupting their placid manner of life. He probably resented this rejection, which may account for his never giving any details regarding those three years, except that he spent them "in Arabia." This presumed expulsion supposedly was the end of the fourth Paul -- Paul the Essene novitiate.

However, this was by no means the end of Paul, the Essene. The three years of Essenic indoctrination overshadowed the short period of instruction in Jesus' religion previously given by Ananias in Damascus. Chief evidence for Paul's having spent those years in that monastery is found in the number of distinctive Essene words that became woven into Paul's theology -- terms and concepts not found in the religion of Jesus. Comparison of Paul's letters with the Damascus Fragment and the Dead Sea Scrolls shows that he had become saturated with Essene perspectives that became a permanent part of his religious outlook.

PAUL'S ATTEMPTED TAKEOVER OF THE JERUSALEM CHURCH

Since Paul must have feared that the assassination plot against him in Damascus would be revived, he did not stop in that city on returning to the outside world. He rushed on to Jerusalem where he hoped to win support of the parent church to his apostleship. This was the fifth Paul -- Paul the aspiring leader of the Jerusalem church.

The account of that visit is referred to with amazing terseness in Galatians 1:18-19. Upon arrival in

Jerusalem he went to confer with Peter, who in Acts and
Paul's letters goes under three different designations.
Simon was his real name. Peter ("rock" in Greek) and
Cephas ("rock" in Aramaic) were titles conferred on him.
Strange as it may seem, that chief of the apostles virtually imprisoned this guest for the fifteen days of
his stay in that city. Paul was not allowed to see any
members of the Jerusalem church except James, the brother of Jesus. Paul must have been outraged by this inhospitable treatment which he received from pillars of the
Jerusalem church.

The account in Acts of that reception, unfortunately, has been confused with a later trip. The portion
applying to this first postconversion arrival in Jerus-
lem is presumably:

> And when he was come to Jerusalem, he attempt-
> ed to join himself to the disciples; but they
> were all afraid of him, not believing that
> he was a disciple

and "they brought him down to Caesarea and sent him
forth to Tarsus" (Acts 9:26, 30).

If it is true that Paul had been at the Essene monastery for the previous three years, he likely was immersed in Essenic theology and freely dispensed this to
his Jerusalem hosts. Probably because Peter and James
did not trust his gospel, they muzzled Paul by not allowing him to reveal his subversive doctrines to any
other member of the Jerusalem church.

It is regrettable that nothing has survived concerning the conversations that went on between those
three church leaders during those fifteen days. Only
slight intimations are observable in Acts and Galatians
regarding the tumultuous conflicts of that historic
fortnight. Paul probably came to Jerusalem with the
intent of taking control in that area. However, Peter

and James did not choose to surrender their leadership
of the apostles and the Jerusalem church. These two officials not only rejected Paul but also appear to have
sent him home with the admonition that he refrain from
any further ministry in the name of Jesus.

Paul must have returned to Tarsus a completely
crushed man, and likely remained in that condition for
some years. The only time-key is the "fourteen years" in
Galatians 2:1 (presumably reckoned from his conversion):
three, in Arabia; eight, in seclusion at Tarsus; one,
at Antioch; and two, on his first missionary journey.
General statements that are supposed to suggest preaching during the eight silent years appear baseless, for
there is no specific evidence that Paul founded any
church during those years in Syria, Cilicia, or even
in his home city of Tarsus. This was the sixth Paul --
the Paul who was depressed, inactive, and silent for
at least eight years.

The radical changeableness displayed in these six
Pauls makes it questionable whether an unstable person
of such fits, starts, and eventual collapse, could have
been capable of being a valid channel for the divine
spirit and a competent Christian interpreter.

THE REACTIVATED PAUL OF THE MISSIONARY JOURNEYS

Advent of the seventh Paul occurred in A.D. 46 when
Barnabas was sent by the Jerusalem church to Antioch
of Syria for the purpose of investigating developments
that were occurring in the church at that place. Upon
arrival in Antioch, Barnabas recalled the story of that
earlier man from this north country who supposedly had
been converted but had been discredited by the Church
and had been sent back to his home in Tarsus. Barnabas
decided that he would cross the bay to Tarsus and see
if he could find Paul.

The search was successful. Barnabas apparently was
impressed with Paul and his account of how he had been
mistreated and silenced by Peter and James. Barnabas
concluded that this convert could be of service to the
Church and persuaded Paul to return with him to Antioch.

> And it came to pass that even for a whole year
> they were gathered together with the church,
> and taught many people, and that the disciples
> were called Christians first in Antioch (Acts
> 11:25-26).

It may be guessed that Paul's Essenic theology,
plus the news spreading from Jerusalem about Peter's
and James' antagonism toward him, gradually eroded the
initial flash of his ministry in Antioch. By the end
of that year it appears that both Paul and Barnabas had
become discordant elements among the leadership of that
church. The congregation therefore seems to have sought
at least temporary relief by having these two controversial men take to Jerusalem the money raised for Palestinian famine relief (Acts 11:27-30). The Antioch leaders may have hoped that Peter and James would administer
to Paul the correctives which they felt he needed.

The record of this second postconversion trip of
Paul to Jerusalem unfortunately has been displaced from
chapter 12 back into chapter 9. Upon arrival in Jerusalem Paul and Barnabas apparently found Peter, James,
and all the disciples as antagonistic toward him as the
two leaders had been on the first visit.

This time the bad reception was salvaged by Barnabas who

> took him and brought him to the apostles, and
> declared to them how he had seen the Lord in
> the way, and that he had spoken to him, and
> how he had preached boldly in the name of
> Jesus at Damascus (Acts 9:27).

It is notable that Barnabas did not mention any preaching by Paul in Syria, Cilicia, Tarsus, or even Antioch
but only at Damascus, immediately after his conversion.
In time Paul was allowed to speak in public:

> And he was with them, going in and going out
> at Jerusalem, preaching boldly in the name
> of the Lord. And he spoke and disputed a-
> gainst the Hellenistic Jews, but they were
> seeking to kill him (Acts 9:28-29).

This emerging death plot probably caused that pair of
visiting apostles to leave more quickly for Antioch than
had been planned (12:25).

Paul likely became inflated somewhat by the new
prestige he had gained in Jerusalem and, upon returning,
became even more offensive to the other church leaders
in Antioch. Therefore, it was decided that Paul, and
his supporter Barnabas, had better leave for other
fields. However, this discord was wreathed in seemingly
innocuous theological language and procedures.

> Now there were prophets and teachers at Anti-
> och, in the church that was there: Barnabas,
> and Symeon who was called Niger, and Lucius of
> Cyrene, and Manaen the foster brother of Herod
> the tetrarch, and Saul. And as they ministered
> to the Lord, and fasted, the Holy Spirit said,
> "Separate for me Barnabas and Saul for the
> work whereunto I have called them." Then, when
> they had fasted and prayed and laid their
> hands on them, they sent them away (Acts 13:1-
> 3).

Although Paul had a successful first journey, upon
returning to Antioch he found himself in conflict with
delegates from Jerusalem who demanded full law observance. This controversy ended in "no small dissension
and questioning with them" (Acts 15:2). It therefore was

advised that Paul and Barnabas go to Jerusalem, to the
mother church, and get this matter settled. That strategy resulted in the Jerusalem conference, essentially the
first ecumenical council of the Christian Church, as
described in Acts 15.

In delivering the opening address, Peter claimed
credit for having begun mission to the Gentiles (Acts
15:7-11). That assertion irked Paul who insisted that he
himself had been entrusted by Christ with the "gospel
of the uncircumcision" as Peter was with the "gospel
of the circumcision" (Gal. 2:7). Since the Acts 15 report of that meeting records statements only by Peter
and James, it is likely that Paul was slighted and that
he resented such treatment. In his own account of those
Jerusalem deliberations Paul was insolent by referring
to these leaders as "those who were reputed to be pillars" of the church, and stating that "those who were
reputed to be something . . . imparted to me nothing"
(Gal. 2:9, 6).

After that conference Peter evidently followed Paul
to Antioch, to straighten out the situation there himself. At Antioch Paul accused Peter of hypocrisy -- having a double standard, according to whether he was with
Jewish or Gentile Christians. "But when Cephas came to
Antioch, I resisted him to the face, because he stood
condemned." On that occasion even Barnabas sided with
Peter (Gal. 2:11-13). Paul's antipathy toward Mark
brought the final break with Barnabas, Paul's only
strong support during those tumultuous years (Acts
15:37-40).

THE BATTLE OF THE APOSTLESHIPS

In contrast with Peter and other church leaders,
who had been privileged to have direct contacts with the
historical Jesus, Paul found himself pressed down into

an inferior status. At the ill-fated meeting in Jerusalem, following the "three years in Arabia," Peter and James presumably had attempted to supply this recent convert with information regarding the life and teaching of Jesus, which they assumed Paul needed in order to become a proper interpreter of the Gospel. To all such supposed informative sessions, during those fifteen days, Paul apparently had lent only a deaf ear. Why should he, the trained theologian, pay attention to the words of an illiterate fisherman?

Paul countered with vigor by asserting that he had been entrusted with an apostleship that was superior to theirs. Peter and James may have seen and heard the historical Jesus, but Paul had an apostleship to which he had been commissioned directly by the heavenly Christ on the Damascus Road.

To Paul the Christian story began not at a manger in Bethlehem but at the cross when, through sacrificial death, God's Son was exalted by the Father to become the immortal Christ. According to this view, all that went before Calvary (the life of the historical Jesus and his Gospel) was of no consequence -- actually an impediment to the real gospel, Paul's gospel (II Cor.5:16).

Paul was interested only in what he considered the dynamic present -- the influence of the immortal Christ as manifested in the supposed continuing day-by-day communications Christ was issuing to his followers. Since Paul prized himself as the recipient and dispenser of such revelations, he felt certain that he had been entrusted with the only true apostleship. Whatever status the other leaders had enjoyed for a time was now superceded by him.

This insistence landed Paul in a head-on collision with the Jerusalem church. In the light of this ever-widening rift, Paul eventually gave up the Palestinian

segment as virtually lost to what he considered valid
religion. This gulf divided the movement that had begun
in Galilee into the Syria-Palestine-Egypt orbit against
the Asia Minor-Greece-Rome orbit.

Challenge to the validity of his apostleship continued to plague Paul throughout his mission endeavors.
One of his greatest opponents was Apollos, a brilliant
young man from the church center of Alexandria in Egypt,
"a learned man" who "was mighty in the Scriptures." He
founded the Ephesian church and, in Corinth, attacked
Paul's theology by proclaiming the inadequacy of those
who, converted by him, "had believed through grace."
Apollos

> had been instructed in the way of the Lord
> and, being fervent in spirit, he spoke and
> taught accurately the things concerning Jesus
> (Acts 18:24-28).

Paul never had the courage to face Apollos, but
attempted to nullify his influence by writing epistles.
Although this ominous rival is referred to by name seven
times in I Corinthians, sprinkled through the whole Corinthian correspondence are unlabeled barbs and jibes
directed against this eloquent evangelist and his followers. The three chapters of II Corinthians 10 to 12
were devoted especially to condemning those opponents.
He regarded Apollos as a false apostle who was "corrupt-
ing the word of God" (2:17). Apollos felt the same way
about Paul.

Paul used varying techniques in trying to defeat
his critics. At times he worked on their sympathies,
by resorting to self-depreciation, hoping thereby to
shame his critics into supporting his apostleship:

> For I am the least of the apostles, who am not worthy
> to be called an apostle . . . . who am less than the
> least of all the saints (I Cor. 15:9; Eph. 3:8).

Then again, he took the opposite tack of asserting the
superiority of his apostolate and disparaging his com-
petitors.

> For I reckon that I am not a bit behind the
> very chiefest apostles. . . . For such men
> are false apostles, deceitful workers, fash-
> ioning themselves into apostles of Christ.
> . . . . Are they ministers of Christ?. . .
> I more; . . . for in nothing was I behind the
> very chiefest apostles (II Cor. 11:5, 13, 23;
> 12:11).

Because Paul was so unreceptive to others, so vigorous in pressing his views, and so bent on excelling,
he invariably found himself embroiled in controversy. He
knew that if he were to visit Corinth, his presence
there would erupt into "strife, jealousy, wraths, fac-
tions, backbitings, whisperings, boastings, tumults"
(II Cor. 12:20).

As a headstrong individualist who knew no compro-
mise, Paul's overweening ambition made it difficult for
him to cooperate even with other workers. He eventually
cast aspersions on all his associates except Timothy,
whom he cited as the only one who was completely loyal:

> For I have no man likeminded, who will care
> truly for your state, for they all seek their
> own, not the things of Jesus Christ (Phil.2:20-
> 21).

Paul was determined to save the new Greek churches
from the supposed pernicious influences, so disparaged
by him, which were emanating from the Palestinian sector. He seized an important advanced position in this
skirmish by blanketing the mission world with his avalanche of correspondence. Largely through this writing
of letters, Paul finally won the battle of the apostle-
ships. Through the succession of disruptive confrontations,

from the Damascus road and onward, Paul's religion became forged out on the anvil of controversy.

THE FIVE-STEP PATHWAY TO SALVATION

In contrast with the multipurpose religion of Jesus,
Paul's religion had only one objective -- getting people to Heaven. Toward this end he devised three distinctive paths to salvation, possibly not realizing that
they were mutually exclusive.

Paul's more rigid theological structure rested on
the foundation of predestination. He concluded that all
things relating to Christianity had been predetermined
and "foreordained before the ages unto our glory"
(I Cor. 2:7). "For those whom he foreknew he also foreordained to be conformed to the image of his Son"
(Rom. 8:29). God

> chose us in him before the foundation of the
> world: . . . having foreordained us unto a-
> doption as sons through Jesus Christ unto him-
> self, according to the good pleasure of his
> will, . . . having been foreordained accord-
> ing to the purpose of him who works all things
> according to the counsel of his will(Eph.1:4-5,
> 11).

Focus was on those individuals whose names had been
placed by God on his list of persons who are predestined
for salvation -- the list he made out before the world
was created.

Such predestinarian belief is the basis for Paul's
doctrine of human inability, that no person of himself
or herself can choose to embark on the pathway to salvation. According to this theory, if an individual's name
is not on that list, nothing can be done to get it on.
On the other hand, if a person's name is included, God

will direct that man's or woman's life in such a way
that they cannot get off the list.

As the second step, all who have been predestined
from before the world began must be "called" by God to
that salvation. In this religion of divine initiative
only God can "call" people "into the fellowship of his
Son Jesus Christ our Lord" (I Cor. 1:9). As on the
Damascus road Paul was "called to be an apostle," he
went on to say, "you also are called to be Jesus
Christ's (Rom. 1:1, 6). Paul asserted that those whom
God "foreordained, them he also called" (Rom. 8:30).
The importance of being "called" is illustrated_ by
I Corinthians 7:18-24, where the term "called" occurs
seven times in the course of seven verses.

The company of those who have been "foreordained"
and "called" are designated by Paul as "the elect," i.e.,
those who have been elected to salvation. These are
"God's elect, holy and beloved" (Col. 3:12). Paul gave
his life for the elect:

> Therefore I endure all things for the elect's
> sake, that they also may obtain the salvation
> which is in Christ Jesus with eternal glory"
> (II Tim. 2:10).

After the individual has been predestined, called,
and elected, the fourth stage on that path toward salvation is termed sanctification. "God chose you from the
beginning unto salvation in sactification of the Spirit"
(II Thess. 2:13). Being "sanctified by the Holy Spirit"
(Rom 15:16) is the condition of holy sinlessness, the
state of being exempt from temptations, sin, and all
carnality. Paul's first letter to the Corinthians (1:2)
was addressed to "those who are sanctified in Christ
Jesus, called to be saints." Paul's great concern was
that his followers be in that state of sanctification
(I Cor. 1:30; 6:11; I Thess. 4:3-4; II Tim. 2:21). These

sanctified people were commonly referred to by this
apostle as the "saints."

This succession led to the fifth stage, the ultimate of perfection. Paul felt that God's power was made
perfect in him (II Cor. 12:9). This apostle began his
Corinthian correspondence by urging perfection and ended
it by praying for "their perfecting" (I Cor. 1:10;
II Cor. 13:9, 11). To the Thessalonians Paul expressed
concern that he might "perfect that which is lacking
in your faith" (I Thess. 3:10). He was trying to unite
the Colossians in the "bond of perfectness" (Col. 3:14).
His letter to the Philippians holds up perfection as
the ideal toward which to strive, Ephesians was written
"for the perfecting of the saints," and Romans declares
the "perfect will of God" (Phil. 3:12; Eph. 4:12;
Rom. 12:2). Since its members were sanctified unto perfection, the Church itself was conceived of as "glorious,
not having spot or wrinkle or any such thing; but that
it should be holy and without blemish" and "unreprov-
able" (Eph. 5:27; Col. 1:22).

JUSTIFICATION BY FAITH, GRACE, AND BELIEVING

In Paul's more thoughtful moments he must have
questioned the validity of his cherished five stages
of salvation that rested on predestination. If that system were true, God would have sole jurisdiction in dis-
pensing salvation and there would have been no point in
Paul's widespread missionary endeavors of enlisting converts to Christianity. Under such criteria, Christian
evangelism might even be construed as going against
God's will by getting into the Church people God does
not want to be in it.

To escape this anomaly, Paul developed a variant
theology in which the achievement of salvation is the
product of human initiative so that every person may

pursue it. According to this approach, faith in Christ became the credential for obtaining salvation. That concept of "justification by faith" became a favorite alternative doctrine in Paul's arsenal of theological beliefs.

The letter to the Romans, in chapters 3 to 5, gives the most definitive treatment of his justification theme. Paul began with "the promise to Abraham . . . that he should be heir of the world, but through the righteousness of faith." Since he "did not waver through unbelief, but grew strong through faith, . . . it was reckoned unto him for righteousness" (Rom. 4:13, 20-22; cf. Gal. 3:6-22). When Paul was in this theological mood, he could find no other justification than through faith. He accordingly could write,

> We reckon therefore that a man is justified
> by faith . . . . God is one, and he shall
> justify the circumcision through faith and
> the uncircumcision through faith. . . . Being
> therefore justified by faith, we have peace
> with God through our Lord Jesus Christ (Rom.
> 3:28-30; 5:1).
> The righteous shall live by faith; . . . that
> we may be justified by faith (Gal. 3:11, 24).

However, Paul's subconscious belief in human inability again intervened by suggesting that justification by faith, of itself, would not be sufficient to obtain salvation. Even the most mature faith could not be effective unless supplemented by that strange divine contributory which Paul called grace (Rom. 3:24). Since he came to regard this additive as the indispensable ultimate in achieving salvation, it is understandable how this concept of grace meant so much to Paul.

According to this apostle, grace is a benevolent willingness on the part of deity to give something

344 The Twelve Religions of the Bible

extremely valuable to believers without anything approaching full deservingness on their part or ability to render any compensation that might even begin to approach adequacy. Since grace is a free gift which is bestowed individually upon the justified person (Rom.5:15; Eph. 3:7), Paul could write to the Corinthians "of the exceeding grace of God in you" and could conclude with, "Thanks be to God for his unspeakable gift" (II Cor. 9:14-15). The climaxing statement regarding grace is in Ephesians 2:8: "For by grace you have been saved through faith, and that not of yourselves -- it is the gift of God." Paul was not clear as to the origin of grace. Usually it is ascribed to God, but often to Christ, and sometimes to both.

Occasionally Paul seems to have abandoned completely his elaborate five-rung ladder of salvation that rested on a base of predestination as well as his other path through justification by faith and God's awarding salvation through the gift of grace. Sometimes he made it extremely easy and quick to obtain salvation. The ultimate is found in Romans 10:9 and 13 where it is stated that

> if you will confess Jesus as Lord with your
> mouth, and shall believe in your heart that
> God raised him from the dead, you shall be
> saved

and

> Whoever shall call upon the name of the Lord
> shall be saved.

Little wonder that this is the favorite passage of Paulists in all ages on this subject! Upon hearing the message and expressing belief, one who has never even heard of Jesus before can be assured of eternal salvation in a few moments of time, without waiting for baptism, good ideas, gift of the Holy Spirit, grace, or anything else.

Such is the message of salvation, reduced to its most simplistic form.

At other times Paul slipped back into his Jewish groove by making provision for salvation through law observance as he stated that "the doers of the law shall be justified" (Rom. 2:13).

AVOIDANCE OF JESUS' RELIGION

The basic concepts which formed the foundation of Paul's most distinctive systems of salvation were completely absent from the thought of Jesus. This divergence is shown by the Synoptic Gospels (Matthew, Mark and Luke) where one never encounters on the lips of Jesus the words, in their varied forms, which Paul found so precious: foreknew, foreordained, predestined, called of God, elected, justification, sanctification, adoption, saints, covenant, perfected, and grace. For example, this favorite term "grace" occurs 102 times in the Pauline sector but was never used by Jesus in the Synoptic Gospels. Even the pivotal word "believe," in Paul's third system of salvation, was never used by Jesus in that sense.

Three other theological terms also were Pauline favorites. Each of these is ascribed to Jesus only once in the Synoptic Gospels, but in each instance there are reservations. Jesus' only use of the term "salvation" was in speaking to Zacchaeus. There, however, the designation does not refer, in the Pauline sense, to a next life but to Zacchaeus' being saved for constructive living in his community (Luke 19:9).

In chapter 10 it was shown that "perfection," so loved by Paul, never was commanded by Jesus except in Matthew's mistranslating as "be perfect" what Luke renders properly as "be merciful" (Matt. 5:48 cf. Luke 6:36).

Third in this subsidiary trilogy of favorite words was "redemption." While Paul made extensive use of the Old Testament words "redeem" and "redemption," employment of this term is attributed to Jesus only in Luke 21:28, part of a dubious apocalypse which probably was inserted into that gospel at a later date.

How could Paul conceive that the vocabulary used by the revealing heavenly Christ should have been so different from the words which the incarnate Christ, according to Pauline theology, used while on earth? These sharp contrasts as to fundamentals indicate that Paul's religion was almost wholly at variance with the religion of Jesus as they moved in different theological worlds.

Perhaps the greatest divergence between Jesus and Paul lay in the availability of what each had to offer. The spirit of Jesus was that whosoever will may come and partake of the water of life freely. His objective was to transform all life by having it lived in harmony with God's spirit. Jesus envisioned all people becoming "sons of God," i.e., godly individuals.

By contrast, in his two standard systems Paul considered the granting of salvation an extremely selective matter. On the pathway of foreordination, salvation is possible only for the spiritual aristocracy God has predestined to receive it. When thinking in terms of grace, Paul felt that this priceless gift would be bestowed only upon the relatively few people whom God chooses individually to grant his special grace, "a remnant according to the election of grace" (Rom. 11:5). Paul's other extreme, making achievement of salvation so easy that it can be obtained in a moment of conversion and declaration, contrasts with Jesus' program of lifetime spiritual culture as laid out in the Sermon on the Mount.

Although faith was the foundation of Jesus' religion, it was not faith in himself but in God. Paul shifted the object of faith from God to the immortal Christ. Another great difference lay in what faith accomplishes. To Jesus, faith in God was the means by which a person is transformed into physical and spiritual wholeness. By contrast, Paul regarded faith and belief in Christ as the means of getting believers into a Christian Heaven.

Where did Paul pick up his collection of favorite concepts and basic theological terms that were so foreign to the ideas and words of Jesus? One finds a considerable portion of the answer in the Damascus Document and the Dead Sea Scrolls, particularly the Psalms of Thanksgiving and the Manual of Discipline. Those scrolls that were sectarian in nature abound in the use of Paul's key concepts and subsidiary terms. His system of salvation therefore appears not to be Christian but basically an Essenic brand of Old Testament theology. Even though the year spent in the church at Antioch may have modified his views somewhat, the basic perspectives of Paul, to the end of his life, remained Essenic rather than from the teachings and religion of Jesus. The divergences show that Paul was like a comet, moving ever farther out into theological space, away from the historical Jesus and his religion.

From Peter, James, and the Jerusalem church, more of Jesus' religion percolated into Pauline thought than he would have admitted. However, his general ignorance concerning the life and teachings of the historical Jesus, refusal even to hear anything pertaining thereto, and almost fanatical opposition to all that savored of the Gospel, raise the question whether it was possible, with such serious handicaps, for Paul to be a reliable guide. This apostle also was lacking in many qualities which made Jesus' life and religion the epitome

of spiritual achievement. All these disabilities should
be borne in mind in appraising Paul's theological system.

CHRIST, CREATOR OF THE WORLD AND DIRECTOR OF HISTORY

When in his advanced Christological mood, Paul
traced the origins of his supernatural Christ back to
the beginning of time, to the primeval mythological age
in polytheistic antiquity. Then, it was believed that
male and female gods married and were given in marriage
as they procreated and gave birth to sons and daughters.
Paul accordingly grafted into Christianity the sexual
concept that Christ is God's Son, his only Son, and this
has continued as a basic belief in the Church.

Shortly after Christ was begotten, God handed over
all dominion and authority to his Son. This newly empowered Christ at once seized the initiative by performing
the first great act of his administration -- creating
the universe and everything in it. The most complete
description of Christ's origin and early acts is found
in Colossians 1:13-17, where he is portrayed as

the Son of his love, . . . the firstborn of
all creation, for in him were created all
things in the heavens and upon the earth,
things visible and things invisible, whether
thrones or dominions or principalities or powers. All things have been created through him
and unto him, and he is before all things,
and in him all things exist.

This is the pre-existent Christ of whom Paul could say,

Jesus Christ, through whom are all things,
. . . . For of him, and through him, and unto
him, are all things (I Cor. 8:6; Rom. 11:36).

Some forty years after Paul's death, the author
of the Fourth Gospel in his famed prologue re-emphasized
this Pauline view by stating that Christ (speaking of

him philosophically as the *logos* or "word")

> was in the beginning with God. All things were
> made through him, and without him was not any-
> thing made that has been made (John 1:2-3).

Under continuing Pauline influence that same author re-
emphasized the pre-existence of Christ by placing on
the lips of Jesus the words, "Before Abraham was born,
I am" (8:58).

Christ's second great act, less spectacular but
more arduous and exacting, lay in being the deity who
ordered and sustained the whole creation through the
millennia of Old Testament history and intertestament
times. Christ was the manna in the wilderness wanderings
and the water that Moses brought from the rock for the
Israelites, as

> all ate the same spiritual food, and all drank
> the same spiritual drink, for they drank of
> a spiritual rock that followed them, and the
> rock was Christ (I Cor. 10:3-4).

"When the fullness of the time came," God "sent
forth his Son" into the world to be "born of a woman"
(Gal. 4:4). Christ descended to earth not to transform
mankind by teaching people how to live spiritual lives.
Rather, he came with the sole purpose of offering himself as a sacrifice on Calvary. His dealings and ministering to the multitudes were but advance dramatizations
of his impending glory.

God "spared not his own Son, but delivered him up
for us all" by seeing to it that his innocent Son was
crucified to take away the sins of the world which had
been initiated by Eve and Adam and through them had become fastened upon all humanity. Judas and the Roman
officialdom in Jerusalem were God's special agents in
ending the world domination of sin by bringing about
his desired sacrifice. Through the shedding of Christ's

blood "we have our redemption, the forgiveness of our
sins" (Col. 1:14 cf. Rom. 3:24-25; Eph. 1:7). These proceedings followed the Old Testament priestly insistence
that no sin can be forgiven unless an innocent animal,
bird, or person be sacrificed. Such action implemented
the belief that without the shedding of blood there can
be no remission.

    In recompense for this obedience unto death, God
resurrected Christ as the firstfruits of the grave.
Thereby the possibility of resurrection and hope of immortality were brought to all believing mankind. This
redemption and grant of immortality purchased by God's
Son on Calvary may best be described not as religion
but as Christ magic.

    God then exalted his resurrected Son to occupy the
position of prime jurisdiction in both heavenly places
and on earth. Christ therefore has been in control of
the universe since the first Easter and will continue
that rule until the end of time.

        Wherefore also God highly exalted him, and
        gave to him the name that is above every name,
        that in the name of Jesus every knee should
        bow, of things in Heaven and things on earth
        and things under the earth" (Phil. 2:9-10).
God
        raised him from the dead, and made him to
        sit at his right hand in the heavenly places,
        far above all rule, and authority, and power,
        and dominion, and every name that is named,
        not only in this world, but also in that which
        is to come, and he put all things in subjec-
        tion under his feet (Eph. 1:20-22).

    The Pauline inspired Great Commission, in a final
paragraph appended to the Matthean gospel (Matt. 28:18),
expresses the same transfer of jurisdiction as the

resurrected Christ is made to say, "All authority has
been given to me in Heaven and on earth."

When all evil finally is eliminated, and Christ
shall have made all powers in existence subject unto
himself, he will turn the jurisdiction over to his Father, who will then become God of the completely subjugated universe.

> Then comes the end, when he shall deliver up
> the kingdom to God, even the Father, when he
> shall have abolished all rule and all authori-
> ty and power, for he must reign until he has
> put all his enemies under his feet (I Cor. 15:24-
> 25).

REVEALING CHRIST, MYSTICAL CHRIST, INDWELLING CHRIST

Paul also found the immortal Christ to be a deity
who reveals himself and his desires to his followers.
This apostle wrote concerning "the exceeding greatness
of the revelations," especially when he was

> caught up even to the third Heaven. . . . into
> Paradise, and heard unspeakable words, which
> it is not lawful for a man to utter   (II Cor.
> 12:1-7).

By reason of Paul's assertion that he had direct communication with Heaven, he insisted that he could present
questions and receive directives in answer. His important dealings were claimed to have been with the immortal Christ.

For instance, Paul said his formula for administering communion of the bread and wine had been given him
directly by Christ: "For I received of the Lord that
which I delivered unto you . . . "(I Cor. 11:23). Paul
was certain that most of his teaching had been received
by direct commandment from Christ. This claim is expressed where he advised all to "take knowledge of the

things which I write to you, that they are the commandment of the Lord" (I Cor. 14:37). Or again,

> For I make known to you, brethren, as touching
> the gospel which was preached by me, that
> it is not after man. For neither did I receive
> it from a man, nor was I taught it, but it
> came to me through revelation of Jesus Christ
> (Gal. 1:11-12).

Occasionally Paul mentioned having "no word" from
Christ, as "I have no commandment from the Lord, but
I give my judgment as one who has obtained mercy of the
Lord to be trustworthy" (I Cor. 7:25). Two more times
in that same chapter Paul spoke "not of commandment"
and "to the rest I say, not the Lord" (7:6, 12). By contrast, in verse 10 he said, "I give charge, not I but
the Lord."

For his Christology Paul was indebted chiefly to
the mystery religions of the Greek world, with which his
readers and people in his audiences were quite conver-
sant. As each of those cults was oriented about its particular dying-rising god, Paul made his Christ into another dying-rising deity.

Under the influence of those Greek mystery religions, Paul presented the work of Christ as a mystery.
This apostle considered it his task "to speak the mystery of Christ" (Col. 4:3). His presentation was

> according to the revelation of the mystery
> which has been kept in silence through times
> eternal, but now is manifested. . . . unto
> all the nations. . . " (Rom. 16:25-26).

This is "the mystery that by revelation was made known
unto me, . . . the mystery of Christ" (Eph. 3:3-4).

The never-failing love that is bestowed upon the
believer by this mystical Christ is best described in
Paul's letter to the Romans.

Who shall separate us from the love of Christ?
Shall tribulation, or anguish, or persecution,
or famine, or nakedness, or peril, or sword?
. . . In all these things we are more than
conquerors through him who loved us. For I
am persuaded that neither death, nor life,
nor angels, nor principalities, nor things
present, nor things to come, nor powers, nor
height, nor depth, nor any other creation
shall be able to separate us from the love
of God which is in Christ Jesus our Lord
(Rom. 8:35-39).

The pantheistic aspect of the mystical Christ is
manifested in his being alive and everlastingly present
among us. Paul was certain that Christ lives in intimacy
within each believer, whose old self has been crucified
with Christ unto newness of life. Paul wrote,

I have been crucified with Christ; and it is
no longer I who live but Christ lives in me,
and that which I now live in the flesh I live
in faith which is in the Son of God, who loved
me and gave himself up for me (Gal. 2:20).

Paul spoke "in Christ" (II Cor. 2:17). To the one in
whom Christ dwells, conduct is no problem:

And if Christ is in you, the body is dead with
respect to sin, but the spirit is life because
of righteousness (Rom. 8:10).

Wherefore, if any man is in Christ, he is a
new creature: the old things are passed away,
behold they have become new (II Cor. 5:17).

Paul therefore advised his readers to "put on the Lord
Jesus Christ" (Rom. 13:14).

The mystical Christ resides also in the company of
believers, the Church, which is the body of Christ

(Col. 1:24; 2:17). The members of the Church are bound
together in Christ: "So we who are many are one body
in Christ, and severally members of one another"
(Rom. 12:5). "Now you are the body of Christ, and members each in his part" (I Cor. 12:27).

After Paul's many utterances on the work of Christ,
the love of Christ, the day of Christ, and the gospel of
Christ, the final word on the mystical indwelling Christ
is found in Colossians 3:11-16:

> there cannot be Greek or Jew, circumcision
> or uncircumcision, barbarian, Scythian, bond-
> man, freeman: but Christ is all, and in all
> . . . . And let the peace of Christ rule in
> your hearts, . . . Let the word of Christ
> dwell in you richly.

FROM MONOTHEISM TO DEISM AND POLYTHEISM

The figure of deity has suffered in three ways at
the hands of Paul's Christological innovations as this
apostle has denigrated God and radically limited his
power.

In the first place, Paul set up competition through
adding Christ as a new and more vibrant deity to the
heavenly jurisdiction. Thereby Paul was chiefly responsible for dissipating Jesus' monotheism into a Christian
orthodoxy which has become the world's leading humanistic religion -- in the sense of giving worship to a
human being, the humble prophet-teacher from Nazareth,
as the virtually superior deity of the universe. In so
doing, Paul departed from the monotheistic heritage of
Judaism by recognizing two major gods.

As previous sections have shown, Paul's second serious blow to God's prestige consisted in conceiving of
him as fully God, in supreme charge of the universe,
at only three points in cosmic existence: (1) the time

before creation of the universe, (2) the few years while
his Son was on earth, and (3) after the endtime when
God will rule in the final consummative kingdom handed
over to him by Christ. Except for the years from Bethlehem to the first Easter, the Pauline God is mainly a
protological and eschatological deity, operating fully
only before the advent of historic time and after the
close of history.

Paul's third discounting of God consisted in abandoning theism in favour of deism for most of historic
time. According to the essence of deism, God only started the universe going and ever since has been content
to leave its operation in other hands. In such deistic
fashion, except for the approximate thirty-one or
thirty-three years of Christ on earth, God was thought
of by Paul as having virtually abandoned the chief
scene of action from the primeval past to the most distant future. During all these aeons God has remained
only the honorary chief of the universe while Christ
has been, is, and will continue to be the all-important
executive officer. Paul never claims to have received
special directives from God but only from Christ.

Although such were Paul's theorizings when in a
Christological mood, in daily practice he usually remained the monotheistic Jew, indebted to God for daily
routine guidance and inspiration. As such, Paul mentioned God approximately twice as often as he mentioned
Christ, the more potent deity. The benedictive closings
to his letters indicate that Paul was considerably confused with regard to deity. None of these mention God
alone. Four (Romans, II Corinthians, Ephesians, and
Philippians) have both God and Christ. Three (Colossians, I Timothy, and Titus) contain no deity ascrip-
tions. The remaining six include the name of Christ only.

Many contemporary evangelical churches forget about Paul's theology and remember only his Christology. In such services one seldom or never hears the name of God, but only "The Lord Jesus Christ." This one-sided Pauline influence is seen also in the prayer of a chaplain who said, "Lord Jesus, thou who answerest our prayers and supplies all our needs," followed by imploring "Lord Jesus" a half dozen more times, but with no mention of God in the entire prayer.

Paul's confusion with regard to the object of his faith was compounded by the role he gave to his third important deity, the god of evil. The Ephesian correspondence describes Satan's world government with his myriad of sub-rulers. To resist that vast invisible empire, believers are advised to

> Put on the whole armor of God, that you may be able
> to stand against the wiles of the devil. For
> our wrestling is not against flesh and blood
> but against the principalities, against the
> powers, against the world-rulers of this dark-
> ness, against the spiritual hosts of wicked-
> ness in the heavenly places. Wherefore, take
> up the . . . shield of faith with which you
> shall be able to quench all the fiery darts
> of the evil one (Eph. 6:11-13, 16).

Satan is alluded to as "the god of this world" and "the prince of the powers of the air, of the spirit that now works in the sons of disobedience" (II Cor. 4:4; Eph.2:2). To the Corinthians Paul expressed the hope

> that no advantage may be gained over us by
> Satan, for we are not ignorant of his devices,
> . . . for even Satan fashions himself into an
> angel of light.

Although Paul boasted in his apostleship, he did not consider even himself exempt from Satan's power, for he said, "there was given to me a thorn in the flesh, a messenger of Satan to buffet me" (II Cor. 2:11; 11:14; 12:7). According to Paul, deistic God has delegated to Christ, through future history, the major task of conquering Satan's empire and eliminating his evil jurisdiction from the world. After that victory is accomplished, Christ will turn over government of the world to God and both the deism of the millennia and the power of Satan will come to an end (I Cor. 15:24-25).

Candidate for a fourth deity was the Spirit, so frequently mentioned in the letters. To Paul, the Holy Spirit was the radiation of divine influence. This apostle always was puzzled whether, like grace, "the Spirit" emanated from God, from Christ, or from both. Although Paul's Holy Spirit was not yet personalized to the point of being an individual sitting on a heavenly throne, his positing two members to the harmonious godhead made it much easier eventually to add a third. With Christ and Satan having such important jurisdictions, addition of the inevitable Holy Ghost or Holy Spirit at Nicea in A.D. 325, plus later galleries of saints in both the eastern and western medieval churches, God often became almost ignored.

Paul's polytheism eventually was to destroy Christianity from most of the Christian heartland. When Islam came, with its strong monotheistic message that "There is no god but God," Christianity quickly capitulated ideologically in Palestine, Syria, Asia Minor, and North Africa. Archaeologists dig up the images and great cathedrals that once existed throughout that area, but few Christians remain in those countries today.

AUTHOR OF THE ANTINOMIAN HERESY

Paul's three favorite paths to salvation (predestination and election, justification by faith plus grace, and salvation through belief) combined to lead him into the heresy of antinomianism. The latter part of this term comes from the Greek word *nomos* (law). The whole word grew from antipathy toward law-observance as a means of salvation.

Paul saw value in the "law" only during Old Testament days when it had been "ordained through angels by the hand of a mediator" as "our tutor to bring us unto Christ" (Gal. 3:19, 24). When, in the fullness of time, the era of faith through Jesus Christ dawned, the law became not only obsolete but an impediment, imprisoning Jews in bondage by keeping them from justification through faith in Jesus Christ (Gal. 3:23-5:26).

As a religious crusader, this belated apostle traveled over the Graeco-Roman world proclaiming religious freedom, setting Christians, and especially Jews, free from bondage to law. His message was "For freedom did Christ set us free" from the "yoke of bondage" (Gal.5:1).

In theory, Paul saw only one alternative -- people are "justified" either "by the works of the law" or "through faith in Christ" (Gal. 2:16). He was certain that law and faith cannot coexist, "for if righteousness is through the law, then Christ died in vain. . . . for the law is not of faith"(Gal. 2:21; 3:12). Paul even regarded those who advocated law-abiding as "under a curse" (Gal. 3:10-13).

Wonderful as this great emancipation from law sounded, it landed Paul in a rather disastrous predicament, one which he never fully comprehended. Unfortunately, he did not distinguish between man-made ritualistic laws and the eternal moral laws of the universe. He did well to demolish the absurd ritualistic and Pharisaic legal structures that were enslaving their followers. But when Paul, without making any distinction, left the impression that the same condemnations applied to Old Testament moral law and the legal structures of the Graeco-Roman world, his movement became mired in the quicksands of lawlessness.

By denouncing "law" as bad, Paul seemed to give his readers warrant for leading lives of permissiveness. As might have been expected, many people in his churches construed liberation from law as license to pursue whatever unseemly form of conduct they might choose. In this way his churches often became dens of corruption as his declared "saints" concluded that conduct was an irrelevancy in religion (I Cor. 5-6; Rom. 13:13-14). They could enjoy their assurance of Heaven and at the same time carry on all manner of immoralities here and now.

Paul was shocked by these conditions in his churches as his admonitions reveal the conduct deficiencies. He pled with the Romans to walk "not in revelling and drunkenness, not in chambering and wantonness, not in strife and jealousy" (Rom. 13:13). The "works of the flesh," to which the Galatians were addicted, were

> fornication, uncleanness, lasciviousness, i-
> dolatry, sorcery, enmities, strife, jealous-
> ies, wraths, factions, divisions, parties,
> envyings, drunkenness, revellings, and such
> like, of which I forewarn you (Gal. 5:19-21).

Comparable indictments of conduct in his churches are found in Paul's other letters.

There is no indication that Paul, or his inner circle of helpers, were guilty of moral inadvertences. As a zealous Orthodox Jew he had been reared and educated in a system of strict compliance, and he evidently continued to follow the fundamental moral and ethical principles of his native Judaism to the end of his days.

At this point Paul was greatly misinterpreted, and remains tragically misunderstood today. He was not stating that ethical conduct is irrelevant in religion.

Rather, he was concerned with priorities. Instead of the legalistic view that ethical living brings salvation, Paul said salvation produces ethical living. He felt moral living would come as a matter of course to any person who is "in Christ." Therefore, Paul spent all his effort in bringing people through faith to Christ.

Nevertheless, the misconception that Paul divorced ethical living from religion caused undue damage to early Christianity. This supposed separation amounted to nullifying the superb ethical contributions made by the Old Testament prophets and by Jesus. To correct this damaging effect, Paul urged Titus twice (3:8, 14) to "maintain good works" and felt compelled to include in his letters some prescribed norms of moral and ethical conduct, as in Romans 12:9-21; 13:8-10; Galatians 5:22-25; and Ephesians 4:25-32. However, even such passages were not strong enough to neutralize the more enticing incipient antinomianism in his writings.

To keep the Church from degenerating hopelessly into Paul's supposed antinomian heresy was an important factor in producing the gospel age. By recovering the life and teachings of the historical Jesus, the Jerusalem leaders thought to retrieve the Church from its Pauline antinomian ways and restore it in full allegiance to the Gospel as enunciated and lived by Jesus of Nazareth.

However, the Synoptic Gospels have not been able to extinguish the antinomianism they were called upon to efface. To a large portion of supposed Christians the precepts of Jesus are too specific and demanding. To all such, and they comprise most members of the Church, the more vague abstractions and generalizations of Paul are more appealing, with their chief condemnation of sin rather than sins and their stress on faith rather than works. Consequently, the Church lives more comfortably with Paul than with Jesus. Antinomianism therefore has continued through all these centuries as an ever-present Christian heresy, particularly in the more Pauline segments of the Church. The phenomenal growth of Pauline religion is largely due to the fact that most of its adherents think thereby they can escape the rigorous ethical demands of Jesus' Gospel.

This section may conclude with some continuing echoes of this supposed Pauline antinomianism. (1) In expounding Paul a minister said, "Sin is disbelief, rebellion against God, and lack of faith. Sin has nothing to do with being good or bad." (2) Too many pulpits have spent time ridiculing "the good moral man" who places ultimate trust in conduct, leading the casual listener to think that ethics has no place in religion. (3) The antinomian emphasis generated by Paul, whether intentionally or unintentionally, has led most individuals and segments of the Church to oppose social action movements that are geared toward creating a more Christian society and a better world.

MAJOR DEBITS IN PAULINE RELIGION

In contrast with Jesus, where one finds only good, Paul displayed a strange mixture of good and bad. In addition to the debits already cited, certain others deserve special mention.

A particularly regrettable area concerns the relations of a Christian to the government. In Romans 13:1-7, the major passage on this subject, Paul expressed unquestioning support of every governmental official, for it is twice stated that "he is a minister of God." Christians were not to resist even the tax-farming system since tax gatherers also "are ministers of God's service." Paul's most definitive words regarding a Christian's relationship to the government are,

> Let every person be in subjection to the high-
> er powers, for there is no power but of God,
> and the powers that be are ordained of God.
> Therefore he who opposes the power resists
> the ordinance of God, and they who resist
> shall receive judgment to themselves. For
> rulers are not a terror to the good work but
> to the evil.

Paul never conceived of placing duty to God above duty
to king.

Since Romans has generally been regarded as Paul's
most authoritative letter, this passage has brought
great harm on the supposedly Christian world. Romans
13 became chief warrant for "the divine right of kings"
and oppression of the peasants during the days of the
great European monarchies. That chapter made the German
people into meek supporters of Adolph Hitler in all his
dastardly programs. Romans 13 has led supposed Christians unthinkingly to support wars and militarism in
all its forms. Paul's words have made the Christian
world supportive of governments, even when they do wrong.
It may be asked, Would Paul have withdrawn this "revelation" when he was being executed in Rome, and if he had
foreseen the great Roman persecutions?

Paul's antipathy toward marriage is another major
debit in the Pauline system which permeated the Church
with the belief that sex is sinful. He permitted marriage, but only with grave misgivings, for those who
are unable to follow wise advice:

> It is good for a man not to touch a woman
> . . . . I would that all men were even as I
> myself. . . . I say to the unmarried and wi-
> dows, It is good for them if they remain even
> as I . . . . If you should marry, you . . .
> shall have tribulation in the flesh, and I

> would spare you . . . . But I would have you
> to be free from cares. He who is unmarried
> is concerned for the things of the Lord, how
> he may please the Lord, but he who is married
> is concerned for the things of the world, how
> he may please his wife, and is divided
> (I Cor. 7:1-2, 7, 8, 28, 32-34).

Paul advised marriage only for the oversexed who otherwise would "burn" and be tempted to fornication (7:9).
How strange to have Christianity made into the arch opponent of marriage and the home!

   This was Paul, the Essene monk, who had been fas-
cinated by that manner of life. He at least subconscious-
ly realized that he was on shaky ground, as indicated
by saying four times that these were his own judgments
and not a command given by Christ (I Cor. 7:6, 12, 25, 40).
However, Paul's derogating of marriage, and advice a-
gainst it, became woven into the fabric of Christianity
as monasteries and convents multiplied, with eventual
celibacy of even parish clergy in the Western church.

   Paul's disparaging of women was even more notable.
Because he believed women since Eve to be unreliable, he
insisted that they be ruled by men.

> But I would have you know that the head of
> every man is Christ, and the head of the woman
> is the man, . . . For a man . . . is the image
> and glory of God, but the woman is the glory
> of the man. For the man is not of the woman
> but the woman of the man; for neither was the
> man created for the woman, but the woman for
> the man (I Cor. 11:3-9).

Wives are to be "subject to their husbands in everything"
and the wife is to "fear her husband" (Eph. 5:22-33).

   Although in Galatians 3:2 Paul was carried away
by his zeal for freedom into proclaiming the spiritual

equality of all people, he consistently denied to women their human rights and dignity, considered them unfit to become Christian teachers, and ordered them to keep their heads covered and their mouths closed in church.

> Let the women keep silent in the churches,
> for it is not permitted unto them to speak;
> . . . And if they would learn anything, let
> them ask their own husbands at home, for it
> is shameful for a woman to speak in the church
> (I Cor. 11:5-13; 14:34-35).

This was the carryover of Paul the Jew who, by contrast with Jesus, made Christianity, like the Judaism of that age, into a religion of men, by men, and for men, in a man's world.

Although some aggressive individuals in his churches broke out of the sex barrier, Paul was able to keep most women in their place of subservience and obscurity. In this respect Paul's religion contrasted with the Greek religions of that day, in which women were relative equals with men and there were priestesses as well as priests. Paul was tragically successful in ridding Christianity of the regard Jesus showed toward women. As a result, for almost two thousand years women have been consigned to second-class citizenship in the churches -- excluded from ordination and participation in ecclesiastical hierarchies. How Paul could have failed so completely to grasp the significance of Jesus' Gospel in this regard remains a mystery. In so doing, this apostle inflicted upon Christianity one of its major handicaps through the ages.

Paul also supported slavery. He told slaves to remain such "even if you can become free." By considering slavery a divine "calling" Paul gave warrant to owners to pursue their enslavement of human beings.

> Let each man remain in that calling wherein
> he was called. Were you called, being a slave?
> Do not be embarrassed for it. No! even if you
> can become free, use it rather. For he who
> was called in the Lord, being a slave, is the
> Lord's freedman: . . . let each man, wherein
> he was called, abide therein with God (I Cor.
> 7:20-24).

He advised Titus to

> Exhort slaves to be in subjection to their own
> masters, and to be well-pleasing to them in
> all things; not gainsaying, not purloining,
> but showing all good faithfulness, that they
> may adorn the doctrine of God our Savior in
> all things (Titus 2:9-10).

> Slaves were urged that they be faithful to their
masters.

> Slaves, be obedient unto those who according
> to the flesh are your masters, with fear and
> trembling, in singleness of your heart, as
> unto Christ (Eph. 6:5; cf. Col. 3:22).

Since Paul regarded slaves as property, he advised that
runaway slaves be returned to their masters. To this
end Paul sent even Onesimus back to his master Philemon
(Philem. 10-18). On the other hand, slave masters were
urged to treat their slaves fairly and refrain from
"threatening" them (Eph. 6:9).

Paul's pronouncements in support of slavery have
been made slightly more palatable by translating "bond-
servants" or simply "servants" instead of "slaves." However, throughout the centuries Paul's words in support
of slavery have been well understood and treasured by
slave-owners. In this way Paul led supposed Christians
to support slavery for some eighteen hundred years.

On the basis of an isolated passage, Paul has been
prostituted by churchmen into giving warrant for opposing social programs and welfare payments. "If any man
will not work, neither let him eat" (II Thess. 3:10).

By convincing the churches that the second coming
of Jesus would take place during Paul's lifetime, he
committed a regrettable error. The supposed immediacy
of the second advent was one of his reasons for opposing
marriage, since Christ's coming was so near that it
would be distracting to take on the added burden, as
all effort should be directed toward preparing for the
great day (I Cor. 7:29-31). The most decisive passage
on this subject is found in I Thessalonians 4:15-17.

> For this we say to you by the word of the Lord,
> that we who are alive, who are left unto the
> coming of the Lord, shall in no wise precede
> those who are fallen asleep. For the Lord him-
> self shall descend from Heaven with a shout,
> with the blast of the archangel, even with
> God's trumpet, and the dead in Christ shall
> rise first. Then we who are alive, who are
> left, shall be caught up in the clouds togeth-
> er with them to meet the Lord in the air, and
> so shall we ever be with the Lord.

Paul has been responsible for causing the people
of every Christian generation since his day to be entrapped in the illusion that the end of the world was
at hand and that they would witness the second advent.
Fastening the mania of adventism upon Christendom has
resulted in an ecstasy of expectation that has tended
to distract the Church from its real tasks through all
these centuries and probably will continue so to the
end of time. That this dramatic event would occur during
Paul's lifetime was at least one declared revelation
from Christ that proved erroneous.

Although Paul was an extreme intellectual, he contributed his influence toward making Christianity dis-
count education by glorifying the gift of tongues in
the Corinthian church. This practice enabled illiterate
persons to command attention in the congregation to what
they claimed to be the highest manifestation of the
spirit. Paul told the Corinthians, "Now I would have
you all speak with tongues" and "I thank God I speak
with tongues more than you all" (I Cor. 14:5, 18).

However, this practice soon got so out of hand in
that congregation that the apostle devoted three whole
chapters in trying to restrain that charismatic movement
(I Cor. 12-14). In his exasperation he said,

> In church I had rather speak five words with
> my understanding, that I might instruct others
> also, than ten thousand words in a tongue
> (I Cor. 14:19).

Paul evidently did not repeat his Corinthian mistake
elsewhere, for silence on this subject in his other letters suggests that tongue-speaking did not get started
in his other churches. It is an anomaly that many segments of the twentieth-century church ignore Paul's admonitions as tongue-speaking becomes a widespread phe-
nomenon.

At all these points, where Paul clearly went a-
stray, one might wish that he had received valid revelations from Christ. These major debits cast serious doubt
on Paul's credibility. When he failed so completely in
treating the mundane, in the midst of which he was living, how can he be trusted in expounding things heavenly?

THE GREAT APOSTLE TO THE GENTILES

The Bible consists basically of two great streams
of contradictory thought that flow from Genesis to Revelation. One of these currents considers both mankind

and the entire creation as good. This stream has its
origin in Genesis 1 where six times one finds the statement "and God saw that it was good." These refrains were
followed by a benediction on the whole creation, "And
God saw everything that he had made, and, behold, it
was very good." When this strand is intercepted in
Psalms one finds,

> What is man that you are mindful of him? And
> the son of man that you pay attention to him?
> For you have made him but little lower than
> the gods, and crown him with glory and honor.
> You make him to have dominion over the work
> of your hands; you have put all things under
> his feet (Ps. 8:4-6 [5-7 in Hebrew]).

This view that mankind is essentially good, and but little lower than deity, is taken up in the New Testament
by Jesus, who regarded all people as basically good and
responsive.

The other stream regards humanity as vile and sinful. It began in the Garden of Eden where Eve and Adam
ate the forbidden fruit and brought themselves and all
subsequent mankind under the conviction of sin. As one
intercepts this polluted stream in the Psalms one finds
the statement, "Behold I was brought forth in iniquity,
and in sin did my mother conceive me" (Ps. 51:5 [Hebrew
vs. 7]). Paul continued that stream which disparages
humanity and looks upon the supposed unregenerate human
race as wallowing in sin.

> All have sinned and fall short of the glory of
> God. . . . Therefore, as through one man sin
> entered into the world, and death through sin;
> and so death passed unto all men, for that
> all have sinned

and

no good thing dwells in my flesh (Rom. 3:23;
5:12; 7:18).

This fundamental divergence shows that, in their respective appraisals of mankind, Paul held a position dia-
metrically opposite to Jesus' view.

In further contrast, while the religion of Jesus
consisted in the full and undivided impact of God's
spirit upon that young man from Nazareth, Paul's religion has been seen to be a composite derived from diverse sources. It may be described most graciously as
an elaborate tapestry, made up of varying strands and
colors.

In spite of his experiences on the Damascus road
and afterwards, this apostle to the end of his life remained basically a Pharisaic Jew in his ethical principles, reverence for God, and regard for the Old Testament as illustrated by his copious quotations from it.
The constituent elements in his two main systems of salvation, and subsidiary theological terms, were derived
mostly from the Essenes with whom he presumably spent
his "three years in Arabia" and became indoctrinated
in their theological perspectives. His Christology, and
orientation of Christianity around the resurrection
theme, came from the Greek mystery religions as he
transformed the historical Jesus into another dying-
rising god, supplemented by his own personal mystical
experiences with the heavenly Christ. In I Corinthians 2,
and   more or less throughout his letters, according
to contemporary Pauline scholars, this whole theological
complex was freely seasoned with the heretical Gnostic
thought which was in vogue at that time.

Because of the diversity of these conflicting influences upon Pauline thought, his religion was an enig-
ma to the early church and remains such today. Not consistent with himself, his letters are a series of riddles.

For instance, when in his Jewish mood Paul thought God was in charge of the universe, when in his Christian mystical experiences he was certain Christ ruled and sustained the world and everything in it, but when in his depressed states Paul regarded Satan as the ruler of this world and age. It is puzzling how he could be so anti-Jesus, virtually pronouncing his life and teachings anathema, and yet be so powerfully pro-Christ. The tantalizing nature of the apostle's writings, on these and other subjects, has made his letters enticing as a favorite field of exercise for so-called Christian theologians from that day to the present.

Paul was a whirlwind, a dynamic person, an irresistible force. Charged with the love of Christ, completely committed, and hurrying to do his work, wherever Paul went there was action. He gave up everything for what he thought was Christ. He was wholly devoted and knew no defeat. He was

> pressed on every side, yet not halted; perplexed, yet not unto despair; pursued, but not overtaken; smitten down, yet not destroyed (II Cor. 4:8-9).

This apostle was a man of physical handicaps that would have reduced most people to silence. As intimated in his letters, he was short of stature, not appealing in looks, and not fluent in speech. He appears to have been afflicted with malaria and epilepsy, his "thorn in the flesh." Apparently trachoma almost blinded him, so he could write only with "large letters." In addition, he encountered an avalanche of unspeakable physical and mental ordeals during the course of his journeys (II Cor. 6:4-10; 11:23-28). In spite of all these handicaps and hardships, he never relaxed in pressing "on toward the goal to the prize of the high calling of God in Christ Jesus" (Phil. 3:14).

Paul likely gave the name to the Christian Church during the year he worked in Antioch. Since he resented everything connected with Jesus, this apostle apparently was annoyed with having the movement called "the Way," i.e., the way of Jesus (Acts 9:2; 18:25-26; 19:9; 22:4; 24:14, 22). Since Paul was devoted to the immortal Christ, the new name Christian seemed more appropriate and "the disciples were called Christians first at Antioch" (11:26).

The monumental task of spreading Christianity over the Graeco-Roman world was accomplished by Paul, largely singlehandedly. In so doing he really both founded and built the Church. He also organized it -- establishing deacons, presbyters, and bishops (I Tim. 3:1-13; 4:14). Since the Church is based more essentially on Pauline theology, rather than the religion of Jesus, it might more properly have been called "The Paulist Church."

Paul not only founded, organized, and probably named the Christian Church but also, by both intent and inadvertence, supplied most of the Scriptures for its New Testament. His own writings, during the missionary years from A.D. 48 to 61 or 64, became treasured by the congregations he started. These letters were avidly read, copied, exchanged among the churches, and became regarded quickly as at least semicanonical -- the first Christian Scriptures. As such, the thirteen "Pauline letters" formed the nucleus around which the other fourteen books came to be grouped, a New Testament that is indebted to Paul as its founder.

Largely due to Paul's vigorous influence, both negative and positive, all four gospels were brought into existence as the second major stage in New Testament growth. By his cascade of letters Paul provoked the opposition into writing also. Although this apostle undoubtedly hoped that no such documents as gospels ever

would be written and thought that production of such
would be an unspeakable calamity, his attempt to oblit-
erate from the early church all memories of the historical Jesus backfired. This recoil eventuated in an age
of gospel writing when "many" (Luke 1:1-4) historical
gospels were produced, especially during the two decades
of A.D. 65 to 85. Of those, Mark, Luke, and Matthew have
survived.

These Synoptic Gospels were an attempt by the better elements in the Church to combat the Pauline influence in the churches. The intent was to free the Church
from bondage to Paul's Essenized brand of faith, his
antinomianism, his rejection of the Gospel, and his disregard for the historical Jesus. These gospels were offered as a protest against that apostle's leading the
Greek church out ever farther on such theological
tangents.

On the positive side, the three Synoptic Gospels
were written to bring the Greek church back to the fundamentals of the Gospel as demonstrated by Jesus in his
life and enunciated by him in his teachings. Paul's perhaps greatest contribution to the development of Christianity, although by inadvertence, consisted in his virtually forcing the Church into its age of gospel production.

Paul's impact in this regard did not stop with pro-
voking Mark, Luke, and Matthew into existence. At approximately A.D. 100 his continuing influence inspired
production of the Fourth Gospel, which might appropriately be called the Pauline Gospel. That belated writing
represents Paul's religion as reinforced and elaborated
by some four decades of further growth. This Gospel of
John displays a Paulinism blended with Christian Gnostic
heresy as Christ's discourses became transformed into
the favorite Gnostic dialogue style of presentation,

so well illustrated by the newly discovered Nag Hammadi
documents. The John who wrote the Fourth Gospel is the
most brilliant writer in the New Testament. This Pauline-
based writing at once became the most popular gospel
in the Church, and remains such today.

Through the centuries the Church has continued to
be Pauline rather than the church of Jesus. Paul has
monopolized even the contemporary pulpit. This takeover
is indicated by the fact that approximately eighty per
cent of the New Testament sermons preached in supposed
Christian churches are based on the Pauline and Pauline-
inspired Johannine writings. By contrast, few sermon
texts are taken from the Synoptic words of Jesus as recorded in the Gospels of Mark, Luke, and Matthew. Paul
at least deserves credit for having originated the New
Testament's most popular religion.

PINNACLES OF THE PAULINE ACHIEVEMENT

In his more mellowed moments, a few words or re-
flections of Jesus appear to have filtered into Paul's
writings.

> For the whole law is fulfilled in one word,
> even in this: You shall love your neighbor
> as yourself. . . . Bear you one another's bur-
> dens and so fulfill the law of Christ. . . .
> Be not deceived, God is not mocked: for what-
> soever a man sows, that he shall also reap
> . . . . And let us not be weary in well-doing:
> for in due season we shall reap, if we faint
> not. So then, as we have opportunity, let us
> work that which is good toward all men (Gal.
> 5:14; 6:2, 7, 9-10).

A little sermon on the mount is found in the thirteen verses of Romans 12:9-21:

> Abhor that which is evil, cleave to that which
> is good. . . . Bless those who persecute you,
> bless and curse not. . . . Render to no man
> evil for evil. . . . Avenge not yourselves,
> beloved, . . . But if your enemy hungers, feed
> him; if he thirsts, give him to drink: . . .
> Be not overcome of evil, but overcome evil
> with good.

The more typical Pauline ethical pronouncements are
veiled in generalities.

> In love of the brethren be tenderly affection-
> ed one to another, in honor preferring one
> another, in diligence not slothful, fervent
> in spirit, serving the Lord, rejoicing in hope,
> patient in tribulation, continuing steadfastly
> in prayer, communicating to the necessities
> of the saints, given to hospitality. . . .
> Rejoice with those who rejoice, weep with
> those who weep, be of the same mind one toward
> another. Set not your mind on high things,
> but condescend to things that are lowly. Be
> not wise in your own conceits. . . . Take
> thought for things honorable in the sight of
> all men. If it be possible, as much as in you
> lies, be at peace with all men (Rom. 12:10-18).

In the same Pauline mood of generality are
some of his final words to the Philippians:

> Finally, brethren, whatever things are honor-
> able, whatever things are just, whatever
> things are pure, whatever things are lovely,
> whatever things are of good report; if there
> by any virtue, and if there is any praise,
> think on these things (Phil. 4:8).

On the subject of life survival after death Paul
penned the best passage in the Bible. Treasured words

from I Corinthians 15 accordingly are read at every
Christian funeral or memorial service.

> That which you yourself sow is not germinated
> unless it dies: . . . So also is the resur-
> rection of the dead. It is sown in corruption,
> it is raised in incorruption; it is sown in
> dishonor, it is raised in glory; it is sown
> in weakness, it is raised in power; it is sown
> a natural body, it is raised a spiritual body
> . . . . flesh and blood cannot inherit the
> kingdom of God; . . . For this corruptible
> must BE put on incorruption, and this mortal
> must put on immortality. . . . then shall
> come to pass the saying that is written,
> Death is swallowed up in victory.
> (I Cor. 15:36; 42-44, 50, 53-54).

Dealing with the crisis of tongue-speaking in the
Corinthian church drew forth the finest words of this
apostle. After classing tongue-speaking as the least
worthy of all spiritual gifts, he moved into his immortal encomium on the trinity of supreme spiritual gifts.
It remains a mystery how such a stern and unloving person as Paul could have produced what may be the greatest
poem on love ever written. If Paul was ever inspired,
he certainly was doubly inspired when writing Corinthians 13, the greatest chapter in the New Testament outside the Sermon on the Mount. It charts the higher levels and mountain peaks of spiritual attainment in a marvelous manner. It rightly serves as the benediction to
Paul's religion.

> If I speak with the tongues of men and of an-
> gels, but have not love, I am become sounding
> brass, or a clanging cymbal. And if I have
> prophecy, and know all mysteries and all know-
> ledge, and if I have all faith, so as to

remove mountains, but have not love, I am
nothing. And if I give away all my wealth to
feed the poor, and if I give my body to be
burned, but have not love, it profits me
nothing.

Love suffers long, and is kind; love envies
not; love vaunts not itself, is not puffed
up, does not behave itself unseemly, seeks
not its own, is not provoked, takes not account of evil, rejoices not in unrighteousness
but rejoices with the truth; bears all things,
believes all things, hopes all things, endures
all things.

Love never fails: but whether prophecies, they
shall be done away; whether tongues, they
shall cease; whether knowledge, it shall be
done away. For we know in part and we prophesy
in part, but when that which is perfect is
come, that which is in part shall be done
away.

When I was a child, I spoke as a child, I felt
as a child, I thought as a child. Now that
I have become a man, I have put away childish
things. For now we see in a mirror darkly,
but then face to face; now I know in part,
but then shall I know fully even as also I
was fully known.

But now faith, hope, and love endure, these
three, and the greatest of these is love.

THE APOCALYPTIC RELIGION OF THE REVELATOR

The Bible's twelfth and final religion is found principally in its closing book. There is fairly general agreement that the most likely time of production was during the final two years of the Emperor Domitian's brutal persecution of Christians, A.D. 95 to 96. The main purpose in writing was to inspire Christians to abstain from emperor worship and to remain faithful to God and Christ during those difficult times.

Many parts are written in code so Christians alone would be able to understand the message. The Lamb is Christ; the great red dragon, the Roman Empire; the vicious beasts, the Roman emperors; etc. The book's seeming innocuousness, as a collection of animal stories, was intended to prevent its being seized and destroyed by arresting officers and other government authorities. Hopefully, they would not comprehend that, from their point of view, Revelation was in reality a highly seditious document. The way to resolve its meanings was passed on orally among underground groups of Christians.

Revelation at best is a puzzling book, since the key to much of its interpretation has been lost. These myriads of uncertainties led Saint Jerome, A.D. 340(?)-420, to remark in the introduction to his commentary on Revelation that this last book of the Bible has "as many mysteries in it as it has words."

Revelation purports to have been written by the disciple John, imprisoned on the Isle of Patmos (Rev. 1:1-2,9). It probably was a pseudonymous writing, but the author's identity was known in some quarters. Because

he was a questionable person, combined with the nature
of the book, storms of controversy swirled around Revelation from the beginning. Various groups in the early
church

> stated that Revelation was composed toward
> the end of the first century by a heretical
> Jewish Christian named Cerinthus, who wrote
> under the name of John to give his work apos-
> tolic sanction. Likewise, some of the more
> orthodox . . . were inclined to question both
> the canonicity and the apostolic authorship of
> Revelation. Among these was a certain Caius
> of Rome who, around the year 210, . . . re-
> jected Revelation -- . . . like others he at-
> tributed the work to Cerinthus.[1]

In his history of the early church the great historian Eusebius wrote (III, xxvii. 2),

> Cerinthus, through revelations professing to
> have been written by a great apostle, brings
> before us marvels which he falsely claims were
> shown to him through angels, asserting that
> after the resurrection there would be an
> earthly kingdom of Christ, and that men dwel-
> ling in Jerusalem will again be subject to
> desires and pleasures. And being an enemy to
> the Scriptures of God, he said that a period
> of a thousand years would be spent in nuptial
> festivities.

There was great sentiment in the early church a-
gainst including the Book of Revelation in the New Testament. Although some western churches accepted Revelation early, the Marcionites, Alogi, Chiliasts, Montan-
ists, and Bishop Dionysius of Alexandria (A.D. 247-264)
rejected Revelation as not canonical. Dionysius

observed that many did not accept Revelation
as canonical, while some said that it was not
by an apostle, but by Cerinthus.
The Council of Laodicea at A.D. 360 did not include Revelation in its canon of Scripture. Bishop Cyril of Jerusalem, who died in A.D. 386, forbade the reading of Revelation in both public and private. It was not included
in the Syriac New Testament, produced by Bishop Rabbula
of Edessa (A.D. 411-435), and did not appear in the Armenian or early Coptic versions. The decisive move in
establishing its canonicity occurred when influential
Bishop Athanasius of Alexandria, in his pastoral letter
of A.D. 367, included Revelation in the list of twenty-
seven New Testament books. Even so, the absence of Revelation in many Greek manuscripts indicates "lingering
doubts concerning its right to be in the canon."[2] (*Inter-*

Adverse judgments against Revelation resurfaced
in the Protestant Reformation. In the Preface to his
translation of 1522 Luther expressed strong aversion
to Revelation, declaring it neither apostolic nor prophetic. He said,

My spirit cannot adapt itself to the book,
. . . Christ is neither taught nor recognized
in it, which is what an apostle ought before
all things to do.

Luther regarded Revelation as

a hidden dumb prophecy, unless interpreted,
and upon the interpretation no certainty had
been reached after many efforts.

The Protestant reformer Zwingli did not regard Revelation as a biblical book and Calvin ignored it.[3] (James

Revelation may well have been produced in several
stages. Chapters 1 to 3 contain rather thoughtful

pastoral letters to the seven churches of Asia. Chapters 4 to 20 offer a collection of weird visions regarding God's programming of future world events. Chapters 21 and 22 picture the new Jerusalem. Some of this author's visions and predictions may have resulted from flighty dreams experienced while he was maddened by torture and imprisonment. Other visions are so fantastic, incoherent, and often inconsistent as to suggest that the Revelator envisioned them while under the influence of drugs. If the book were a valid divine revelation, as claimed, one would have a right to expect greater consistency between its various parts.

It seems strange that in the late twentieth century, an age of supposed enlightenment, many segments of Christianity, especially the electronic church and the evangelicals, consider Revelation the most important book in the Bible. In some quarters it is regarded as even more valuable than all the remainder of the Bible combined. In light of the strong feelings pro and con, it seems best that the author of Revelation be allowed to present his religion largely in his own words. Consistency must not be expected. At best, one can bring only partial order into such a hodgepodge of confused imageries.

THE COSMIC CHRIST OF REVELATION

Rather than the historical Jesus, Revelation features the cosmic Christ. The birth of this heavenly being is portrayed as having taken place not in a Bethlehem stable but in the sky in sight of all the world. Male involvement and attandance has been entirely eliminated as neither Joseph, nor shepherds, nor wise men appear at a manger. Instead of the humble maid of Nazareth, Mary has become transformed into the queen of Heaven.

And a great sign was seen in Heaven: a woman
arrayed with the sun, and the moon under her
feet, and upon her head a crown of twelve
stars, and she was with child; and she cries
out, travailing in birth and in pain to be
delivered (Rev. 12:1-2).

Herod, the child-slayer, has been transmuted into
the Roman Empire, the intentioned Christ-devourer. The
"great red dragon," representing that empire as the incarnation of Satan, is shown facing the expectant mother
at the celestial nativity:

and the dragon stands before the woman who
is about to be delivered, that when she is
delivered he may devour her child (Rev. 12:3-4).

While in Matthew's gospel the holy family fled into
Egypt to escape from Herod's slaughter of the innocents,
in Revelation the queen of Heaven was separated from
her newborn child at the moment of birth, before the
dragon could devour the infant. "And she was delivered
of a son, a man child, . . . and her child was caught
up to God, and unto his throne." After his safe keeping
was thus assured, the bereft mother also sought safety.
"And the woman fled into the wilderness, where she has
a place prepared by God" (Rev. 12:5-6).

Practically all that Jesus was in the Synoptic Gospels has vanished. Instead, the Revelator has presented
a series of variant portraits describing the adult
Christ and his work. Sprinkled through Revelation one
finds the Jesus of the second coming whose advent on
earth, in a dramatic role, was expected very soon. The
book announces

The things which must shortly come to pass:
. . . for the time is at hand. . . . For, behold, he is coming with the clouds and every
eye shall see him, . . . (Rev. 1:1-3, 7).

This Jesus is quoted as saying,

> Repent therefore, or else I come to you quick-
> ly, . . . I will come as a thief, and you
> shall not know what hour I will come upon you
> . . . . I come quickly: hold fast that which
> you have, . . . Behold, I come as a thief
> . . . . to show unto his servants the things
> which must shortly come to pass. And behold,
> I come quickly. . . . for the time is at
> hand. . . . Behold I come quickly, and my
> reward is with me, to render to each man ac-
> cording as his work is. . . . He who testifies
> these things says, "Yes, I come quickly" (Rev.
> 2:16; 3:3, 11; 16:15; 22:6-20).

At times the Revelator followed Paul's belief in
a Christ who was pre-existent, who created the world,
who has ordered history until now, and who will continue
to do so until the end of historic time. To this end
Christ is made to introduce Revelation by saying,

> I am the Alpha and the Omega, . . . I am the
> first and the last, and the Living one; . . .
> and I have the keys of death and of Hades (Rev.
> 1:8, 17-18).

The Revelator ended his book with a similar assertion,
"I am the Alpha and the Omega, the first and the last,
the beginning and the end" (22:13).

A portrait of this ever-existent Christ is supplied, showing him

> clothed with a garment down to the feet, and
> girt about at the breasts with a golden gir-
> dle. And his head and his hair were white as
> white wool, as snow; and his eyes were as a
> flame of fire, and his feet like unto burnish-
> ed brass, as if it had been refined in a fur-
> nace; and his voice as the voice of many waters.

And he had in his right hand seven stars, and
. . . his countenance was as the sun shines
at its brightest (Rev. 1:12-16).

There is also the spectacular, regal Christ with
the serpentine mouth and a slashing two-edged sword for
a tongue. He is "the ruler of the kings of the earth
. . . . and out of his mouth proceeded a sharp two-edged
sword." He is "the Lion that is of the tribe of Judah,
the Root of David" (Rev. 1:5, 16; 5:5). This is the conquering Christ, who is made to say, "I will make war
against them with the sword of my mouth." Added also
is God's commissioning of his great warring general:

to him I will give authority over the nations,
and he shall rule them with a rod of iron,
as the potter's vessels are broken into
shatters (Rev. 2:16, 26-27).

This is the ruthless militaristic Christ, of the blood-
spattered garments, who is destined "to rule all the
nations with a rod of iron" (12:5; 19:13).

At twenty-seven places in Revelation Christ is
found in a completely variant role as the meek Lamb of
God who has taken away the sin of the world. The Lamb
appears in chapter 5 when God has a book that

no one in the Heaven, or on the earth, or under the earth was able to open . . . And I
saw in the midst of the throne and of the four
living creatures, and in the midst of the elders, a Lamb standing, as though it had been
slain, having seven horns, and seven eyes,
which are the seven Spirits of God sent forth
into all the earth. And . . . the four living
creatures and the four and twenty elders fell
down before the Lamb, having each one a harp,
and golden—bowls full of incense, which are
the prayers of the saints. And they sing a

new song, saying, "You are worthy to take the
book, and to open the seals thereof: for you
were slain and did purchase unto God with your
blood people of every tribe, and tongue, and
people, and nation" (Rev. 5:6-9).

According to this vision, the chief activity in
Heaven consists in worshiping the Lamb.

And I saw, and I heard a voice of many angels,
round about the throne, and the living creatures and the elders, and the number of them
was ten thousand times ten thousand, and thousands of thousands, shouting with a loud voice:
"Worthy is the Lamb who has been slain to
receive the power, and riches, and wisdom,
and might, and honor, and glory, and blessing."
And every created thing which is in the Heaven,
and on the earth, and under the earth, and
on the sea, and all things that are in them,
I heard saying: "Unto him who sits on the
throne, and unto the Lamb, be the blessing,
and the honor, and the glory and the dominion,
for ever and ever." And the four living creatures said, "Amen." And the elders fell down
and worshiped (Rev. 5:11-14).

A RELIGION OF HATRED FOR THE ROMAN EMPIRE

A leading element in Revelation religion consists
in hatred for Rome and gloating over her hoped-for downfall. That empire was regarded as the incarnation of
Satan on earth.

The whole of Revelation 13 is devoted to describing
the Roman emperors as a succession of beasts. Of one
"beast" it is said,

And the dragon (Satan) gave him his power,
and his throne, and great authority . . . .

and the whole earth was lured after the beast,
and they worshiped the dragon because he gave
his authority unto the beast, saying, "Who
can compre with the beast and who is able to
war with him?" . . . And he opened his mouth
for blasphemies against God, to blaspheme his
name, and his tabernacle, even those who dwell
in the Heaven. And it was given unto him to
make war with the saints, and to overcome them.
And there was given to him authority over every
tribe and people and tongue and nation. And
all who dwell on the earth shall worship him
(Rev. 13:2-8).

Although Roma is not mentioned by name, chapter 17
is directed against that goddess of Rome. She is the
"great harlot" (vs. 1) "with whom the kings of the earth
committed fornication" (vs. 2) by submitting to Roman
trade, culture, government, and religion.

And upon her forehead a name is written: MYS-
TERY, BABYLON THE GREAT, THE MOTHER OF THE
HARLOTS AND OF THE ABOMINATIONS OF THE EARTH.
And I saw the woman drunken with the blood
of the saints and with the blood of the wit-
nesses of Jesus (vss. 5-6).

The Revelator tells how the kings of the earth, who
joined in worshiping the goddess Roma and her succession
of deified emperors, "shall war against the Lamb, but
the Lamb shall overcome them" (Rev. 17:14). Then follows
the more detailed description of how Rome would be annihilated by Christ and his heavenly armies:

And I saw the Heaven opened and, behold, a
white horse and he who sat thereon, called
Faithful and True, and in righteousness he
judges and makes war. And his eyes are a
flame of fire and upon his head are many

diadems; . . . And he is arrayed in a garment
splattered with blood, and his name is called
The Word of God. And the armies which are in
Heaven followed him on white horses, clothed
in fine linen, pure white. And out of his
mouth proceeds a sharp sword, that with it
he should smite the nations, and he shall rule
them with a rod of iron, and he treads the
winepress of the fierceness of the wrath of
God, the Almighty. And he has on his garment,
and on his thigh a name written: King of Kings
and Lord of Lords (Rev. 19:11-16).

Revelation 18:1-5 is devoted mostly to the grief of
Rome's multitude of trading partners when it finally
can be said that

Fallen, fallen is Babylon the great, . . .
And the kings of the earth, who committed
fornication and lived wantonly with her, shall
weep and wail over her, when they look upon
the smoke of her burning, . . . saying, "Woe,
woe, the great city, Babylon, the strong city!
for in one hour has your judgment come." And
the merchants of the earth weep and mourn over
her (Rev. 18:2, 9-11).

The Revelator gloats over Rome's anticipated downfall and calls for punishments to be heaped upon her.

Treat her even as she treated, and double,
the double according to her works: in the cup
which she mingled, mingle unto her double.
However much she glorified herself and waxed
wanton, so much give her of torment and mourning

in payment for "the blood of prophets and of saints,
and of all who have been slain upon the earth" (Rev.
18:6-7, 24).

Even Heaven was called upon by this author to rejoice over Rome's downfall:

> Rejoice over her, you Heaven, and you saints,
> and you apostles, and you prophets; for God
> has executed your judgment on her.

There followed the assurance that Rome's annihilation
would bring great rejoicing in Heaven.

> After these things I heard as it were a great
> sound of a great multitude in Heaven, saying,
> "Hallelujah, salvation, and glory, and power
> belong to God: . . . for he has judged the
> great harlot, her who corrupted the earth
> through her fornication, and he has avenged
> the blood of his servants at her hand. . . .
> And the four and twenty elders and the four
> living creatures fell down and worshiped God
> who sits on the throne, saying, "Amen, Halle-
> lujah." And a voice came forth from the throne,
> saying, "Give praise to our God, all you his
> servants, you who reverence him, the small
> and the great" (Rev. 18:20; 19:1-5).

Then was to come the great wedding and the marriage
feast of Christ and his gathered church,

> for the marriage of the Lamb has come, and
> his wife has made herself ready. And it was
> given unto her that she should adorn herself
> in fine linen, bright and pure, for the fine
> linen is the righteous acts of the saints.
> And he said to me, "Write, Blessed are they
> who are invited to the marriage supper of the
> Lamb" (Rev. 19:7-9).

The undependability of the Revelator's visions is
shown by the fact that the end of the Roman Empire in
A.D. 476 did not occur, as anticipated in Revelation 19,

at the hands of the blood-smeared conquering Christ and his heavenly armies.

Persecution usually is thought to purify religion by forcing adherents into greater devotion, but the reverse had taken place by A.D. 96. Roman religion became sadistic to the degree it persecuted Christians, finding ultimate joy in torturing followers of Christ and feeding them to the lions. Such cruelty produced the reciprocal reaction of causing Christianity in the Ephesus region to rejoice in an unholy manner over everything which might contribute toward the downfall of Rome. The New Testament thereby is made to end in a malevolent religion of rejoicing over the anticipated fall of that empire. Although the Roman persecutions did not succeed in destroying Christianity numberwise, they caused its Revelation manifestation to degenerate into a sadistic religion.

A RELIGION OF UNSPEAKABLE TERROR

The Revelator's sadism became projected far beyond the Roman issue to the future of the universe itself, presented as the impending victim of God who is portrayed as ultrasadistic. Revelationism thereby became a religion of revelling over the anticipated God-inflicted terrors of the future.

This author expected that, at a designated time, God would outplague the plagues of Moses in Egypt. Those ten plagues had been showered indiscriminately upon both guilty Pharaoh and the millions of innocent Egyptian citizens. Except for the locusts in Revelation 9:4, the coming myriads of plagues are scheduled to victimize the entire cosmos and all its people, regardless of guilt or innocence. They will serve as a megalomanic display of God's power before all the universe. Since

the Revelator claims to "have seen" these visions, they
are described in the past tense.

According to this visionary, these ghastly and horrible terrors are programmed to be executed in three
stages. First will be "the great day" of "the wrath of
the Lamb" (Rev. 6:16-17) which will begin by taking
"peace from the earth, and that they should slay one
another" (6:4). The horsemen of the apocalypse (6:8-17)
will be given

> authority over the fourth part of the earth,
> to kill with sword, and with famine, and with
> death, and by the wild beasts of the earth
> . . . . and there was a great earthquake,
> and the sun became black as sackcloth of hair,
> and the whole moon became as blood; and the
> stars of Heaven fell unto the earth, . . .
> And the Heaven was removed as a scroll when
> it is rolled up, and every mountain and island
> were moved out of their places. And the kings
> of the earth, and the princes, and the chief
> captains, and the rich, and the strong, and
> every bondman and freeman, hid themselves in
> the caves and in the rocks of the mountains;
> and they say to the mountains and to the rocks,
> "Fall on us and hide us from the face of him
> who sits on the throne, and from the wrath
> of the Lamb, for the great day of their wrath
> has come, and who is able to stand?"

All this is expected to be but a trial run, after
which will follow a second major succession of cosmic
convulsions, the great tribulation. Each of its six cycles of world catastrophes is to be heralded by a trumpet blast from an announcing angel.

> And the *first* blew, and there followed hail
> and fire, mixed with blood, and they were

showered upon the earth; and the third part of
the earth was burned up,and the third part
of the trees was burned up, and all green
grass was burned up (Rev. 8:7).

And the *second* angel blew, and as it were a
great mountain burning with fire was cast into
the sea: and the third part of the sea became
blood; and the third part of the creatures
in the sea, those that had life, died; and
the third part of the ships were destroyed
(Rev. 8:8-9).

And the *third* angel blew, and there fell from
Heaven a great star, burning as a torch, and
it fell upon a third part of the rivers, and
upon the fountains of the waters; . . . and
the third part of the waters became wormwood;
and many men died of the waters, because they
were made bitter (Rev. 8:10-11).

And the *fourth* angel blew, and the third part
of the sun was smitten, and the third part
of the moon, and the third part of the stars,
that the third part of them should be darkened; and the day should not shine for the third
part of it, and the night in like manner. And
I saw, and I heard an eagle, flying in mid
Heaven, screaming with a great voice, Woe,
woe, woe, for those who dwell on the earth
(Rev. 8:12-13).

And the *fifth* angel blew, and I saw a star
from Heaven fallen onto the earth: and there
was given to him the key of the pit of the
abyss. And he opened the pit of the abyss,
and a smoke went up out of the pit as the
smoke of a great furnace, and the sun and the
air were darkened by reason of the smoke of

the pit. And out of the smoke locusts came
forth upon the earth; and venom was given them,
as the scorpions of the earth have venom (Rev.
9:1-3).
These superlocusts were sent to hurt
    only such men as have not the seal of God on
    their foreheads. And it was given to them that
    they should not kill them, but that they
    should be tortured five months, and their tor-
    ture was as the torture of a scorpion, when it
    strikes a man. And in those days men shall
    seek death, but shall in no wise find it; and
    they shall desire to die, but death shall flee
    from them. And the shapes of the locusts were
    like unto horses prepared for war; and upon
    their heads as it were crowns like unto gold,
    and their faces were as men's faces. And they
    had hair as the hair of women, and their teeth
    were as of lions. And they had breastplates,
    as it were breastplates of iron; and the sound
    of their wings was as the sound of chariots,
    of many horses rushing to war. And they had
    tails like unto scorpions, and stings, and
    in their tails was their venom to hurt men
    five months. They have over them as king the
    angel of the abyss: his name in Hebrew is
    Abaddon, and in the Greek he has the name
    Apollyon (Rev. 9:4-11).
    And the *sixth* angel blew, and I heard a voice
    from the horns of the golden altar which is
    before God, . . . "Loose the four angels who
    are bound at the great river Euphrates." And
    the four angels were loosed, . . . that they
    should kill the third part of mankind. And
    the number of the armies of the horsemen was

twice ten thousand times ten thousand. . . .
And thus I saw the horses in the vision, and
those who sat on them, having breastplates
of fire and of hyacinth and of brimstone; and
the heads of the horses were as the heads of
lions, with fire and smoke and brimstone proceeding out of their mouths. By these three
plagues the third part of mankind was killed,
by the fire and the smoke and the brimstone
that proceeds out of their mouths. For the
venom of the horses is in their mouths, and
in their tails: for their tails are like unto
serpents and have heads, and with them they
bite (Rev. 9:13-19).

Then, for twelve hundred and eighty days, "fire
proceeds out of" the

two olive trees and the two candlesticks,
standing before the Lord of the earth. . . .
These have power to shut the Heaven, that it
rain not during the days of their prophecy;
and they have power over the waters to turn
them into blood; and to smite the earth with
every plague, as often as they shall desire.

Then

the beast that comes up out of the abyss shall
make war with them (the righteous who have
gathered at Jerusalem), and overcome them,
and kill them. . . . And from among the peoples and tribes and tongues and nations do
men look upon their dead bodies three days and
a half, and suffer not their dead bodies to
be laid in a tomb. . . . And in that hour
there was a great earthquake, and the tenth
part of the city fell; and seven thousand persons were killed in the earthquake (Rev. 11:4-13).

These terrors, that God is expected to perform during the great tribulation in response to the six angel
calls, boggle the mind. The horrible decimations to be
caused by these series of deadly plagues seemingly will
be intended to bring such "fright" upon the earth that
its inhabitants will "give glory to the God of Heaven"
(Rev. 11:13). However, to have a cruel God display such
fiendish power is a strange type of evangelism. If these
ghastly deeds will be displays of deity, who on earth
would want anything to do with godliness or desire to
enter the Heaven of such a brutal God?

CALM BETWEEN THE STORMS

Unbelievable as it would seem, the maze of barbar-
ous atrocities inflicted upon earth and humanity in this
great tribulation will terminate with great rejoicing
in Heaven.

> And the *seventh* angel blew, and there followed
> great voices in Heaven, and they said, "The
> kingdom of the world has become the kingdom
> of our Lord, and of his Christ, and he shall
> reign for ever and ever." And the four and
> twenty elders, who sit before God on their
> thrones, fell on their faces and worshiped
> God, saying, "We give you thanks, O Lord God,
> the Almighty, who are and who was, because
> you have taken your great power and did reign
> . . . . and there followed lightnings, and
> voices, and thunders, and an earthquake, and
> great hail (Rev. 11:15-19).

Updating Ezekiel's vision of the valley of dry bones
(Ezek. 37), the Revelator records that a considerable
number of victims will be resurrected and taken to Heav-
en even before the great tribulation will be ended. These
will comprise a multitude of the faithful whose corpses,

slain by "the beast," will lie unburied in the streets
of Jerusalem for three and a half days while "they who
dwell on the earth rejoice over them, and make merry;
and they shall send gifts one to another." At that point
God will come into the picture:

> And after the three days and a half the breath
> of life from God entered into them, and they
> stood upon their feet, and great fear fell
> upon those who beheld them. And they heard
> a loud voice from Heaven saying to them, "Come
> up here." And they ascended up into Heaven
> in the cloud, and their enemies beheld them
> (Rev. 11:7-12).

The faithful, who survive the great tribulation,
will be transported bodily to Heaven.

> After these things I saw, and behold, a great
> multitude, which no man could number, out of
> every nation and of all tribes and peoples
> and tongues, standing before the throne and
> before the Lamb, arrayed in white robes, and
> palms in their hands; . . . These are they
> who come out of the great tribulation, and
> they washed their robes, and made them white
> in the blood of the Lamb. Therefore they are
> before the throne of God: and they serve him
> day and night in his temple, and he who sits
> on the throne shall spread his tabernacle over
> them. They shall hunger no more, nor thirst
> any more; neither shall the sun strike upon
> them, nor any heat, for the Lamb who is in
> the midst of the throne shall be their shep-
> herd, and shall guide them to the fountains
> of waters of life, and God shall wipe away
> every tear from their eyes (Rev. 6:9-17).

THE OUTPOURING OF GOD'S WRATH

This intervening calm will be for a limited time
only. The great tribulation, frightful as it will be,
is rated by the Revelator as mild compared with the ultimate terrors God is expected to inflict upon humanity
when he pours the final measure of his wrath upon the
earth. Every one who joins in emperor worship "shall
drink of the wine of the wrath of God which is prepared
unmixed in the cup of his anger" (Rev. 14:10).

However, the same chapter has a variant disposition
by which all the evil people on earth are to be crushed
into extinction in the great winepress of God's wrath.

And the angel cast his sickle into the earth,
and gathered the vintage of the earth, and
cast it into the great winepress of the wrath
of God. . . . and blood came out from the
winepress, even unto the bridles of the horses,
as far as a thousand and six hundred furlongs
(Rev. 14:19-20).

Reduced to contemporary measurements, the blood of these
people who are to be slain by God's wrath is five or
six feet in depth and extends to a distance of two hundred miles in every direction.

Although chapter 14 recorded elimination of all
wicked people by (1) being tortured forever in the lake
of fire and brimstone, and (2) being crushed to bloody
extinction, chapters 15 and 16 offer a third type of
disposition by the seven plagues poured from the seven
bowls of God's wrath.

And I saw . . . seven angels having seven
plagues, the last, for in them is finished the
wrath of God. . . . seven golden bowls full
of the wrath of God

with directions to "pour out the seven bowls of God's
wrath onto the earth" (Rev. 15:1, 7; 16:1).

In succession, these seven bowls brought (1) "noise-
some and grievous sores upon men," (2) the seas became
blood "and all the living creatures that were in the
sea died," (3) all "the rivers and the fountains of the
waters; . . . became blood," (4) "it was given unto him
(the sun) to scorch men with fire," (5) "the beast, and
his kingdom was darkened, and they gnawed their tongues
for pain," (6) "the great river, the Euphrates" was
dried up so "the kings of the whole world" could gather
for "the war of the great day of God, the Almighty" at
"Armagedon," and (7) lightnings, thunders, hail, and
"a great earthquake such as there was not since there
were men upon the earth" split the city of Rome "into
three parts, and the cities of the nations fell" (Rev.
16:2-19).

The great tribulation and the successive pourings
forth of God's wrath upon mankind terminate with the
Revelator's description of "the great supper of God."
This triumphal cannibal feast of the end-time will occur
after the brutalized Christ shall have completed "tread-
ing the winepress of the fierceness of the wrath of God,
the Almighty." At that heavenly banquet they will

> eat the flesh of kings, and the flesh of cap-
> tains, and the flesh of mighty men, and the
> flesh of horses, and of those who sit thereon,
> and the flesh of all men (Rev. 19:15-18).

There eventually will be the day of resurrection
and judgment, with vanishing of the conventional Heaven
and the conventional earth.

> And I saw a great white throne, and him who
> sat upon it, from whose face the earth and
> the Heaven fled away; and there was found no
> place for them. And I saw the dead, the great
> and the small, standing before the throne.
> And the books were opened: and another book

was opened, which is the book of life, and
the dead were judged out of the things which
were written in the books, according to their
works. And the sea gave up the dead who were
in it, and death and Hades gave up the dead
who were in them, and they were judged, every
person according to their works. And death
and Hades were cast into the lake of fire.
This is the second death, even the lake of
fire (Rev. 20:11-14).

Although Revelation has the wicked destroyed by
God's wrath many times over, attention finally focuses
on that lake of eternal torture that "burns with fire
and brimstone" as the showpiece of divine vengeance.
Into that place of endless torture will be cast all

the fearful, and unbelieving, and abominable,
and murderers, and fornicators, and sorcerers,
and idolators, and liars

who managed to escape God's many decimations (Rev. 21:8).
All such eventually will find themselves in that "lake
which burns with fire and brimstone" in which "they
shall be tormented day and night for ever and ever"
(Rev. 20:10). There they

shall be tortured with fire and brimstone in
the presence of the holy angels and in the
presence of the Lamb, and the smoke of their
torture shall go up for ever and ever, and
they shall have no rest, day or night. . . .
And if any was not found written in the book
of life, he was cast into the lake of fire
(Rev. 14:10-11; 20:15).

The brutal deeds ascribed to God and the Lamb in
Revelation religion are sufficient to curdle the blood
of any spiritually sensitive person. The very concept of
God became depraved through his being degraded into such

an insane ruthless punisher. This is a fiendish God
whose chief delight consists in torturing those whom
he regards as wicked -- experiencing joy at seeing them
suffer his unspeakable tortures. The terrors that rev-
elationists joyfully expect God to inflict upon the inhabitants of earth in the anticipated great tribulation,
and in the pourings out of his divine wrath, are unworthy of any religion.

This is the God of vengeance who never heard of
love or the forgiveness that Jesus taught and practiced.
It is significant that, after the letters to the churches, the word *love* occurs only once (Rev. 12:11) in the
remaining nineteen chapters, and there only in the martyrdom context of a Christian's not loving his or her
own body. By its barbarism Revelation has vitiated the
love that was the heart of early Christianity. No longer
could the Church say, "For God so loved . . ."

THE POWER AND THE GLORY OF SATAN

The Revelator adopted Paul's concept of Satan as
the god of this world and became infatuated with sa-
tanology. This author of the Bible's last book believed
that God shared the heavenly domain with Satan until
the birth of Jesus. At that moment Satan appeared in
the sky as "a great red dragon, with seven heads and
ten horns, and upon his heads seven diadems." In anger
over the impending birth of Christ this great Satan-
dragon with "his tail swept the third part of the stars
from Heaven and cast them to the earth" (Rev. 12:3-4).

Presumably in punishment for attempting to destroy
the Christ child, Revelation posits a war in Heaven
which resulted in Satan and his hosts being driven from
Heaven to earth.

> And there was war in Heaven: Michael and his
> angels warring with the dragon, and the dragon

> warred, and his angels; and they did not pre-
> vail, neither was their place found any more
> in Heaven. And the great dragon was cast down,
> the old serpent, he who is called the Devil
> and Satan, the deceiver of the whole world;
> he was cast down to the earth and his angels
> were cast down with him (Rev. 12:7-9).

But

> Woe for the earth and for the sea, because
> the Devil has gone down unto you, being very
> angry, knowing that he has but a short time
> . . . . And the dragon grew angry with the
> woman, and went away to make war with the rest
> of her seed, who keep the commandments of God
> and hold the testimony of Jesus.

Except for these Christians, "the whole earth . . . worshiped the dragon" (Rev. 12:12-13:4). The Revelator
accordingly assumed that in his day, and since, Satan
has been in virtual control of the earth.

The Bible's terminal author believed that this influence of Satan in the earth will be stopped for a
thousand years when God will choose to imprison the
tempter for that coming millennium.

> And I saw an angel coming down out of Heaven,
> with the key to the abyss and a great chain
> in his hand. And he laid hold on the dragon,
> the old serpent, which is the Devil and Satan,
> and bound him for a thousand years, and cast
> him into the abyss, and shut and sealed it
> over him, that he should deceive the nations
> no more, until the thousand years should be
> finished: after this he must be loosed for
> a little time (Rev. 20:1-3).

At the same time that Satan will become imprisoned
for his sentence of a thousand years, God will resurrect

all the martyrs who met death by holding out for their
faith during the Roman persecutions. These, who will
be summoned in the "first resurrection," will sit on
heavenly thrones of judgment and reign with Christ for
the thousand years.

> And I saw thrones, and they sat upon them, and
> judgment was given to them: and I saw the
> souls of those who had been beheaded for the
> testimony of Jesus, and for the word of God,
> and such as worshiped neither the beast nor
> his image, and received not the mark upon
> their foreheads and upon their hands; and they
> lived and reigned with Christ a thousand years
> . . . . This is the first resurrection. Bles-
> sed and holy are those who have part in the
> first resurrection: . . . they shall be
> priests of God and of Christ, and shall reign
> with him a thousand years (Rev. 20:4-6).

This doctrine of the millennium is one of the most
distinctive elements in Revelation religion. With Satan's power and evil eliminated from the universe, all
people on earth will share an idyllic existence for those
thousand years. However, at the conclusion of those days
God will release the jailed one and Satan will rampage
over the earth, deceive all humanity, and subject it
to wickedness once more "for a little time" (Rev. 20:3).

> And when the thousand years are completed,
> Satan shall be released out of his prison and
> shall come forth to deceive the nations which
> are in the four corners of the earth, Gog and
> Magog, to gather them together to the war -
> - the number of whom is as the sand of the
> sea. And they went up over the breadth of the
> earth and encompassed the camp of the saints

about, and the beloved city; and fire came
down out of heaven and devoured them (Rev.20:7-9).
However, Satan is to receive preferential treatment,
if such it may be called, with the other two evil nota-
bles:

> And the Devil who deceived them was cast into
> the lake of fire and brimstone, where also
> are the beast and the false prophet, and they
> shall be tortured day and night for ever and
> ever (Rev. 20:10).

Watching Satan battle the fiery brimstone may be the
eternal chief tourist attraction of the redeemed.

Certain questions remain. Is Revelation's Satan
a surviving primeval god of wickedness with whom God has
been battling rather unsuccessfully for power through
all ages and presumably will continue so to the end of
historic time? Or, if God created everything, why did
he create a Satan or allow him to develop? If God has
been all-powerful over his creation from the beginning,
why has he permitted that tempter to corrupt virtually
all humanity, except for the coming millennium, from
that strategic tree in Eden to the end of the future
age? If God has power to imprison Satan for a thousand
years, why will he grant him a parole to deceive the
nations and torment his saints during earth's final
days?

In Revelation religion it appears that God lost
control of his creation already in Eden and has had to
subsist, at least partially, on the crumbs that have
fallen from Satan's table ever since. Christ came along
to bail out his Father, but another thousand or more
years will be required before the moment of final triumph will arrive. Whether at A.D.96 or today, Revelation
religion recognizes Satan as a counter deity of evil,
almost as powerful as God.

THE GLORIOUS CITY OF GOD IN A PERFECTED EARTH

To have the Bible end in a religion of practical
atheism is amazing. Although the Revelator assumed that
a theoretical God exists, this terminal biblical writer
did not believe in a God who is strong enough to keep
his creation going properly. Since the God of Revelation
has made a virtual mess of his world, he is represented
as about to go into bankruptcy proceedings and call it
quits, insofar as historical time is concerned.

This Revelation type of religion therefore anticipates a "day of the Lord" when the entire creation "shall
pass away." That terminal liquidation of Heaven and earth
is best described in the associated writing of II Peter.
There it is stated that the entire universe will be dissolved with fire in a terminal *great bang* when

the heavens shall pass away with a great noise,
and the heavenly bodies shall be dissolved
with extreme heat, and the earth and the created things that are therein shall be burned up

when "the heavens being on fire shall be dissolved, and
the heavenly bodies shall melt with extreme heat" as
"we look for new heavens and a new earth in which righteousness dwells (II Peter 3:10-13). How the righteous
are to survive this destruction of the total creation
is not stated.

The final thirty-two verses of vision in Revelation
21:1-22:5 are devoted to describing the reorganized salvaged world as anticipated by the Revelator. And what a
change of mood! After all his sadism, and the myriad
of ways in which he is expected to wreak destruction
on his creation, even God seems to have become touched
a bit with the true Christian spirit in this final vision. Like the calm that follows a violent storm, Revelation ends in the description of a perfect creation,
with all semblance of wickedness purged from it. This

transformation is conceived to consist in bringing Heaven down to earth in the most dramatic unveiling of the ages.

> And I saw a new Heaven and a new earth, for the first Heaven and the first earth are passed away, and the sea is no more. And I saw the holy city, new Jerusalem, coming down new out of Heaven from God, made ready as a bride adorned for her husband. And I heard a great voice out of the throne, saying, "Behold, the tabernacle of God is with men, and he shall dwell with them, and they shall be his peoples, and God himself shall be with them, even their God: and he shall wipe away every tear from their eyes, and death shall be no more; neither shall there be mourning, nor crying, nor pain any more, the former things are passed away." And he who sits on the throne says, "Behold, I make all things new. And . . . I will give unto him who is thirsty of the fountain of the water of life freely. He who overcomes shall inherit these things; and I will be his God and he shall be my son (Rev. 21:1-7).

The Revelator imagined this "holy city Jerusalem" as a fantastic cubical structure "twelve thousand furlongs" (1500 miles) in every dimension (Rev. 21:16). Imagine a high-rise apartment towering to such dizzying heights, equal to the distance from New York City to Bismarck, North Dakota! In light of this unimaginable size one can understand how the author of the Fourth Gospel, writng perhaps four or five years later could say, "In my Father's house are many rooms" (John 14:2).

This new Jerusalem is of "pure gold" and even its street is of "pure gold" (Rev. 21:18, 21). The city is surrounded by a protective jasper wall some seventy-three

feet high, resting on a twelve-layered foundation, each
layer constructed of a type of precious stone, such as
emerald, amethyst, etc. (vss. 17-20). The twelve entrances are arranged three to the side, each portal made
through a giant pearl, with a guardian angel at every
gate (vss. 12-13, 21). Everything in the new Jerusalem
focuses on the two deities:

> and the throne of God and of the Lamb shall be
> therein; and his servants shall serve him, and
> they shall see his face, and his name shall
> be on their foreheads (Rev. 22:3-4).

This is the city of perpetual day, with its light
illuminating the whole earth.

> And the city has no need of the sun, nor of the
> moon, to shine upon it, for the glory of God
> did lighten it, and the Lamb is the lamp there-
> of. And the nations shall walk amidst the light
> thereof: . . .And there shall be no more night
> and they need no light of lamp, nor light of
> sun, for the Lord God shall give them light:
> and they shall reign for ever and ever (Rev.
> 21:23-24; 22:5).

It is notable that in his new Jerusalem the Revelator
has discarded everything which he formerly "saw" in the
heavenly Jerusalem except God and Christ. Gone are the
twenty-four thrones of the twenty-four elders, "the seven
spirits of God," the "four living creatures full of eyes
before and behind," and the "many angels round about
the throne" numbering "ten thousand times ten thousand,
and thousands of thousands" (Rev. 4:4-5:11). Even the temple is gone: "And I saw no temple therein, for the Lord
God, the Almighty, and the Lamb, are the temple thereof"(21:22).

The primeval river and the two pivotal trees, although both now construed as trees of life, are brought
from the Garden of Eden to provide a park.

> And he showed me a river of water of life,
> bright as crystal, proceeding out of the throne
> of God and of the Lamb, in the midst of the
> street thereof. And on this side of the river
> and on that was a tree of life, bearing twelve
> crops of fruit, producing its fruit every
> month; and the leaves of the tree were for
> the healing of the nations. . . . Blessed are
> those who wash their robes, that they may have
> the right to the tree of life, and may enter
> in by the gates into the city (Rev. 22:1-2,14).

A JEWISH BRAND OF CHRISTIANITY

The emerging rift between Jewish Christianity in Jerusalem and gentile Christianity in Antioch is recorded in the early chapters of Acts, with Peter representing the former and Paul, the latter. Acts 15 and the Galatian letter reflect a turbulent stage in that conflict.

Revelation shows Jews having a virtual monopoly on the inner sanctums of Christianity. This might have been expected in a book, as shown earlier, that likely was written by the converted Jew Cerinthus. The angel, "having the seal of the living God," asked that the great tribulation be postponed until

> we have sealed the servants of our God on
> their foreheads. And I heard the number of
> those who were sealed, a hundred and forty-
> four thousand, sealed out of every tribe of
> the children of Israel.

Then follows a list of the twelve tribes, with twelve thousand saved from each (Rev. 7:2-8).

These hundred and forty-four thousand Jews, who were destined to withstand the Roman persecutions, are portrayed as Christ's elite. They are the twelve Jewish disciples of Jesus multiplied by twelve thousand.

> And I saw, and behold, the Lamb, standing on
> Mount Zion, and with him a hundred and forty-
> four thousand, having his name, and the name
> of his Father, written on their foreheads
> . . . . those who had been purchased out of
> the earth. These are the ones who were not de-
> filed with women, for they are virgins. These
> are the ones who follow the Lamb wherever he
> goes. These were purchased from among men as
> the first fruits unto God and unto the Lamb
> (Rev. 14:1-4).

According to the Revelator's view, celibacy already has
become the hallmark of Christianity.

Presumably the same hundred and forty-four thousand
"servants of our God," who were sealed "on their foreheads" in Revelation 7:3-8, will be the special attendants at "the throne of God and of the Lamb." These
"servants shall serve him, and they shall see his face,
and his name shall be on their foreheads" (22:3-4). It
therefore seems assured, according to Revelation, that
no one but celibate Jewish men who have embraced Christianity will be allowed to minister in God's presence
in the New Jerusalem and see his face.

The material structure of the golden building called the new Jerusalem, its surrounding wall, and outlying regions, are described in considerable detail. By
contrast, nothing is said as to who will occupy that
fantastic high-rise, except for the occupants of the
throne area. Will the other rooms be for those hundred
and forty-four thousand Jewish celibate men who are
God's special servants (Rev. 7:3-8; 14:3-4; 22:4)?

The terminal vision is not clear as to whether only
Jewish-Christians will be allowed to enter the golden
city and live in it, but this conclusion seems a

possibility. Since each of the twelve gates to the new
Jerusalem is to have the name of one of the twelve Israelite tribes over it, each of the Jewish entrants may
need to come in through his own tribal entrance, checked
by the admitting angel at each of these portals. That
Jewish Christians will have a monopoly on the holy city
is suggested further by the names of the twelve Jewish
apostles that will be inscribed on the twelve foundations of the city wall (Rev. 21:12-14).

Not schooled in Jewish history, Revelation's author
apparently was unaware that ten of the twelve Israelite
tribes had perished in the exile through becoming absorbed into the Arab populations of Syria, Iraq, and
Iran. Since only the Judah and Levi tribes remained intact to form Judaism, only these two surviving tribes
will be able to supply their respective twelve thousands.
This would tally up the total number of saved Jewish
firstfruits as only a possible twenty-four thousand
rather than the hundred and forty-four thousand anticipated in Revelation.

This new Jerusalem seems conceived by the author
as an overtone of the historical temple in Palestinian
Jerusalem. In that structure Gentiles were not permitted
to enter the inner courts and the sacred Holy Place.
Gentiles were allowed only in the outermost court, the
Court of the Gentiles. Similarly, since only the hundred
and forty-four thousand Jewish "servants of our God"
with "his name on their foreheads" will be privileged
to "see his face" (Rev. 7:3-4; 14:1-4; 22:4), it is
questionable whether Gentile Christians will even be
admitted to the holy city.

The final statement before the descent and unveiling of the new Jerusalem is that "if any was not found
written in the book of life, he was cast into the lake
of fire" (Rev. 20:15). Therefore, the "nations" (21:24)

that will encircle the new Jerusalem apparently will be made up of saved Gentiles. It will be possible for them to enjoy the eternal light that will radiate from the city to the whole world. They will be able to come and admire the golden city and its gemmed walls and present their offerings but at least may not behold God or enter into those sacred precincts where he presides.

Since in Jewish terminology "nations" and "Gentiles" are synonyms, access of these people to the new Jerusalem may be translated as follows:

> And the Gentiles shall walk by the light thereof, and the kings of the earth shall bring their glory to it. . . . and they shall bring the glory and the honor of the Gentiles to it, and there shall in no wise enter into it anything unclean, or he who makes an abomination or a lie: but only those who are written in the Lamb's book of life (Rev. 21:24-27).

The division between Jewish and Gentile Christians therefore seems envisaged as continuing in and around the new Jerusalem. Although the saved Gentiles may continue as peripheral nations, they are permitted only this second-class Christian salvation outside the holy city. By reason of their uncircumcision they are "unclean," and "there shall in no wise enter into it anything unclean" (Rev. 21:27).

The author of Revelation, presumably the Jewish convert Cerinthus, as introduced at the beginning of this chapter, finally settled the feud of the decades between Jewish Christians and Gentile Christians, to his own satisfaction. In the final vision that heretic consigned Gentile Christians to their supposed divinely ordained inferior status in perpetuity.

THE ILLUSORY NATURE OF APOCALYPTIC ESCHATOLOGY

The Revelator continued neither Jesus' work of building the kingdom of God nor the work of Paul in spreading the gospel of Christ and evangelizing the Greek world. Instead of devoting itself to spiritual culture in transforming self and society, Revelation religion's main concern is with what God is going to do in the future, so worshipers may escape his wrathful terrors and obtain his gift of immortality. This futuristic quest is called eschatology, the study of last things. Its cousin, apocalypticism, deals with the cosmic cataclysms that supposedly will end this age and initiate the escatological era.

Revelation represents the climax of a long eschatological trend. This emphasis in religion began before biblical time in the Sumero-Akkadian mythological writings, especially *Enuma Elish* (the *Seven Tablets of Creation*) and the *Gilgamesh Epic*. In the Old Testament the prophet Ezekiel, the father of biblical eschatology, and Daniel, the father of apocalyptic, gave the first definitive biblical treatments of supposed futuristic events. The other major Old Testament development was initiated by the Eschatologist who interpolated such materials rather systematically at places in the so-called Minor Prophets, Isaiah, and Jeremiah. This approach to religion came to its cliamx in the intertestament writings of the *Apocrypha* and *Pseudepigrapha*. Especially notable are I and II Enoch, II Esdras, II Baruch, Jubilees, and the Sibylline Oracles.

Chapter 9 dealt with John the Baptist's expectation of God's immediate coming to earth, slaying all the wicked, and establishing righteousness in the earth. Chapter 11 revealed certain eschatological phases in Paul's religion, especially the second coming of Christ during that apostle's lifetime. Mark 13, largely copied by Luke and Matthew, probably is a small apocalypse, not by Jesus but inserted from some other source into the Marcan gospel.

The author of Revelation was an apocalyptic devotee who was somewhat familiar with most of the works listed in the two previous paragraphs. He may be described as attempting to become a systematic eschatologist, gathering gleanings from the unfulfilled eschatological and apocalyptic expectations of previous millennia. He reactivated and amplified those visions with the maze of conflicting fantasies which he added, producing a confused conglomerate of speculations regarding the future.

This religion of revelationism specializes in trying to discover every item in the supposed predetermined timetable of God's future action, especially the programming of events leading to the assumed final consummation of this age. Such endeavor runs into the fact that the secrets of the future, as pointed out by Jesus, presumably remain undisclosed in the hidden counsels of God, and he has not chosen to divulge them. This roadblock makes of the Bible's final effort an escapist religion of illusion and untruths that have little or no substance. Hope is one thing, but vain hope is quite another.

Such pyramiding of apparently baseless expectations is not only an exercise in futility and a waste of time, but is also a travesty on valid religion. Revelationism is a religion that enmeshes its devotees ever deeper in the false satisfactions that come from being unduly charmed by visions of a supposed eschatological future. Wherever found, in the Old Testament, intertestament literature, New Testament, or today, eschatology is an artificial phantom search that tends to incapacitate its adherents for real religion.

This religion of fantasy has led every generation
since A.D. 96 to *know* that it was living in the *last
days*. Also, every present and future generation that
follows Revelation religion will continue to place its
faith in this illusion throughout all future time.

This pursuit is like that of desert travelers who
follow the shimmering mirage of a supposed beckoning
oasis. They may have great excitement and hope at be-
holding its palm trees, enticing lagoons of water, and
lush gardens that loom on the horizon. But as the trav-
eler advances toward these mirages, they recede ever
farther into the desert, leaving the deluded pursuer
ever more famished and hopeless. Similarly, those who
follow the lures of Revelation's eschatology and apocalyptic visions are likely to meet only illusion and spiritual death.

BIBLICAL RELIGIONS IN COLLAPSE

One seemingly would have had a right to expect that
the New Testament would end in a grand climax, with the
Bible's twelfth and final religion rising to higher levels than those preceding it. Instead, one finds the
Scriptures terminating in an anticlimax of almost total
collapse. This terminal biblical manifestation is a pov-
erty-stricken product that is devoid of most basic elements in religion, as the good components in the eleven
preceding biblical faiths are largely missing. It is
anomalous that, in the guise of an ultimate super-
religion, this controversial apocalypse, with its degenerate form of Christianity, has become the concluding
book and religion of the Bible.

Three passages in the final chapter are especially
disturbing. One of these is found in Revelation 22:11.

> He who is unrighteous, let him continue to
> do unrighteousness: and he who is filthy, let
> him continue to be made filthy.

Even though these words were spoken as a moratorium on
evangelism, because of the supposed immediate "second
coming," this embarrassing admonition continues as part
of Christianity's final benediction to the world.

Revelation 22:15 is a strange footnote to the description of the new Jerusalem.

> Without are the dogs, and the sorcerers, and
> the fornicators, and the murderers, and the
> idolators, and every one who loves and makes
> a lie.

The Revelator has forgotten that in 20:15 he had the
creation cleared of all wickedness as all evil people
were cast into the lake of fire to be tortured eternal-
ly. By contrast, this final verse of the terminal vision
makes of the new Jerusalem but an idyllic oasis in the
midst of a world ghetto of wickedness and depravity.

A third troublesome passage consists in denying the
possibility of God's spirit being able to inspire mankind after the Revelator concluded his writing.

> I testify unto every man who hears the words
> of the prophecy of this book. If any man
> shall add unto them, God shall add upon him
> the plagues which are written in this book:
> and if any man shall take away from the words
> of the book of this prophecy, God shall take
> away his part from the tree of life, and out
> of the holy city, which are written in this
> book (Rev. 22:18-19).

In Revelation religion there is an almost complete
moratorium on ethics, since pursuit of speculations a-
bout the future has left little or no time for attention
to religious duties here and now. One can hardly rate

as ethical even the immediate objective, to resist the
Roman persecutions, escape God's wrath, and obtain proper reward for faithfulness under trial. "Fornication"
is the great sin in Revelation, but fornication in this
religion consists in patronizing the Roman state cult
by indulging in emperor worship, conceived as "harlotry."
In this terminal religion the most important question
is, Whom do you worship? This concern contrasts with
the Synoptic Gospels, where the main question is, How
do you live? In revelationism the Bible has come full
circle, for this terminal manifestation is an ethically
bankrupt religion that is pre-Christian, pre-Jewish,
pre-prophetic, and pre-Mosaic -- stampeding back through
history to the early pre-ethical chapters of the Bible.

In line with Paul's antagonism to the life and
teachings of Jesus, it seems evident from Revelation
that the Synoptic Gospels, which came into being between
A.D. 65 and 85, made no impact among the seven Pauline
churches of Asia. It may even be doubted whether the
gospels were being circulated in that metropolitan
Christian center of Ephesus. At any rate, Jesus' *Gospel*
plays no role in Revelation religion. This neglect is
as true today as at A.D. 96, even though at both ages
the naming of Christ may be profuse on the lips of worshipers in that type of religion.

Adding the Book of Revelation to the New Testament
probably was the greatest mistake made by the postapos-
tolic church and the greatest calamity that has come
to Christianity. This decomposition from within has been
more disastrous than the Roman persecutions which the
book was to withstand. Revelation represents a brand
of supposed Christianity that has succombed to malignancy in which the healthy elements have largely withered
as the cancerous cells have flourished and taken over.

414   The Twelve Religions of the Bible

However, even the Revelator had a few moments of wholesome illumination at the unusual places where a slight
shaft of light from Jesus shines through temporary rifts
in the forbidding clouds. Christ is quoted as saying:

> Behold, I stand at the door and knock: if any
> man hears my voice and opens the door, I will
> come in to him and have supper with him, and
> he with me (Rev. 3:20).

> And the Spirit and the bride say "Come." And
> he who hears, let him say, "Come." And he who
> is thirsty, let him come: he who will, let him
> take the water of life freely (Rev. 22:17).

> And I heard a voice from Heaven saying,"Write,
> Blessed are the dead who die in the Lord from
> henceforth: yes, says the spirit, that they
> may rest from their labors, for their works
> follow with them" (Rev. 14:13).

NOTES TO CHAPTER 12

1.   *Interpreter's Bible*, Vol. XII, 1957, p. 352

2.   *Ibid.*, pp. 352-353.

3.   James Hastings, *Dictionary of the Bible*, Vol. IV,
p. 241.

IN RETROSPECT AND PROSPECT

Religion is like fingerprints. No two persons ever have had or will have the same religion. Similar variance is equally true of collective spiritual manifestations. By treating only the twelve most outstanding religions in the course of biblical history, the many lesser developments have had to be passed over. The differences between these religions have been due largely to their unique founding persons and circumstances, plus the various ways in which each has subsequently been ethnicized, ritualized, theologized, officialized, and institutionalized.

Religion itself is very simple, and has been seen to consist in the triple search. First is the quest for God -- the attempt to discover more of his spiritual laws, that govern our material and spiritual world, and respond to the divine influences that radiate from deity. Second is the outgoing search for fellow persons, with the whole gamut of ethical living that makes possible a harmonious and constructive society. Third is the inner search into one's self, to develop a life of personal integrity, self-respect, and inner harmony through soul culture.

At times the Scriptures have been seen to portray great forward movements but, all too often, these have been followed by declines or even tragic regressions. From this study it appears that it is difficult for any religion to maintain high levels for a prolonged period of time. Although there has been some progress through biblical centuries, the ultimate net gain has been disappointing.

These twelve major biblical faiths have presented a panorama of landscapes. Seven of these religions may be described as more or less fertile valleys. Joshua's religion of genocide and the Revelator's collection of apocalyptic horror visions and eschatological fancies form the forbidding canyons of the Bible. At the other extreme, three of the biblical religions represent challenging mountain peaks of spiritual attainment.

Towering high was the religion of Israel's prophets with their courage, social concerns, passion for justice, and increasing discovery of God's nature and will. The lyrical and nonritualistic religion of Israel's humanists and sages formed another mountain peak, with their devotion to spiritual living, reverence for God, observing nature as the stage on which the deity acts, their educational zeal for conserving the ethical heritage of the ages in proverbs, and passing on its achievements untarnished to each rising generation of youth. The religion of Jesus became the great triumph with its Beatitudes, Sermon on the Mount, golden rule, love to both God and man, establishing inner controls, building the kingdom of God as the rule of God in daily life, passion for redeeming the lost segments of humanity to constructive living, and concern for sinners, the poor, downtrodden, women, and children.

The pressing imperative is to be more selective in dealing with the Bible -- veering away from its lesser portions and giving renewed devotion to the superb elements of its more excellent parts. It would seem that the time has come when the more worthy biblical religions should come into their own through becoming transformed into a more mature religion for a more mature humanity.